This Book Is Ded

My parents,
Norbert & Marion Sabisch

A simple Christmas present they gave me more than 40 years ago has turned into a life-long passion that has afforded me the opportunity to search for lost valuables on almost every continent in the world, make many amazing finds and meet countless treasure hunters that have become lifelong friends. It's hard to believe that a simple metal detector costing less than $30 ordered from the back of a magazine so many years ago has unlocked a world of adventure with no end in sight.

Special Thanks To:

Bill Paxton

Over the years I've known Bill, we've shared a lot of ideas that have helped both of us become better treasure hunters in our own right. We've worked together on development projects with major metal detector manufacturers that resulted in better equipment used by detectorists worldwide. He's also helped me on several writing projects such as books, magazine articles and web editorials including the final proofing & review of this book. Thanks again Bill for your friendship!

© 2010; P&L Publishing

All Rights Reserved. No portions of this book may be reproduced in print or transmitted electronically without express written permission of the author.

Library of Congress Control Number: 2010901732

PUBLISHED BY:
P&L Publishing; http://www.SabischBooks.com

Cecly Sebh
8/13/10

Table of Contents

CREDITS 5

INTRODUCTION 6

WHAT THIS BOOK IS & IS NOT 8

THE WORLD OF TREASURE HUNTING 9

DEFINING YOUR GOALS .. AN ESSENTIAL FIRST STEP 15

THE FORMULA FOR SUCCESS 22

RESEARCH – FINDING PRODUCTIVE SITES! 26

YOUR EQUIPMENT – TIME TO UPGRADE OR SIMPLY MASTER WHAT YOU ALREADY HAVE? 48

TARGET RECOVERY – REMEMBER THE MATH! 68

GENERAL TREASURE HUNTING TIPS & TECHNIQUES 75

SPECIALIZED TREASURE HUNTING TIPS & TECHNIQUES 86
    COIN HUNTING 87
    RELIC HUNTING 93
    BEACH & SHALLOW WATER HUNTING 104
    UNDERWATER TREASURE HUNTING 110
    PROSPECTING 115
    CACHE HUNTING 121
    COMPETITION HUNTING 125
    BOTTLE HUNTING 130
    DOWSING 135

DOCUMENTING YOUR SEARCHES 137

IDENTIFYING YOUR FINDS 141

CLEANING, PRESERVING & DISPLAYING YOUR FINDS 145

CASHING IN OR SELLING YOUR FINDS 149

"STATE-OF-THE-ART" TREASURE HUNTING TECHNIQUES 154
    GLOBAL POSITIONING SYSTEM (GPS) UNITS 154
    MAP CALIBRATION SOFTWARE 154
    AERIAL PHOTOGRAPHY & STREET-LEVEL PHOTO MAPPING 155

TREASURE HUNTING TRIPS & OUTINGS 158

METAL DETECTING CLUBS 160

WORLDWIDE METAL DETECTING ORGANIZATIONS 161
    THE FEDERATION OF METAL DETECTOR AND ARCHAEOLOGICAL CLUBS (UNITED STATES) 161
    NATIONAL COUNCIL FOR METAL DETECTING (NCMD) (UNITED KINGDOM) 162
    FEDERATION OF INDEPENDENT DETECTORISTS (FID) (UNITED KINGDOM) 164

TREASURE HUNTING LAWS 165
THE UNITED STATES 165
WORLDWIDE 166

2010 TREASURE HUNTING EQUIPMENT BUYERS GUIDE 168
AQUASCAN INTERNATIONAL, LTD. 170
BOUNTY HUNTER 172
C.SCOPE METAL DETECTORS 177
DETECTORPRO ELECTRONICS 180
FISHER RESEARCH 183
GARRETT ELECTRONICS 189
J.W. FISHERS 196
MINELAB ELECTRONICS 199
NAUTILUS METAL DETECTORS 206
NEXUS METAL DETECTORS 209
SAXON METAL DETECTORS 212
SECON METAL DETECTORS 214
TEKNETICS 217
TESORO ELECTRONICS / LASER DETECTORS 222
VIKING METAL DETECTORS 228
WHITES ELECTRONICS 231
XP DETECTORS 240
COMPARISON CHARTS 244

CREDITS

I would like to thank all of those that provided input to this project in the form of photographs, search techniques, tips and resources. Without this assistance, the book would not have contained the wide range if valuable information it does. The willingness of treasure hunters worldwide to freely share information to help others become successful themselves is one of the great aspects of this exciting hobby.

- Bill Paxton
- Barry Wainright
- Velius Constantine
- Brian Stamm
- Bill Stirling
- Earl Stevens
- Brian Geddes
- Hardy Rusell
- Jim Vokes
- Larry Shirah
- Gary Drayton
- Miguel Rivera
- Charles (Upstate NY)
- Jim Walsh (Golddigger)
- Jim Sellers
- Roger Tuohy
- Bobby Ellis
- Steve Johnson
- Aaron Riggs
- Steve Hersbach
- Mike Scott
- Mark Sweberg
- Adam Staples
- Rick 'Meech' Burchfield
- Captain Dan Berg
- Martin Wright
- Brian Anderson
- Denny Koutouzis
- Ed & Brenda Williamson
- James H (south Texas)
- Larry Childress
- Gerry Denton
- Eric Johnson
- Bryce Brown
- Doc Lousignant
- Gary Storm
- Bill Sarver
- Doug Virgin
- Tom Perry
- Steve Alter
- Graeme Smith
- William Ferguson
- Bob Sickler
- John Edmonton
- Bob Afina
- Brian Phillips
- John Benfield
- Jim Harnick
- Ken Williams
- Stuart Rainford
- Dennis Jones
- William Jeffers
- Josep Mandek
- Randy Horton
- Wayne Burton
- Bill Grey
- Jerry Troiano
- Dave McCracken
- Bill Jameson
- Bob Jargeson
- Lloyd Sadler
- Greg Zayas
- Martin Sykes

This book was not intended to be static in terms of its content and annual updates to this book are planned. Treasure hunters are encouraged to submit their own techniques, tips and find photos along with suggested reference material, suppliers or equipment they have found to help in the field for possible inclusion in future editions. Full credit will be given if used . . . simply send them electronically to Handbook@SabischBooks.com.

Cover Design by Velin Saramov

INTRODUCTION

Over the past 60 years, treasure hunting has grown from an activity practiced by a secretive few to a mainstream hobby pursued by millions worldwide. While some have made treasure hunting their profession, the majority of us simply enjoy it much as others enjoy golf, tennis, cycling or fishing. It's a hobby that knows no limitations due to age, sex or geographic location.

Today's modern metal detectors are as close to real life "time machines" as we can get. What other device allows anyone to scan the ground near where they live and uncover examples depicting what life was like 50, 100 or even 1,000+ years ago? Virtually everywhere people have been over the centuries, lost items in the form of relics, coins, jewelry and the like wait for a detectorist to return them to the light of day and tell their story. Combine this with the natural "targets" such as gold nuggets, silver ore, float copper and even meteorites and you would be hard pressed to find an area that does not hold some form of treasure waiting to be found.

I started treasure hunting in 1965 when I received an inexpensive metal detector as a Christmas gift. That was back in the days of non-discriminating BFO detectors . . . my parents spent $19.95 when they ordered it from an advertisement in the back of a Popular Mechanics magazine. I'm sure they figured it would wind up in the back of a closet within a few weeks, but my brother Chris and I stayed with it and hunted every possible spot we could get to - school yards, parks, churches, private yards, the local beach, etc. Over the next 6 months we came up with a meager 26 coins and a ton of trash but we stuck with it. In the ensuing years I upgraded equipment, honed my research & hunting techniques and started to build an impressive collection of coins, jewelry and artifacts. My interest in treasure hunting has remained high over the years. I've been fortunate enough to have traveled to virtually every corner of the world as part of my job as well as on personal trips and hunted for all types of lost and buried treasure. Wreck diving along the East Coast, the Caribbean and the Mediterranean, prospecting for gold throughout the Western United States, Georgia and Alaska, detecting the old ghost towns in the United States, Canada, Mexico and eastern Europe; hunting for bottles in New England and the deep South; searching for military artifacts from wars dating back over 2,000 years; beach & coin hunting throughout the United States, Mexico, Europe and South America and attending 100's of competition hunts & shows - treasure hunting has an truly become an integral part of my and my family's life!

Over the years I have talked with literally 1,000's of treasure hunters worldwide and many of the questions they pose have been quite similar - usually related to how they can be more successful on a consistent basis or to best use the equipment they already own. The content of this book is intended to be different than any other published on the subject. It is not simply a book covering treasure hunting in generalities but one that contains specific tips to compliment the focused brand-neutral information applicable to treasure hunters worldwide.

My intent is to provide you with a "road map" that, if followed, will ensure you are successful in the field regardless of the type of treasure hunting you are involved in or type of equipment you use. Even many seasoned treasure hunters find the quality and quantity of their finds fall far short of their expectations. This book provides you with the tools necessary to develop a solid formula that will improve your success rate and can be repeated time and time again to ensure your success continues no matter where in the world you might be hunting.

It is also the first book to cover treasure hunting from a worldwide perspective; i.e., Europe, the United States, Canada, Australia, etc. Metal detecting has become a mainstream hobby worldwide and as you will see throughout this book, there are many tips and techniques that treasure hunters can share among ourselves. I received input from dozens of avid detectorists, dealers and manufacturers from all parts of the world and was extremely impressed at the wealth of information that was freely provided to assist other hobbyists. The sharing of the knowledge gained from hours of experience is truly unique to the metal detecting fraternity.

In addition to the tips and search techniques contained in this book, there are lists of books, videos, magazines, Internet resources, equipment suppliers and manufacturers in most chapters. These will provide you with a ready source of additional information if you still have any unanswered questions or see the need to add some new equipment to your treasure hunting arsenal.

The 2010 Treasure Hunting Equipment Buyers Guide provides a comprehensive overview of the equipment currently available and allows you to compare features of any piece of equipment you might be interested in. The Buyers Guide - as well as other portions of the handbook itself - will be updated on a regular basis so that you will always have an up-to-date reference tool to help you find more with the time you have in the field.

To get the most out of this book, you should read the first several chapters and then select the chapters that focus on the specific type(s) of treasure hunting you are interested in and the equipment you have or might be considering owning.

Best of luck to all of you in the field!

Andy Sabisch

What This Book Is & Is Not

This might be a strange title for the first chapter in a book but it provides you with a quick synopsis of what the focus of this book will be so that you are not looking for something that it does not contain.

This book is a bit different than the myriad of other books currently available on the subject of treasure hunting in that it covers virtually every facet of the hobby but does not delve into them in minute detail. Real life examples are interspersed throughout the book to show how specific techniques have been put into practice and with some thought, how you can do the same. The intended audience of this book ranges from novices who may have never even picked up a metal detector and are looking for advice on how to get started to seasoned hunters with years of experience under their belt looking for those bits of information that will give them an edge over the competition.

My personal treasure hunting library contains close to 3,000 books and many more magazines going back more than 50 years. I often find myself picking one up and skimming through it looking for even one tip, technique or idea that I had not considered or had forgotten about and see how I could apply it apply it to a current search. As people that are passionate about any subject that do the same have said, *"If I get just one great idea from a book or magazine, its cost was more than justified."* Well, in the case of treasure hunting, even one idea that might lead you to a site that would have otherwise gone undetected can net you finds that would exceed the cost of the book 100 times over.

As you go through this book, you will be presented with numerous tips and techniques used by successful treasure hunters the world over. See which ones will work for you based on the type of hunting you are interested in and your personal preferences in terms of conducting research, gaining access to sites and hunting styles. Look over the Reference Resource Bibliography at the end of most chapters where information on more specific books, magazines and websites is provided as well as contact information for manufacturers and suppliers of equipment proven to help increase your success rate in the field. It's worth mentioning that manufacturers and suppliers are listed in alphabetical order and the order in which they appear does not indicate one is better than another. All of the companies and products listed throughout the book have been used by treasure hunters around the world and are determined to be of value. Selecting specific products is a matter of personal preference.

This handbook has been designed to be a "one stop shop" for all forms of treasure hunters looking to improve their success no matter where they live and what type of targets they might be searching for. It focuses on the type of treasure hunting done everyday by people worldwide . . . and does so in a format designed to help all treasure hunters be more successful.

The book also makes extensive use of photos of finds made by fellow treasure hunters. The finds serve to bring the many examples provided to life so to speak as well as motivate all of us to get out and make some of those finds ourselves.

OK, let's get started!

The World Of Treasure Hunting

Many people have the misconception that Treasure Hunting is strictly limited to searching for lost mines in the Southwest, hidden payrolls or sunken Spanish galleons. While there are people and entire companies engaged in this form of treasure hunting, it is only one small facet of the world of treasure hunting and not the information intended to be covered in this book.

After all, if you look up the word **TREASURE** in the dictionary, you will find a definition such as the one below contained in the American Heritage Dictionary:

> ### *TREASURE:*
> - Valuable or precious possessions of any kind
> - Accumulated or stored wealth in the form of money, jewels or other valuables
> - Something of worth or value

As the definition suggests, today's treasure hunters search for and collect a wide range of items such as military items spanning 1,000's of years, bottles, household artifacts from towns long-forgotten, mining memorabilia, coins, tokens, jewelry, license plates, dog tags, tools . . . the list is virtually endless! As I mentioned in the Introduction, this book will provide you with tips and techniques that apply to all forms of treasure hunting as well as information specific to most "specialties" such as Civil War relic hunting, bottle hunting, ghost-towning, European field hunting, beach hunting, electronic prospecting, etc.

This chapter will provide an overview of many of the more popular forms of treasure hunting and maybe give you some new areas to explore that might never have caught your attention. As with other chapters throughout the book, there will be some very impressive finds submitted by treasure hunters from all parts of the world which not only show what can be found but will very likely get you "fired-up" to go out and make similar finds in your area. So here's a high-level list of some of the many types of treasure hunting done by today's hobbyists which you may wish to try for yourself.

Coin Hunting	Relic Hunting	Beach & Shallow Water Hunting
Underwater Treasure Hunting	Electronic Prospecting	Cache Hunting
Bottle Hunting	Competition Hunting	Dowsing

This list was not intended to be all-inclusive as there are many facets of treasure hunting that just a small number might partake in or it might be very regional in nature. As you go through this book, explore many of the resources provided and talk to others in the hobby, find out what interests you and learn all you can about that type of treasure hunting. Remember, first-class finds combined with your enjoyment of being in the field will be the true measure of success - after all, if you come home tired, frustrated and dreading the next in-field expedition, is this really what you had thought treasure hunting would be? Most of us get enough of that at our 9-5 job so treasure hunting should be - and is for many - an escape and ideal way to relax. It is probably the only hobby out there that can, and often does, pay for itself.

COIN HUNTING:

Coin hunting is the most popular form of treasure hunting worldwide after all; coins have been lost anywhere people have been for literally 1,000's of years. The most obvious areas for finding coins are those sites that are still in use on a regular basis which includes school yards, parks, ball fields, picnic areas, churches . . . the list is almost endless. While most of the coins found at sites still in use will be modern and worth little more than face value, the experience you gain here will pay off when you search sites that contain the older, more valuable targets. Many veteran detectorists take the time to hunt these easily accessible sites on a regular basis to sharpen their skills. On occasion, you might even pick up a piece of jewelry, relic or an old coin or two depending on the age of the site itself. If the site has been in use for decades or longer, there will likely be older coins to find even if the area has been heavily hunted for years thanks to the performance edge provided by a combination of the latest technology and proper search techniques.

The beauty of coin hunting is that it can be done virtually anywhere people have been – from yesterday to 2,000 years ago. Some coin hunters focus their efforts on finding elusive quality specimens such as the 1830 Bust Half Dollar found by Brian Stamm in Vermont or 1562 Hammered silver coin from Lithuania found by Velius Constantine in Germany. Many others enjoy a day at the local schoolyard or playground picking up a pocketful of common coins. Then there are those that do both depending on the mood they might be in.

RELIC HUNTING:

Coin hunting may be the most popular form of treasure hunting but relic hunting is the most diverse in terms of the types of targets that can be unearthed. You do not have to live in an area containing ghost towns from the old West or historic military battlefields as relics can be virtually anything ranging from everyday household items dating back 100's or even 1,000's of years to mining equipment, military gear, wagon parts, trade beads, horse shoes, early civilization copper tools, Medieval artifacts, Roman relics . . . simply add any item you can imagine and someone out there will be looking for it and finding it with one of today's metal detectors. Examples of the types of relics being sought include artifacts from military campaigns covering periods such as the Revolutionary War, Civil War, French & Indian Wars, Crusades World War I & II, and Roman conquests; westward expansion in the United States, the Middle Ages in Europe, items from everyday life spanning 1,000's of years. Look around your own area, delve into the local history and see just how many different types of relics you can find within just a short distance of your house.

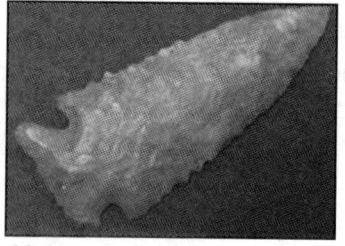

BEACH & SHALLOW WATER HUNTING:

Beach hunting is probably the only form of treasure hunting where anyone can go out and find items worth $1,000's just a short drive from their house. Most importantly, one is able to do so on an ongoing basis as valuable targets are continually being lost at beaches around the world. With very few exceptions, there will be a beach or at least a spot where people have gone swimming near virtually any location around the globe and unless pollution has rendered the nearby water unfit, you will find these sites remain popular year after year. Don't forget about the effect storms have on beaches either. Valuable targets such as coins and jewelry may be far below the detection depth of metal detectors but when a storm strips feet of sand off the shoreline, these targets are now within range of even a low-cost machine. The pair of rings below – one platinum with a large emerald and the other 14KT gold with a birthstone – were recovered by Charles from Upstate New York on a New Jersey beach after a 'Nor'easter struck the beach. Items spanning the centuries are found regularly as the 1775 gold Spanish half escudo recovered by Miguel Rivera in the surfline on a beach in Puerto Rico attests to.

UNDERWATER TREASURE HUNTING:

This form of treasure hunting is not for everyone but for those who are comfortable underwater and are looking at doing something other than simply swimming around looking at fish and coral; this can be a highly addictive and potentially profitable activity. While metal detectors intended for underwater use are designed to withstand pressures experienced in excess of 100 feet, the vast majority of your time will be spent searching the bottom in 50 feet or less . . . and in many cases, just over your head. An obvious starting point would be at any of the countless beaches worldwide. Are there floats or docks that sit in deeper water? Divers have made impressive finds from these sites but it does not stop there. Searching the waters off the shores of old hotels, piers, railroad bridges and towns turn up relics of all types on a regular basis. Scanning the bottom around wreck sites can also uncover maritime artifacts such as brass portholes, bells, tools and more. Obviously you should not try to get involved in underwater treasure hunting before getting the appropriate training but if you are willing to take the challenge of searching underwater, the rewards can be truly outstanding.

ELECTRONIC PROSPECTING:

Over the past 20 years or so, metal detector technology has improved significantly in terms of being able to detect targets in even the most severely mineralized ground and as a result, they have proven themselves to be an extremely effective tool in the prospecting arena. For many, the first image that comes to mind when prospecting is mentioned is an old grizzled miner with a pick & shovel on his trusty mule and a gold pan in his hand. Well, that may have been the case 100 years ago, but the equipment used and types of ore being sought have changed dramatically since that time. A nominal investment in today's equipment and some time in the field can produce amazing results . . . . but you may find yourself quickly becoming a collector and unwilling to part with any of your beautiful finds – I know I have yet to sell any of the specimens I've found over the past 30 years while out prospecting.

While gold has the greatest allure when it comes to what people hope to find, there are many treasure hunters searching for countless other specimens – some of which can be worth far more than a piece of gold. Copper can be found in naturally-occurring nuggets in many areas, and specimens weighing in excess of 2,000 pounds have been found by detectorists searching in the right location. Silver ore and beautiful nuggets can be found . . . often in areas where gold can be found doubling your chances for making a memorable find. A rapidly growing facet of electronic prospecting is the search for meteorites which have been found in every corner of the globe. It takes a bit of practice to recognize one but with values of more than $200 a gram for certain specimens; meteorites can actually be worth a good deal more than gold.

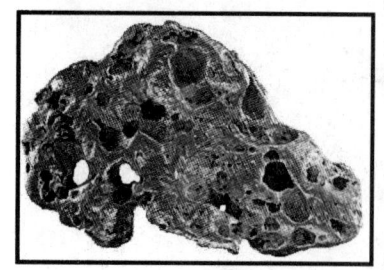

Examples of what today's electronic prospectors find on a regular basis
Gold, silver & copper nuggets and meteorites

CACHE HUNTING:

With a bank on literally every corner in most towns, you might wonder why anyone would hide valuables rather then keep then secure in a vault designed for that purpose. Well, it's been said that between 1 and 3 houses out of 5 hold some form of valuables hidden in or around it. Prior to the Great Depression, banks were not insured and if one was robbed or burned down, any money that had been deposited was in essence lost. As a result, many depositors kept some of their money and secreted it somewhere that they could get to it if they needed without fear of a bank folding overnight. In many cases, illness or a sudden accident took the life of the person that hid the valuables and what they hid has remained undiscovered for decades. Even today, there are many that do not trust banks or may have earned their money in less-than-honest enterprises and prefer to keep their money where they can get to it quickly or with no questions asked. While those that seek out forgotten caches are not successful every time they go out it is a unique form of treasure hunting that has an allure all to its own. If you have the patience, caches can be found anywhere people have lived as they have been hidden for 1,000's of years and the excitement that one receives from recovering a cache is indescribable!

BOTTLE HUNTING:

Bottle hunting is an extremely popular form of treasure hunting that sprang up decades ago and can be done anywhere people have lived since glassware was first used on a wide-scale. Obviously larger cites offer more possible locations to search for bottles and other discarded items but even small dumpsites at isolated farmhouses can be veritable treasure troves of antique and often valuable artifacts. There is a wide range of shapes, colors, embossing messages and even materials in the bottles, glassware and crockery found while bottle hunting and many who start out in this facet of treasure hunting find themselves avid collectors in short order. The chapter on Bottle Hunting will cover possible locations to search, equipment used by successful bottle hunters and provide references to additional resources to aid in your hunt.

COMPETITION HUNTING:

Competition hunting is unique when it comes to treasure hunting in that you and a group of fellow treasure hunters pay an entry fee and then race across a field searching for targets that have been planted by hunt organizers. In a way, competition hunting can be equated to events such as golf and fishing tournaments where strategy, skill and some good ol' fashioned luck come into play to determine the winners at the end of the day. These types of hunts may not be for everyone but the camaraderie experienced at these events among hunters along with the tips and techniques that are shared and the value of prizes that are up for grabs makes them extremely popular worldwide. The chapter on Competition Hunting will provide some proven tips that can increase your odds of being successful in these events and possibly bring home a pocketful of old coins or a brand new metal detector in addition to the new friendships that you've formed in the time between each event.

DOWSING:

Dowsing is probably the most controversial form of treasure hunting with two distinct camps: those that firmly believe it works and those who don't. There is little doubt that dowsing has been proven to work for some people for centuries and their successes have been well documented. Countless water wells have been located through the use of a simple set of rods or a forked stick in the hands of a dowser. Veins of gold and deposits of precious metals have been located by dowsers for more than 1,000 years including the Spanish conquistadors exploring the New World. If you have an open mind, spend some time looking over the information in the chapter on Dowsing. You can start out with an inexpensive set of dowsing rods and if you experience some degree of success, you may find that dowsing becomes an addictive activity and that you may have the talent to find items that might otherwise have gone undiscovered without this technique.

REFERENCE RESOURCE BIBLIOGRAPHY

Books

- **Buried Treasure You Can Find - How & Where To Find Treasure In All 50 States** by Robert Marx
- **How to Find Lost Treasure** by Charles Garrett
- **Metal Detecting for Beginners** by Ed Tisdale
- **The New Metal Detecting, The Hobby** by Dick Stout
- **Treasure Hunting for Fun and Profit** by Charles Garrett
- **Treasure Hunting Pays Off!** By Charles Garrett
- **Where to Find Treasure** by Dick Stout

Magazines

- **American Digger Magazine**; Covers a wide range of topics; http://www.americandigger.com/
- **Detection Passion**; French metal detecting magazine; http://pagesperso-orange.fr/detection.passion/
- **Lost Treasure Magazine**; The #1 treasure hunting magazine in the U.S.; http://www.losttreasure.com
- **The Searcher**, Another magazine from the United Kingdom; http://www.thesearcher.co.uk/
- **The Treasure Depot Magazine**, For treasure hunters . . . by treasure hunters – a full color magazine covering all aspects of treasure hunting; http://www.thetreasuredepot.com/
- **Treasure Hunting Magazine**; Britain's best selling metal detecting magazine; http://www.treasurehunting.co.uk/
- **Western & Eastern Treasures**; Published since 1966; http://www.treasurenet.com/westeast/

Internet Resources

- **Detecting – United Kingdom**: http://www.detecting.org.uk/forum/index.php
- **Gary's UK Detecting**: Excellent site filled with useful information; http://www.garysdetecting.co.uk/
- **Stan Grist's Adventures into the Unknown**: http://www.stangrist.com/
- **UKDetectorNet**: Started in 1994, this is one of the oldest treasure hunting sites on the web covering United Kingdom metal detecting; http://www.ukdetectornet.co.uk/

Defining Your Goals . . An Essential First Step

The first step in being successful in the field is to define what area you want to focus in on. Many people I talk to at club meetings or treasure hunting shows express the desire to 'find-it-all'. They look at displays made by fellow detectorists and their enthusiasm grows accordingly. Several years ago I was a speaker at a large annual treasure hunting show in Keene, NH called *'The Best of the Northeast' Show & Hunt* or BONE for short. As with many larger shows, BONE encourages attendees to bring displays of their finds and gives awards for them in several categories. The number and quality of the displays that I saw walking through the exhibit hall were truly amazing. Bottles dating back to the 1600's, well-preserved Revolutionary War relics, Colonial artifacts, coin collections worth $1,000's, display cases filled with gold & silver jewelry and much more. The displays got me fired-up and observing the people wandering through the exhibition hall, they had the same effect on them as well. At one of the presentations I gave throughout the day I started out by asking the audience what type of treasure hunting they primarily did and what type of targets they searched for. The vast majority of people kept their hand up as I rattled off the various types and targets. Curious as to how successful they were in their searches, I asked them how well they had done over the past year. Not surprisingly, most said that they had found an occasional "keeper" or two but in general had not made the type of finds that were on display in the exhibit hall downstairs.

What I said next took them many of them by surprise which was the old saying *"You are the jack-of-all-trades but the master of none."* In treasure hunting today this saying is directly related to how successful one is in the field.

If you want to become successful and start building a collection on-par with those you see in magazines or at shows, you need to select one or two types of treasure hunting or specific targets and focus all your efforts on them. For example, many of you will recognize the name of Ed Fedory who is probably the most well-known Revolutionary War relic hunter today. His collection contains literally 1,000s of artifacts from the 1700s and he has helped many other detectorists build similar collections over the years. The secret to his success is that he focuses solely on this period of history when conducting research or actual in-field searches. You won't see Ed searching for coins at the local park one weekend, beach hunting the next and maybe driving to Virginia to try hunting for Civil War relics the third. The period leading up the American Revolution is the only one that captures his attention and his knowledge of this era gained over the years is what ensures his success when he starts swinging his detector.

So, before we get into how best to conduct research, proper search techniques, documenting your searches and identifying your finds, you need to define what you want to focus on throughout the rest of the book. Revisit the list provided in the previous chapter to zero in on the type(s) of treasure hunting you plan on focusing your efforts on; but do not simply say "they all look interesting" or you will find yourself drifting from one to another and not making high quality finds on a consistent basis. Again, while the list covers a wide spectrum of treasure hunting possibilities, do not look at it as being all-inclusive. If you have an interest in something not listed, by all means add it to the list. Think about the history of your area. While you might have an interest in Civil War relics or medieval coinage, if you live in Los Angeles, California or Bogotá, Columbia, the chance of finding what you are looking for without extensive travel will be slim at best! Select two or three <u>SPECIFIC</u> types of detecting you are interested in and they will form the basis of your research and search activities. If you travel, you might want to add one or two types of detecting that you can do when you reach your destinations such as Revolutionary War relics in New England or the Carolinas, old coins from parks in local towns you visit or old mining relics in Alaska, Idaho or Nevada.

I have a number of friends that have specialized in what they search for and in doing so; both the quality and quantity of their finds have increased dramatically. Larry Childress is a treasure hunter I know from eastern Idaho who focuses solely on caches hidden in and around the old gold mining camps. He does his research and, while he does he have a fair number of dry runs, he is successful more often than one might expect. His finds include coins dating back to the mid-1800's with a generous sprinkling of silver dollars and gold coins. Would this be the type of success you might be interested in?

Just a few of the gold & silver coins Larry Childress has recovered from long-forgotten caches in the many ghost towns that jot the wilderness in Idaho. A good metal detector and the right techniques have allowed Larry to recover a number of these caches left by miners more than 100 years ago.

Now that you have defined what TYPE of treasure hunting you want to start focusing in on, you need to further define what type of targets you would like to find.

As I mentioned above, one thing that continually surprises me as I travel around the country talking at various club meetings and attending treasure hunts is the number of detectorists that have considerable experience in the field, two-to-three years or more, telling me that they have yet to find a coin from the 1800s, a piece of gold jewelry or even a relic from a time of turbulence in our country's history. At the same time, I see other club members or show attendees with case after case of impressive and often quite valuable items recovered from the same area that the individual with nothing but modern finds frequents. In many cases, these members are relative newcomers to the hobby but have learned how to focus their efforts to produce the best results. They have developed techniques on their own which many seasoned hunters may have never thought of trying and their results speak for themselves.

The purpose of this section is to have you start building an easy-to-follow road map that will help you find some of those valuables that have eluded you . . . even if you are a newcomer to the hobby. The **GOAL SHEETS** you develop in this chapter will help you focus your efforts as you read through the remainder of this book and spend time in the field with your detector.

In my discussions with treasure hunters that express disappointment in not being able to find the type of "goodies" they see pictured in magazines or brought in to their club meetings, the common denominator always seems to be where they are hunting. Recently I was talking with some detectorists at a club meeting in central Illinois. I had been in the area on business for a few days prior to the meeting and had gotten a chance to hunt around the foundation of an abandoned home which netted 7 coins from the 1800s along with some artifacts and additional coins from the early 1900s. A few other sites I had identified using some of the techniques covered in this book turned up more coins, a nice silver locket and several interesting relics. Several club members looked at my finds and were awe-struck when I told them they had come from sites within five miles of the meeting hall and less than three miles from my hotel. One of them had been hunting for nearly two years and had NEVER found a silver coin! When I asked where they were hunting, they gave me a list that included the three local schools (none older than 1972), a lake used for cooling a nearby power plant (built in 1984) and a park on the outskirts of town (built on land donated to the town in 1976). They had found literally 1,000s of targets; however, with the exception of a stray wheat cent here and there, everything they had found was modern. It does not take a Ph.D. to deduce that the reason they had not found any old coins was because they were not hunting the old sites where old coins were lost.

If you want to start finding some of the items most treasure hunters only dream of finding, you need to start re-focusing how and where you hunt. Unless a new park was built on the site of an old Civil War battle site or a school built on an old fairground, the chances of finding what you are hoping to find in these areas is slim to none.

OK, enough preaching, let's start working on that road map that I mentioned earlier. This system has worked for literally 100's of treasure hunters I have presented it to over the years so I am confident that it will work for you as well no matter how much experience you have under your belt.

Make a copy of the GOAL SHEET titled "**SUMMARY PAGE - MY TREASURE HUNTING FIND WISH LIST FOR 20XX.**" Then, start listing the items you would like to find throughout the coming year and be specific! Don't just say a silver half - define it by listing the item as a Walking Liberty Half Dollar. The same applies to relics including military artifacts, bottles and even gold nuggets. Use the same process of **specifically** identifying what you want to find as this will help you zero in on the type of sites that will hold the targets you are looking for.

Some of the items on my lists over the years have included: Seated Liberty quarter (1840 - 1891); Flying Eagle cent (1857 - 1858); Georgia Military Institute button (1850s - 1864), a U.S. Eagle breast plate (1860 – 1865), one ounce of natural gold, a 14KT gold ring with a diamond larger than ½ carat and a cache of silver coins. Your list does not have to contain any "rare and exotic" type of items or those that others have on their lists but rather what interests YOU! For example, a few years ago my son Paul's list had a few hard-to-find items but the ones at the top of his list were simply dollar amounts of clad coins with things he wanted to buy in parentheses including a scientific calculator, a video game and an MP3 player. You may simply want to put down "*Enough clad coins to pay for the detector.*" In order to make the list manageable and worthwhile, do not put down more than 20 items as it will be impossible to really focus on everything and as a result, you will fall back into the same old trap of "*looking for whatever you happen to come across.*"

One word of caution however, is to make these goals realistic! All of your actions from this point on will be to meet your goals and then set new ones . . . an on-going process that will make you a treasure hunter who is consistently successful in your searches. For example, if you are a coin hunter in the Northeast, having a Connecticut copper, bust dime, large cent, two cent piece and a piece of Spanish silver on your list are all achievable based on the age of your area. However, if you live in Hawaii, goals like these would be extremely unreasonable resulting in little more than frustration at the end of the year. There is one exception to this and that is if you travel extensively. A number of treasure hunters I have shared this methodology with are retired and as such spend several months out of the year in a different part of the county or even elsewhere in the world. In this case, having two sets of Goal Sheets – one for each area you spend time in – will pay off nicely!

While the examples I provided above focus on U.S. coins and relics, I know of many treasure hunters around the world who have used these forms to improve their success searching for native gold, ancient artifacts in Europe and jewelry on distant beaches. The key will be to define precisely what items you would like to add to your collection and use that as the starting point for conducting research and in-field searches. The rest of this book will provide you with all of the tools to make your goals easily achievable no mater where you might live or how many other detectorists might be searching the surrounding area.

Once you have your "wish list" on paper, the next and MOST IMPORTANT step takes place. Make enough copies of the **Goal Sheet – Detail Page** for each of your goals and transfer each item to a separate copy of the page. One of the most important pieces of information to capture before you even think of doing any research is to identify the date range when the item you are hoping to find was used. You will start developing a list of sites that were in use when the item you are looking for was in general use. Let's look at the list of some of the items I had wanted to find. Searching a school built in the 1970s hoping to find a Seated Liberty Quarter would be a waste of my time - I needed to hunt a site that was in use during the time period of the 1840s to the turn of the century. The same holds true with the Georgia Military Institute button I hoped to find. Here not only did I need to find a site that was in use during that time but now my desired target is also regional in nature. Hunting a site in Alabama from the 1850s would probably NOT turn up what I was looking for. On a simpler note, searching for – and finding – the Eagle breast plate required me to find locations that had been frequented by the troops that carried them. Even my son had to search the right sites to meet his goal of gathering enough clad coinage to buy some high-dollar items. He focused on sites that were in constant use, had a reason for people to handle coins and were close by so that he could spend his time hunting and not traveling.

If you are a prospector, this methodology will still work for you. For example, if you want to find a ½ ounce gold nugget, you need to focus your attention on areas where larger nuggets have been found in the past rather than simply hunting nearby sites where most of what you'll find is in the grain-size range.

> ⚠ **REMEMBER:** In order to find ANY type of target you are interested in, you need to spend your time searching those sites where the specific target is most likely going to be found. While this may seem to be common knowledge, many treasure hunters seem to forget this basic message when heading out in the field . . . don't waste valuable hunting time searching non-productive areas!

So, on each page you will start building a list of potential sites that fit the date range and geographical area in which the specific item you are hoping to find would have been in use. This will start to focus your research to look for sites that fit the criteria you need. If you are drawing a blank as far as what sites you should be adding to your list, pick up a few of the books listed in the specific chapters that cover the type of treasure hunting you are interested in. As you read over these books, jot down sites that the authors mention as being productive on your list – after all, if they produced well in say Indiana, there's no reason why they would not be as productive in Virginia (unless of course the type of targets you are searching for are highly area-specific).

Feel free to use additional pages if you find more sites that meet your criteria than the form allows you to enter. The chapter on Research will provide step-by-step instructions on finding the sites that fit the criteria that you have written down. Then, as your list of sites starts to grow, you can give up hunting the convenient school or park down the street that really does not produce and start hitting the type of sites that hold targets of greater interest. If you follow these simple steps, you will find that you will be recovering more of the type of targets that interest you and will be more excited about treasure hunting itself because you will be coming home with keepers in your pocket.

I have received feedback from many people I've presented this technique to over the years and the types of finds people have made are truly amazing. One of the best examples of how the Goal Sheets can help you focus your efforts to areas where you have a higher probability of success was given to me by Jim Sellers from upstate New York. He knew he lived in an area rich with history dating back to the early 1700's; however, other than an isolated Indian Head penny or Barber dime, his finds had all been from the 1900's. Well, he wrote down a dozen items on the Goal Sheets and then delved into the history books at his local library to identify the sites most likely to hold the targets he wanted to find. It took less than six months for Jim to cross all of the items off his list and begin a second one. In that period of time he found more than 20 coins from the 1700's, pewter buttons, Revolutionary War bullets and insignia, shoe buckles and more! The 1768 Spanish 8 Reale from the Mexican mints shown came from a small wooded site near his home that Jim found with some simple research techniques we will cover in upcoming chapters. Throughout the book I will be providing similar experiences provided to me for your benefit.

Gary Drayton from southern Florida started out as bottle hunter traveling to England each summer to search the river banks for their glass treasures. After finding a gold guinea in the mud, he switched to metal detecting for coins on these annual trips and then to searching for – and finding - Spanish treasure on Florida beaches. Wanting to be successful on a more consistent basis, he switched his focus again to searching for jewelry lost by the more affluent patrons of the southern Florida beaches in his area. He spent the time learning where the appropriate clientele spent their days, when the optimal conditions existed and how to set his equipment to get the best performance it could provide. By not jumping from coin hunting a local park one day, searching for relics the next time out and selecting a random beach the following weekend Gary found that the quality and quantity of his finds really picked up. In 2006 he found 123 gold rings followed by 230 gold rings in the 2007, 178 gold rings in 2008 and 130 gold rings partway through 2009.

Aren't these the type of finds we are all hoping to make? The ring on the left – dubbed the "*Starship Enterprise*" by Gary's wife – is platinum with 142 diamonds! The coin ring is 18KT gold surrounded by 40 diamonds. The other two are platinum containing a myriad of diamonds

You need to be realistic in terms of what you write down - after all if you are hoping to find a $5, $10 and $20 gold coin from the early 1800s and you live in an area that was not settled until the early 1900s, your chance for success is quite remote. Also, by focusing on one or two specific forms of treasure hunting, your efforts will by more apt to pay off in the field. I try to make my annual lists challenging but not unrealistic - after all, you don't want to finish up the year so frustrated that you toss the ol' detector in the trash pile.

GOAL SHEET
Summary Page

MY TREASURE HUNTING FIND GOAL-LIST FOR 20____

List the particular items you are interested in adding to your collection in the form below. In order to help focus your research efforts, be as SPECIFIC as possible when you enter your goals. Rather than simply writing down "Silver Coin" or "Civil War Relic", narrow it down with descriptions such as "Barber Dime", "Confederate Cavalry Spur", "Gold Ring" or "Roman Coin." To keep the subsequent forms manageable and your research from becoming too fragmented, limit your list to 20 items. As you find items on your list, you can add new "challenges" on an ongoing basis.

GOAL #	DETAILED DESCRIPTION OF ITEM (BE SPECIFIC!)
1	
2	
3	
4	
5	
6	
7	
8	
9	
10	
11	
12	
13	
14	
15	
16	
17	
18	
19	
20	

GOAL SHEET
Detail Page

Goal #: _____   Item Description: _____

When was the item in general use (Be specific!): _____

_____

_____

Where was the item predominately in use (Be specific!): _____

_____

_____

_____

_____

Detector settings that optimize the detectability of the item, if known. This includes discrimination level, sensitivity, probable target id readings, etc: _____

_____

_____

As you conduct research focusing on sites that meet the criteria you have defined above; i.e., in use when and where the item was in use, document the sites you find below for further follow-up. The forms provided in the Research chapter should be used to document additional information on each of the sites you determine hold the best potential for holding the specific items you are looking for:

SITE #	SITE DESCRIPTION	Additional Info. Available (Y/N)	Site Hunted (Y/N)

The Formula for Success

In the previous chapter the importance of defining specific goals to ensure that your time in the field was spent productively was discussed. The remainder of this book will provide you with the tools and guidance necessary to make sure that your goals become reality on a regular basis.

I'm sure the title of this chapter caught the attention of everyone that read it. After all, wouldn't it be great if being successful simply meant applying a formula written down in a book? Well, I am not even going to try to say that there is a simple formula for succeeding in any endeavor; however, in terms of treasure hunting, the formula discussed in this chapter and expanded on throughout the book will make you successful in whatever type of hunting you are involved in.

Simply put, the 4-part formula looks like this:

Sites + Equipment + Search Techniques + Target Recovery = SUCCESS!

Now before you shake your head and continue on, let me explain what each term means and how it plays a key role in determining your overall success in the field on a regular basis. The individual terms may seem blatantly obvious; however, it has been my experience in talking with treasure hunters worldwide for more than 30 years that they are typically ignored and the mediocre results experienced by many of them show what happens. The four parts of the formula will be expanded on throughout the book with specific tips and techniques to ensure you apply it on a consistent basis and reap the rewards it can offer.

SITES

The sole purpose of completing the Goal Sheets in the previous chapter was to come up with a list of the <u>types</u> of sites that are most likely to hold the items you want to find. Let's say you are a coin hunter and after listing 20 nice key coins from the 1800's you are interested in finding, you started to build a list of sites where the coins would have been in use (see the second section of the Goal Detail Sheet). You may have listed sites such as picnic areas, local fairs or festivals, resorts, religious revival grounds . . . the list should be comprehensive and based on what was common in your area at the time the coins were in use. But, this is only half of what you will need for the first term of the 4-part formula.

Once you have come up with a list of the <u>types</u> of sites you should be searching, you need to come up with a list of <u>specific</u> sites that meet this criterion. For example, under the heading of **PICNIC AREAS**, you will start to list actual sites used for that purpose in your area; i.e., Roaring Brook Picnic Grove, etc. In order to find these sites, you will need to conduct research and that is the subject of the next chapter. I know, we've all heard that research is essential to finding good spots but who likes digging into dusty books only to often come up with nothing of value. Well, the chapter on research will show you new ways of conducting research that are not only easier to use but will produce more leads than what you have been doing in the past.

So simply stated, the first part of the formula requires that you be able to identify productive sites for your preferred facet of treasure hunting. Searching sites that have little chance of holding the type of items you are hoping to find or have been heavily hunted for decades will do little to improve your success but rather, waste time that would be better spent elsewhere and in many cases cause you to give up the hobby out of frustration. How many potential areas to hunt do you see in the photo above? This book will show you how to see spots others overlook.

EQUIPMENT

If you ask a craftsman how he or she is able to produce high quality products on a consistent basis, they will more than likely say "*By using the right tool for the right job*". Well, this expression applies to treasure hunting as well; however, it's only half the answer. They should have said "*By using the right tool for the right job **AND** knowing how to use it*".

With the technology in today's treasure hunting equipment, it's amazing that everyone is not making outstanding finds on a regular basis. Compared to what many of us "ol' timers" started out with years ago, anyone should be able to find what we missed with our "antiquated" equipment. To really date myself, the youngster in the photo here is me some 45 years ago with my first metal detector along with the meager finds which were the results of my first 6 months in the field! Amazingly I stuck with it and my success increased with each passing year. So if that's the case why isn't everyone successful? The answer is simple - either they are not using the equipment best suited for the specific application they are trying to use it for or they are not using it correctly.

Here's an example that demonstrates how both the proper equipment and know-how combine to equal success in the field. Several years ago, a co-worker expressed an interest in metal detecting after seeing some of what I found and had brought into the office. I offered to take him to a spot that had been the site of a military drill field from the late 1800's to the mid-1970's. It had been hunted by others but there were still plenty of targets to find. For the first hour he followed me around and was amazed at how much lay just under the ground. We then swapped off and I told him when a signal was worth recovering. One trip was all it took to get Colin hooked on the hobby. He opted to go with a decent but low-cost starter unit and when it arrived, we again visited the old drill field. Going our separate ways, we met about an hour later. You could see the frustration in his eyes as he emptied his pouch and showed me a pile of trash along with three recently-lost coins. When I showed him my finds which included silver coins, wheat cents and some military insignia, he was ready to give up. Of course the first thing he said was that I had sold him a lemon and I had a better detector. While my machine was more expensive, I tried to tell him that understanding what the detector was telling you played a bigger role than the price tag. He did not want to hear it. So, I offered to switch detectors with him for the rest of the day and he jumped at the offer. Well, an hour or so later and he was back. He had found more trash and still only a few newer coins. When I showed him a pile of finds similar to what I had made with my detector earlier, he started to realize that it was not just the detector that mattered but how well the operator could use it that dictated success. Over the next few months Colin and I spent quiet a bit of time together and in the end, he could out-hunt other detectorists with years of time in the field using more expensive detectors simply because he took the time and mastered his original detector. As I penned this chapter, I called Colin and not surprisingly, he said he still owned that detector and could still find "keepers" in areas others had written off as "worked out".

Do not interpret the meaning of this section as a call for you to sell your equipment and buy the latest, most expensive equipment available. Before you make any rash decisions be sure to read the chapter entitled "*Your Equipment - Time to Upgrade or Simply Master What You Already Have?*" and you may find you already own everything you need to be successful on a regular basis.

The chapters dealing with the type of treasure hunting you are interested in combined with the brand-specific chapters will ensure you have the right equipment and know how to get the most in terms of performance from it under any conditions.

SEARCH TECHNIQUES

The third part of the formula has to do with ensuring that you use the best search techniques for the type of hunting you plan on doing in the area you will be doing it in. All too often treasure hunters know that the site they are at has strong potential; however, when they get out of their vehicle and look at the expanse of beach, grass or woods before them, they simply wander off hoping to get lucky. This is one of the main reasons good finds can still be made at sites that have been heavily hunted for decades . . . if no proven search pattern or technique is used, there are bound to be areas containing buried valuables that even a small army of treasure hunters would miss. Remember that most detectors use concentric coils which although they offer good performance in most areas (see the discussion on search coils in the Equipment chapter); their detection field gets smaller than the diameter of the coil the deeper the signal goes. On a typical 8" concentric coil the detector may only be "looking" at a 4" or 5" diameter search area at 6" or so. Since the deeper targets are generally the older ones, unless you conduct your searches in a systematic manner that ensures deep targets are not inadvertently overlooked, you'll probably see some of those finds at the next club meeting or treasure hunting show in someone else's display case. Changes in sweep speed, subtle adjustments to some of the settings on your detector or even a trick or two in specific types of sites can often make the difference between a mediocre day and a red-letter day at the same location.

As you read through the various chapters in the book you'll see different proven search techniques for specific types of treasure hunting. The techniques that may be ideal for hunting an old park in town will be far different than what works when searching a forgotten battle site, the shallow waters off an abandoned beach or dry desert dry wash holding gold nuggets. See what others have found to work in the type of hunting you do and in the areas that you search and then fine-tune them to best suit your personal preferences.

TARGET RECOVERY

The first three parts of the formula are fairly straight-forward but you're probably wondering what Target Recovery has to do with being successful. After all, if you've spent the time researching productive sites, learning how to use your equipment and honing your skills, don't you simply go out and bring home the "goodies"?

Well, it all comes down to math. If you have an hour to hunt a given location, the longer it takes you to recover a target your detector has located, the less time you will have to continue detecting and locate the next one. This philosophy holds true in any form of treasure hunting. If you are a relic hunter, coin hunter, water hunter, bottle digger or even a prospector, your goal should be to become as proficient as possible in pinpointing and recovering targets in the least amount of time so that your in-field time is spent locating new targets and not trying to find what you have already located. The chapter aptly entitled *"Target Recovery – Remember the Math!"* will cover some generic tips and techniques and then specific tips will be provided in each Chapter on the type of hunting you are interested in.

Another example will help exemplify the importance of this part of the formula. While living in Atlanta, I belonged to three different metal detecting clubs and spent a great deal of time hunting for Civil War relics with some of the members. Most of them were extremely proficient in the use of their detector and had some impressive finds to support that observation. As I spent time with a few of them, I watched how they recovered targets they detected. The digging tool of-choice was either a short-handled pick or Army entrenching shovel. They were effective for digging in the Georgia red clay; however, they typically dug a rather large hole in search of the target. It then took them a while to find the target as they sifted through the dirt piled up alongside the hole. On the other hand, by spending a few seconds to more accurately pinpoint the target or possibly use one of the new pinpointing probes, they could have cut the recovery time significantly. Over the course of an afternoon they could have spent more time locating additional targets rather than trying to locate ones they'd already detected.

Hopefully this chapter has shown you that being successful on a consistent basis is really not that difficult and the remainder of this book will provide you with all the tools necessary to become part of the **"5% of the treasure hunters that make 95% of the great finds"** . . . . a statement that the late legendary treasure hunter Karl Von Mueller made 30+ years ago which still holds true today.

Research – Finding Productive Sites!

The problem most treasure hunters have today is locating the older sites that hold the types of targets they hope to find. After all, unless the site has been in constant use for the same activity for the last 150 years or more, the site of the old school, park, beach or battlefield you are looking for has probably long since faded into obscurity. The trick to finding these sites is a word feared by most treasure hunters - <u>RESEARCH</u>!

I'm sure most of you will immediately think back to your days in school sweating to finish a project or term paper at the last minute. Well, researching metal detecting sites can actually be an enjoyable pastime especially when you see the fruits of your labor on the kitchen table after a successful hunt.

In the previous chapters we covered the importance of setting realistic goals for yourself in terms of what you would like to find over the next 12 months or so. Over the past decade or two I have discussed the method of setting goals as an important part of one's pre-search activities at club meetings and treasure hunts that I have spoken at. The feedback I have received - often months or even years later - has been overwhelmingly positive.

In talking with many treasure hunters at shows, in the field or by phone over the past 20+ years, I can sense the feeling of fear creep into the discussion whenever I bring up the subject of research. But, without doing your homework, the quantity and quality of your finds will rely on your being lucky in selecting the sites you hunt rather than being assured of a productive site every time you head out.

The aversion to research probably comes from the pain associated with researching papers and assignments in school as we were growing up. Well, if you combine having to read through pages and pages of dry facts & figures with getting a topic that probably was not the least bit interesting to start with, its little wonder that most of us would rather go the "drive around and hope we find a good site" route rather than doing some research to find a better one. Don't worry, finding productive sites through research is a lot easier than you might think and the rewards are much better than simply seeing that "A" on your term paper was years ago in school.

Brian Geddes, a detectorist who I met a few years back at an organized treasure hunt in South Carolina, is a good example of how setting goals and then focusing you research efforts can pay off. He had been searching for Civil War relics near Charleston for years yet despite the fierce battles and extended sieges in the area, his collection was meager at best. Well, he used the forms and identified 10 very specific relics he was interested in finding. Most of what he listed was related to the Calvary activity that swept through the low country. This forced him to learn about the equipment, troop movement, battle tactics and skirmish sites in his immediate area. I ran into him at another competition hunt about nine months later and he came up to me holding a wooden box and smiling from ear-to-ear. Even with all my years being involved in treasure hunting, the contents left me speechless. Every one of the 10 items he had listed along with many more were in the box including Confederate spurs, rosettes, bridle bits, buttons, unit insignias and even two beautiful CSA rectangle buckles worth more than $5,000 apiece! Obviously I can't take all the credit for his finds; however, Brian did say that the Goal Sheets forced him to focus his energy into finding the sites that were most likely to contain what he was hoping to find and based on his collection, it paid off in spades!

The question that most people ask once they start to fill out the Goal Sheets is *"Where do I find the sites to add to my Detail Page?"* The rest of this chapter will cover where you can find the information you need to pinpoint dozens of sites that hold the type of targets you are looking for - even if they may be from 100's or even 1,000's of years ago. The chapters that deal with specific types of treasure hunting later in the book contain additional sources that can provide you with leads for follow-up in the field. Look over the Reference Resource Bibliography section at the end of each chapter and pick up a few titles for your library. They have been selected based on personal use and feedback from other successful treasure hunters based on the information they contain. So, start by reading this chapter and then select the chapter(s) that pertain to the type of treasure hunting you are interested in to compile a comprehensive list of potential sites to search.

Before you delve into the sources described in this chapter and elsewhere throughout the book, make copies of the **Goal Sheet** from the previous chapter and **Research Form** provided later in this chapter and place them in your notebook. You can then enter any relevant information you come across directly into the forms. If you are a "21st Century Treasure Hunter" you might want to re-create the form electronically and then either use a laptop to record all of your research information as you do your research or record the information on your desktop when you get home. While not a requirement, using a computer will greatly simplify your research activities – both in terms of conducting the research as well as compiling & sorting the information you obtain. Most of the techniques contained in this book work just as well with a pad of paper & file folders as they do with a state-of-the-art computer system . . . use what works for you!

The Pen Scanner

If you are a "computerized" treasure hunter, you should take a close look at one of the pen scanners currently available. This pocket-sized device allows you to scan information from reference material - including that which can not be checked out – and then download it into your computer when you get home. Holding up to 1,000 pages of information at a 95%+ accuracy rate, it is an excellent way to collect useful research material for later use.

As you start doing the research needed to find the sites that hold the items you are looking to find, you need to think "a little outside of the box" as they say in selecting the material you want to review. Unlike the research you might do for a paper where you are looking for facts to support your assignment, you are looking for information that will lead you to specific sites to search with your metal detector which may be hidden amongst pages of unrelated information. The rest of this chapter will cover different sources of leads that can identify sites that have been searched lightly if at all.

Before getting into the specific sources of leads to productive sites, let's start out with a scenario and see if it sounds at least a bit familiar. Joe is an avid coin hunter and really enjoys unearthing coins such as Mercury dimes, Wheat cents, Buffalo nickels and other coins no longer in circulation which is what got him interested in metal detecting in the first place. He's been using a top-of-the-line detector for almost 3 years now and gets out as much as he can, weather permitting. The town he lives in dates back to the late 1800's and many of the older homes and parks have been untouched by progress. There's a small treasure hunting club in a town about 25 miles away and Joe has seen several people detecting sites such as the community ball field, village park and a few of the schools in his area. Since he's lived here most of his life, he really has not done much in terms of researching new sites since after all; the old sites are still visible no? Joe's done OK in his searches; over the past 3 years he has found about 50 silver coins, 200+ wheat cents and a few older coins dating back to the 1800's. Today Joe has a few hours to spare and opts to head out to ball field located between his home town and a neighboring hamlet – about a 15 mile drive. It's a well-known & well-hunted site but as we all know, no site is ever really hunted out right? The radio is playing a few of his favorite songs and before he knows it, he arrives at the field. Two hours go by and Joe feels he had a good day with 3 wheat cents and a silver dime in his pouch. Nothing spectacular but in his mind, a good day none the less. As he pulls into the driveway, he thinks "*I wish I lived in one of the areas where people find all those neat coins and artifacts they post on the Internet forums or show in magazine articles!*" Well, he figures there's always next time.

Do you think Joe is reaping the full potential of his area? If you do, then this chapter should help you boost your finds with a minimal amount of effort.

Let's contrast Joe with a friend of mine, Hardy Russell. Hardy got into detecting a few years ago and about a year ago upgraded to a top-of-the-line detector. I spent some time with him teaching him how to get the most out of it and his finds started to increase in the areas we would hunt together. With different work schedules, Hardy started to head out on his own whenever he had some free time as he was quickly becoming "hooked" on the hobby. As a coin hunter, he was finding quantity searching the obvious sites such as the local schools still in-use, the grassy / wooded areas around a local pool or two, and some of the ball fields but in general quality finds eluded him. We talked and went over a few simple concepts that have been proven over the years to identify sites that have not had 100's of other detectorists visit them before him and held a much higher potential to hold the type of targets Hardy (and most of us) would like to find. Over the next few months, Hardy started coming by my house with better and better finds from sites that had clearly not been hunted to any great degree or if they had been, his skill with his equipment gave him an edge over those who had come before him. What were some of the techniques that Hardy found to payoff in the field? Well, let's revisit the Four Part Formula for Success covered in the previous chapter.

Sites + Equipment + Search Techniques + Target Recovery = SUCCESS!

This chapter will delve into proven sources of information that will lead you to sites that were in use at the time the type of target you are hoping to find was in use. If you hoping to find some Indian Head cents, searching the local high school built in 1954 will not be an effective use of your time (unless there was an earlier structure at the site). Another friend who is an avid coin hunter, Bill Jameson from upstate New York, loves digging Wheat cents and silver so by starting to focus on sites built and in-use during the first half of the 1900's, his total number of coins went down but the quality went through the roof. Write down what kind of coins you are hoping to find (or any target for that matter) along with a date range of when they were in-use. Then start a running list of sites that meet that criteria and focus your efforts on them. You will see an immediate jump in what you bring home each day! Remember, hunting sites that were not in use when the types of targets you are looking for were in regular use is a sure-fire recipe for failure.

Look back at Joe's trip to the ball field where he was relaxing as he listened to his favorite songs on the radio. While he may have been focusing on the road, he had tuned out everything else he passed including a section of sidewalk being torn up near the old downtown district, four vacant houses dating back to the early 1900's, a vacant lot with an overgrown set of cement steps leading up from the street and a large old home that had a For Sale sign in the front yard. As you drive around for any reason, be observant of your surroundings and look for potential sites to search. Hardy said that after we had talked about a number of local sites that I had found to be solid producers and had not been heavily hunted, he had started to look for similar sites to hunt and quickly saw that they were everywhere. A few years ago I was taking my daughter to a swim meet in central Pennsylvania and as I drove by a field, I saw what looked like the remains of an old baseball backstop overgrown with vines. A few days later I got back and after talking to the property owner, learned that it had in fact been a ball field from the 1920's to the 1960's for a now defunct factory. He gave me permission to hunt it and over a 3-month period I pulled out more than 200 coins and other items. As an interesting side note, this site - which clearly had never been hunted - was located less than 30 miles from a local club that has been in existence for more than 15 years with a membership of more than 50 hunters. If the site is privately owned, try using some of the techniques covered in the General Treasure Hunting Tips & Techniques chapter to gain permission to search them. Many people are reluctant to ask permission but as I always say, what's the worst thing they can say? If they say NO, you simply thank them and drive on . . . you did not have permission before you asked and did not get it when you did, but you will find that with the right technique and approach, you will get permission upwards of 90% of the time.

> **REMEMBER:** If you want to start locating and hunting the sites that 95% of the competition overlooks, you need to start using methods that 95% of the competition does not use including research techniques. Try to think of unique angles to find these sites and you will be one of the 5% that finds 95% of the "goodies"!

The sections that follow cover a number of effective and innovative sources of finding sites to search. There will not be a long list of the same tired old sites that you will see published everywhere including places such as local schools, parks, beaches, playgrounds, fairgrounds, picnic areas, amusement parks and ball fields as they are quite obvious and more than likely, if they are still in use have been searched by 100's of people before you. This is not to say that there are still not targets to find but the purpose of this chapter is to steer you to areas that have been overlooked by the vast majority of other hobbyists. Some of these well-known types of sites will be ones you are looking for but the difference is that you want to find the schools, parks, picnic areas, home sites and beaches that have been abandoned for decades or longer as they will be the ones that hold the targets that get one's heart racing when they come out of the ground. The message you need to keep at the front of your mind as you start looking for new sites to search in order to find what others have overlooked is . . .

THINK OUTSIDE THE BOX

"KEEPING YOR EYES OPEN"

A surprisingly effective and simple technique that you should get into the habit of using on a regular basis can best be described as simply "*keeping your eyes open*". While this may seem to be an unusual name for a way to find new sites, it's one that many detectorists don't use at all.

Do you typically load all your gear into the truck, pull out of the driveway, turn on the radio and think about life in general as you drive to the site you've targeted to hunt? If so, you're not alone . . . most people tend to find themselves arriving at their destination with little memory of what they passed on the way. The next time you drive anywhere – for detecting, shopping, work – start looking around with the purpose of identifying possible sites to search.

Not long ago, my family and I were visiting relatives in Charleston, SC, an old city with a rich history. Rather than hunting the beaches as I typically did, I opted to look for some sites downtown to search.

I drove along the waterfront in the older section of Charleston and started looking for potential sites. Suddenly, I drove past a series of abandoned buildings and saw something that made me hit the brakes. In between two buildings that dated back to the turn of the century was a decrepit structure that obviously pre-dated the surrounding buildings by at least 100 years! And the best part of what I saw was that there was a narrow strip of grass that led from the street to the building itself. Parking across the street, I spent a productive 30 minutes searching this area. While there was a fair amount of trash present, the coins and other items I found made it well worth the effort. Several Indian Head pennies, a Shield nickel, three Barber dimes, some coins from the 1900's, a pocket knife and a brass key all wound up in my pouch. Satisfied with my finds, I packed up the gear and headed off in search of another site to hunt.

A short distance away, I found another building that was in the process of being torn down. Asking the crew working inside if I could hunt the grass outside, they said as long as I stayed clear of the building itself I could hunt the property. There was not much grass to hunt as many of the homes in this part of town took up most of the lot but a brief search turned up several wheat cents, a few Indian Head pennies and some interesting Victorian-era artifacts. Continuing my drive, I saw what turned out to be an abandoned school building waiting to be razed. Parking along the street, I spent 45 minutes searching the area with similar success . . . as a matter of fact, the first signal I hit turned out to be a silver Mercury dime!

The moral of this story is that there are still some great sites out there if you just take the time to go out and look for them. You'd be surprised at how often treasure hunters pass literally dozens of productive spots on the way to the same old hunted-out park or school they head to every weekend. Keep your eyes open for potential sites when out driving around - not only when you are in new territory but even when you go to some of the sites you typically visit. You'll be amazed at what's still out there waiting for an astute treasure hunter with a sharp eye. The type of sites you should be alert for are not just limited to urban areas either. As you drive around in the country, look for old stone walls, trees planted in straight lines where a house no longer stands, a baseball backstop long since forgotten, cellar hole depressions, flowers in the middle of an empty field or wooded area indicating a house was once there – the list is endless. A large percentage of these sites were never written about in the history books so even the most diligent researcher will not discover their whereabouts. An astute treasure hunter who keeps his or her eyes open as they drive to a site may just stumble across a site even more productive than their intended destination. Has it become harder to find good targets in the sites that seem to attract treasure hunters on a regular basis? Yes, but by looking for what others have overlooked before you, finds that others can only hope to find will start showing up on your hunts.

Keep a small notebook or even an inexpensive digital camera in your vehicle to capture details on these sites when you see them. You will typically come across a "killer" site when you have no time to even do a cursory search and unless you capture the details when you see it, you will likely forget to return until you hear about the great finds someone else made there. With the location recorded, you can do some research to find out about the history of the site as well as who the current owner is in order to get permission to search it.

INEXPENSIVE DIGITAL CAMERAS

The price of digital cameras has plummeted in the past few years and now you can pick up a basic model which is ideal for capturing site information for later follow-up for under $25. These cameras can be left in your glove box so potential sites or historical markers can be captured, followed up on and easily added to your research library.

LIBRARIES & HISTORICAL SOCIETIES

The first stop any treasure hunter should make is their local library. It always surprises me when I give a talk and ask how many people visit the library that very few hands go up. Almost all libraries have a local history section. While most of the material can not be checked out, a few dollars worth of photocopying can give you more than enough leads to sites to hunt for the next few months. Ask to see books or pamphlets on the history of your area. Learn to skim over the material looking for references – in words or pictures - to the types of sites that might hold the kinds of targets you are searching for. If you are a coin hunter, keep your eyes open for references to old schools, church picnics, scenic overlooks, a section of town that may have died when the new highway came through on the other side of town, a baseball field, small amusement parks or traveling circuses that may have come to town. If you are a relic hunter, look for references to sites such as military skirmishes, campsites, monuments or muster grounds. If you're a water hunter, look for references to beaches – large or small, swimming holes or even public pools that may now simply be a grassy lot. I find a highlighter to be useful in flagging the sections worth following up on but use whatever method works best for you (and obviously, do not use a highlighter on a book you need to return to the library).

Spend some time talking to the desk librarian. They are trained in conducting research and are usually more than willing to assist you in tracking down information. Let them know you are trying to find details on old recreation areas, schools, parks, churches, swimming holes or even military activity in your county and you'll be amazed at how much information they can help you come up with.

Recently I went to the local library in order to see what research material might be available. Like many libraries today, this one had a small room containing all sorts of information pertaining to the history of the town, county and state dating back to the 1700's. In less than 4 hours, I had obtained copies of several detailed hand-drawn maps showing Revolutionary War troop movements and campsites within 25 miles of my house, details of old parks and picnic groves long since abandoned and two swimming lakes that closed in the 1940's . . . more than enough sites to keep me busy for some time to come. None of these sites were found in books labeled "TREASURE HUNTING HOT SPOTS" but rather typewritten church histories, newspaper clipping files and even a well-worn local travel guide from 1946 – the type of material that most treasure hunters would not even give a second glance to!

The county historical society is another resource that you should make use of. They will typically have a collection of maps and other material covering the local history dating back to when the first settlers reached the area. Most of this must be used at the historical center itself; however, a notebook, pen scanner or digital camera can help you capture the information you need to pinpoint potential sites.

You should also consider joining the local historical society or at least offer to give a talk about the hobby. Bring some of your finds and equipment to show as part of your talk. Let attendees know about your shared passion in history. Pass out some business cards and offer to work with them in searching some of the properties they may have control of. Put together a display of what you find and donate it to the society's museum or visitor's center. With the notoriety gained from this type of positive work, it will be much easier to gain permission to search other older sites in your area as well as meet people who can provide you with a wealth of local history and potential sites to search.

LOCAL TRAVEL GUIDES

Another source of leads that I have used successfully many times, especially when I am traveling and want to find a productive site in an area I am not familiar with, are local travel guides or booklets. Next time you see a visitor's center on the interstate or coming into a town, stop in and look over the many guides that are in the racks on display. If there are any historic attractions in the area, you will usually find something related to the site. While some will likely be off-limits to detectorists, drive by and see what is available in the area. If the site is an old one, it is probably in the older section of town and there will usually be a number of productive sites nearby which may be hunted with permission. Two years ago I found out about a Revolutionary War battle site near an area I was going to on business from one of these guides and while the site itself was designated as a historic site, a large area across the road was being cleared for a low-income housing project. Needless to say, permission was readily obtained and a number of relics from the 1700's were easily uncovered. My son, an avid metal detectorist in his own right, almost always comes back to the car with a few guides containing leads to sites. A few years ago we picked up a newspaper-type publication at a rest area off I-81 in Virginia with 20 pages of Civil War sites and tours in the area. While we did not have the time to hunt them on that trip, I did go back about a year later and found a small virgin Union campsite just by driving along one of the detailed tour guides in the paper . . . recovering more than 50 relics in a single afternoon. Others have spent countless hours researching the local area . . . no need to repeat their effort and it is quite simple to leverage that work into a successful hunt in a new area.

LEADS FROM OTHERS

One of the best and easiest source of leads to productive sites are local residents, with the "ol' timers" usually the ones who can be your biggest asset. After all, who better to tell you where the old parks, schools, picnic groves, amusement parks, carnival grounds, beaches or even battle sites were than the people who actually used them or heard about them from their parents or grandparents.

Over the years, I've given talks at senior citizen centers and have always come away with many solid leads that produced finds I would not have made otherwise. Most centers welcome presentations that may be of interest to their residents. You can share your interest in treasure hunting with the residents at the same time you get new sites to hunt; a win-win situation for everyone involved. Another advantage is that you may talk to people who actually grew up in another area and can provide you with a number of sites worth traveling to hunt that you would otherwise have been unaware of. Think about putting on a follow-up presentation showing some of the finds you might have made at the sites provided earlier and you will usually wind up with even more sites to search that had been previously forgotten.

A tip that fellow treasure hunter Gerry Denton provided me a number of years ago has proven to be a consistent producer no matter where I have moved since. Gerry recommended talking to those active in the outdoors such as hunters, fisherman, hikers, canoeists or kayakers and tell them about your interest in local history. Ask them to let you know if they come across old foundations, abandoned roads, rock fences, partially submerged piers, bottle dumps, swimming holes, dilapidated bridges or ferry landings when they are out in the woods. I've taken the tip one step further and put up flyers in several local gun or outdoor shops offering a $5 store voucher for any site that I am able to gain access to . . . a win-win for both of us. Many of the sites I have been steered to this way have never been hunted and were not documented in any material I could have uncovered doing hours of tedious research.

If you are not from the area or don't know anyone in the area you are planning on hunting, drive around and keep your eye out for some of the older residents . . . then simply ask them for a little of their time. A few choice questions such as where were the old schools, parks or beaches can often uncover sites that no amount of formal research would have uncovered. Another way to meet these "information resources" in smaller towns is to stop at a local diner or corner restaurant – you can almost always find a group of residents socializing and most will be more than willing to talk about the history of the area.

Another easy-to-use and effortless technique to find some productive sites is to talk about your hobby to friends and co-workers. Let them know you are always looking for older sites to search and see if they are aware of any that you could gain access to. The type of sites worth asking about include old family homes, vacant land where homes or buildings once stood, foundations on their property far from any road, swimming holes, old informal ball fields, etc. Over the years I have found many very productive sites simply by asking a few pointed questions and listening to the responses. Most people love to reminisce and if you listen for leads, you will have more sites than you could hunt going at it on a full-time basis. A word of caution here: be sure not to mention that you are also hoping to find valuable coins and jewelry. People tend to get odd when money is involved so focus on collectibles and the historical significance of what you are looking for when you ask about possible sites to search.

HIKING, CAMPING & OUTDOOR BOOKS

This is another example of how "thinking out of the box" can pay off. Look for books written for an entirely different audience that can often provide treasure hunters with an easy-to-follow road map to countless productive sites that likely have never seen a metal detector skim across their grounds. Be creative in the titles you look for and you will find a stack full with little effort. Let's talk about a few examples to get you started.

Sites that have consistently produced many exceptional finds over the years have been spots along abandoned railroad lines. They can include bunkhouses for workers, small hotels and stores on long-forgotten routes or supply bunkers left to fall into disrepair. There is an excellent book that was written for railroad enthusiasts entitled "*Right-of-Way; Guide to Abandoned Railroads in the United States*" by Waldo Nielsen. It covers all the states in the U.S. and provides specific details that in combination with a modern topographic map, allow you to easily locate productive sites that have often never been hunted. I've found several sites dating back to the 1800's with this book and a few hours of detecting turned up coins dating back over 100 years and some railroad collectibles including a silver railroad watch that now has a place in one of my display cases. The book is out of print but a search on sites such as Amazon.com can usually turn up a copy or two. On the same line, hiking and biking along abandoned railroad lines has become a popular pastime worldwide. There are several companies in Europe that actually run tours using specially-fabricated bicycles to ride the old rails and there are a number of books that detail the lines and interesting waypoints . . . translation – possible sites to search (as long as there are no restrictions about hunting them).

How about another example which easily identified a number of sites with very little effort? In the first half of the 1900's, the Catskill Mountain region north of New York City was famous as a resort destination and the most prevalent ethnic group visiting the area were the Jews from the city. There were all sorts of options ranging from low-cost motels to grand hotels and bungalow colonies. Virtually every one of these has closed their doors and in many cases are simply overgrown areas that time has passed by. Items such as collectible coins, jewelry, trinkets and other relics would have been lost in the heyday of the resorts. Figure all the sites have been hunted out? Well in fact, there still are some that have never been hunted and others still produce with a bit of hard work. Waiting in the airport terminal in New York, I wandered through a bookstore and came across a book that chronicled a number of these old resorts from the personal perspective of the author who grew up in the midst of this era. Over 300 pages in length, it contained a list of more than 900 resorts and details on a number of them. Returning from my trip, I took three days and visited the area. I was able to get permission to search five of the old resorts and it was immediately apparent that two had never been hunted based on the number of coins that turned up. With countless other sites in that one book that required no difficult research to locate, research does not have to be painful to be productive.

Other subjects that have helped identify sites over the years include books on hiking trails (look for references to old towns, military engagements, unused roads and the like), water trips (look for mention of swimming sites, old resorts or long-forgotten towns); canoeing or kayaking trips (towns that once existed on the water, popular swimming sites or picnicking locations). Be creative and see what you can come up with.

LOCAL HISTORY BOOKS

If you are still looking for more sites to search, the next step is book research – reading through local history books in search of any mention of the type of sites you are looking for. As mentioned before, you can find a number of local history books in your library and should start there. They may even be able to request a specific title through the Inter-Library system if they do not have it on their shelves. Keep your eye out for local history books that might be offered as fundraisers by historical society's church groups or small towns. Typically a limited run of only a few 100 copies will be produced and when they are sold, that's all there will be. Often these books will include personal photographs submitted by long time residents and the only place you will find the photos will be in the book. Can you imagine thumbing through a small local history book and seeing a photo of a group of families picnicking along side of a nearby creek with a rope swing visible in the background? It happens and in most cases you will be the first one to hunt the area.

Let's say you are a coin shooter and would prefer to find a few quality coins from the 1800's rather than a pocketful of clad coins lost in the past few months. Your research needs to focus on finding sites that were popular in the 1800's, and if possible, no longer in use (fewer people will know about them and hence you will be more likely to find the targets you are looking for with less competition). You probably won't find a book entitled "*Forgotten but once Popular Sites from the 1800's in Anytown, USA*", but there are countless books that hold the key to becoming a more successful detectorist that could just as well have that title. Virtually every county and many towns and cities have had history books written about them, typically in limited quantities and distributed through the local historical society or offered to commemorate something about the area such as its centennial or bicentennial. Typically out-of-print, they can be found at the historical society, local library or even at garage sales and flea markets. An example will help make the point. Several years ago I came across a book on the history of a small town in Pennsylvania near where we lived at a *"Friends of the Library"* book sale. It had been published in 1976 and was about 150 pages in length containing a number of old photographs of the town. Going through the book, I read about the old high school that had burned in the 1920's, a ball field that was popular in the 1930's and 1940's, a swimming hole on a nearby creek and several church picnic grounds that had been packed every month during the summer months. The school was my first stop and as I came upon the site, I was happy to see it was still an empty field and better yet, the old flagpole was still standing in a group of trees along once side. Well, to make a long story short, my first signal turned out to be an 1899 Barber Quarter, and over the next 3 months, my partner Brent Parrett and I recovered more than 500 coins dating back to the 1870's along with a number of other items including gold jewelry, tokens and artifacts. Other sites in that one book kept us busy for the better part of a year - and we never saw another detectorist at these sites despite two metal detector dealers and a major distributor having storefronts within 40 miles of the town.

If you can not find what you need there, contact one of the book dealers listed in the Resource Reference Bibliography section. Let them know what your interests are, where you are planning on searching and have them recommend material that will meet your needs.

POSTCARDS

In the years before the Internet and glossy full-color travel brochures, postcards were the most common form of advertising used by resorts around the world. Postcards gained popularity during the late 1880's with most of these early examples being hand drawn or simple black-and-white. By the early 1900's, many of the most postcards were available in color and typically showed the amenities they offered along with easy-to-follow directions for those that wanted to vacation there. These old post cards can often be found at antique shops, flea markets and swap meets as well as on the Internet. Most dealers have cards separated by subject matter and / or location. Keep you eye out for sites worth searching such as beaches, amusement parks, swim clubs, ski resorts, motels with wide expanses of grass . . . use your imagination as you thumb through the cards. The cost of these cards is typically quite reasonable considering what information you can get from just one of them.

Once you have found out that a site worth searching existed, a little additional research will easily provide you with its location and current use. Many older sites are now abandoned and just waiting for someone to search them with a metal detector and recover the valuables they still contain. Often old postcards will show a site such as a beach in its heyday and may show you that the old area was in a different location than the current in-use location. Other features to look for in post cards include ball fields which may now just be an overgrown field, defunct picnic groves, a popular motel that faded into obscurity when the highway bypassed the area it was situated in, swimming pools at motels that were filled in yet the grassy area that surrounded it is still present and docks or piers that no longer exist.

A good example was provided by Earl Stevens, an avid detectorist and over-the-road truck driver from Iowa. He came across the postcard shown here and knew that the motel was still in operation from having seen it in his travels; however, he could not remember ever seeing the pool. The next time he was in the area he stopped, showed the owner the postcard and asked about the pool. He was told it had been filled in some 20 years earlier due to insurance liability concerns and maintenance issues. Permission was granted to search the grassy area between the building and over the next 6 months - hunting it each time he came through the area - Earl recovered more than 400 coins including almost 60 pieces silver. All found simply by looking at a post card and recognizing the potential it presented.

So for a simple method of finding potential sites to hunt, give postcards a try. The Reference Bibliography at the end of this chapter contains some websites that can steer you to postcards for your area. Even a search of E-Bay for items such as "Amusement Park Postcard" or something more specific can turn up listings that can point you in the direction of a site that might just be un-hunted. In the case of finding a card online, you do not even have to buy it but rather simply note the location and pinpoint its location with a little more research. Post cards truly give credence to the old saying, "*A picture is worth a 1,000 words.*"

REAL ESTATE GUIDES & WEBSITES

An area that is consistently productive yet is avoided by most treasure hunters is the yard of private homes. Knocking on a homeowner's door and asking for permission to search their yard is not the most popular thing for a detectorist; however, my experience has shown that on the average 9 in 10 will say yes. Additionally, once you get permission from one property owner, getting their neighbor to say yes is usually simply a matter of walking next door and asking.

In sticking with the common thread of this chapter in finding sites with a minimal amount of work, this section has been proven to be a consistent producer worldwide. With countless homes being placed on the market on a regular basis, you have a source of leads that is continually updated and readily available. Have you ever noticed the many free real estate guides at supermarkets, gas stations or restaurants? Well, next time you do, pick one up.

So what are you looking for in these guides? How about homes or properties for sale dating back 50 years or more. Once you have the address of a home that has been listed, stop by and talk to the property owner. I have found that even owners of well-kept homes with manicured lawns are more amenable to allowing someone to hunt the property knowing that they will soon be leaving than they might otherwise have been. Come up with a great speech when asking for permission and you will get to hunt 90% or more of the properties you try to access. Be careful not to stress that you are looking for valuables but rather your interest in historical artifacts. Offer to return any personal items you come across and you should be good to go. And when you are done (make sure you leave **NO** sign you were there), see if the owners can give you the names of the surrounding residents and you might have several homes to hunt.

Are you into computers? Well, if so, log onto Realtor.com and do a search of your local area. If you go to the Advanced Search page, you will see an option to select homes at least 51+ years old. Simply select this option and run your search. It will return the older homes for sale with a map & directions available for each one - what could be easier? You can expand the scope of your search to include neighboring towns through the Nearby Areas tab. The following photo collage shows two houses that were easily found with the Realtor.com search engine. In less that a few hours at each location, more than 50 coins with some dating back to the mid-1800's were recovered.

I have used real estate guides and the computerized search engine on the last few business trips I have been on to find homes that turned up some great finds including Indian Head pennies, a few large cents, more than two dozen silver coins and other trinkets . . . with virtually no effort other than skimming through some guides at dinner or a few clicks of the keyboard!

REALTOR.COM WEBSITE

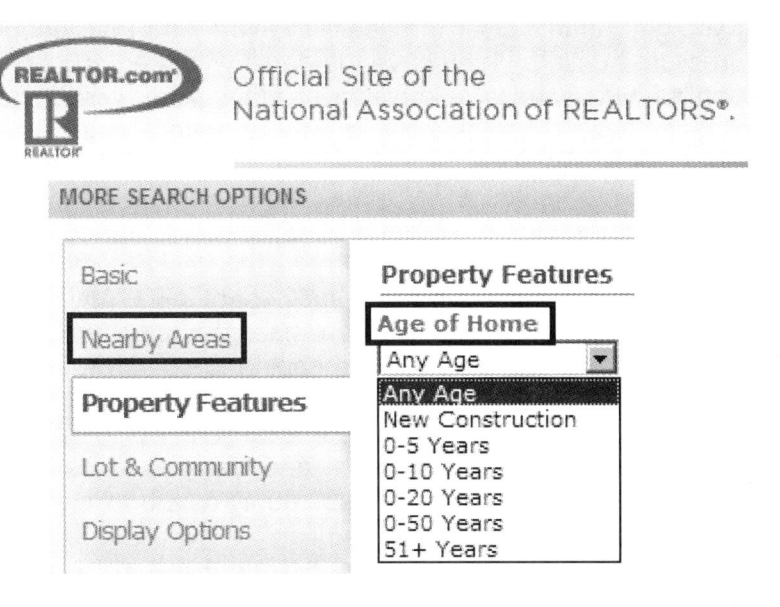

RESULTS OF A FEW CLICKS FOLLOWED BY A FEW PHONE CALLS

MAPS

The use of maps to find productive sites should come as no great surprise but do you really think there are maps with the proverbial big "X" emblazoned on them and the annotation "Dig Here for Treasure"? Well the signs might not be quite so obvious but there are many maps that are readily available that can lead you right to an untouched site with little or no additional effort. This section will cover two types of maps – old, historical documents and current ones – as well as how to obtain copies of both and then interpret what they tell you to find the sites you are hoping to discover.

Maps are excellent tools for all types of treasure hunting. Potential sites can be plotted and then when actually checked, annotated as to their productivity. Old roads, canals, wagon paths or trails can be drawn onto the map and vacant areas worth checking become readily apparent. Take your maps – new and old - with you when you visit the library or talk to some ol'timers in the area . . . it's a lot easier to pinpoint sites with a detailed map in hand than trying to plot conflicting or confusing directions later when you get home. Over the years I have found that topographical maps are the maps best suited for treasure hunting. They have the detail you need and by showing the contour of the land, you can often tell where trails, campsites or other sites were located using some basic common sense. Laminating them is an inexpensive way to protect your research and allows you to take them into the field for ready reference.

OLD MAPS:

Unless the area you live in was only settled in the past 50 years, older maps will be the ones that hold the greatest chance of leading you to virgin sites. New maps are great and as you will see later in the section, are in fact useful tools, but the sites you are hoping to search will typically not be shown on any current map. If they were, it's extremely unlikely that you would be the first - or even the 100th - person to hunt it. As discussed earlier, stop off at your local library or historical society and see what maps they might have available. Another excellent and often overlooked source of maps is the county clerks' office or the tax assessor's office at the county courthouse. Most counties have maps dating back to when they were initially laid out and while you will not be able to take them home with you, you can often get copies of sections you might be interested in. I have taken high-resolution digital photographs of some of these maps and reviewed them on my computer at home to pinpoint productive sites.

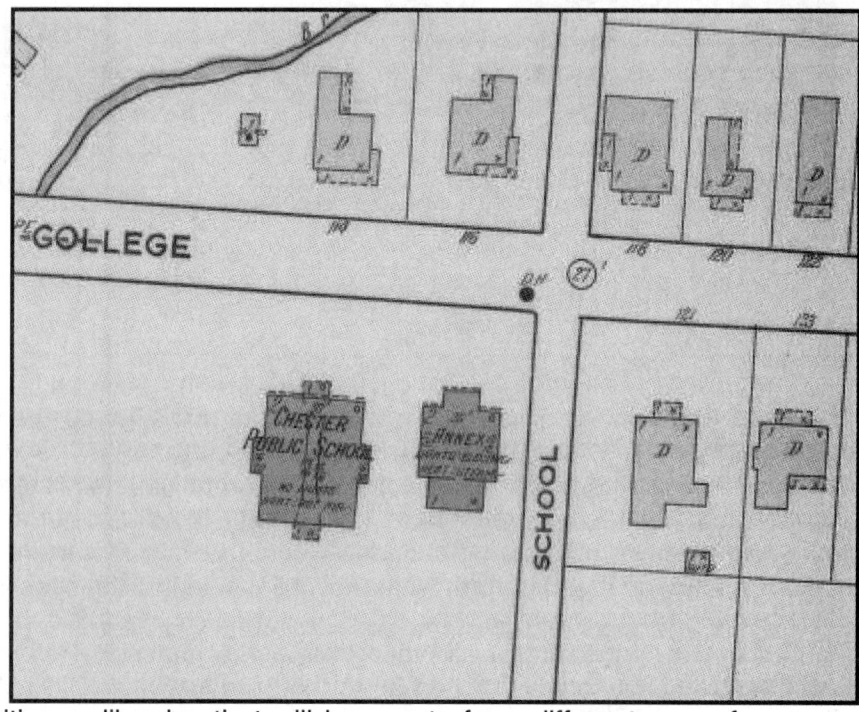

Thanks to technology, many map collections that were once accessible only by appointment and in-person are now available via the Internet. The Reference Resource Bibliography at the end of this chapter contains several sizable map collections that can be accessed at no charge from your home computer. Many can be saved for later reference but all can be viewed and printed when interesting sites are identified. One of the best maps that treasure hunters can use is known as the Sanborn Fire Insurance Map collection or simply Sanborn Maps for short. The Sanborn map collection consists of a series of scale maps, from 1867 to the present showing commercial, industrial, and residential sections of some twelve thousand cities and towns in the United States, Canada, and Mexico. The maps were designed to assist fire insurance agents in determining the degree of hazard associated with a particular property and therefore show the size, shape, and construction of buildings including sheds, outhouses (more about that later) and barns. They also show the street names - many of which are the same today – and what commercial buildings were used for. If a piece of property was being used for a park, ball field or something else, it will be shown as well. The entire Sanborn collection includes some fifty thousand editions of fire insurance maps comprising an estimated seven hundred thousand individual sheets. A search on the Internet for Sanborn maps of your area or state should produce at least one or two sites such as universities or libraries that will have sets from different years for you to review. In late 2008, I looked over the collection covering areas around my home which consisted of more than 50 maps dating back to the early 1900's in search of sites to do some coin hunting. It was a simple matter to identify sites such as neighborhood parks and wooded areas surrounded by homes on the old maps and transcribe their location onto a modern-day street map since virtually every road name was the same on both maps. Finding some of these small out-of-the-way sites was quite easy and more than 150 coins dating back to the turn of the century turned up over the course of the next 3 months.

Another source to explore are book or map dealers - either local businesses or those found on the Internet listed in the reference section at the end of this chapter. These companies offer copies of maps for most areas of the country dating back to the early 1800's. Many of these maps have sites such as parks, horse racing tracks, schools and battlefields clearly marked on them. You can usually find copies of old topographical maps as well as county or city maps at libraries or the town hall office and these maps will also contain countless sites that can be transferred to a current map. When you start looking for old maps, here are some types that have proven to hold keys to the sites we are all hoping to find . . . use this as a starting point and see what you can turn up. Make a list of the following: early U.S. maps, old railroad maps, county and city maps, Indian trail and camp maps, trapper trails, old fort locations, maps of the Pony Express routes, military maps . . . the list is virtually endless, customize it to fit the specific history of your area.

If you come across old maps, be sure to read the chapter entitled "*State of the Art Treasure Hunting Equipment & Techniques.*" It describes the use of some innovative computer programs that can take long-forgotten sites from old maps scanned into your computer and translate them into waypoints that can be easily transferred to a GPS unit. Once you have them loaded into your GPS unit, you can walk right to the site and start recovering the "goodies"! I have used this combination of old maps and new technology on a number of occasions to find once vibrant sites that are now nothing more than an overgrown field or wooded stand of trees that would otherwise not even warrant a second glance. This is yet another example of thinking outside of the box to find sites that have never seen a metal detector yet hold countless artifacts just waiting to be recovered.

A highly recommend source of research material is the archives of K.B. Slocum Books. They have an amazingly extensive library of maps dating back to the 1700's for most areas of the United States. The maps come in small collections or kits and show towns, roads, ferry landings and railroad lines to name just a few features that can help you find local sites. A friend of mine, Bill Stirling, from Connecticut recently purchased a map of the township he lives in from K.B. Slocum Books that showed a picnic grove down the road from a church less than five miles from his house that was still standing. He obtained permission from the current landowner and quickly discovered that no one else had ever hunted the site. Over the next few weeks he recovered more than 100 coins dating back to the 1860's with very little trash. Even a single site such as this in your area could recoup the cost of dozens of maps! The 1872 Seated half dollar is just one of the superb coins Bill recovered from a site that took very little effort to locate.

Lost Treasure Magazine's on-line map store has maps not found elsewhere that can quickly pinpoint sites worth searching – and they are adding new maps on a regular basis.

NEW MAPS:

Street-level maps or road atlases can also be useful in finding new sites to search. Print versions can be perused to look for places such as schools, parks, beaches, historical sites (not to search them directly but to see what open land surrounds them), hiking trails, campgrounds . . . the list is limitless. Taking the print atlases or maps high-tech, there are a number of low-cost computer mapping programs that offer some useful features such as being able to search for places like schools, parks, beaches and specific street names (see the tip below on how streets were often named) as well as being able to add notes tied to locations where you can save your research material. Several of these programs are also listed in the Reference Resource Bibliography.

Place names are another quick and often unused technique to locate long-forgotten sites worth searching. In days gone by, names of streets, towns, bridges or even landmarks were given based on what their use was. For example, near Atlanta, Georgia there are several roads that end in ferry; i.e., Powers Ferry, Paces Ferry, Johnson Ferry, etc. Care to hazard a guess as to where they got their names? Each of these roads now have modern bridges that cross the Chattahoochee River; however, 100 years ago, they were roads that ended at a privately run ferry crossing run by a person whose name is still associated with the road. Now in the area of major cities, the possibility of finding anything at the site of the old crossing is quite slim, but you can find these types of sites in less populated areas by simply looking at a local map. Many times I have come across roads or landmarks with names such as Battle Hill, Bloody Pond Road, Deep Mine Road, Cornwall Avenue, Fetch Hill School Road, etc. In many cases, I have found sites that were never hunted or at least hunted superficially with little or no additional research required to pinpoint the site other than drive to it and find the location of whatever it was that gave it its name. Pick up a local map and skim through the street index highlighting those that have names warranting closer scrutiny. If you have a mapping program such as Streets & Trips or Street Atlas, you can type in words such as those listed above in the search window and see what turns up . . . you might be amazed at the number of sites you can find with little or no effort.

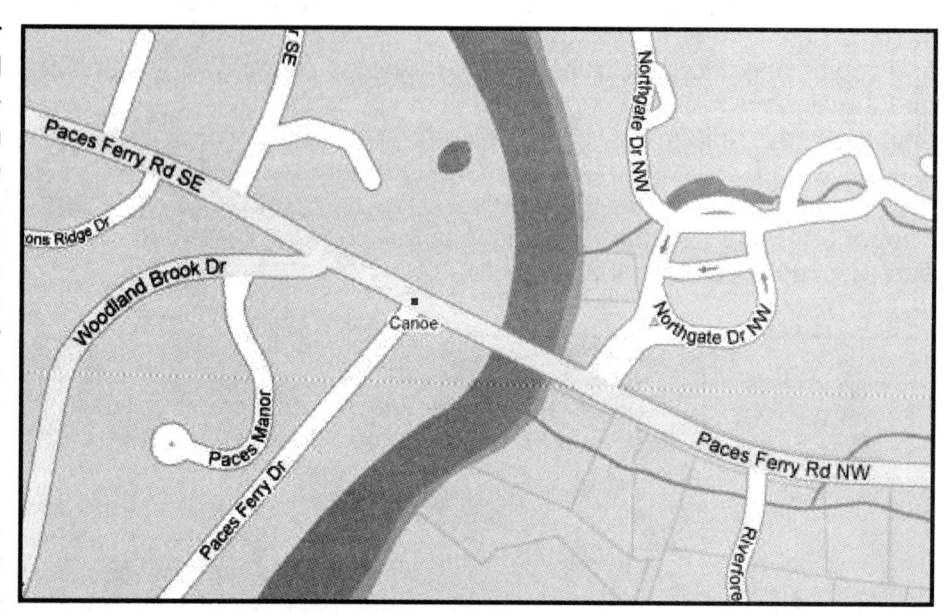

Topographical maps are extremely useful as a treasure hunting aid. Older maps show the location of houses and other buildings that are no longer there. Even modern maps often show abandoned structures and if they are located some distance from the nearest road, you may just be the first one to search them. Most countries have some sort of national mapping program and they are usually the source of official printed maps. A number of 3rd party printers have assembled books containing detailed maps of states or countries that are excellent companions in the field. Delorme is a U.S.-based company that produces both print and electronic versions of topo maps. Another excellent source of maps from around the world at all different scales is East View Cartographic. Contact information for both of these companies is provided in the back of this chapter. There are also websites that provide on-line topo maps which can be used when researching a specific site and you do not need to purchase a complete collection of maps.

GEOGRAPHIC NAMES INFORMATION SYSTEM (GNIS):

An extremely useful tool available to treasure hunters is an online database known as the Geographic Names Information System or GNIS for short. It contains name and location information on more than two million physical and cultural features located throughout the United States and its territories. It was developed by the United States Geological Survey in cooperation with the United States Board on Geographic Names to promote the standardization of feature names. What does this mean to treasure hunters looking for possible sites to search? Well, you simply call up the search page for the GNIS database, select a state and refine the query to a particular county, scroll through the drop-down menu to pick a particular feature such as beach, canal, church, mine, park or school to name just a few of the choices and click on SEARCH. The results appear in tabular form and provide the feature's name and coordinates. Many of the locations contained in the GNIS database are denoted as being <u>HISTORICAL</u> which often means it is not longer in use. .. just imagine the possibilities these sites can hold! The coordinates can then be plugged into a computerized or on-line mapping program or entered in a handheld GPS receiver and quickly located with a minimal amount of effort. The screen shot below shows part of the results of a representative search for schools located in Georgia's Cherokee county - note that there were 62 school sites identified in that one county (including historical sites), more than enough to keep a group busy for months or longer!

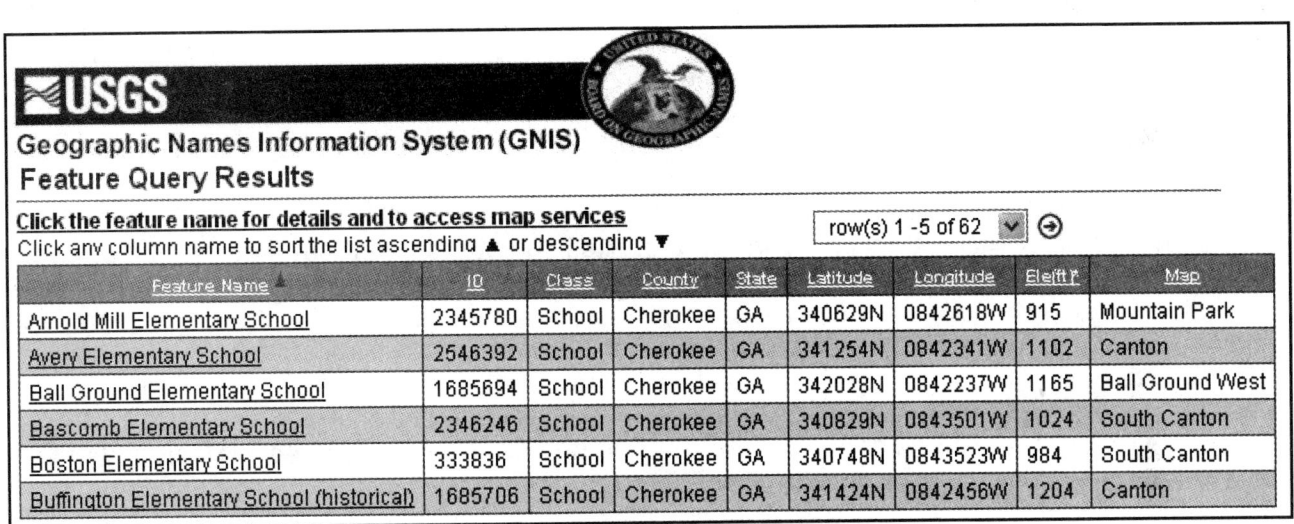

≋USGS
Geographic Names Information System (GNIS)
Feature Query Results

Click the feature name for details and to access map services
Click any column name to sort the list ascending ▲ or descending ▼   row(s) 1-5 of 62

Feature Name ▲	ID	Class	County	State	Latitude	Longitude	El(ft)"	Map
Arnold Mill Elementary School	2345780	School	Cherokee	GA	340629N	0842618W	915	Mountain Park
Avery Elementary School	2546392	School	Cherokee	GA	341254N	0842341W	1102	Canton
Ball Ground Elementary School	1685694	School	Cherokee	GA	342028N	0842237W	1165	Ball Ground West
Bascomb Elementary School	2346246	School	Cherokee	GA	340829N	0843501W	1024	South Canton
Boston Elementary School	333836	School	Cherokee	GA	340748N	0843523W	984	South Canton
Buffington Elementary School (historical)	1685706	School	Cherokee	GA	341424N	0842456W	1204	Canton

NOTE: To enter the coordinates provided by GNIS into a GPS receiver or mapping program you need to use the following format (take Avery Elementary School for example): N 34 12 54 W 084 23 41.

U.S GenWeb PROJECT

This is another example of a resource developed for a use that is completely unrelated to treasure hunting yet contains information that many in the hobby have used to locate sites that have been overlooked by others in their area. The USGenWeb Project was created to provide a compilation of genealogy websites used for genealogical research in every county and every state of the United States and offers access to all the information at no charge. Local genealogists compile the information which includes maps, county and town histories, census reports, church newsletters and other sources of possible sites to search. Some areas have more detailed material than others but more is being added all the time. The portal to start your search is accessible from the Internet at http://www.usgenweb.org/. Other countries around the world have similar websites . . . a simple Internet search will turn up a number of sites that were created for genealogical needs yet can be used to find sites to search.

NEWSPAPERS

As with maps, newspapers – both old and new – can be great sources of leads if you know what to look for and approach them from a perspective different than other treasure hunters.

OLD NEWSPAPERS:

Almost every library carries microfilmed copies of local newspapers that date back to the earliest days of the paper having been published. With the press of a button on the viewer, you can get a copy of any interesting lead you come across and add it to your research library. As you select sections to review, think about what you are looking for . . . references to sites that may be lost in time yet hold the types of targets you are searching for. If you are a coin hunter, look for references to picnics held in wooded groves, schools celebrating graduations that are no longer in existence, circuses coming to town or church revivals put on by traveling preachers to list just a few. Are you interested in beach or shallow water hunting? How about looking for outings to local beaches and swim clubs – many of which have been closed down for decades? Another different tact to try is to pull up the classifieds and look for the Lost & Found section. A simple entry reporting a lost ring or other valuable may be the only tip you need to track down what might have been a popular site many years ago. As you skim through the old papers – either in hardcopy or electronically – look for photos that show groups of people enjoying time outdoors. As they say, a picture says a 1,000 words and seeing people at a site long since abandoned may be a roadmap to an untapped bonanza.

NEW NEWSPAPERS:

Many papers – especially those published in smaller towns – run a weekly area history column. Read through them and look for references to the type of sites you are focusing on. I've found many sites with this method ranging from schools long since torn down to Civil War and Revolutionary War relics from small, little-known skirmishes and even old mine sites. Several successful treasure hunters have taken this one step further and contacted the columnist asking for additional details on sites covered in the articles or information on similar sites not yet put to paper.

Keep an eye out for stories detailing new construction projects. When the area is cleared, you may have a narrow window to search the site without having to fight your way through thick underbrush. If there was any activity of interest in the area, you may find it amazingly easy to recover artifacts that have lain undisturbed for years.

As mentioned in the section above on old newspapers, don't pass up the Lost & Found section in the classifieds. Recovering and returning a lost ring, watch or other valuable will often result in a reward and you never know what else might turn up while searching for the item that brought you to a specific location in the first place. A year ago my hunting partner was asked to look for an engagement ring that a recently married woman had lost off the edge of a public boat dock. Strapping on his dive gear and dropping to the bottom, he found a ring almost immediately . . . but when he surfaced, she said it was not hers. Well, he went back down and found another ring which also turned out to not be hers. The third ring was the charm but in addition to the $100 reward Cory was given, he left with two nice gold rings from a location neither of us would have thought twice of hunting.

BULLETIN BOARDS & CLASSIFIED ADS

As we discussed in the "Leads From Others" section above, often finding out about a productive site simply requires letting others know about your interest. Eric Johnson, a veteran detectorist from upstate New York tried an interesting approach more than 20 years ago while searching for some new sites to hunt. He put a small classified ad in his local newspaper that simply read "*Are there lost or hidden valuables on your property? Call 555-1212 to find out."* In the first two days the ad ran, he received more than 20 calls from interested property owners and was given permission to search the grounds of seven. A pocketful of old coins and other items wound up in his collection even after giving the people who gave him permission some of what he had found. In drafting this book, I called him and he said that he still uses that simple technique to find new sites to hunt when he's run out of other areas. Placing a simple ad in a local paper like the one Eric started using years ago costs but a few dollars yet can open up areas you might never have thought of hunting. Another no-cost option can be found at most grocery stores or neighborhood markets. Next time you go in, see if there is a bulletin board near the doors where you can put up an index card-sized announcement of your interest and see if you get any bites.

Taking this into the digital age, there are a number of local classified websites that allow you to post ads at no charge. Two well-known examples are CraigsList (www.Craigslist.com) and BackPage (www.Backpage.com). CraigsList covers a worldwide audience so if you are looking to find sites outside of the U.S., this would be a great site to start with. See if there are any small, local websites that can give you additional exposure for little or no cost and let people know of your interest. The ad below came from a local CraigsList posting and shows what these websites can offer you.

> I am searching for property to metal detect on. I will gladly give you first pick of anything that I may find. I do have an extra detector if anyone that would allow me to detect would be interested in trying it out. I will cover any areas that I search in, will gladly dispose of any trash metal I may come across. Thanks!

RESEARCH PAPERS

Another source of information that is seldom used is college research thesis papers. Students pursuing American History degrees often select the interesting periods as the subject for their research papers. Copies of these manuscripts are usually retained by the school for reference purposes. If there are any universities nearby, call the library to determine if they maintain copies of research papers for public use. If so, they may produce a lead to sites overlooked by most relic hunters. Many of these papers are extremely detailed and contain excerpts from personal documents that may not be available to the general public. A few years ago a friend of mine gave me a copy of just such a paper done on a county in Georgia. The student had divided the country into individual lots and plotted them on a country map. Then for each lot, a detailed history was provided. This document provided leads that were easy to locate and pinpointed Civil War sites, old foundations, mill works, river crossings and more. This one paper contained enough sites to search to keep an entire club active for years!

THE "RESEARCH RADIUS"... CLOSER IS USUALLY BETTER

In talking to many treasure hunters over the years that have learned how to conduct effective research and find productive sites, there is one aspect that is rarely considered in selecting sites: the distance the site is from one's home base. You may want to search for items that are not typically found in your immediate area; i.e., Civil War relics if you live in Oregon or gold nuggets if you live in Texas, but these goals should be used to plan an annual vacation rather than take time away from searches you could make any day of the week in your area. There's a joke that I've heard told many times that describes this phenomenon. Joe was an active treasure hunter who lived in City A. He had done research that revealed that a park in City B – 200 miles away – dated back to the 1800's and had been quite popular. Steve lived in City B and had also done his homework. He found a church revival site near City A that had hosted large crowds in the 1800's. Both treasure hunters packed their gear and spent 4 hours driving to the other city, passing each other near the halfway point. Since they had an 8 hour round trip, they only had time for a few hours of actual hunting. Both Joe and Steve made some nice finds; however, if each had hunted the site in their immediate area, they would have found much, much more! All too often we look for sites miles away figuring they would not have been hunted as much as nearby sites and then spend valuable hunting time driving to see what they might hold.

To be honest, I used to be in that mindset - often spending hours driving to sites that turned out to be mediocre at best. After all, with the rise in popularity of treasure hunting over the last 20 years, you would be hard pressed to find any area of the country where you can't find at least a few "hard core" treasure hunters. And similar to the story above, I would find out later that treasure hunters from the area near where I had gone had driven to my town with mediocre results similar to mine. Charles Garrett wrote in one of his books many years ago that there was more treasure within a 25 mile radius around anyone's home than one could recover in year of full-time treasure hunting. Despite the fact that there are more treasure hunters out there today, this statement still holds true.

Several years ago I visited a small town in southern Nebraska on business. The town which dated back to the late 1800's had a population of fewer than 5,000 people. I ran into a local treasure hunter, Joe Harpham, who started telling me about his finds. I was stunned when he showed me his collection which included more than 7,000 coins, jewelry, keys, relics and more - all found within the town limits over a 4-year period! Another point that really surprised me was when he told me that there at least 10 or 12 other detectorists active in the area. Learning how to use his detector and taking the time to find out about the town itself was what Joe attributed his success to. Here's a slogan that pays to remember when you start thinking about going on one of those 200-mile one-day trips: - "*Find more by driving less.*"

YOUR RESEARCH IS COMPLETE . . . OR IS IT?

Doing research is the first step. Putting it in a form you can actually use and then applying it is the follow through many treasure hunters fail to do and wind up frustrated when the finds they had hoped for fail to materialize.

Let's look at fellow Civil War relic hunter Larry Shirah from Atlanta. He's been a friend of mine for a many years and has made some impressive finds searching Civil War sites throughout the eastern United States. While he has been detecting for more than 25 years, he'll be the first to admit that research has not played a role in his success. Well, I offered to take him to a few sites I had researched the next time I visited Atlanta and he readily agreed. We met at a gas station and before we headed to the first site I had selected, I asked Larry what he knew of the specific troop locations and movements in the area around where we were standing. Despite having lived in the area for more than 50 years, he quickly realized that he was not as familiar with the details as he thought he had been. I described what regiments had been camped in specific locations surrounding us, where both the Union and Confederate troops had come from and moved to throughout the 3-week period surrounding the Battle of Kennesaw Mountain and what types of artillery had been used by both sides. Larry started to see the benefit of researching an area to identify sites rather than relying on luck which many treasure hunters tend to do. Over the years I have transcribed all of this information onto laminated topographical maps which have become an invaluable tool in determining what areas are worth searching and which are more than likely barren of Civil War relics. In addition, if troop movements cross an area where research has not shown anything to be, one can make a few focused trips to see if anything might be found. The maps also allow me to see what areas are not worth spending time searching even if construction is clearing them. On many occasions I have seen relic hunters detecting these "barren" areas and when I stopped to talk with them, had my maps confirmed when they said that nothing had turned up yet. One of the sites we hit that afternoon was a long ridge which had been occupied by Confederate troops in early July of 1864. Before we even took our detectors out of the truck, we talked about where the troops had been dug-in, where the Union troops had been located and even what the ground cover had been like some 139 years earlier. Why not just start hunting? Well, there was a lot of ground we could cover but we needed to focus on those areas where relics would be found. Again, knowing where both sides had been camped was essential to selecting a starting point. Walking down a section of the ridge that Larry had previously ignored, we started to recover relics in short order including various bullets, buttons, watch parts and an Indian Head penny. Not bad for less than an hour from an area that was readily accessible yet not obvious unless you knew where the activity had taken place. Larry said he and many other relic hunters had searched another section of the ridge on numerous occasions with little success and after our discussion before our hunt, he could see why they had come up empty handed so often - other than a stray soldier walking through the area, there was little reason for anything to have been lost there!

Maps with your research information transcribed onto them are extremely useful when you are driving to a site and your bearings get turned around (I'm sure we've all been there before). As we drove around the area and I described the troop movements and pointed out sites to hunt, I had to stop and reorient myself in terms of where the battle lines had been and where each army had been entrenched several times. Without a map and/or compass, you can easily find yourself searching a great looking spot that holds nothing. Remember, your success in the field comes down to basic math . . . how many good finds do you make in a given period of time; i.e., per hour. You need to ensure that your in-field time is spent in sites where targets are plentiful unless you are just out for the exercise.

Think outside of the box and look for the sites that have not been hunted by everyone with a metal detector for decades. Finding them does not require a degree in research as many might think. Once you have used the techniques covered in this chapter to identify the sites that were in use during the time period the item(s) you are looking to find were being used, you shouldn't have much trouble making the finds you read about in the magazines or see others make month after month at your club meetings. There are still 1,000's of unsearched sites out there just waiting for a treasure hunter with the willingness to do some research and locate them – why not make this the year you find your own "untapped glory spot?"

REFERENCE RESOURCE BIBLIOGRAPHY

Books

- **Site Research for Detectorists, Field Walkers & Archeologists** by David Villanueva (a U.K. book but applicable to anywhere in the world)
- **Successful Detecting Sites, Locate 1,000's Of Superb Sites & Make More Finds** by David Villanueva
- **United States Treasure Atlas** by Thomas Terry (State specific information containing details on literally 1,000's of sites including ghost towns, forts, ferry landings, lost treasures and more)

Book & Map Suppliers

- **Big Ten, Inc.**, Box 321231-W, Cocoa Beach, FL 32932-1231 (321) 783-4595 http://goldmaps.com
- **Carson Enterprises**, 861 Sunbonnet Lane, Las Cruces, NM 88007, (505) 541-1732; http://www.waybilltoadventure.com/
- **Delorme;** Supplier of print and electronic maps and GPS equipment; http://www.delorme.com
- **East View Cartographic**; Supplier of a wide range of current maps covering the world; http://www.cartographic.com
- **K.B. Slocum Books**, 4401 Bouvet Court, Austin, TX 78727; (800) 521-4451 http://kbslocumbook.com/K.B. Slocum Books and Maps/
- **Lost Treasure Magazine's Book Store**: Collection of books for treasure hunters, many long since out of print;; http://losttreasure.com/catalog/40
- **Maps of the Past**, 4979 Cornwell Court, Bloomington, IN 47403, (877) 353-6891 http://www.historicmapsrestored.com/
- **Research Unlimited**; P.O. Box 219, Oscoda, MI 48750; (989) 739-3294; http://www.research-unlimited.com/
- **The Northern Map Company**, P.O. Box 129, Dunnellon, FL 34430 (800) 314-2474
- **True Treasure Books**; 43 Sandpiper Road, Whitstable, Kent, CT5 4DP United Kingdom (+44-(0)-1227-274801); http://www.truetreasurebooks.com/

Internet Resources

- **AtoZee Postcard Collecting Web Directory**; http://www.atozee.com/web/postcards/
- **ACME Mapper:** Powerful, intuitive and free on-line mapping tool; http://mapper.acme.com/
- **Bing Maps**: Street level and aerial photo mapping for the world. Many locations have street views that allow you to scout out a new area from your keyboard. GPS coordinates can be entered to get directions to sites; http://www.bing.com/maps
- **Geographic Names Information System (GNIS)**: http://geonames.usgs.gov/pls/gnispublic
- **Google Maps**: Street level and aerial photo mapping for the world. Many locations have street views that allow you to scout out a new area from your keyboard. GPS coordinates can be entered to get directions to sites; http://maps.google.com/
- **Postcard Pages – United Kingdom**; http://www.postcard.co.uk/
- **The Postcard Shoppe**; http://postcardshopping.com/
- **Reminiscene (UK postcards)**; http://www.reminiscene.co.uk/

Maps

- **British Towns & Villages Network**: Excellent site offering research material and maps of England, Scotland, Wales and Northern Ireland; http://www.british-towns.net/
- **Digital-Topo-Maps.com**: Free onscreen topo maps you can print or you can order custom maps covering larger areas. http://www.Digital-Topo-Maps.com
- **East View Cartographic**: Detailed maps including topo maps, satellite images and nautical charts for most areas of the world; http://www.cartographic.com/
- **Lost Treasure Magazine's Map Archives**: Large collection of research maps in a single location; http://losttreasure.com/catalog/55
- **MyTopo**; Topo and aerial maps covering the US plus print maps you can order; http://mapserver.mytopo.com/
- **The Library of Congress American Memory Collection**; http://memory.loc.gov/ammem/
- **The University of Texas Worldwide Map Collection**; http://www.lib.utexas.edu/maps

Computer Programs

- **Delorme Street Atlas & Topo USA**: Street-level and topographical mapping programs covering the U.S., Mexico & Canada; http://www.Delorme.com
- **Microsoft Streets and Trips**: Street-level mapping program covering the U.S. & Canada; http://www.microsoft.com/Streets/
- **TeleType**: Providers of computer and PDA based mapping software (street & topographical options) with bundles available for all areas of the globe. http://www.teletype.com/

RESEARCH FORM

SITE NAME:

LOCATION & DIRECTIONS:

continued ☐

| Ownership: | Public: ☐ | Private: ☐ | Site still in use? | ☐ |

| Owner: | | Contact Info: | |

Checked Out In Person: ☐ **Date(s):**

Searched Site: ☐ **Date(s):**

SITE DESCRIPTION / HISTORY:

continued ☐

SITE CONDITIONS:

continued ☐

REFERENCE SOURCE(S):

continued ☐

ATTACHMENTS:

☐ : Site History   ☐ : Pictures   ☐ : Reference Material   ☐ : Site Find Log

Your Equipment – Time To Upgrade Or Simply Master What You Already Have?

So far you have compiled a list of finds you would like to make in the form of goals and spent some time researching where these finds would most likely be found. Hopefully you are beginning to see that it is possible to start making the kind of finds that you had previously only seen pictured in a treasure hunting magazine or in someone else's find box at club meetings.

This chapter will cover the second part of the Success Formula – "**EQUIPMENT**". As the chapter entitled "*The Formula for Success*" discussed, you need to not only have the right tool for the type of treasure hunting you will be doing but know how to use it in order to be successful on a consistent basis. This chapter will cover how to ensure you have the best equipment for your needs as well as the ability to master the equipment so you can make it work under all conditions.

The decision to replace your trusty detector with one of the new models being introduced on a regular basis by the various manufacturers is one that even seasoned treasure hunters struggle with every time they see an advertisement for a new model. Metal detectors have benefited greatly from the huge technological advancements being made in the computer field today. The circuitry has been made smaller and at the same time is able to perform at much higher levels than detectors even a few years old. Microprocessors are being incorporated into many of today's detectors and they are able to automate many of the complex adjustments once needed in order to be proficient in the field. This new technology is even included in the starter units from many of the manufacturers enabling these low-cost units to perform as well as some of the higher-priced units did years ago. All in all, as far as the detectors currently on the market go, they are definitely superior in virtually all aspects to those produced even a few years ago. Improved detection depth, discrimination, overall stability and reduced weight combine to help treasure hunters find more in areas that were previously considered to be "worked out."

Now before everyone that reads this decides they have to get rid of their current detector and buy a new one, let's put on the brakes and look at the whole picture. First of all, you need to think about how often you use your detector and what you use it for. If you have a mid-range detector and really only get it out when you and the family head to the beach in the summer or you hunt the newer parks and playgrounds for modern coins and other goodies, then you might not need a new detector. But, if you have detector that is more than five years old and you hunt year-round, then you may want to consider taking a look at some of the new models that are available. If you fall into that category, you might be somewhat taken aback by the number of choices out there but there are a few things that you should keep in mind as you start thinking about upgrading your current detector.

While a metal detector will be the biggest single expense as far as treasure hunting equipment goes, there are a myriad of other accessories available for various applications. This section will cover those that directly affect the metal detector itself . . . other chapters will cover additional accessories that will further improve your success rate in the field.

48

To start with, none of the major manufacturers build a "bad" unit – after all, if they did, they would quickly go out of business. There are two main reasons why they have different models in their line. First, some of the models are designed for a specific specialized application such as electronic prospecting, water hunting, or cache hunting to name just a few. Second, manufacturers need to have less-expensive, entry-level units for people who want to try their hand at treasure hunting yet do not want to spend hundreds of dollars initially. Remember, even the basic units will perform well in the field if you understand how to use them. What they lack may be the added discrimination or depth capabilities of the more expensive models or features such as target id, interchangeable coils, and multiple search modes. I personally know several treasure hunters that use mid-range detectors and are quite successful. The reason is that they have learned what their detector is telling them and understand what its limitations might be.

There is no one detector that can excel in all forms of treasure hunting despite the claims you might read or hear from other detectorists. While some of the newer detectors come close, there will always be certain detectors that stand out in certain types of treasure hunting and you should try to get one that is best suited for your style of hunting and for use in your area. I hate to tell people this but I personally have over 20 different metal detectors hanging on the wall and with the exception of a few collectible units, each one is used for a specific type of detecting in specific environments. For example, relic hunters tend to look for a detector that offers maximum detection depth to find deeply buried targets; however, the ability to identify individual targets is not a feature or capability they need. On the other hand, a coin hunter would find discrimination and target identification "must-have" features – even at the expense of raw depth.

So, before you start pouring through manufacturer literature or the Buyers Guide portion of this book, there are a few points you should think about. Until you define what your needs will be, shopping for new equipment will more than likely produce disappointing results and cost you money in the long run. Read over the following questions and use your answers to fill out the Equipment Buyers Research Form provided at the end of this chapter. If answered with some thought, this form will prove to be invaluable in ensuring your final selection is a sound one. Many of those I have shared this with over the years came back later to say that it had actually made them rethink the model they were going to purchase and in hindsight, the model they finally selected was a much better fit for their specific needs. It may also show you that simply buying an optional coil or other accessory for the detector you already own may give you the boost you need to be more successful in your searches. By having the information handy when you start shopping around, you will be able to avoid being steered into something that won't best serve you in the field or wind up draining your wallet unnecessarily. Being an informed consumer is always the best approach.

- **What type of hunting will you be doing MOST of the time?** There is no true all-purpose detector no matter what you might have been told so you need to determine what you will be doing most of the time; i.e., coin hunting, beach hunting, relic hunting, etc., and select the BEST detector for THAT application. If you truly plan on dividing your time equally among two or more types of detecting, then you will probably need to spend a little more and get a detector that is more versatile than say an entry-level or starter unit or buy two units. The form at the end of the chapter will help you define what your interests are and your intended use will be. There are a few rules of thumb that one can apply to a buying decision.
    o If you plan to focus on coin shooting, discrimination is essential. Coin hunting in countries outside the U.S. is more like relic hunting with regard to key features due to the wide variation of coins in terms of composition.
    o For relic hunting, factors such as detection depth, basic discrimination; i.e., ferrous or non-ferrous and the ability to compensate for wide variations in ground conditions are key.
    o For cache hunting, excellent depth and the option of larger search coils will be needed.
    o If your main interest is prospecting, you'll need to be able to ground balance the highly mineralized ground in the areas you will be searching.

- o If you are a beach or shallow water enthusiast, items such as solid construction, comfort due to the added weight, and performance in salt water / black sand environments will rise to the top of your list.
- **Where you will be hunting MOST of the time?** Some brands / models perform better in certain locations than others – even 100 miles apart – due to vastly different ground conditions. Let's look at a real-life example. A number of years ago when Compass Electronics was a major player in the market, they released a detector called the Coin Scanner Pro. It proved to be unbeatable in the areas containing dark, rich soil around my home in southern New Jersey in terms of hitting deeply buried valuables and accurately ID'ing them. Well, we moved to Atlanta and I quickly discovered that the red clay there rendered the Coin Scanner virtually unusable and detection depth was reduced to mere inches. The moral to this example is be careful about selecting a detector based on the recommendation of someone 100's or 1,000's of miles away who is unfamiliar with the ground conditions you will face – their ideal detector may become nothing more than a doorstop in your area. Ground conditions can change from one area to another and factors such as clay, alkali ground, salt water, black sand and iron ore can affect different detectors differently so ask questions, do your research and choose wisely.
- **What is your budget?** For a given price point, a particular brand / model will have an advantage over other models intended for a specific application in that price range. Don't forget, spending more does not necessarily mean a better detector. Unless you have unlimited funds, stick to your budget - there are some excellent detectors that cost a fraction of high end units that for many may do a fine job. If you are simply looking for a detector to spend some time searching for recently lost coins and an occasional piece of jewelry, investing in a top-of-the-line unit is probably not justified. On the other hand, if you plan to focus on searching for Medieval or Roman coins buried for centuries in fields across Europe, a starter unit will most likely leave you with little to show for your time other than frustration.
- **Who will be using the equipment . . . are weight and complexity factors that need to be considered?** If you are looking for a detector for someone who might not be able to swing a heavier or less well-balanced unit for any period of time or find that simply turning the detector on and not making any "fine tuning adjustments" is more what you want, make sure you consider these points in making your final selection. Some detectors feel far heavier than they really are due to less than optimal balance or do in fact weigh more than the competition. At times, this can be addressed through hip mounting the control housing but that configuration may not be one you are comfortable with or might not be available. The versatility afforded by some of the high-end units comes with a price in terms of the learning curve associated with mastering them. Even some of the more simple units have tricks that can help you find more. There are also books, videos and Internet forum sites that can provide you a great deal of user-based information to help you get more out of the detector you opt to use. Finally, don't forget the value provided by your local dealer if you think there might be a problem fully mastering your new detector. You may save some money buying mail order; however, if not understanding how best to use the detector caused you to miss a rare coin, relic or piece of jewelry worth $1,000 or more, how much did you really wind up saving?
- **Have you considered the equipment's reliability and warranty?** In an ideal world, whatever you buy should last forever but as we all know, that is not even close to being reality. Treasure hunting equipment takes a ton of punishment in the field yet despite this treatment holds up amazingly well. There are many 20+ year old detectors that are still going strong and finding goodies which is a testament to the quality used by detector manufacturers. It is quite aggravating to wait weeks to get a detector back from service, especially at the height of the detecting season. Talk to fellow detectorists and see what their experience has been in terms of reliability and service with their detectors. Call the manufacturer's service department and ask what their typical turn around time is as well as what the cost for service might be after the warranty expires. If this is a key factor in your decision making process considering the cost of some detectors, then check with your local dealers to see if they offer a loaner in case yours

needs to go in for repair or if they will help expedite the work if possible. Warranty periods range from 1 year to the unique lifetime warranty offered by Tesoro and with few exceptions, are not transferable which comes into play when buying a used detector.

Once you have defined your criteria by answering the questions listed above and filling out the Equipment Buyers Research Form, you will be able to better narrow down your choices. Be sure to think about factors such as the unit's weight & balance, layout of the controls (this may in fact make a big difference if you are left handed), how it actually feels as you swing it, ease of assembly and changing coils, what accessories are available and their cost, how visible the display or meter is in sunlight or dim / no light, how complex the unit is to adjust, overall construction, pinpointing accuracy and the warranty to name just a few. If you put the sheet together and grade different detectors in each aspect as you check them out, you will be able to make an educated decision that will serve you well in the field. The whole purpose of getting out with your detector is to enjoy your time and see what you can find. If you are uncomfortable with your equipment or get frustrated due to factors such as complexity, balance or performance, you have defeated the whole reason you got into the hobby in the first place.

I hate to admit it but even I have bought a detector or two over the years that caught my attention based on a well-written advertisement or brochure that after using it for just a short period of time, I realized that there were too many negatives to actually enjoy using it. Detectors range in price from under $100 to $1,000's and spending more does not necessarily mean you are getting a detector that will better serve your needs or preferences. Take your time, don't rely solely on the recommendations from someone clear across the country regardless of their reputation, and let the answers to the questions guide your decision making process.

As you read through the manufacturer's literature, you can easily find yourself overwhelmed by the different terminology and claims it contains. Circuit and searchcoil designs, shaft configurations and operating frequencies are just a few features that can leave your head spinning and make it difficult to make an informed decision as to what equipment is actually the best choice for your needs. Two excellent sources of easy-to-understand information well worth the time it takes to read are Tesoro's Metal Detector Information Booklet printed annually and Charles Garrett's book "*The Modern Metal Detectors*". Both provide non-brand specific information that will help you determine what's important to you and what's not. Websites from both Garrett (www.Garrett.com) and Tesoro (www.Tesoro.com) website (www.Tesoro.com) contain a Frequently Asked Question section that provides much of the information one might need to start interpreting specifications and literature. The next few sections of this chapter will cover two specific design features that should be understood when assessing your current equipment or looking at buying something new.

DETECTOR CIRCUIT CHOICES

Rather than taking up several pages going through the various circuits that have been used on metal detectors since they were first invented, we'll stick with the circuits found on detectors currently on the market namely the Very Low Frequency (VLF), Multiple-Frequency and Pulse Induction (PI) circuits. The rest of this section provides an overview of these circuits; however, if you want or need a more detailed description of how they actually work in terms of processing signals, picking up a copy of Charles Garrett's highly acclaimed book, *Modern Metal Detectors* is recommended.

The most common circuit found on detectors today is the VLF. First introduced in the mid-1970's, the big advantage the VLF detector had over its predecessors was the ability to compensate for the adverse affect ground mineralization had on detection depth. While most detectors could pick up a coin several inches from the coil, once it was buried in even the mildest of ground that detection depth dropped markedly. The VLF detectors allowed users to adjust for the mineralization present and greatly improve the depth at which targets could be located. Over the years the circuitry that compensates for ground conditions has been improved upon by every manufacturer and there are now detectors that can actually sample the ground electronically and automatically adjust for the ground mineralization to ensure the detector is providing the best possible performance for the conditions present. Even those that require the adjustment to be done manually have become simple enough that precise settings are possible even by those with little or no experience.

The frequency at which a VLF detector operates can have an effect on how well it can detect certain types of targets as well as how it handles specific types of soil conditions. Today's VLF detectors operate across a band of frequencies ranging from 2.5 kHz to 100 kHz. The specific frequency a manufacturer selects for a particular model is based on its primary intended purpose, what optional coils might be available and in the end what the engineers at the factory simply feel will "work best". Again, while there are no really bad detectors or manufacturers on the market (they'd be gone in short order if there were), some just perform better for certain applications and in certain ground conditions than others. The operating frequency does come into play in determining how a detector will perform and the following is a guideline that can be used when looking at different models, but remember, you need to make sure the one you chose works in your area and if there is only a slight difference between the frequencies of the models you are looking at – say 5kHz or so – the actual performance difference will be minimal solely on the basis of their operating frequencies.

- **Lower frequencies** tend to be more sensitive to higher conductive targets such as those made of silver and brass. They also tend to detect larger targets (coin-sized and up) deeper than higher frequency VLF detectors.
- **Higher frequencies** tend to be more sensitive to low conductive targets such as those made of gold, platinum and lead. They do a better job of detecting tiny targets that might be missed by a detector using a lower frequency.

What some manufacturers have done in the quest for a better metal detector circuit is to design metal detectors that operate at two or more frequencies to gain the advantages offered by each. This obviously does not come without a price and these detectors are at the upper end of the price scale; however, the performance they offer in areas with severe ground conditions or with a wide range of target composition is an expense worth evaluating.

The other feature that most detectorists have come to take for granted is the ability to accept or reject specific types of targets through a discrimination circuit. Decades ago – when some of us ol' fossils first started treasure hunting – metal detectors did just what their name implied: they detected any form of metal. We sure dug a lot of targets and the ability to ignore some of the trash was a dream many of us had. Well, as the technology evolved for manufacturers to develop circuits that could distinguish one type of target from another, that dream became a reality. Virtually all VLF detectors out there today – with the exception of some designed solely for prospecting where all targets warrant investigation – have a discrimination circuit of some sort. Basic models may only have a knob that as you increase the setting, more and more targets are rejected based on their electrical properties. More advanced models allow users to define specifically what they want to accept or reject with a high degree of precision. Unfortunately a point that needs to be remembered when searching for deeply buried targets is that ground mineralization and target depth as well as multiple targets in close proximity to each other can cause a good target to be missed if too much discrimination is used. The rule of thumb that should always be applied is to use as little discrimination as the site you are searching allows ensuring you are not passing over a "once-in-a-lifetime" find. The level of discrimination can also vary at a specific site from visit to visit depending on how much time you have available to search, how much patience you might have on a given day or what types of targets you are looking for. There have been times when I've searched the same old park or military campsite which is littered with iron trash one time in all metal and on the next visit at a discrimination level that rejects the iron recognizing that I might be missing targets masked by the trash due to limited time or my mood. The actual amount of discrimination you choose to use at any site you visit should be selected based on what you are hoping to find, how much trash or unwanted targets are present and how much digging you either feel like doing or will be allowed to do. Let's look at two examples and use the meter from an older Whites metal detector shown below to visualize the points.

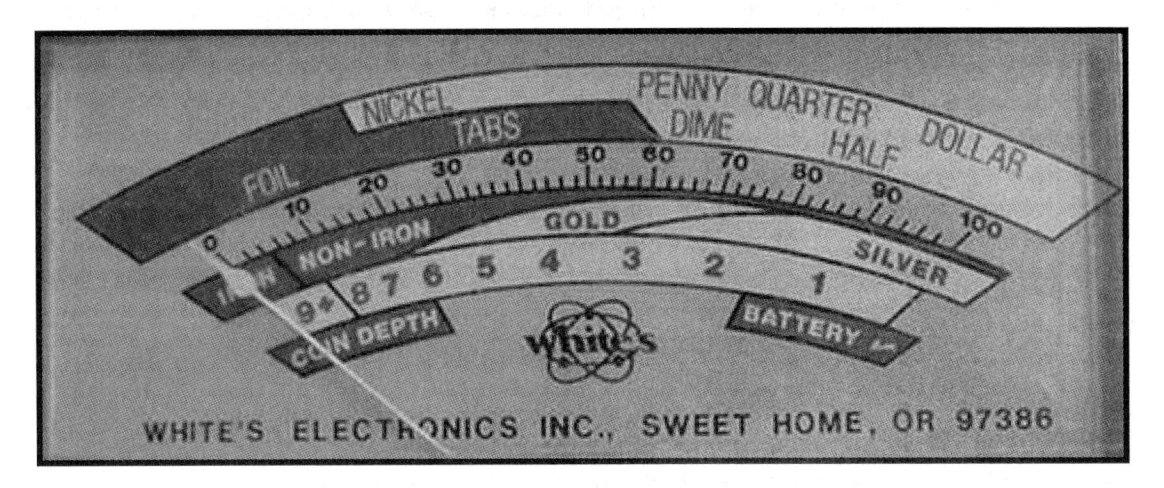

- John is a beach hunter and visits the local beach on a Monday morning following a hot summer weekend where crowds had filled the area. He starts out around the volleyball court and soon finds dozens of pull tabs. Well, his detector has a discrimination control and he turns it up until the tabs are all rejected. After a few hours he empties his pouch and counts out $8.63 plus a nice heavy silver medal. Happy with his take, he heads home. Unfortunately by rejecting the tabs, John more than likely passed up what he had been hoping to find – a piece of gold jewelry. Looking at the target ID meter, you can see that by rejecting tabs, most gold will also be rejected so in John's case, a bit more patience could have paid off handsomely.
- Bill is a coin hunter who is happy with a pocketful of clad coins and frequents local playgrounds and ball fields – both very productive locations. He knows enough to avoid over-use of the discrimination control from books and articles he's read so he sets his at FOIL. A 4 hour hunt turned up more than $10 in coins along with an apron-full of trash including pull tabs, wads of tin foil, shredded soda cans and the like. Had Bill looked in his pouch and seen that he had only found 2 nickels amongst the 150+ coins and piles of trash, he might have increased the discrimination to TABS, spent less time digging trash and doubled the number of coins recovered in the same amount of time.

Subsequent chapters on specific types of treasure hunting will discuss how much discrimination, if any, other successful hunters use but the final call will be up to you. Just remember, less discrimination can in fact produce more in the right location. Hunting in all-metal at the trashiest site you can find will often produce little more than frustration so think about each site you visit and adjust your discrimination accordingly.

The Pulse Induction or PI circuitry is even better suited for adverse ground conditions than a VLF model and is commonly found in detectors used for searching black sand salt water beaches or in highly mineralized areas where gold, silver and other ores are sought by prospectors. Unlike VLF detectors that are sending out a continual signal from a Transmit coil and processing the returning signal picked up in the Receive coil, the PI detector sends out a pulse and then switches over to "listen" for a returning signal. This "send-listen" cycle is typically very short . . . with today's PI units sending out between 100 and 1,000 pulses per second. While PI detectors tend to be unaffected by ground conditions which would appear to make them the ideal detector when looking for maximum detection depth, they have very limited discrimination capabilities. If you are searching a trash-filled site such as a park, home place or campsite containing ferrous trash and non-ferrous valuables, the time spent recovering trash at extreme depths may outweigh any benefits the PI technology might have afforded you in terms of tackling severe ground conditions. Salt water beach hunters, gold prospectors and relic hunters searching in highly mineralized ground are often willing to accept this trade-off to gain additional detection depth and as you will see in the photos contained in the chapters covering these forms of treasure hunting, the rewards are most definitely there. One interesting aspect of PI detectors is that search coils can be made far larger than what you will find on VLF detectors and even the largest coils are still fairly sensitive to smaller targets. As they say, the more ground you cover per hour, the more finds you can make and with a large PI coil, this is most certainly the case. One coil manufacturer actually produces a 20"x40" search coil for PI detectors!

There are some other detectors on the market that utilize variations of these two circuits or attempts to marry the two; however, since they tend to be used by a very small number of hobbyists and have little wide-spread testing to assess their true effectiveness, these are not covered in this book

SEARCH COILS

Manufacturers typically equip their detectors with a search coil that will provide optimal performance under most conditions; however, it will not really EXCEL in all applications. The typical coil that comes with a detector today ranges from 8" to 10" in diameter; however, optional coils are available for most detectors optimized for specific conditions or applications from both the detector manufacturer as well as several after-market vendors. But what are the pros and cons of coils in different sizes or internal design?

COIL DESIGN

Well first let's look at coil design. There are two main designs used on metal detector coils today, the concentric coil and the Double-D or Wide Scan coil. The difference between these two designs lies in how the transmit and receive windings are mounted inside of the coil shell itself.

As shown in the adjacent picture, while both coils utilize a "transmit" and "receive" winding, the electrical field sent out by each coil design is markedly different due to how the windings are mounted inside of the coil shell. The concentric coil, found on many detectors over the past 40+ years, uses an outer transmit coil and an inner receive coil that sends out a cone-shaped field focused around the center of the coil. On the other hand, the Double-D coil has two identical D-shaped coils – one being the transmit and the other the receive winding – which overlap down the center of the coil.

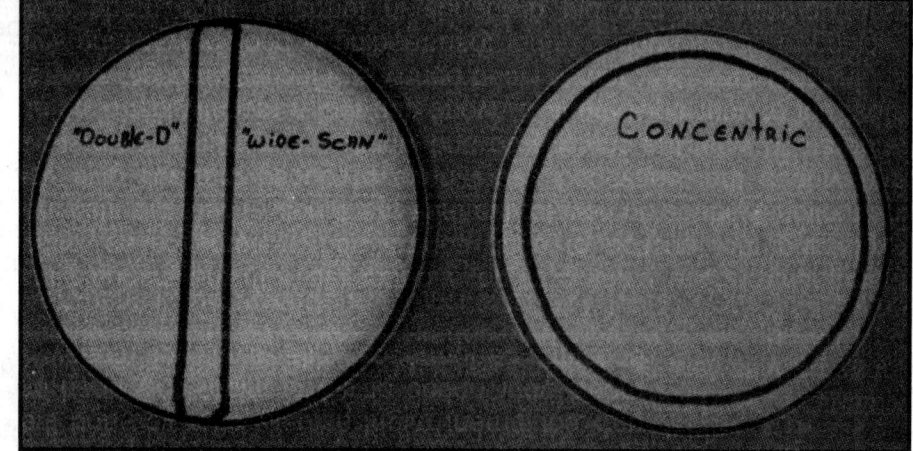

Both coils do a great job of detecting targets near the surface. However, since the concentric coil's detection field shrinks the farther you get from the coil, the potential to miss a deeply buried target increases with a concentric coil when compared to a Double-D coil. If the targets you are looking for are deeply buried, you need to hone your search style to ensure you do not miss them. On a standard 8-inch concentric coil, you are actually only scanning an area 5" in diameter at a depth of 6" or more. Without overlapping each sweep, you may in fact be missing many of the targets you are walking over!

On the other hand, Double–D coils send out a signal that is quite narrow but reaches into the ground across nearly the entire width of the coil. While the pattern may seem a bit unusual, as you sweep the coil from side-to-side it provides almost 100% coverage without requiring you to overlap each sweep. Another advantage of the Double-D design is that in highly mineralized ground it is somewhat less affected by the mineralization than a concentric coil which can mask targets. It also minimizes electrical "chatter" allowing a weaker signal to be more easily detected which means more detection depth in bad ground; i.e., the worse the ground becomes, the better the Double-D coil performs in comparison to a concentric coil used in the same conditions. The figure below shows the electrical signal pattern sent out from the two types of search coils.

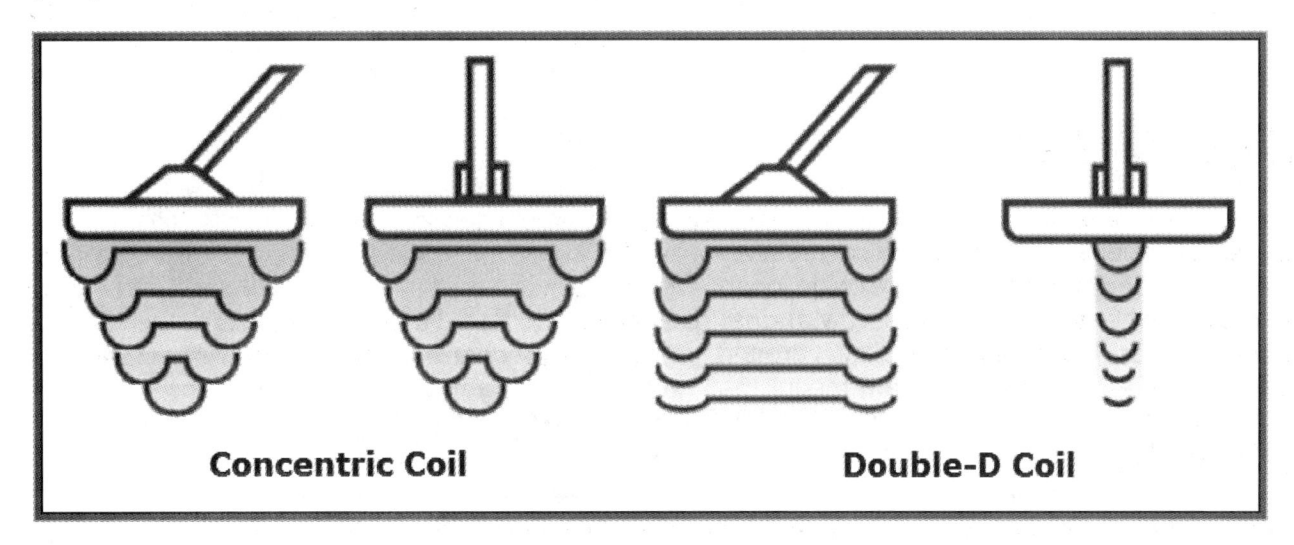

Concentric Coil   **Double-D Coil**

At this point you are probably asking "*If the Double-D coil is so good, why don't all metal detectors come with one as standard equipment?*" A downside to Double-D or wide scan coils is that pinpointing targets is a bit different than when using a concentric coil. For many users that have extensive experience with concentric coil detectors, making the switch can be a daunting task. People who have never used a detector before tend to master pinpointing faster with a Double-D than those with years of in-field experience under their belts using other coils. Another advantage of the concentric coil design is that they tend to provide more accurate target identification than Double-D coils so depending on what type of detecting you plan on doing, you may tend to favor one design over the other.

Remember, the advantage of the Double-D design is that it provides maximum detection depth across the entire width of the coil down the strip where the two D-shaped coils overlap. This pattern minimizes the possibility of inadvertently missing a target by not overlapping each swing but the pattern also requires one to alter how to accurately pinpoint a target's location. A target that produces a signal can be located <u>ANYWHERE</u> under the center strip that runs from the front edge to the back edge. By comparison, on a concentric coil the strongest response from a target will always be in the center of the two windings or the center of the coil itself. This is the main reason most detectors come standard with a concentric coil. It makes pinpointing much easier for the new user. Tips to improve the ease and accuracy of pinpointing targets with either coil design will be presented in the Target Recovery chapter.

The last point regarding search coil design that you should consider is that by selecting one of a different design than the one that came stock with your detector, you can often get a new level of performance out of the same detector in different sites or ground conditions. Virtually every manufacturer today as well as several third-party vendors offer optional coils in the two designs which provides a great deal of flexibility when it comes to changing how a detector performs simply by swapping a coil rather than buying a new detector. The Brand-Specific chapters will provide information on all optional search coils that might be available for your equipment.

COIL SIZE

If the choice of coil design is not confusing enough, we also have the size & shape of the coil to consider. Coils range in size from as small as a one-inch probe to a whopping 18"x15" or larger and many sizes in between as well as shapes that include round, elliptical and even square. A large number of choices for sure but there are places for each and depending on your style of hunting; you can narrow down your options in short order.

As we started out saying, the manufacturers equip their detectors with what they feel will be a solid all-purpose coil capable of searching most areas with a decent level of performance. Based on what users find on a regular basis, this decision is typically a sound one. However, if you tend to hunt areas that are littered with trash, have decades or centuries of soil built-up resulting in targets being very deep, are wide open expanses where targets may be few and far between or have challenging ground conditions, a different coil can mean the difference between a day with little to show for your efforts and one which goes down as a super hunt. The photo to the right shows four different sized coils from Tesoro showing the flexibility available by selecting the right coil for a specific application.

Smaller coils see less of the ground with each sweep and while this requires more sweeps and hence time to cover an area, if it is littered with trash, a smaller coil will in fact produce more than a larger coil might. A metal detector is not a magical device and until we have detectors that can show us a photo of what is underground, we need to work within the inherent limitations of the current technology. If you frequent extremely trashy sites such as well-used parks, old foundations or military sites filled with ferrous targets, you can experience what is known as "target-masking". If there are multiple targets under the coil at the same time such as a silver coin, a few nails and a wad of tinfoil, the signals from the trash targets can override or mask the signal from the good target and as a result, you wind up leaving the coin for the next treasure hunter. A small coil – 6" or less in diameter – will allow you to pick out good targets from amongst the trash and find valuables that other detectorists have passed over for years.

Small concentric coils tend to be a bit more sensitive to small objects yet loose some detection depth when compared to a stock-size coil . . . that's just the nature of the coil design and what happens as they are scaled down. Conversely, larger concentric coils will go deeper but tend to be less sensitive than the stock coil. An interesting characteristic of Double-D coils is that unlike concentric coils, smaller coils do not have an appreciable loss of detection depth when compared to the stock coil. This means you can still find deeper targets with a small coil while eliminating the possibility of missing something due to target masking. Larger Double-D coils are also not prone to the typical loss of sensitivity to smaller targets that one sees on larger concentric coils. Many users of the larger Double-D coils report finding small artifacts or even coins on edge at impressive depths.

Sites that have produced well in the past such as military campsites, schools, parks, etc., all have one thing in common . . . they have all had large numbers of people cross their ground. In order for the site to contain a large number of good targets, there had to be a high concentration of people there to lose them but also lose a pile of trash targets as well. Unfortunately, many treasure hunters have thought that in order to find "keepers" in heavily hunted areas, they need to use a larger coil and try to get a bit more depth out of their detectors. While this may work well in areas where targets are few and far between, in trashy sites, you will actually find less than with the stock coil due to increased target masking. To put this in perspective, let's look at some concentric coils. Looking at coverage, a 9" coil will "see" 64 in^2 of ground while a 6" coil will "see" 28 in^2 and a 12" coil will "see" 113 in^2. As you can see, the larger the coil the more likely masking is to occur so in sites littered with trash, go smaller for more finds. Recently a friend of mine, Bob Jargeson, who just started metal detecting, purchased a 5-inch coil for his detector and went to a city park that has been hunted for more than 30 years by virtually every treasure hunter within 50 miles. Some of the oldest areas were also the most trash-filled and this is where he opted to try out the smaller coil. By moving slowly and checking questionable signals, he was able to recover more than 30 coins dating back to the mid-1800's including Indian Head pennies, Shield nickels, Barber and Seated silver coins and a few local trade tokens over a month-long period. An interesting point that he mentioned was that more than half of the targets were less than 5 inches deep and could have been easily detected by almost any detector that had gone through the area. The heavy concentration of trash had masked them from detectors using larger coils. I think we would all agree that these are the type of finds we would all like to make on a regular basis so think about the sites you hunt and see if a small coil may give you the edge over the competition.

On the flip side, a larger coil will allow you to cover more ground with each sweep and in the case of a concentric coil, detect targets that would be out of range with a stock coil. In areas that are not littered with multiple targets in close proximity, a larger coil can help you find more "keepers" per hour. Larger coils are also well-suited for searching wide open areas such as ocean beaches or battlefield areas where your success-rate will increase proportionally with the amount of ground you can cover in a given amount of time. Before ordering the largest coil you can find, consider that as the coil size increases, so does the weight which can throw off the perfect balance of your detector and make what was once fun to use for hours uncomfortable after even a short period of time. Also, using a large coil in overgrown sites can be an effort in futility resulting in little more than frustration. But, in the right location, larger coils may turn into your primary coil. The photo here shows three choice silver coins and a some Indian Head pennies found in one outing by veteran detectorist Bryce Brown using a 10"x12" coil on his Minelab Explorer SE. He exclusively hunts parks near his home in Illinois that others consider to be "worked-out" and makes finds such as these on a regular basis by combining the right equipment, well-honed skills and perseverance.

GROUND BALANCE CIRCUIT OPTIONS

In the early years of treasure hunting, metal detectors would often detect targets at impressive (at the time) distances on a workbench or table; however, when the adverse affect of ground mineralization was factored in, the true detection depth was cut dramatically. In the early 1970's, the ability to design a metal detector that could compensate for the ground effect resulted in a considerable increase in detection depth under even the most severe conditions. I can still remember my father and I driving 75 miles to the nearest dealer that had one of the new Whites Coinmaster V Supreme detectors in-stock and both of us standing there with our mouths open when it easily detected coins at several inches while the units we had brought with us never even beeped. There was no question as to our buying it and on the way home we stopped at an old church we'd hunted many times before. I can still remember the first target was a V nickel almost 8 inches deep and that was just the start. Those early ground-compensating detectors were a giant leap in detector technology but mastering the tuning procedure to ensure it was set properly and remained so took some time. A good number of treasure hunters simply wanted to swing their detector rather than continually tweak it for optimal performance. Well as time went on, manufacturers took one of three paths in designing new detectors when it came to ground compensation. All detectors today that operate on the VLF principle feature a form of ground compensation and understanding which one a particular detector has along with the strengths and weaknesses the particular form used has is key to getting the most out of your equipment and time in the field.

The first option most lower-priced models have is the fixed or preset ground balance. While this does offer some degree of compensation, the inability to make any adjustments can cause a drop in performance if conditions are significantly different than the mineralization level selected by the manufacturer's engineers. Most detectors with fixed ground balance work well in parks, schools, woods and the like that do not contain red clay, black sand, alkali ground found in many desert locations or salt water beaches.

> **TIP** If you have a fixed ground balance unit and want to try using it in these types of areas, try dropping the sensitivity below where you would normally run it and/or hunt with the coil off the ground an inch or two to minimize the effect the ground has on the detector's circuit. Selecting a smaller coil or opting for a Double-D design can also help as the detector will "see" less ground and hence be less affected by the mineralization.

The next step up in the world of ground compensation circuitry is the adjustable circuit. Here you are given the ability to make changes to the ground balance setting as ground conditions change. Unlike the original manual ground balance circuits, the current manual ground balance detectors are much simpler to adjust and keep adjusted as ground conditions change at the hunt site. If you are hunting areas that contain highly mineralized ground and want to be able to compensate for the adverse affect it has on detector performance, this should be the minimum you should settle for in terms of ground balance circuitry when selecting a detector.

The third option is typically found on the higher-end models from most manufacturers and provides for automatic setting and adjustment of the ground balance circuit. Taking any guesswork out of selecting the proper setting for a wide range of ground conditions, these detectors are able to handle even the worst ground conditions. Most have computerized tracking capabilities which continually monitor the ground and make adjustments automatically as conditions change. There are times when you may not want this auto-tuning function to be operating as will be discussed in some of the chapters dealing with specific types of treasure hunting and on most detectors with this feature it can easily be turned off.

> ⚠️ **BEWARE OF AIR TESTS:** Be careful when checking out new equipment that you don't base your purchase decision solely on how it performs in an air test demonstration. While air testing will show you how it responds to specific targets, they rarely show how it will perform in the field. Some detectors can detect targets at great depths in the air but fall far short of that performance in the ground. Others air test poorly because their circuitry needs to see the ground matrix in order to function properly. Don't rely on air tests – ask to see how it works in the ground and preferably in the type of ground you plan on using it in.

MASTERING YOUR EQUIPMENT... NEW OR NOT

Remember the example of Hardy Russell in the previous chapter? The first and most important lesson Hardy learned was the need to "become one" with his detector. Until you know what each adjustment is used for and how best to set it for <u>different</u> conditions, you will not be getting the maximum potential out of the detector as you go from site to site, even if the sites are fairly close together; i.e., within the same town. Hardy and I had hunted a site that dated back to the early 1900's for several weeks and done fairly well in terms of finds. Opting to try another site some 40 miles away, we started hunting and after 30 minutes or so, Hardy came over and asked if I was ready to try somewhere else as he had been skunked so far. Well, after showing him a few Wheat cents and a Barber dime he asked what he was doing wrong. I had him check the next good signal I received and he said he would not have dug it. I asked him what settings he was using and he said the same ones we used at the other site . . . big mistake! This site had soil comprised of clay rather than dark dirt at the earlier site and the trash content was far higher. Both of these conditions required some adjustments to be made. After making a few tweaks, Hardy started hunting and almost immediately pulled out a Mercury dime from amongst some nails at 8" deep. Since then, we have discussed the specific options on his detector and how each should be set to optimize performance under different conditions. Knowledge is power as they say and in the case of your detector, knowing when to make an adjustment – even a small one – can often mean the difference between success and failure at the end of the day. Unless you travel extensively, the conditions in your immediate hunting area will not change dramatically but differences in soil conditions and trash content will dictate changes to your usual settings.

> **YOU MAY ALREADY HAVE THE "PERFECT" DETECTOR:** The equipment you already have may in fact be the right equipment for you . . . don't feel that if it is not brand new or the most expensive model available that you have to upgrade. I know a number of treasure hunters that use older, mid-range equipment and make finds that even seasoned detectorists are envious of. Take your time, do the research as to what advantages the new equipment might actually offer you and then decide if what you have meets your needs or if you might only need an accessory item or two to boost the performance while saving you money.

Manufacturers are starting to do a better job with the manuals that come with their detectors in explaining the function of each control and in some cases, either provide a free DVD or sell instructional videos on how to use their machines. There are also many excellent after-market books and videos that seasoned users have produced that will give you the foundation you need to understand what the controls do and when to make an adjustment as conditions change to get the most out of your equipment. Anyone can find a recently lost dime at 2 inches but the skill comes in finding that rare 1877 Indian Head penny at 9 inches amongst several pieces of trash. It's a lot more exciting to be out hunting rather than reading or book or watching a video but the small investment of time up-front will pay big dividends in terms of finds made down the road. Check with the manufacturer of your detector, your dealer or one of the suppliers listed in the Reference Resource Bibliography section at the end of most chapters to see what material may be available to help you <u>really</u> understand your detector and how to best set it for any conditions you might come across. One word of caution in terms of the information available through the many Internet forums – these are great sources of information but when it comes to settings for a detector, you need to remember that what works for someone in one part of the world may in fact be totally useless in your area or for your style of hunting. If you understand what the controls do, you will be able to assess the settings others provide and see if they will work for you without simply blindly loading them and coming home more frustrated than anything else.

LEARN YOUR DETECTOR BEFORE HEADING OUT!

All too often, when people get a new metal detector the first thing they want to do is run out and start digging up treasure. Unfortunately heading out **BEFORE** learning what the detector is telling you virtually ensures you will wind up frustrated or at best with less in your pouch than you might have found with even a minimal amount of practice after you have unpacked the detector. Not to sound repetitive but the following statement from Greg Moscini, veteran detectorist and owner of Trans-Bay Metal Detectors in Foster City, CA, is relevant here. *"How can you hope to be successful when you start detecting without knowing how to set your detector or what type of signal to expect from the types of targets you are looking for or hoping to avoid? Going out in search of unknown targets with a detector you do not fully understand is a guaranteed recipe for frustration and failure. There are simply too many variables for you to be successful."* This is excellent advice for **ANY** detector and is the focus of the following sections.

AIR TESTING

OK, the title of this section is not to see if you read the caution on the previous page about the pitfalls of basing a buying decision on air test results. There is a good use for performing air testing on your detector which is the focus of this section. Those that find the most even in areas that have been hunted for many years are those that have "become one" with their detector and can interpret the slightest nuances which are often the targets we all hope to find. Start by collecting an assortment of the types of targets you expect to come across in your searches – and the items will vary depending on what type of hunting you plan to focus on. Don't forget to include examples of the trash you can expect to come across so you can start to learn what not to dig.

Lay the detector on a table with the coil away from any metal including heating ducts, braces in the table, nearby appliances or even your pockets. Remove your watch and rings. Remember that the coil detects objects above and below it as well as off to the sides. Turn the detector on and start with the discrimination control set at "0". Pass each target at least 4 inches away from the coil going side-to-side. You can also test the target response by bringing the target in towards the center of the coil and then pulling it away. Listen to the audio response. If you detector has an audible threshold, see how it reacts to targets including any changes once the target has been moved away from the coil.

Put together a table using graph paper that will allow you to keep track of what discrimination setting results in specific targets – good and bad – being rejected. While most instruction manuals have tables that provide that information on a high level and controls often show points where items are rejected, you will find that there are slight differences from unit to unit and you want to know exactly where those points are on **YOUR** detector. Experiment with various adjustments and repeat the air tests to see how the changes affect the responses received. Keep a notebook handy to record your results and see if slight changes can make the responses easier to interpret when testing the specific targets you hope to uncover.

TEST GARDENS

Alright, let's assume that you have either found out that your detector fits the bill or you have opted to retire ol' Bessie and purchase a replacement. Have you really mastered the detector for the type of hunting you will be doing? With today's equipment, virtually anyone can find a coin, ring or relic at 4" in neutral soil but do you know what a silver coin at 8" next to a rusted nail, a thin gold ring in bone dry soil or a tiny gold nugget beneath a hot rock sounds like? These are the subtle differences that will help ensure you place consistently at the "find-of-the-month" competition in your club or just among your fellow treasure hunters. If you answered no or are uncertain, an excellent practice tool is the

"Test Garden". Having a spot in your backyard that provides a way to not only learn what different signals sound like as ground conditions (i.e., moisture content) change but to practice pinpointing these targets can really help give you the edge over 95% of the competition. A test garden is quite easy to construct and the benefits are immeasurable.

As many successful detectorists can attest to, building a test garden – and more importantly, using it – is probably one of the most important things you can do to become familiar with your detector. You can also learn how changing ground conditions like rain or drought periods affect the way the detector responds to targets in the ground. You can also perfect your pinpointing technique before you try venturing out into a well-manicured lawn or park which builds on the Target Recovery portion of the success formula.

Where Is It?

The first thing you should do is collect samples of the types of targets you search for and expect to come across in your searches. If you are a coin hunter, get examples of the coins you will be looking for as well as the type of trash targets you expect to find. If you are a relic hunter, do the same for those types of targets. If you dabble in a bit of everything, then by all means, get some coins, relics and if you can bear to part with it, some gold jewelry for your test garden. If you are starting out and do not have coins or relics to use, stop by your local coin / relic shop and see if they have what are called cull coins (damaged / worn) or ugly relics. As long as they are representative of what you are looking for, their condition is irrelevant. You can also check out some of the on-line sites such as E-Bay for inexpensive test objects for your test garden.

Next, select an area that will be used for the actual test garden plot. In order to make sure there are no "unknown" targets that can cause confusion down the road, setup your detector for maximum sensitivity and zero discrimination. Search the area thoroughly and remove any target you come across. Next, using a ruler to ensure the targets are at known depths, bury each of the targets you have selected about 12 inches apart at the depths you have selected – usually ranging from 2" to 8"+. Mark the exact center of the target using a golf tee. This will help you refine your pinpointing skills. Document what target each tee marks including the depth so that you can see how different settings or ground conditions change the target response. Sometimes REDUCING the sensitivity setting can actually result in INCREASED detection depth depending on the type of ground conditions that exists. A test garden will let you see how adjustments to each control affects the response you get from a target. A sample test garden layout for a coin hunter is shown below. If you search for other targets, simply replace the ones shown with targets better suited to your preferred style of hunting. Remember, the more you use the test garden, the more proficient you will become!

1	Silver 10c at 5"	2	Nickel at 6"	3	Screw Cap at 3"
4	Zinc 1c at 5"	5	Thin Silver Ring at 6'	6	Pull Tab at 4"
7	Tin Foil next to a silver 10c at 3"	8	Large rusted nail or bolt at 6"	9	Silver 25c on edge at 4"
10	Gold charm at 4"	11	Indian Head 1c at 6"	12	Copper 1c next to nail

REMEMBER, EACH SITE YOU SEARCH IS DIFFERENT

Since each site you hunt will differ in terms of trash content, mineralization, moisture content and types of targets, another technique that will improve the quantity and quality of finds you make is assess the signals you get and dig those that have the potential to be keepers based on their depth or even intermittent "good" signals. What you will find is that many of the questionable signals that you (and other treasure hunters) typically pass up will turn out to be the targets you see in the magazines – old coins extremely deep or on edge, valuables adjacent to trash or odd-shaped goodies. Mike Moutray, an extremely successful treasure hunter from St. Louis, makes finds on a regular basis that many treasure hunters have not made even after years of detecting. What is his secret? Learning how to interpret what his detector is telling him, hunting in a methodical manner and digging marginal signals that he knows might be the older targets has allowed him to amass an enviable collection of large cents, bust silver, antique jewelry and other artifacts from parks that have been hunted since the 1960's.

On many occasions I have found that the level of mineralization present causes me to use a different group of settings than I would have otherwise based on some quick testing before I started to hunt a new area. As an example, I recently received a call from a friend of mine, Larry Shirah, who is an avid relic hunter near Atlanta, Ga. He consistently makes finds most of us would love to make and has taken the time to master his detector for the type of hunting he does. He and his partner were hunting a Civil War site for the first time and after an hour, stopped to compare finds. Larry had not found anything while his partner had several nice relics. What he discovered was that with his detector set the way he normally had it set, he was barely able to detect a bullet lying on top of the ground. The ground conditions were far different than the surrounding sites they had visited and required significant adjustment before he could successfully hunt the area again. Had he not had some one with him to compare signals with, he would have hunted all day and then written the site off as non-productive. A simple test before you start hunting can make the difference between a great day and a total washout.

See if any of your fellow treasure hunters have the detector model you are looking at and see how they like it. If at all possible, try to find a local dealer that carries the model you are planning on purchasing. There's a big difference between seeing what detector someone that lives 1,000's of miles away from you is using or what looks good in a catalog and what feels comfortable in your hands or will work well in your area for the type of hunting you plan on doing. If you already have a detector, bring it with you and make sure you are actually getting more detection depth, discrimination or just general comfort out of the new unit by doing a side-by-side comparison.

PROS & CONS OF THE VARIOUS BUYING OPTIONS

There are several options available to get some new equipment including buying from a local dealer, buying from a mail-order firm or buying used equipment from a fellow treasure hunter and each has its pros and cons.

The first option we'll cover will be buying used equipment. Obviously the biggest benefit one receives is buying the equipment at a considerable savings over what you would pay for it new. But before you jump on something advertised at a super low price, keep a few points in mind. First, unless you are fairly experienced and know what to look for, it may be difficult to tell if it is operating properly. Clearly if it looks like it has not been well cared for (and I have seen some detectors that look like they were dragged behind the truck to and from hunting sites), you should probably walk away unless the price is so low that even if it dies soon after you buy it, it will not cause a financial hardship. For the most part, used detectors do not come with a warranty (Whites Electronics does allow warranties to be transferred which is a good point to remember when looking at used detectors) and repair costs can be quite expensive, especially on specialty models such as those for underwater use. If you do find yourself with a used detector in need of repair, one of the repair centers listed at the end of this chapter can repair just about any detector ever made . . . just ask for an estimate before the repair begins. A few other points to consider if buying used equipment include the following. First, most private individuals may not be willing or able to provide much if any instruction on how to use the equipment and in fact this may be why they are selling it. Second, technology especially with detectors changes on a continual basis so buying a piece of equipment 5+ years old may not give you much of an edge when it comes to finding what others have missed before you. In many cases, the value of what you don't find could have easily covered the difference between what you paid and the price of a newer unit. Finally, buying from someone who has equipment on a site such as E-Bay 100's of miles away forces you to make a decision based on a photograph and I have talked to many people who did not get what they thought they had bought. Being able to lay your eyes on it before putting down the cash has value in itself.

The next two options pertain to buying new equipment. The first option we will cover is buying from a local dealer. The one drawback to this avenue is that not everyone has a local dealer in their area or if they do, the dealer may not carry the brand of equipment they are looking for. To see what you have in your area, start with the Yellow Pages and if you do not see anything listed, contact the manufacturers using the contact & web site information provided in the Buyers Guide section of this book to get the names of local factory-authorized dealers. Outdoor Outfitters is a multi-line distributor in the U.S. that can put you in touch with many independent dealers that often are not listed with the manufacturers. Joan Allen Electronics based in England can provide referrals to local independent dealers in that part of the world. Another option is to try an Internet search to identify your local dealers that may not appear on the manufacturer's website. Most local dealers are usually active treasure hunters themselves and can tell you what models tend to work better in your area. Remember, a metal detector that may excel in one part of the country and be highly recommended by everyone that uses it may be virtually useless in another part that has significantly different ground conditions. Another advantage of going to a local dealer is that you will be able to actually try out various competing models before you buy and may find that weight, balance, feel or even simply the appearance can sway you from your initial choice. Also, since most mail order firms are not setup to accept trade-ins, if you have something that you need to put towards a new piece of equipment, trading it in might be easier than trying to find a buyer first. Another positive attribute of local dealers is that most offer services after the sale that may not seem important when you are looking to buy but having someone to go to when you have a problem can be invaluable in the middle of a productive year. Often they can provide you with a loaner detector if yours needs to head back in for warranty service. Being able to demonstrate how to best operate your new equipment and even steer you to some possible sites to hunt are other advantages to a local dealer.

The third option is purchasing your equipment from a mail-order firm. The Internet has greatly changed the way many people shop and the treasure hunting arena is no different. Mail order companies now range from a sideline operation run from a spare bedroom in an apartment to huge storefronts employing dozens of full-time employees. A simple Internet search will provide you with a number of these dealers to choose from. Of course the most obvious benefit of buying from a mail order dealer is usually a lower price since the dealer knows that they will not have to spend a great deal of face-to-face time that a local dealer might need to spend. Combine a lower price with no sales tax and free shipping, mail order dealers are attractive to many who know what they want and are willing to forgo some of the services local dealers can provide. Many of the larger mail order firms have staff members who use what they sell so that they can answer your questions and help steer you into the right equipment for your needs. Keep in mind however that since they will not be based in your area, what they recommend may be ideal for them in their location but might not be the best choice for you. Get some local recommendations when drafting your list of possible choices before you start contacting mail order dealers. If you feel like they are trying to steer you to a specific model despite your initial choice, you are best to simply try another dealer since they may be trying to move a particular model or may have received better pricing on that brand than what you might have called about. Other services offered by some of the larger mail order firms include toll free technical support lines, maintaining a sales staff that has been trained at the factory on the brands they carry, trade-up polices that allow you to upgrade if you feel you need a better piece of equipment than the one you purchased and having fresh inventory due to the volume they sell. If these services are of importance to you, see if your local dealer will match them as many will and the convenience of having a local dealer is a valuable commodity in itself.

A final option that can boost the performance of your current equipment is to have it modified by one of the companies that specialize in tweaking particular models for increased performance. There are a few experts that have found ways to modify a detector to gain detection depth and this option can in essence give you a new detector for a fraction of the cost associated with buying a new one. Just realize that if you still have any warranty in effect, modifying the unit will void that coverage. But if your detector is no longer under warranty or you want to get more out of it and accept the warranty implications, you may want to look into one of the companies that offer modification services.

In summary, you should weigh all of the pros & cons of the various options before you decide where to buy your equipment. There are good and "not-so-good" dealers in both the local and mail order markets. Unless you are certain that you will not need any assistance after the sale, find out before you put any money on the table exactly what services each dealer will provide. Make up a list of questions that you feel are important and ask them of each dealer you contact using their answers to make your final decision as to where to make your purchase. For some price may be the primary factor, while for others being able to drop in and ask a question face-to-face may be the factor that seals the deal.

IS IT POSSIBLE TO MAKE A DETECTOR FEEL LIGHTER?

While most detectors are designed to be durable but lightweight typically weighing between 2-to-4 pounds, they can feel like they weigh much more as the day goes on. The ergonomics of a particular model may also make it feel heavier than it really is which can force you to opt to not use a detector that may in fact be ideal for your needs or cut your hunting time short. There is a simple solution to reducing these apparent weight and balance issues that can allow you to stay in the field longer or choose a detector that might otherwise not have been an option.

Several companies produce a support system using bungee-type cords, straps and clips to relieve the weight of the detector from your wrist, elbow and shoulder. The harness is fully adjustable for user height and hunting style and can be used in either a left or right handed configuration. A slight change in one's swing is required but being able to swing it by holding the handgrip with just the lightest touch of your fingers makes believers out of most who try them. While this concept has been used on a number of gold detectors for several years, the advantage this system could provide to the general treasure hunter was recognized and the concept was modified to work on virtually any detector out there. By not being made for a specific model it allows you to quickly and easily switch it from one detector to another as the need arises or as your detector arsenal changes.

Another third-party product that greatly improves the overall balance and ergonomics of many detectors on the market is known as the "straight shaft". By replacing the common S-shaped shaft assembly with a straight design and in some cases relocating the battery pack, a detector can feel markedly lighter allowing it to be used for hours longer than the stock shaft allows. A listing of models that can be equipped with one of these shafts is provided in each manufacturer-specific chapter later in the book. If you have a detector that can be fitted with a different shaft, they are well worth looking into.

HEADPHONES

Headphones are another item that most detectorists should devote some time in selecting the right set for their application. Hopefully most of you recognize the importance of using a set of headphones and use them on a regular basis. They enable you to hear the fainter signals that typically indicate smaller, deeply-buried targets, conserve detector battery life and allow you to politely ignore the incessant questions you invariably get when hunting public areas. But all headphones are not created equally. In addition to the wide assortment of headphones produced by both the metal detector manufacturers and treasure hunting accessory companies, there are dozens of headphones made and sold for non-treasure hunting applications that work just as well as the specialized ones. Each model of headphones will produce a slightly different signal when connected to your detector so selecting a specific set will be a matter of personal preference. For example, my kids and I use different brands of headphones and this was based on trying out several different types to find those that were both comfortable and produced audio signals that were easy to distinguish. The advantage of some of the headphones designed for treasure hunters is that they are built to withstand the wear-&-tear of everyday use in the field and in many cases, are easily repairable with replaceable cords and plugs. Check out your local metal detector dealer as well as sources such as Radio Shack, Wal-Mart, K-Mart, stereo stores and the like. I have actually had friends take their detector into Radio Shack to try out the various headphones before buying a pair – this is definitely a purchase that you want to try-before-you-buy if at all possible. As with selecting a detector, be careful about making your selection based on what you may have picked up on an Internet forum or read in an advertisement. Some of the metal detector headphones can run well over $100, and while they are quality products, if they produce a sound that is not to your liking or are not comfortable to wear, you will regret the purchase long after you have paid the bill. For example my son has opted to use a fairly inexpensive set of lightweight headphones when participating in competition hunts and a more substantial pair of detector headphones when heading out for some serious coin or relic hunting with me. The better headphones just weren't comfortable when he was rushing across a field kneeling down every 30 seconds to recover a target so he has a specific pair for a specific type of hunting.

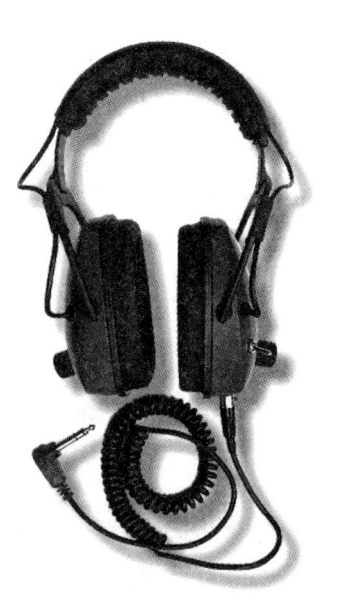

In the subsequent chapters dealing with specific types of treasure hunting, there will be compilations of additional accessories that have been proven highly effective in the field and can significantly increase both the quality and quantity of your finds along with contact information for the companies that produce them. The brand-specific sections of the Buyers Guide will provide references to books & videos covering particular models as well as model-specific accessories and Internet websites where additional information, assistance and tips can be obtained.

REFERENCE RESOURCE BIBLIOGRAPHY

Books & Videos

- **Advanced Detecting** by Norfolk Wolf [UK book]
- **Beginners Guide to Metal Detecting** by Julian Evan-Hart [UK book]

- **Comprehensive Guide to Metal Detecting** by Bob Bailey
- **Handbook for Detectorists** by Gert Gesink [UK book]
- **Modern Metal Detectors** by Charles Garrett
- **Metal Detecting Down to Earth** by Mike Pegg (DVD or VHS)

Internet Sites

- **1000 Metal Detectors.com**: Reviews of various metal detectors from users worldwide + useful tips; http://www.100metaldetectors.com
- **Find's Treasure Forums – Modifications**; Forum is for people that have either wanted to or have already modified their detector's original setup; http://www.findmall.com/list.php?22
- **Find's Treasure Forums – Metal Detector Classified Forum**: http://www.findmall.com/list.php?34
- **Geotech; Technology for Treasure Hunting**; Forums intended to answer questions and exchange information on all types of metal detectors & modifications; http://www.geotech1.com/forums/
- **Lost Treasure Magazine's Field Tests:** Field test reports on detectors from all the manufacturers going back to the 1980's; http://www.LostTreasure.com
- **Metal Detector Reviews**: Site providing independent reviews of metal detectors & accessories; http://metaldetectorreviews.net/
- **Miliron Detector Test Info**: Independent tests of most major brands and models showing in-field performance; http://www.detectortest.info/
- **TreasureNet – Head-to-Head Comparison Forum**: Compare detectors to one another – good buying reference site; http://forum.treasurenet.com/index.php/board,316.0.html
- **Treasure Spot – Buy/Sell/Trade Forum**: http://www.mytreasurespot.com/main/list.php?7
- **The Treasure Depot – Classified Ads**: Space to buy, sell or trade treasure hunting equipment; http://www.thetreasuredepot.com/cgi-bin/classifieds/classifieds_config.pl

Headphones Designed for Metal Detectors

- **B&B Distributors, LLC.**, (205) 752-5523; http://www.KillerBPhones.com
- **Detector Electronics**; (800) 446-0244; http:/www.MetalDetector.com
- **DetectorPro**, (845) 635-3488; http://www.DetectorPro.com
- **Jimmy Sierra, Inc.**; (415) 488-8131; http://www.JimmySierra.com
- **Sun Ray Detector Electronics**; (319) 636-2244; http://www.SunRayDetector.com
- **Timberwolf Headphones**, (888) 272-7325; http://www.timberwolfheadphones.com

Harness Systems to Improve Detector Weight & Balance

- **E-Z Swing**: Treasure Products, Inc.; (877) 304-7788; http://www.treasureproducts.com/
- **Lejermon Harness System**: Dixie Metal Detectors; (615) 860-4333; http://www.dixie-metal-detectors.com
- **Swingy Thingy**: Profile Prospecting Supply; (702) 732-8000; http://www.kamakazi.com

Other Sources & Suppliers

- Metal detector repair / service and performance enhancing modifications:
  - **East Texas Metal Detectors** (Keith Wills); (903) 734-7773; http://www.BrokenDetector.com
  - **Surfscanner Detectors** (Mr. Bill); (508) 457-4805; http://www.surfscanner.com
  - **Link Technologies**; Performance-enhancing modifications and non-warranty repairs for Minelab gold detectors. Australia (61-03-90175549) http://detectormods.com/
  - **Pentechnic**: The leading factory-authorized repair center in the UK; http://www.pentechnic.co.uk/
  - **Rebel Metal Detectors**: Repair work as well as unique conversions of land detectors to waterproof versions; (843) 763-1115; http://www.rebelmetal.com/
- Local dealer referral options in addition to the manufacturer's websites:
  - **Outdoor Outfitters**; (800) 558-2020; http://www.OutdoorOut.com
  - **Joan Allen Electronics, Ltd.**; +44 (0)1959 571255; http://www.joanallen.co.uk/

EQUIPMENT BUYERS RESEARCH FORM

Type of hunting you will be doing (enter %'s . . . ensure the total equals 100%)

	Coin Hunting		Relic Hunting
	Prospecting		Beach Hunting
	Shallow Water Hunting		Underwater Hunting
	Bottle Hunting		Cache Hunting

Where do you / will you be hunting most of the time; i.e., the specific area(s) as this will allow you to quantify the ground conditions you will be facing?

	YES	NO
Are weight, ergonomics and complexity factors that will need to be considered based on who will be using it?		
Do you have equipment now? Have you used a metal detector before?		
What brand and model?		
How old is it?		
What condition is it in?		
Will you want to sell or trade your current equipment?		
Will support after the sale be important to you?		
What is your budget / Is price an important factor?		

POTENTIAL METAL DETECTORS TO CONSIDER

Target Recovery – Remember The Math!

So far we've discussed 1) finding productive sites that the competition has not worked for years and 2) ensuring that you're using the proper equipment and using it correctly. Well, even if you have the right equipment and are hunting in the right location, you still might not be coming home with as much as you could be. As a matter of fact, based on discussions with detectorists from around the world, target recovery is still the one area of treasure hunting that causes the most frustration . . . second only to conducting research.

The truly successful treasure hunters are those that use a detector designed for the type of hunting the do most of the time, know how to adjust it for any conditions they may encounter, search sites most likely to contain the type of targets they want to find **and** then are able to recover the targets with the least amount of effort. As we've said before, success is a matter of numbers. . . simply being in the right location with the right equipment is not enough. The most successful detectorist is one who can pinpoint & recover a target in the least amount of time. After all, you only have a limited amount of time to spend detecting and the more time you spend finding targets and the less you time you spend recovering them means you will have more in your pouch on the way home than someone who struggled with target recovery. Making a few changes to how you recover a target once you've found it with your detector that shaves even a small amount of time from how long it takes to recover each one adds up over the course of a typical hunt and that is the intent of this chapter.

Let's take a look at an example and see which person you can relate to. Joe and Steve have both been metal detecting for a few years and get out on a regular basis. Joe has put together a test garden in his back yard and uses it quite frequently to ensure he is proficient at accurately pinpointing what his detector passes over. Steve on the other hand feels that his time in the field has given him the skill he needs to be successful . . . in other words, practice is no longer necessary. On a sunny Saturday afternoon, the two of them head out to a local park to do some coin hunting. They head in opposite directions agreeing to meet in a few hours near the ball field. They both hit signals on a consistent basis; however, Joe spends less than 30 seconds recovering each one. Steve on the other hand takes considerably longer to find each target . . . digging wider, deeper holes and combing through the dirt trying to find what he located. Even if they both are searching areas of the park that contain the same number of targets, who do you think will find more in the time they have? Since it takes Steve at least 4 or 5 times longer to find his targets than Joe, Joe has an immediate edge over Steve. Well, they meet at the ball field and compare finds. Joe has 62 coins, a small gold ring and a few nice "trinkets". Steve looks surprised as he counts out 24 coins and a brass key. What made the difference . . . recovery time!

Effective target recovery actually is a two part process. The first part is being able to <u>ACCURATELY</u> pinpoint where the target is once you've detected it. It doesn't do you any good to have learned the finer points about your detector, spent hours conducting research and then driven 20 miles to a productive spot only to spend a considerable amount of time trying to find the target your detector has located for you. As we discussed in the Equipment chapter, detectors today have search coils ranging in size from less than 4" to 18" or more. Even if you know that there is a good target beneath the coil of your detector, you will be wasting a lot of valuable hunting time trying to find it if you do not know how to precisely pinpoint the signal.

Let's start out with a question: *"How accurately do you think you are able to zero in on a target you've located with your detector?"* Do you know exactly where a target is beneath the coil when you get a signal? Do you think you could put your finger on top of the target? How about within a few inches of it? Surprisingly, even treasure hunters who have been detecting for years can't identify the exact spot on their coil where targets will produce the strongest signal and hence enable them to pinpoint targets in the field. The rest of this chapter will cover some proven techniques to improve your recovery rate and reduce the impact you might have on a site when you recover a target (thereby ensuring you get invited back). In addition, we'll cover the selection of equipment or tools that can take away some of the frustration you tend to experience when spending an inordinate amount of time trying to find what your detector has located.

> ### ◆ CHALLENGE ◆
> Many once-productive sites have been closed to metal detecting due to the highly visible actions of a few hobbyists who left the area with huge, gaping holes or patches of dead grass visible to anyone passing by. The challenge is to look at your recovery techniques with a critical eye and if you find yourself digging holes larger than 2" – 3" across in a grassy area or just a bit larger in a wooded location, spend time practicing with some of the techniques provided in this chapter to improve your accuracy & reduce the potential damage to the area done when recovering a target.

PINPOINTING TARGETS WITH DIFFERENT COIL DESIGNS

Remember the section in the previous chapter on the different coil designs (concentric vs. Double-D / wide scan)? This section will cover some of the tricks that can help you pinpoint targets faster and with more accuracy which will result in more finds at the end of the day. Let's start by looking at the Double-D coil.

DOUBLE-D or WIDE SCAN COILS

Despite what may seem like a shortcoming with the Double-D or Wide Scan coil design, with a little practice you will find yourself pinpointing targets with accuracy equal to or better than your fellow detectorists can with a concentric coil. As proof of this statement, Doc Lousignant, a seasoned detectorist and well-known dealer from Las Vegas, put on a demonstration at a dealer convention a few years ago. Many attendees expressed negative comments about the 15" Coiltek WOT coil's pinpointing capabilities. Doc proceeded to show the people how to pinpoint targets to within a 1"-2" diameter area and do so in less time than it would take using a small concentric coil. It was obvious that Doc knew his coil but with a little practice anyone can do it.

There are a few highly-effective techniques used to pinpoint targets with all Double-D coils and you should try each of them. Pick the one that works best for you in the specific type(s) of hunting you will be doing, possibly switching between them as conditions dictate. Testing your detector's response in a test garden will prove to be invaluable as you master it. If it takes you 5 minutes to actually find a target that you have detected, you will have far less in your pouch at the end of the day than if it had only taken you a minute or two. Practicing before you head out and then again periodically to keep your skills sharp will pay off when you hit the field. This is especially true if you are trying to recover targets as quickly as possible without damaging the target or the area you are searching.

A technique that works well with Double-D coils has been called *"The Wiggle"* by many users. Remember that the sensitive area of the coil lies under that narrow strip running from the front of the coil to the rear of the coil where the two "D-shaped" windings overlap. When you receive a signal, "wiggle" the coil side-to-side about an inch or so, just enough to produce a consistent signal. This tells you that the target is somewhere under the center "hot strip" as shown in the following photo.

Then while "wiggling" the coil, slowly pull the coil toward you listening for the point where the signal drops off and finally disappears. When this occurs, it means that the "hot strip" has moved off the target. It will be located just beneath the tip of the front of the coil as shown by the coin in the photograph to the right. Another way to use this technique is to slowly push the coil away from you while wiggling it side-to-side and when the signal disappears, the target will be beneath the rear edge of the coil. This technique is commonly used 1) where speed is of the essence in applications such as competition hunts, 2) where getting to the touchpads may be difficult due to the control panel being covered such as when hunting ocean beaches or 3) in non-trashy sites. Some detectorist's use this technique at all times so use what works best for you and it may change based on the site conditions or type of targets you are searching for.

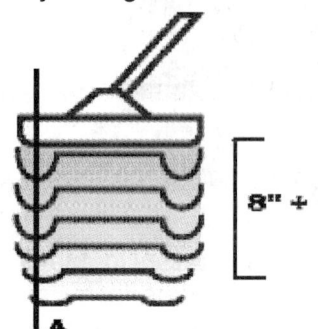

A point to remember when using the "Wiggle" method to pinpoint is that deep targets pinpoint a tad off due to the shape of the electrical field generated by the coil. The signal tends to curve inwards slightly at the edge of the detection field which results in targets pinpointing at a point an inch or so IN from the edge of the coil. If you receive a signal showing that the target is deeply buried (8"+), cut your plug with the center being just in from the edge of the coil. This effect is shown to the left with deeply buried targets being represented by the "A".

Another extremely effective technique used by many Double-D coil users for pinpointing is to "kick" the coil up on edge when a target is detected – especially a shallow one – and use the tip of the coil as shown in the photo to zero-in on the target. Remember, the "hot strip" will result in a very narrow area of detection on the coil assisting you in pinpointing the target. At the same convention, "Doc" Lousignont demonstrated this technique to a packed room full of dealers, many of whom had never seen this in practice. He quickly made converts of those who felt pinpointing capabilities had to be sacrificed when using a Double-D coil, especially a larger-than-stock coil.

CONCENTRIC COILS

The concentric coil produces a field that is the easiest to pinpoint with since it is cone-shaped and symmetrical; i.e., the same all the way around, but there are still some tricks that will help detectorists pinpoint targets faster and more accurately. The basic concept of pinpointing with a concentric coil is to find the point where the signal is the strongest and when that is identified, the target should be directly beneath the center of the two windings. You might have noticed that the words "should be" were underlined. While the target should be under the center of the coil (remember on a concentric coil, the transmit and receive windings are intended to be symmetric around the center point), slight variations in the manufacturing process may result in the actual electrical center being slightly off-center from the coil housing center itself. Checking your coil in the test garden or using the technique described in the upcoming section entitled "So Just How Good Are You at Pinpointing" will allow you to verify precisely where the strongest signal from the target is produced and it will pay off in the field as you attempt to recover actual targets.

The easiest way to zero in on a detected target with a concentric coil is to move it in an X-shaped pattern (left & right / forward & backward) as shown in the adjacent photograph and find the point where the strongest signal is received.

Spend a little time in your test garden to see exactly where the electrical center of the coil is. If you find that your coil pinpoints slightly off-center, a dab of nail polish or a dot from a permanent maker can be a useful aid on solid coils. If you have an open coil, marking it is not an option so after checking for the true electrical center of the coil, you'll have to remember to apply any offset to signals in the field to ensure you are digging in the right place.

> **TIP**
> Shallow targets are often harder to pinpoint and locate than deep targets due to the strength of the signal they produce.
> - If you get a strong signal that is difficult to pinpoint, lift the coil a few inches off the ground and try again. With the reduced signal intensity, it will usually be easier to find the center of the detected target.
> - If your detector has a touchpad / pushbutton that allows you to switch in to / out of the pinpoint mode, try using it as the coil approaches the target. By "shrinking" the response, you will be able to zero in on the target and accurately pinpoint where to dig.

Pinpointing deeper or smaller targets tends to be an easier task due to the smaller signal you are dealing with. Listen for the point where the strongest signal is received with a concentric coil or use the "wiggle" with a Double-D coil. With a little practice in your test garden or with the practice technique described on the following page, you should be able to put your finger above the target every time!

TARGET DEPTH INDICATION

Many of today's metal detectors have the ability to provide a probable target depth indication – either via a meter or LCD screen. When some of us ol' timers started out, a seemingly basic feature like this would have been far-fetched at best but it has become a real asset in reducing the time spent recovering a target by knowing how deep to dig. Many seasoned detectorists are able to cut a plug to just the right depth so that when it is folded back, the target is either at the tip of the plug or visible in the bottom of the hole. If you are not seeing results like that, try spending a little more time in your test garden or watching the display and learn to interpret what your detector is telling you – your find rate will start going up in short order.

> ⚠ An important point to remember is that the depth indication circuitry on all detectors has been calibrated for coin-sized targets. If you detect a larger target such as a belt buckle or a can, the indicated depth will be <u>SHALLOWER</u> then the target's actual depth. Conversely, if you come across a small target such as an earring, piece of aluminum or tiny nugget or pass over a coin on edge, the indicated depth will be <u>DEEPER</u> than the target's actual depth. Keep this in mind as you start recovering targets. Check the target's depth so that you do not inadvertently damage a small, valuable target or waste time going after a large piece of trash whose indicated depth will be far shallower than it actually is.

Indicated Depth

1" 5" 8"

Actual Depth 5"

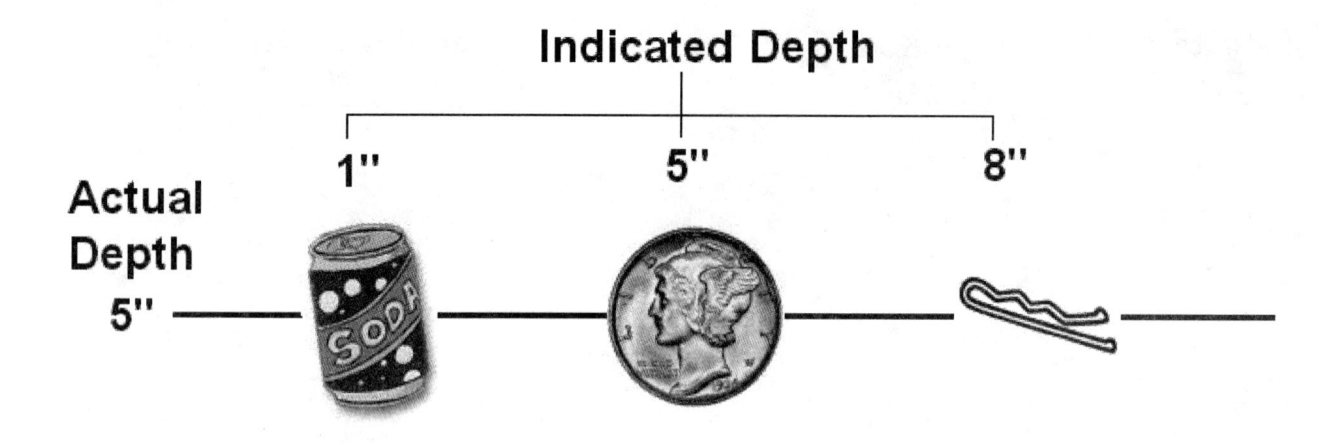

SO JUST HOW GOOD ARE YOU AT PINPOINTING?

Are you looking for an easy way to check your "pinpointing proficiency" regardless of the design or size coil you use? Are you looking for an interesting activity for an upcoming club meeting or hunt? Several years ago I attended the annual hunt put on by the Alaska Treasure Seekers Club near Anchorage. One of the activities they had for entrants was focused on one's pinpointing abilities. They took a large sheet of cardboard and taped a coin to the bottom. Anyone that wanted to compete paid their entry fee and then swept their coil across the cardboard. When they detected the hidden target, they tried to pinpoint it and when they felt they knew where it was, a club member would push a pin through the cardboard at that spot. The cardboard was turned over and the distance from the pin to the center of the coin was measured. The closest to the center won half of the entry fees! This was repeated throughout the two-day hunt and almost everyone I spoke to realized that they had some work to do in terms of pinpointing targets a bit more accurately! Well, this is a great activity to try at home (have your kids or spouse tape the coin in place) or at your monthly club meetings. What I've recommended to many people over the years is to place a mark on their coil (unless it's an open design coil) indicating where the target will be when the strongest signal is obtained. This mark may in fact **NOT** be in the exact center of the coil or where the manufacturer has marked it. Remember, even if you are off by 2-3 inches when pinpointing your target initially, you will be wasting valuable hunting time looking for the target you know is there!

RECOVERY TOOLS

Selecting the correct recovery tool for the type of treasure hunting you do requires more than simply using what came with your detector or what some mail-order company recommended from 1,000 miles away. Ground conditions along with the type of detecting you do will dictate the type of tool(s) you might be using. My basement and garage looks like a small hardware store with the many different recovery tools I have assembled over the years . . . . many were useful for areas I hunted while others turned out to be total disappointments.

Start by talking with treasure hunters in your local area engaged in the same type of hunting you do. After all, someone who searches for Civil War relics in the woods is not going to be able to help you determine what would be best to use for recovering coins from private yards or the local park. Call a few local dealers and see what they carry. They should have what has been proven to work in your area. With the cost of some recovery tools today, you should definitely see if you can try what you are looking at before you buy it. My son, daughter and I are all active treasure hunters and none of us use the same recovery tools when we go coin hunting let alone any other form of treasure hunting. It's a matter of personal preference and if you are not completely comfortable with the tool you've selected, you won't be as efficient as you could be in recovering what your detector has located.

Each of the upcoming chapters on specific forms of treasure hunting will contain a section on recovery tools that have been proven effective by detectorists worldwide as well as suppliers where the tools can be purchased if your local dealer does not have them available.

I'm also a strong proponent of using tools that might not have a "Treasure Hunting" logo on them yet work just as well. For example, coin probes – which are excellent for recovering shallow targets – are similar to ice picks which can be picked up for under $5 at your local hardware store. Low-cost bulb planters work well for retrieving targets in soft, rock-free soil. Army surplus stores usually have a nice assortment of shovels and picks that are ideal for relic hunters or prospectors. This is not to say that you should not pick up a specialized tool designed for treasure hunting as there are many exceptional tools that will make your life easier in the field, just look around to see what's available.

PINPOINTING PROBES . . . RECOVER MORE TARGETS PER HOUR!

You've spent more than a month researching the location of an old picnic ground that had been very popular in the 1800's. After pinpointing its location and obtaining permission to search it, you arrived early one Saturday morning hoping for a productive day. The first signal produced an 1893 Indian Head penny and you knew you had finally found a virgin site. A short time later you received a solid signal that your detector showed as being 8 inches deep, always a good sign. Unfortunately a large root was directly over the target and your frustration rose trying to get it out. Finally after hacking under the root, you see something shiny and pick it out of the hole. A beautiful 1897 O Barber half! As you turn it over, your heart sinks as you see a deep gash from your digger. Later you find that the coin would have been worth almost $1,000 but after hitting it, was worth little more than the bullion content. Think this couldn't happen to you? Well, the number of "what-could-have-been" valuable finds that were damaged during their recovery over the years is truly staggering. Even those of us with decades of experience have been a tad off when pinpointing a target and inadvertently hit it with the digger turning what was a great find into nothing more than a conversation piece. For some reason, one never hits that clad dime or shotgun shell but rather the most valuable find of the day.

Handheld electronic probes designed to help you zero in on a target have been around for many years; however, they have all had a few significant limitations. The first is their limited detection depth. Coin-sized objects had to be quite close to the tip of the probe with most probes providing an inch or less of detection depth. If you were fortunate to have removed a plug with the precision needed to get that close to the target without damaging it great, but in most cases you would need to remove a little dirt and recheck the hole several times before finding your target. Another issue with probes was the way they operated. On most probes, you had to turn it on and tune it each time you wanted to check a hole which quickly became more of a hassle than it was worth. A third issue was tied to the quality of their construction. Treasure hunting places severe demands on the equipment we all use and if it fails to hold up to these demands, the investment soon turns into a disappointment and is tossed in the trash. This is not to say that all probes that have been on the market have been poorly made or provide no benefit to the user. However, many hunters who would have liked to use one found the issues listed above combined with the need to carry along yet another piece of equipment to outweigh the possible benefits a probe could provide.

Many veteran detectorists may feel they are proficient enough in pinpointing targets to not need a probe; however, there are times when even the best of us spends a considerable amount of time trying to find a target due to its size, color that blends in with the soil or having multiple targets in the hole. In these cases, a pinpointer will allow you to quickly locate the target and resume hunting - meaning more targets recovered in the same amount of time in the field. There are a number of electronic pinpointing probes on the market ranging from self-contained units to inline probes that draw their power from your detector. Since each one has a different physical style or mode of operation, it would pay for you to check a few out before you make your selection. I was always one who felt a probe was simply another piece of equipment that I didn't need to drag with me into the field; however, after trying a few of the newer models, I almost feel naked without one anymore. Sales of both stand-alone and in-line probes have skyrocketed in recent years and the reason is quickly apparent when trying one just once. A quality probe can cut recovery time in half and virtually eliminate the risk of damaging targets.

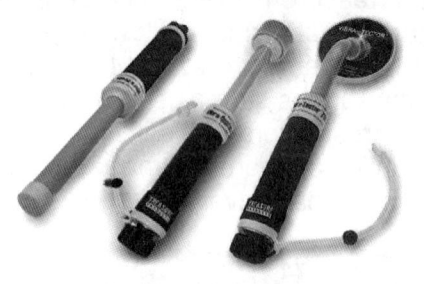

Just a few of the electronic pinpoint probes currently available to aid in recovering targets
Models pictured include Vibra-Probe's lineup (l) and the Garrett Pro-Pointer (r)

With the extreme detection depth afforded by many of the current metal detectors, users sometimes find they need a probe that goes a bit deeper or can be inserted deeper into a hole to zero in on the target. A pulse-induction probe described above or a security-type hand scanner shown below has been proven to provide the extra sensitivity and reach required when recovering a target 2'+ deep. Bottle hunters have also found these larger probes can easily find metal items in the sides of the hole and piles of dirt as they excavate the area . . . recovering coins, jewelry and relics that might have otherwise been missed.

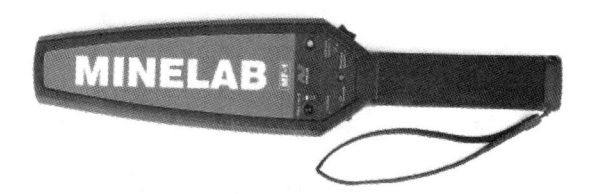

In summary, being able to accurately pinpoint a detected target, quickly recover it without damage and continue searching for the next target will ensure you bring home more at the end of the day. Try implementing a few of the ideas covered in this chapter and you will find that your time in the field is more enjoyable and more productive!

REFERENCE RESOURCE BIBLIOGRAPHY

Pinpointing Probes:

- **Pistol Probe**: DetectorPro; **(**800) 367-1995 or (845) 635-3488; http://www.DetectorPro.com
- **Bounty Hunter Pinpointer**: First Texas; (915) 633-8354; http://www.Detecting.com
- **Garrett Pro-Pointer**: Garrett Electronics; (800) 527-4011; http://www.Garrett.com
- **Automax Precision V4 Pinpointer**: Kellyco Detectors; (888) 535-5926; http://www.kellycodetectors.com/vibra/handhelds.htm
- **GPP Pinpointer:** Secon GmbH; http://www.secon-koeln.de or http://secon-usa.com/
- **Sun Ray Detector Electronics**: In-line probes for Fisher, Garrett, Minelab and Whites detectors powered by the detector; http://www.SunRayDetector.com
- **Vibra-Probe:** Treasure Products, Inc., (877) 304-7788, http://www.vibraprobe.com
- **Bullseye II**: Whites Electronics; (541) 367 6121; http://www.WhitesElectronics.com

General Treasure Hunting Tips & Techniques

This chapter - and the subsequent ones on specific types of treasure hunting - will cover the part of the Success Formula dealing with developing the search techniques that help you find more with your time in the field. There are a number of tips and techniques that successful detectorists have found to be effective worldwide. Aalong with the additional books and other references contained in each chapter, they will help you find more no matter what type of target you are searching for or conditions you are searching under.

SOME DETECTOR BASICS THAT CAN MAKE A BIG DIFERENCE

SENSITIVITY: This one function on metal detectors is probably the most misused control and the biggest contributor to frustration in the field. The very name virtually begs users to crank it to the maximum setting . . . after all; more sensitivity is what we all want, isn't it? Well, under perfect conditions – which only exist in a few select areas or a laboratory – running the sensitivity at its highest level will in fact result in less detection depth and hence fewer targets. A useful analogy would be the headlights on your car. If you are driving along a straight highway on a moonless night, your high beams will allow you to see much farther than the low beams but what if you hit a patch of dense fog like that in the picture? With your high beams, the light winds up being reflected back from the moisture in the fog blinding you and reducing the distance you can see in front of you. Switching to your low beams will allow you to see much clearer even if you are not seeing as far as you had been with the high beams and no fog present. The sensitivity control on your detector works the same way. To get the best overall detection depth, you want to set it at a level that does not produce a great deal of falsing or chatter caused by ground mineralization or outside electrical interference. The optimal sensitivity setting can and often does vary from site-to-site and even from one area of a specific site to another, so unless your detector offers an automatic sensitivity tracking system found on higher-end models, pay attention to this control and make adjustments as needed.

> **TIP**: Sometimes less sensitivity actually produces more. If you are hunting a site where targets are shallow; i.e., recently lost, a thin layer of soil over a hard packed layer, etc., there is no need to run at high levels of sensitivity. A lower sensitivity level can eliminate falsing and make pinpointing shallow targets easier. In high trash, a lower setting can allow the detector to see good targets in close proximity to trash easier than at higher settings

SWEEP SPEED:

If you perform an air test with any metal detector you will find that the electronics tend to process signals so quickly that you will not be able to pass a target across the coil fast enough to have the detector miss it. But this is just another reason not to put a lot of weight in air tests other than to learn how the detector responds to specific targets and where they are rejected as discrimination is adjusted. While a detector can pick up a target passing across the coil at a fast sweep speed, you would not last very long if you tried hunting at that rate all day. Additionally, every detector out there has an optimal sweep speed which is the speed that allows its circuitry to process signals coming back from the ground and if so equipped, monitor and adjust for changes in ground mineralization.

Another use for your test garden is to check the response you receive from the buried targets as you make slight changes to your sweep speed. Shallow targets will be detectable at virtually any sweep speed; however, deeper targets or those in close proximity to trash will respond differently at different sweep speeds. Some models actually have the ability to change the optimal sweep speed as a menu option which allows one to customize the detector based on one's personal preferences. You will find that when hunting in trash-filled sites, a slower sweep speed will enable you to detect good targets amongst the trash.

> **TIP**: When searching sites where targets tend to be deeper, a trick that may help you decide if a signal is worth recovering or not is to "flick" the coil across the target area at a markedly faster sweep speed. This can cause good signals to produce a stronger signal while items on the verge of being rejected tend to breakup or disappear altogether.

Be sure to check the operating manual for your detector as it will let you know what the recommended sweep speed is. For example, the White's M6 manual states that a sweep speed of 1' per second is preferred so a typical sweep from left-to-right should take 4-5 seconds. Other models can be faster or slower so add this to your list of questions when buying a new detector. Buying a new detector and getting tired after an hour or less is hardly the way to enjoy your time in the field.

GRIPPING THE DETECTOR & ADJUSTING THE SHAFT LENGTH: Remember that the main reason the vast majority of us are involved in the hobby is to get out and enjoy the search for what lies just under the surface of the ground . . . the intrinsic value of what we find should be secondary. If you wind up with a cramped arm after just a short amount of time in the field, how much will you really enjoy the search? Many beginners as well as seasoned hunters tend to hold their detector in a death grip which results in cramping in short order. Unless you are forcing the coil of the detector through thick underbrush or shallow water, you should not be gripping the handgrip as if your life depended on it. By ensuring the shaft is adjusted to the right length, you should be able to allow the handgrip to simply rest on your palm and fingers as you sweep from side to side, letting the search coil "float" across the ground. If you find yourself feeling the weight of the detector in your forearm or wrist after hunting for an hour or so, take a good look at how you are holding the detector. Changing the length of the shaft – making it either longer or shorter – and altering how you are gripping it will often make all the difference in the world.

| ➢ Too short ➢ | ➢ Optimal length ➢ | ➢ Too long ➢ |

LEARING A NEW DETECTOR – START SIMPLE: One of the biggest mistakes people with a new detector tend to make is to head for the most challenging site they can find to see how it performs, especially if they have been hunting for a while and are hoping their new acquisition will unlock the vault of hidden valuables. The trashy section of the old fairground may hold the type of coins you are looking for but the amount of junk present will probably cause you to give up in short order and wonder what you spent your hard earned money on. The same holds true if you are a relic hunter, beach hunter or prospector. While your new detector may have the ability to ferret out valuable targets from the trash, it's not as simple as just turning it on and waiting for the finds to appear. Spend some time at the local playground, tot-lot, clean stretch of beach or battle site that is relatively trash-free to learn what the detector is telling you and how slight adjustments can alter the response you get. Then venture into the sites that are more challenging yet still have valuables waiting for you to find.

Martin Wright from Nottingham, England, makes an excellent point about the importance of learning the nuances of a new detector. *"A lot of detectorists think that it's the machine that makes the person a good detectorist, when in fact it's a combination of a good metal detector and having the patience to find how to get the most from the machine and only when the two come together do you have a good detectorist. Whenever I've changed to a new machine I notice that my finds drop off for a while during the learning curve, and then the good stuff starts to surface again."*

TARGET MASKING

A challenge that can frustrate less experienced hunters is trying to separate good targets from junk in trash-filled sites. Not only is it harder to pinpoint a specific target when there are several in close proximity, but what is commonly called "target masking" can actually cause you to miss what could be the find of the year. Target Masking is shown in the following figure and is a major contributor to the number of good targets that still lay hidden amongst the trash in areas that have been hunted for years. If you sweep over the targets shown from left to right, the bottle cap being close to the surface will produce a strong signal. The coil then sees the silver dollar which is a few inches deeper and hence produces a weaker signal. The same holds true as the coil passes over the pull tab followed by the gold ring and then the rusted screw. Unfortunately with metal detector technology, it comes down to which target gives the stronger signal and how much discrimination is being used as to whether the good target will be detected or not. A smaller search coil will result in fewer targets being seen at any one time making it easier to separate multiple targets and identify those worth recovering. Slowing down your sweep speed and overlapping each pass particularly with a concentric coil will also make these areas that others tend to avoid produce again. Bryce Brown, an avid detectorist with close to 30 years of experience, searches the trashiest sections of the Illinois parks surrounding his home almost exclusively and makes finds most of us only dream about on a regular basis using these techniques combined with many hours of in-field experience.

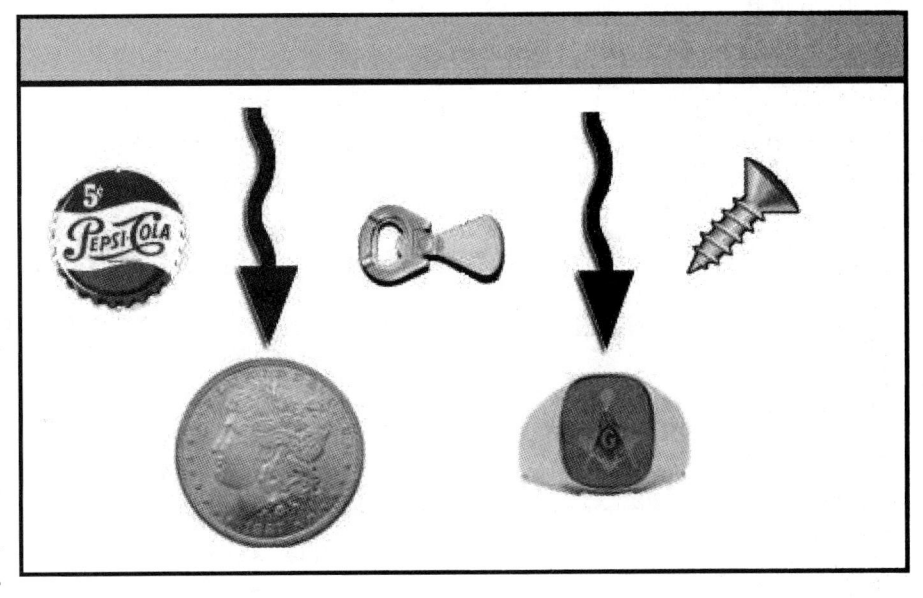

GETTING PERMISSION TO SEARCH PRIVATE PROPERTY

There are many advantages to searching sites on private property such as occupied and vacant homes, pastures, tracts of woods and even resorts. These privately-owned sites are consistent top-producers yet receive very little pressure from other detectorists as most people are reluctant to knock on the door of a stranger and ask to hunt their property. Depending on where you live, items such as Civil War relics, jewelry, tokens, artifacts dating back 100's or even 1,000's of years, old tools & utensils, bottles and more are being found on private property by today's treasure hunters. So let's discuss how best to obtain permission to search these areas.

You might wonder if you could actually get a complete stranger to give you permission to detect their property. Surprisingly, a large percentage of homeowners will allow you to search their yards if you only ask. I am always amazed at how infrequently I have been turned down when asking to hunt a yard . . . after all; I don't know if I would let someone hunt my property if asked. Over the years I have found that up to 9 property owners out of 10 will say yes. Unfortunately many of those that say no have had bad experiences with treasure hunters in the past and as a result, potentially productive sites are now off-limits. As far as obtaining permission, there are two different ways you can approach it. The first is to simply walk up to the front door and speak with the property owner in person. The other is to send the property owner a letter and spell out your request. Both methods have their merits and the one you select is simply a matter of personal preference.

Let's start by taking a look at the direct approach. There are a few basic tips that you should observe if you want to obtain permission and be allowed to keep what you find when you approach the property owner. These include the following:

- When you knock on the door to ask for permission, don't wear your dirtiest set of hunting clothes. Appearance is extremely important. Put yourself in the property owner's place. Would you even open the door if you saw someone caked with dirt standing outside?
- If you are planning on hunting the site with a partner, only one of you should go to the door. Homeowners may be reluctant to open it if they see a crowd standing there; again, put yourself in the shoes of the homeowner.
- If your son or daughter hunts with you, having them with you when you ask for permission usually tips the scale in your favor. Property owners look at the child and see it as a positive spending time in the field rather than sitting inside watching TV or playing video games.
- Have some business cards printed up with your name, address and telephone number on them. People will tend to trust you more if you are willing to leave your name and other information with them. You can get some basic cards printed locally for under $20 or buy some card stock and print them from your computer. Not a bad investment when you consider what you stand to gain from hunting a few prime pieces of private property. A sample is shown below.

North Georgia Historical Alliance

DEDICATED TO THE RECOVERY & PRESERVATION OF GEORGIA'S HERITAGE

Land & Underwater Archeological Surveys
Historical Research - Artifact Recovery

Andrew Sabisch - Team Member
122 West Main Street   Canton, GA   30114
(770) 555-1212

- <u>NEVER</u> mention that you are hoping to find coins or jewelry - simply say that your hobby is metal detecting and you would like to search their yard for lost artifacts. Offer to give them any personal items you might find and make sure you stand behind that statement if you actually find something they may have lost! Often residents have lost keys, jewelry and other trinkets that they would appreciate getting back especially at sites that may be up for sale.
- <u>NEVER</u> use an entrenching tool or shovel to dig with unless you are in a wooded section of the property. The best thing to use is a probe and screwdriver or a knife. Bring along a small sheet of plastic or a dish towel to place the dirt on and then dump it back in the hole as you don't want to leave <u>ANY</u> sign that you were there. Along the same lines, <u>NEVER</u> hunt a private yard during the summer months, as the grass will die leaving brown spots where you recovered targets. Nothing will ruin your reputation in a neighborhood faster than destroying a homeowner's lawn.
- When you start to recover a target, try to position yourself with your back to the house. The homeowner may be watching you and seeing you actually dig a hole may be un-nerving to them. You're not trying to be secretive but rather present the proper image.
- Try to hunt the entire yard in one trip. If you can't, ask if you can come back and when a good time would be. Work on the homeowner's schedule, not yours.

The other method you may want to use to obtain permission to search private property is to send a letter of introduction and request to the property owner. Finding out who owns a piece of property along with their mailing address can be done through the county's tax assessors or collector's office.

The advantage of a letter is that it allows the owner to think about your request instead of simply saying 'NO' and closing the front door. I have used this method on occasion and found that it offers a success rate as high as the 'face-to-face' approach. Jim Vokes, a veteran treasure hunter from upstate New York has developed an effective letter and I appreciate his offer to share it with other detectorists. His letter is shown below for your benefit:

Mr. XXX,

Normally I would prefer to approach you in person; however, I felt that a letter beforehand is a better emissary than just knocking on your door at an inconvenient time and invading your privacy.

In my research I noticed your property at (123 Main Street) was built around (XXXX). I have an interesting hobby that is metal detecting (looking for buried artifacts). I have engaged in this hobby for several years and find it very enjoyable and meet some very interesting people. The thrill of finding something lost for many years is very exciting for me. I am XX years old and have lived in XXX for the past XXX years. I want you to understand that I always respect the property I search and try to leave it in the same or better condition than I found it. Artifacts I recover are usually no more than 5 to 6 inches deep.

I would like to obtain permission for myself and a friend (I do not like detect alone all the time) to detect your property. In addition, I would like to offer my services to you. Perhaps you or someone you know has lost a valuable ring, a cache or farm tool. Perhaps you wish to locate a historical site or relic from the past. I would be willing to assist you just for the thrill of the search.

I have enclosed a self addressed stamped envelope for your convenience and would be happy to meet with you if further discussions are desired.

Thank you for your time and consideration.

Sincerely,

[*Your name, address and telephone number*]

> **TIP:** The tax records for most counties are now available online through the Geographic Information System or GIS for short. To find out if your county provides online access to tax records, do an Internet search using your state and county name along with the word "GIS" or visit the county's website site and look up the tax assessor / collectors office.

You will find that hunting private sites can be extremely productive for a few reasons. First, you will usually be the first person to have hunted it and as a result you will be rewarded with a larger number of finds in a shorter period of time than at the well-hunted sites you typically visit. Second, there will be much less trash than at the local school or park. So if you are looking for a new site to hunt, try asking to hunt some private property . . . you might just get hooked on it!

DISCRIMINATION . . . TO USE OR NOT TO USE

Purists will tell you that running any discrimination will ensure you miss valuable targets and while hunting in all-metal will ensure you do not miss anything, in most areas we tend to search, the amount of trash present makes this an unrealistic option. In certain areas where good finds may have dropped to virtually zero, hunting with little or no discrimination may be an option, especially if you have a detector that has a target ID meter or screen. This allows you to identify each target you come across, and while it may take longer to search the area; it will help you avoid recovering an excessive amount of trash. While great finds have been made with minimal amounts of rejection, hunting in this manner will be a matter of personal preference and may in fact change from one hunt to another depending on how ambitious you feel and how much "noise" you are willing to listen to. On the other hand, discrimination is there for a reason and there are times when higher levels are justified due to having a limited amount of time to search a site, the site containing extreme levels of trash or simply your "state of mind." Learn how slight changes in discrimination levels can affect the response from specific types of targets and use this information to your advantage as you visit different sites.

Doug Virgin, a seasoned detectorist had the following comment on the subject of discrimination, "*I actually adjust my hunting style to the site as needed. I tend to start out in All Metal at a new site just to get a feel for it and tend to dig all targets to get a picture of what's there. If it's too trashy, I make a custom program by using the trash I've dug. Is All Metal the only way for people to hunt? Definitely not but in the right spot it can be the best thing since sliced bread! I am not 'All Metal-All-The-Time', but if you want to see the BIG picture, All Metal will allow that and then you can decide just how much you actually want to dig.*"

PROTECT YOUR DETECTOR

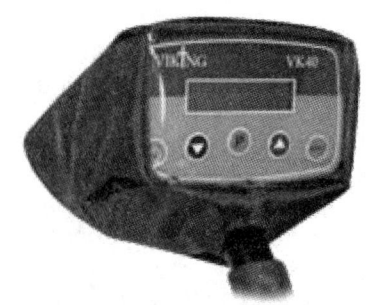

Despite the fact that metal detectors are designed to stand up to the rigors we place on them, a little care up front will keep your detector operating for years to come. An inexpensive accessory available for most detectors is the control housing cover. It slips over the housing and / or meter assembly to keep dirt and moisture from reaching the electronics. When you get home, the cover can be cleaned off leaving the detector looking like new. If you forget to bring a cover with you or there isn't one available for your particular model, a zip-loc bag is a good alternative. Simply pull it down over the instrument, twist it around the stem and secure it with a tie-wrap or some string. A recent addition to the accessory market for detectorists is called the Invisible SHIELD. An ultra-tough clear film, it goes right over the screen and in some cases, around the entire control housing to provide total scratch protection. Adapted from the protection afforded to other portable electronics such as cell phones and MP3 players, it has gained a following in the treasure hunting community and is an inexpensive solution to what could otherwise be an expensive problem. Whatever option you select, protection of some sort is a must when hunting ocean beaches to keep salt spray and sand from getting inside the detector, you find yourself a good distance from the car when bad weather arrives or you have dirt on your fingers and need to press touchpads on an LCD screen.

BATTERY OPTIONS

Some detectors come standard with rechargeable battery systems which do save a good deal of money when it comes to operating costs. If your detector does not come with rechargeable batteries, you can usually buy a system from the manufacturer designed to drop right in. If you want to avoid paying the price some companies charge for their systems, go pick up some 2,000+ mAh NiMH AA or 9 volt cells and a charger to save 50% or more of the price of the factory version. Make sure you get Nickel Metal Hydride (NiMH) batteries rather than older Nickel-Cadmium (NICAD) batteries as the NiMH cells do not develop a memory and can be recharged after 30 minutes or 8 hours of use with no adverse affects. When looking for a charger, get one that indicates it is a rapid charger which means it will fully charge the batteries in under 2 hours. There are also rapid chargers available for use in your car, truck or boat which will ensure you can hunt as long as you want, even when far from the nearest electrical outlet. Recently I came across a set of eight 2,200 mAh NiMH cells and a rapid charger for under $15 after a rebate at an office supply store so watch your sales flyers. You can have all the power you need for a price that won't break the bank.

GRIDING AN AREA

If you have a site that has produced well in the past but the finds have tapered off on recent visits, there's a proven technique that you might want to try before you write the site off for good. Let's look at a typical park, battle site or field holding the remains of a centuries-old village. Focus in on a portion of the site, say one acre in size which equates to an area of approximately 44,000 ft^2. No mater how diligent you feel you might have been in searching the area, with a 9" coil covering but 0.44 ft^2, the likelihood that you have missed a number of targets in your searches is quite high. If you want to spend the time to really work the site and recover as much as your equipment is capable of, gridding may be the answer.

There are a few variations to this technique but all are intended to minimize the potential of inadvertently missing a spot that could hold the best find in the area. The easiest method is to simply pick up a roll of thin colored nylon twine and a few stakes from your local hardware store. Drive two stakes in 50' to 100' apart and run the twine between them on the ground. Then, start on one side of the string and hunt from one stake to the other ensuring you overlap each sweep with the start of each sweep being on top of the string. When you get to the second stake, move to the other side and repeat the process. When you get back to the starting point, move the two stakes over twice the width of your sweep and start all over. You will be surprised at how long it actually takes to thoroughly cover a 100' swath but you will also be amazed at how much you and others have overlooked in random searches. When it's time to head for home, pull the stakes, wind the string around them and put them in your bag . . . . ready for the next trip. If you plan to return, push a golf tee flush with the ground where each stake was when you left off so you continue and not miss anything. Another method involves the use of four stakes where you lay out a square and work it completely in one direction (say east to west) and then rework it at a 90-degree angle (from north to south). Not only does this ensure you cover the entire area as the first method did but by searching it from a different angles, you will make sure that target masking does not cause you to miss a valuable item that may be surrounded by trash.

TREES & UNDERBRUSH CAN HELP YOU FIND PRODUCTIVE SITES

The title of this section probably has many readers scratching their heads wondering how trees can help find productive sites. Well, there are a few tricks successful hunters have found to consistently help them identify areas that hold the items we all hope to find. Nature never plants trees in a straight line so if you are driving through a rural area and see a row of trees running perpendicular to a road, you can be 99.9% certain that there was a structure there at one time. Another use of tress is to use them to estimate the age of a site or estimate the age of the grounds around a site. If you are not able to date trees typically found in your area, ask someone that has knowledge in this field to learn how to do it. For example, if you see a house that may have been renovated, check out the trees that surround it . . . are they old? If so, the house that may look like it's only from the 1960's may in fact predate that time by 50 years or more. If the park or school you are hunting has a field ringed by trees, are the trees as old as the structure itself? If not, there may be a wealth of items just inside the tree line. If you find a park that is heavily wooded, could that have once been an open, grassy expanse where people ate picnic lunches and played? You might just be the first one to hunt it and the finds will make even the most seasoned detectorist green with envy. Be sure to read the example described on page 89 which demonstrates this point. How about that Civil War camp you and every other relic hunter have searched for years. Do you all always park in the same place and then hike into the camp area? A few years ago a friend of mine visited a spot near Resaca, GA that several of us had hunted many times before. We always parked near the farmer's fence but this time Carl arrived alone. He happened to search the area where we usually parked and within minutes turned up a CSA belt plate worth a $4,000. Is there an area overgrown with briars that everyone avoids? Some of these areas have produced impressive amounts of finds easily located simply by looking at the site from a different perspective.

YOU'VE RECOVERED THE TARGET . . . . NOW WHAT?

If you are like 99% of the other treasure hunters out there – and I can honestly say I've found myself doing what I will tell you not to do – the first thing you probably want to do when you recover something from the ground is see what you have found. Sound familiar? Well, unless you are searching a local park built five years ago on virgin ground or a popular swimming beach where all you could hope to find are recently lost coins, you need to put the reigns on and avoid that sudden rush of interest. Never let curiosity get the best of you and start to wipe the dirt off anything you find to see if you can identify it. Dirt is one of the most abrasive substances out there and will easily scratch materials such as silver, gold, brass or copper. When you rub it against the target – even lightly – you can quickly ruin an items value. Want to see just what a "quick peek" can do to an item's value? A few years ago I was hunting with three friends in an old park near Montgomery, Alabama. It had been hunted for years but the targets were there if you worked for them. One of my friends, Howard Wilken, recovered a target and excitedly called us over to see what he had found. It was impressive - an 1896 Barber quarter with an O mintmark that looked like it had been lost soon after it came from the bank. Grading between XF and AU, it was a $600+ coin . . . . except for the noticeable scratches across both sides where Howard had tried to see what the date and mintmark was! What had been a high valve coin had been knocked down to a coin worth $100 or less in seconds.

So what do you do with a target that comes from a site which has the potential to hold valuable items such as silver or copper coins, military relics or old jewelry? The first tip that many veteran detectorists have learned to use (often the hard way and I am no exception - you don't want to see some of the examples I have in my collection of what too much enthusiasm can do to an otherwise pristine object!), is to bring along a plastic 35mm film canister filled with either cotton balls or dry cotton squares. When you find anything other than a recently lost coin or piece of costume jewelry, simply place it between the layers of cotton EXACTLY as you recovered it from the ground until you get home and can get the dirt off without damaging the find. If you have transitioned to digital photography like many of us and do not use 35mm film anymore, stop by any of the locations that process film such as Wal-Mart, K-Mart, CVS, Wal-Greens or a mall camera shop and ask them for any empty canisters they might have laying around. A bag of cotton balls or squares should cost less than $2 at a pharmacy and will be enough to get you through a season or two of hunting.

For items that are too large to fit into the film canister, put a few heavier-gauge Zip-Loc baggies in your pouch or back pocket. When you find something that you do not know what it is or know has value, put it in the bag to keep it from rubbing against your other finds. If you find a truly one-of-a-kind item such as a Civil War belt buckle, gold coin or obviously valuable piece of jewelry, taking it back to the car or even home is the best option. Don't laugh, but I was water hunting off an old resort site on the Chesapeake Bay with some friends. When we stopped for lunch, Brian came up to us grinning from ear to ear telling us about a "killer" ring he had found – a coiled snake holding a loose diamond in its open mouth behind its fangs. Well, his grin turned into stunned silence when he saw that a tear in his bag had let most of his finds spill back into the bay, including the ring. Had he taken 5 minutes and at least brought it back to shore when he found it, he would still have that smile on his face. As a side note, he never did find it again even though he hunted that site for weeks afterwards.

MAINTENANCE & TROUBLESHOOTING

So, you have taken the time and really mastered your detector. You have done the research necessary to zero in on some "first rate" sites that have more than likely never been hunted. You are ready to put those skills you have honed to the test and bring home a pouch full of keepers. It is an hour drive to the site but you know it will pay off when you get there. When you arrive, it looks even better than you had hoped for and the first signal you get after turning your detector on turns out to be a beautiful silver coin over 100 years old. You are on top of the world. Then you hear the threshold disappear and glancing down, the LCD screen has gone blank. Despite your best efforts, it looks like your trusty detector has given up the ghost and your perfect day in the field has turned into the ultimate disappointment. Sound far-fetched? It happens more often than you would care to imagine, yet a little bit of preventive care and some preparations can keep you from missing more than a few minutes of valuable hunting time.

Today's metal detectors have been built to withstand the rigors of treasure hunting but we need to be realistic. We are taking a piece of electronic gear into some of the most adverse conditions imaginable and expect it to continue operating year-after-year. If you run into problems in the field, there are some easy-to-check items that can keep you from loosing a day of detecting.

Let's start with some routine maintenance. As I have said in previous books, despite the number of hours my equipment spends in the field, I often get asked if it is brand new or if I actually hunt with it based on its condition. Several veteran detectorists I know also have gear that could pass as a nearly new "demo unit" . . . compliments of the post-use care they provide. As a result, our equipment operates flawlessly each time we take it out into the field. On the other hand, I have run into hunters who have relatively new detectors that look like they dragged them behind their truck on the way to the hunt site. Then they wonder why they have developed personnel relationships with the repair staff at the factory - no surprise there!

Let's begin with some tips to consider when you get home from a day in the field. Take a few minutes to wipe down your equipment when you come home rather than letting your detector sit in the garage for days – cleanup gets much harder after time has passed. Some of these tips may seem to be common sense but it's often surprising how often they get overlooked.

- Wipe off any dirt or mud using a damp paper towel or soft cloth. Be careful not to rub any dirt across the LCD screen if your detector has one as it will scratch quite easily. Using a control housing cover or screen protector will help keep this part of your detector looking new for years.

- Extend the shaft to the maximum length or disassemble it and wipe it down with a cloth containing a protectant such as Armor All™ or Son-of-a-Gun™. Don't spray it directly onto the detector as it can get inside the coil connector at the housing causing problems down the road.
- Periodically clean the bottom of the coil cover using some steel wool and detergent. Once you have cleaned it, wipe it down with Armor All™, Son-of-a-Gun™ or car polish which makes it easier to clean in the future and allows the coil to glide across the ground. If it really is gouged up, spend a few dollars and buy a new one.
- If you are getting excessive falsing or chatter, make sure the connection between the cable and the control housing is tight. Sometimes it can loosen up and an intermittent connection is a guaranteed problem!

Don't forget about the batteries! It's amazing how often people find themselves at a productive site, recover a few nice targets and then their batteries go dead! Yes, I have done it myself so I am speaking from personal experience but a little preparation is all it takes to prevent it from ruining your day. The advantage of the new NiMH rechargeable batteries is that they do not develop a memory like the old Ni-Cad batteries did. So now if you go out for only an hour or two you can throw the pack back on the charger and top it off so you are ready for the next trip.

A few other tips that will help reduce the chance that you will have problems in the field with your detector include:

- If you are not planning to use your detector for a while, remove the battery pack and store it indoors to prevent the pack from leaking and possibly damaging the electronics in the control housing.
- Never leave your detector in your vehicle during the summer or winter months. Extreme temperatures at either end of the spectrum can permanently damage the electronics of any detector. One tip that a number of detectorists have used to prevent damage in the summer is to place the control housing in a cooler (and that is <u>without</u> any ice!). If you travel with your job and come across productive-looking sites, this will allow you to bring your detector with you and see what turns up.

If you do happen to have a problem that is not easily addressed, look at your manual before boxing it up and sending it back to the factory for repair. The Troubleshooting section may just have a solution to your problem. If that does not fix it, contact your local dealer or your nearest service center and see if they have a solution that does not require you to send it back for repairs. You can also visit some of the Internet forums dedicated to your particular model and post a question. Often, another user – possibly half a world away – will have an idea that can get you back out in the field quickly.

"SAVE-A-HUNT" KIT

For more than 25 years, something I have always assembled and taken with me in the field has helped me fix simple problems on more than one occasion. I call it a "Save-a-Hunt" kit. As mentioned earlier, there is nothing more frustrating and aggravating than driving 50 miles or more to a promising site and then have a detector problem. Many of us assemble kits that allow us to take care of some simple common issues without having to drive home or find a store to buy what we might need. Pickup a small plastic box and stock it with some of the following items:

- **Battery pack and spare batteries**: If your detector uses battery packs, pick up a spare in case something breaks on the one in the detector. Bring along spare batteries but do not install them in the spare pack. Leave them in the packaging they come in to ensure they stay fresh for as long as possible.

- **Car Charger for the Battery Pack**: If you are traveling between sites, a car charger can be used to top off your battery pack - simple yes, but a lot of people find their batteries dead mid-way through the day.
- **Search coil washers**: Frequently the rubber washers that hold the coil in position wear to the point they no longer work and the coil simply flops loosely. This is extremely common when hunting beaches or desert sites where the sand acts as an abrasive that quickly wears out the washers.
- **Headphone plug**: The headphone jacks can crack or the internal wires to the plug can break rendering your headphones inoperable. You can make a temporary repair (until you get home and re-solder the wires) if you have some electrical tape and a spare plug which is available at stores such as Radio Shack.
- **Tools**: Toss in a jeweler's screwdriver, a pair of needle nose pliers and duct tape. A few tools can go a long way if something goes amiss in the field.

REFERENCE RESOURCE BIBLIOGRAPHY

Books:

- **A Guide For Better Treasure Hunting** by H Glenn Carson
- **Buried Treasures You Can Find** by Robert Marx
- **Metal Detecting Previously Hunted Sites** by Vincent C. Pascucci
- **Metal Detecting, The Hobby** by Dick Stout
- **Metal Detecting for Beginners** by Ed Tisdale
- **Permission Impossible, Metal Detecting Search Permission Made Easy** by David Villanueva
- **Successful Treasure Hunting** by Lance Comfort
- **Successful Detecting Sites** by David Villanueva [UK book]
- **The New Metal Detecting The Hobby** by Dick Stout
- **Where to Find Treasure** by Dick Stout

Internet Resources:

- **Detecting UK:** Articles, forums and find photos; http://www.detecting.org.uk/
- **Find's Treasure Forums**: Forums on a wide range of topics; http://www.FindMall.com
- **Friendly Metal Detecting Forum**: Forums on a wide range of topics; http://metaldetectingforum.com/
- **The Treasure Depot**: Forums on a wide range of topics; http://www.thetreasuredepot.com
- **TreasureNet**: One of the oldest forums on the web; http://forum.treasurenet.com/
- **The Treasure Hunter Forum**: Forums on a wide range of topics; http://www.treasurehunterforum.com/

Equipment & Supplies:

- **Mega Batteries**: Complete selection of rechargeable batteries & chargers; http://www.megabatteries.com/
- **Only Batteries**: One-stop shop for a wide selection of rechargeable batteries & home / car chargers; http://www.onlybatteries.com
- **Pelican Cases**: If you need a durable, waterproof case for any application, this company has what you are looking for; http://www.pelican.com/
- **Vista Print**: Low-cost supplier of high-quality business cards, clothing with logos and other items that can you help gain access to sites by giving a positive image; http://www.vistaprint.com/
- **ZAGG Invisible SHIELD**: Scratch-proof patented film to protect your detector. Some custom-cut sets are available for specific detectors or plain sheets can be ordered & cut to fit; http://www.zagg.com/

Specialized Treasure Hunting Tips & Techniques

The sub-chapters that follow are intended to provide additional details on the various forms of treasure hunting practiced around the world and share some of the tips, techniques and photos of finds that have been provided by successful hunters. As mentioned in the chapter entitled "What This Book Is & Is Not", they are not intended to be all-inclusive but rather provide an overview containing information that might not be found elsewhere as well as reference source of books, magazines, videos, equipment, suppliers and Internet sites that will let you obtain additional information to further hone your expertise in a specific area.

As you read through the material covering the forms of treasure hunting that catch your interest, look over the information and see if a slight change to a technique based on your specific circumstances can make it more effective for you. I have found at times that an idea passed along by another treasure hunter who might be living halfway around the world is not directly applicable to my area or style of hunting but it forms the foundation for an idea that with a twist, unlocks valuables that would otherwise have gone undetected. Be sure to go through the Reference Resource Bibliography section at the end of each chapter and look over the material cited there. Many of these references came from others who used the information to help them find more with less effort . . . leverage the time used to assemble them to your advantage.

This book is dynamic in nature and as new information becomes available or references are updated, subsequent editions will reflect those changes. Your input is encouraged and the sharing of information among fellow hobbyists will help all of us improve our in-field success rate.

COIN HUNTING

Coin hunting is by far the most popular form of treasure hunting worldwide. After all, coins have been lost anywhere people have been for literally 1,000's of years.

The most obvious areas for finding coins are those sites that are still in use on a regular basis which includes school yards, parks, ball fields, picnic areas, churches . . . the list is almost endless. While most of the coins found at sites still in use will be modern and worth little more than face value, the experience you gain here will pay off when you search sites that contain the older, more valuable targets. Many veteran detectorists take the time to hunt these easily accessible sites on a regular basis to sharpen their skills. On occasion, you might even pick up a piece of jewelry, a relic or even an old coin or two depending on the age of the site itself. If the site has been in use for decades or longer, there will more than likely be older coins to find even if the area has been heavily hunted for years thanks to the performance edge provided today's detectors. Recovering the older, more valuable coins is not as hard as you might think. But you do need to take the time to understand what the controls do, how a slight adjustment can make a significant difference in terms of performance and how to interpret what the detector is telling you in the field. In other words, **PRACTICE** and **EXPERIENCE**! The adjacent photo shows a few of the first-rate finds made by Jim Walsh hunting sites others considered to be worked out.

Coin hunters in the United States have an advantage over those searching for coins overseas as the type of coins being sought are more standardized so tests can be conducted to determine where they will register. Will there be some variation based on depth, ground conditions, adjacent trash or even how worn a coin is? Sure, but nowhere near the variation experienced when looking for coins spanning 1,000's of years where their composition varies widely and centuries of being underground have altered the signal you will get from them. For the most part, if you are looking for ancient coins as many hunters in Europe and the United Kingdom are, the chapter on Relic Hunting will be of greater interest and relevance to you. On the other hand, if you search parks or similar sites for more recent coinage as U.S. coin hunters do, then this is a great chapter for you to focus on.

SELECTING A DETECTOR FOR COIN HUNTING

As we discussed in the chapter on Equipment, doing your homework to ensure that you select the right detector for a specific application takes some time but having the proper equipment will pay off in terms of finds and overall enjoyment. There are plenty of detectors that will do the job but if you really want to get the most out of your time in the field, make sure you get the right equipment for your type of treasure hunting.

When looking at what features are most important in a detector that will be used for coin hunting, one needs to first determine what kind of coin hunting will be done. There are many detectorists who are thoroughly satisfied with spending a few hours at the local school park or playground in search of clad coins. I have several friends who do just that and in addition to a few $100 in clad coins each year, they come up with an occasional piece of gold jewelry or other valuable trinket adding to the total value of their annual finds. A point worth noting is that while some of them have top-of-the-line detectors, others have what might be considered to be an entry-level model yet all are more than satisfied with their results. Some convert their common date coins into bullion or collectible coins as discussed in the chapter entitled Cashing In or Selling Your Finds. Recently Aaron Riggs, the son of a co-worker, expressed an interest in metal detecting and asked if I could help him with his senior project that he planned to do on the subject of archeology. Lending him a Teknetics Delta 4000, he spent some time getting familiar with its operation and then we tried searching a local school. The results . . . 138 coins in the first few hours he used it. Needless to say, he was ecstatic with the success he experienced starting out and was hooked on the hobby. Obviously the higher-priced detectors offer more features and more performance but if you are not planning on fully utilizing those features or need the additional performance, a good detector with discrimination and possibly target ID may be all you need.

On the other hand, if your goals are more focused on finding older collectible coins, you will need to up the ante to get the performance needed to reach them. Target identification – be it audio, visual or both – is a great tool for the coin hunter, especially those in the U.S. looking for coins of a known composition, as it allows you to pick out "keepers" even at depth. Features that you should look for in a detector when searching for older, deeper coins include its ability to handle a range of ground conditions (and preferably do so automatically), its discrimination capabilities on targets in the ground, overall detection depth, available search coil sizes and designs (hunting the same area with a different coil is often the key to finding more in heavily hunted sites) and target identification capabilities in the ground. See what local hunters use, ask your local dealer for recommendations and see if you can try a few different models out in your area.

SO WHERE DO YOU FIND COINS?

As the opening paragraph of this chapter stated, coins have been lost anywhere people have been for centuries. But while you can find coins anywhere, the focus of your efforts should be to hunt areas where your odds of finding either the quantity or quality of the coins you want exist. Remember the chapter on Defining your Goals? The forms you worked on as you went through that chapter will help you focus on finding the sites that are most likely to contain the types of targets you are looking for. This section will cover some sites proven to be consistent producers and provide some tips to search supposedly hunted-out sites and find what others have overlooked. You won't see the usual "laundry-list" of sites that everyone heads to such as schools still in use, highly visible parks built a decade or two ago, church yards, etc. If you pick up some of the books listed in the reference section of this chapter you will see countless common sites to hunt and many may hold exactly what you are hoping to find. Rather than repeat them here, let's look at some of the sites that are not listed in every book out there or techniques that may help uncover valuables in these sites.

What is the first place most treasure hunters take their new detector to in order to try it out? The local school yard or community park! Because of the accessibility and exposure schools and parks have received over the years, it's doubtful that you'll find a single old school or park still in use that hasn't had at least a few metal detectors skim across its surface. While no place is ever worked out, when the finds become few and far between, you tend to look for new spots to hunt. Before you give up and either look for greener pastures or take up another hobby, stop and look at the site in a different light. What did it look like 50 or 100 years ago? Were those bushes there? Were the trees along the edge of the ball field out as far as they are now? New growth tends to mask productive sites. Try getting on your hands and knees and pushing your coil into these areas. Not only will the coins you find be older but you won't be digging the modern trash you will in the open areas.

Many years ago my brother and I had to hunt sites close to home since all we had for transportation were a pair of bicycles. Our old elementary school had been built in the early 1800's and we unearthed many interesting and valuable items being among the first to ever search the grounds. As others started to get into the hobby, finds dropped off but we took a look at the tree line and realized that they had not always been there. Walking several feet into the trees, we started finding coins and other valuables with virtually no trash. Well, my brother and I moved away and the school was converted into a building for other uses . . . yet I always wondered what might still be waiting to be recovered. About a year ago I came in contact with Roger Tuohy, a detectorist from my home-town area. He indicated that the local sites had been pounded for decades and good finds were getting pretty scarce. I asked Roger if he was interested in trying a few of the spots my brother and I had searched back in the 60's and 70's and he was up to the challenge. When I mentioned the school, he said he had already been there and not really found anything. When I asked if he had hit the woods, he said no. I sent him a map with several areas marked for him to try and a few days later, I received an E-mail telling me that in two short visits, he was stunned at what he had found. Less than 10' into the trees, his first signal turned out to be an 1854 Seated half dollar immediately followed by an 1807 Two Reale. Other finds included 2 Mercury dimes, a Standing Liberty quarter, a silver Victorian bracelet, a sterling toothpick holder, a brass lock and a copper thimble. A simple change in how Roger approached a site that 100's before him had searched and long-since given up on produced some super finds. Try looking at sites from a different perspective than the crowds do and you will be amazed at what can still be found!

If you live in a semi-urban or even a rural area, you probably have at least one exercise trail that has been built in a nearby park or school. These sites typically consist of a jogging trail with exercise stations such as sit-up benches, chin-up bars and stretching posts. As people use this equipment, they often loose items ranging from coins to keys, watches and jewelry. The nice thing about hunting exercise trails is that the areas you need to hunt are well defined and the "goodies" will be replenished on a regular basis. Several friends of mine hunt these areas on a set schedule and consistently find quite a bit in a short period of time,

Another area that has proven to be quite productive not only here in the United States but in other countries as well is the ground around lakes or along rivers. Most communities located along a lake or river have areas set aside for their residents to use for recreational purposes including walking, picnicking, tossing a Frisbee or just relaxing after a hard day in the office. These areas have proven to be consistent producers of items including coins, jewelry and even historic artifacts (rivers have been in use since the early days of our country). Steve Johnson, a detectorist who lives in a small town in

Iowa has found nearly 10 pieces of gold jewelry along with more than 900 coins over the last year since he started hunting the walking trail alongside the river that flows through town. Not bad when you consider there are two treasure hunting clubs within a 30-mile radius of this town and the same complaint - *"there are no good sites left to hunt"* - is heard at every club meeting.

If you live near a larger river that at one time had commercial barge traffic on it, you should think about trying the old tow-paths that date back to the 1700s and 1800s. Before Interstates and the railroads were built, barge traffic was the most common form of moving goods from one area to another. These barges were usually pulled by horse or mule teams plodding along the river bank. In addition to the teams using the paths, local residents and travelers used them for hundreds of years and the variety of items they lost is truly amazing. Brian Anderson, a coin hunter from New Jersey hunts several of the tow paths in eastern Pennsylvania and Maryland and has found more than 200 coins dating from the mid-1700's to the late 1800's along with a number of artifacts from the same time period. One of the most overlooked areas in this type of hunting is the sloping bank going into the water Other hunters may have searched the flat section of the trail, but very few take the time to hunt the bank due to the additional effort it takes to do so.

Another consistent producer that can be found near any smaller town or rural area is the gravel or dirt parking lots near many community fairs, concert areas, restaurants and night clubs. People are always in a rush to get parked and into the event and typically do not notice when they loose something. Go to these areas when there is no event in progress or the business is closed and you may be surprised at what you find. Look for events such as fairs, concerts, shows or festivals and hunt them after the event is over. One thing, make sure that you have permission to hunt the area.

The yards of private homes are among the most productive areas a coin hunter can search. Typically there will be very little trash present and unless it has been hunted before, one can recover a surprising number of coins and other valuables in a relatively short period of time. Getting permission to search yards is actually easier than you might think and the General Treasure Hunting Tips & Techniques chapter provides several ways to gain access to these locations.

Use the Research forms you filled out along with the Goal Forms to zero in on specific types of sites that are likely to hold the types of targets you are hoping to find and as you find what specific types of sites are most productive in your local area, you can further refine your research to locate more of them. The book "*The New Successful Coinhunting*" by Charles Garrett is a must-have for coinhunters worldwide. It contains nearly 260 pages of tip-after-tip and literally 100's of sites to consider searching proven to hold coins just waiting for a today's detectorist.

RECOMMENDED RECOVERY TOOLS & TECHNIQUES

For the most part, coin hunters search sites that are still in use and are being maintained for the enjoyment of others. Sites such as schools, ball fields, church yards, parks, picnic areas, walking trails, fair grounds, private yards and the like will quickly be placed off-limits to metal detecting (and many already have) if holes are left open or the ground left scared due to improper recovery techniques. Being able to accurately pinpoint a target is not only advantageous in finding more targets per hour or search time but will also allow you to do far less damage to the area when making the recovery.

> **TIP**
> Coins buried just under the surface can often be a real challenge to recover quickly and with minimal impact to the grass itself – more so than deep ones. If you get a signal & the depth indication is very shallow, pinpoint it as accurately as possible and use a coin probe (ice pick) to feel the coin and pop it to the surface either with the probe or a flat-head screw driver. Using one of the electronic pinpoint probes can also help considerably as they can detect coins a few inches deep and allow you to quickly extract targets.

Remember the pinpointing challenge posed in the chapter on Target Recovery? Well, being able to recover shallow targets without doing any excavation and deeper ones with surgical precision should be the goal of every coin hunter out there. If the target you have detected is deeper than an inch or two, you won't be able to use a probe or ice pick to recover it. Once you've pinpointed the signal as accurately as possible, there are two methods that most coin hunters use to retrieve the item. If you are not allowed to actually dig in the area you are searching – some parks and private homes may have this restriction – drive a screwdriver into the ground in front of and slightly deeper than the depth of the target. Then force the screwdriver at a 45-degree angle to the left and the right of the target. You should be able to reach into the resulting slit and pull the target free from its resting place – this is where accurate pinpointing comes into play. Once you've recovered it, press the sides of the slit together and step it down before moving on.

If the ground is damp, a three-sided plug will allow you to reach the target and leave little trace that you were there. Leaving at least one side attached will help ensure the grass does not die and turn brown. Gauge the angle at which you cut the plug based on the depth you believe the target is at (either based on the depth indication on the detector or the relative signal strength). If you have judged the depth correctly and zeroed in on the target's location, you should be able to find what you are looking for in the bottom of the plug or at the bottom of the hole. If you need to remove any more dirt to find the target, place the loose dirt on a sheet of vinyl or a wash cloth so that it can be poured back into the hole before the plug is inserted and packed down. Use your fingers to brush away any loose dirt around the hole before moving on and you will find that there will be no signs of your having recovered something, even a depths approaching a foot.

> ⚠ If you are hunting a site still in use and being maintained and the ground is dry, don't attempt to cut a plug or the grass will die! It doesn't matter how careful you are in covering your holes, once the roots are cut, the grass will turn brown in a few days leaving signs you were there. This is a sure-fire way to have an area closed or permission rescinded!

Tesoro Electronics has a section on their website that shows how both of these techniques are done. . . special thanks to veteran detectorist Bob Sickler for providing the artwork.

Some of the tools used by coin hunters are shown in the following photo collage. The knives pictured on the left have a serrated edge to cut through roots and a slightly curved blade to help scoop loose dirt from the hole. The probes can be used to find a target and then extract it with little or no damage to the area. One point to keep in mind is any tool such as a shovel should be left at home. Not only will you damage the area no matter how careful you think you will be but the perception someone will have seeing you in a park or school yard with a shovel will never be a positive one.

DON'T USE!

REFERENCE RESOURCE BIBLIOGRAPHY

Books & Magazines

- **The New Successful Coinhunting** by Charles Garrett (This is the one book all coin hunters need to have in their library!)
- **The Sport of Coin Hunting with a Metal Detector** by Charles Garrett
- **Coin Hunting In Depth** by Dick Stout
- **Coinshooting - When And Where To Do It** by Glenn Carson
- **Coin Hunting II Digging Deeper Coins** by Glenn Carson
- **Coinshooting III** by H Glen Carson
- **The Coinshooter's Manual** by Karl Von Mueller
- **The Standard Catalog of World Coins** by Krause and Mishler (Series of books each covering a century of world coins and their values, updated annually)

Internet Resources

- **ANACS Coin Grading Services:** This is the only service that will grade "dug" coins with environmental damage. If you have a coin that you believe has value, protect your find through the ANACS grading and preservation services; http://www.anacs.com/
- **Professional Coin Grading Service (PCGS):** On-line coin prices for U.S. coins: http://www.pcgs.com/prices/
- **Best Coin:** Another free coin pricing website covering U.S. coins; http://www.bestcoin.com/united-states-coin-pricing-guide.htm
- **Don's Coin World Gallery:** Over 26,000 photos of coins from around the world; http://worldcoingallery.com/
- **Overview of Various Coin Pricing Guides:** http://rg.ancients.info/guide/prices.html
- **Drive-In Theater:** Comprehensive list of drive-in theaters both operating & long since closed .. all great locations to search with permission: http://www.driveintheater.com/drivlist.htm

Recovery Tools:

- **Black Ada Ltd.:** Complete line of rugged digging tools (United Kingdom); http://www.blackada.com/
- **Jimmy Sierra' Metal Detecting Accessories:** Wide range of recovery tools, probes and pluggers; (415) 488-8131; Po Box 519, Forest Knolls Ca 94933 http://www.jimmysierra.com/
- **Kellyco Metal Detector Superstore:** Assortment of digging tools including the Gator Digger line including one model that comes with a lifetime warranty, http://www.kellycodetectors.com/accessories/trowels.htm
- **Predator Tools:** A complete line of target recovery tools; http://predatortools.com/
- **Treasure Wise Products:** Complete line of quality hand-held recovery tools and probes; 824 N Hartwell Ave, Waukesha WI 53186, (800) 558 2020
- **WW Manufacturing Company:** Rugged line of all-metal spades, shovels & hand-held diggers; http://www.wwmfg.com/
- **Wilcox All Pro Tools & Supply;** Complete line of quality hand-held recovery tools; (641) 623-3138; http://www.wilcoxallpro.com/

RELIC HUNTING

Many of you might read the title of this chapter and start flipping to see what's next in the book thinking you do not live in an area containing ghost towns from the old West or historic military battlefields. However, before you pass this chapter up, realize that relic hunting is actually the most universal form of treasure hunting there is. Relics can be almost anything ranging from everyday household items dating back 100's or even 1,000's of years to mining equipment, military gear, wagon parts, trade beads, horse shoes, early civilization copper tools, Medieval artifacts, Roman relics . . . the list goes on and on. Anywhere - and that means anywhere - people have been, lost relics are just waiting for detectorists to find, recover and preserve their story.

Relic hunting was one of the first "recreational" uses of metal detectors. Many of the 'ol timers used surplus World War II mine detectors beginning in the late 1940's to locate artifacts from Civil War sites, pioneer trails, mining camps and the like. Despite the limitations of this early equipment, countless relics were in fact recovered and preserved. When the first detectors with ground balance circuitry were released in the 1970's many sites that were previously un-huntable due to high mineralization were searched effectively. Some relic hunters reported that the problem then was not finding a site to hunt but rather being able to carry all of their finds back out at the end of the day. As a matter of fact, White's Electronics ran a story about several relic hunters testing out their first ground-balancing detector – the Coinmaster V Supreme – near Atlanta, Georgia in the mid-70's. The photograph of the hunters with PILES of artifacts found over a three-day period that included artillery shells, bullets, bayonets, swords and buckles was one to see. I'm sure we all wish we had problems like that today! Many of the well-known battle sites have been hunted for more than 40 years and, while no site is ever completely hunted out, finds are now few and far between. Before you get discouraged and give up relic hunting without even getting started, take heart, as there are hundreds of sites that have never been searched with a metal detector. Proper research will lead you to these locations and the right search techniques will allow you to locate what others have missed.

SELECTING A DETECTOR FOR RELIC HUNTING

As this chapter will discuss, relic hunting is one form of treasure hunting where the least amount of discrimination possible will usually be the most productive setting due to the wide variation of what relics can consist of. Since you will often be hunting in all-metal to avoid possibly missing what might be a great find, the discrimination capabilities of a detector will be secondary when choosing one to fit your needs. The most important factor for most relic hunters will be the overall detection depth afforded by a particular model and the deepest detector will be the one that more often than not finds the most at the end of the day, especially at sites that have been hunted for decades. Relic hunters often spend upwards of $1,000 upgrading to the latest detector if they can coax another inch or two in detection depth from it knowing that it may reopen sites considered to be worked out. Since relic hunting tends to be an all-day activity, finding a detector that you can hunt with for extended periods of time without discomfort should also be a prime factor to consider. I know several veteran relic hunters who have purchased models that are ideally suited for the conditions in their areas; however, they have to switch to something else after just a few hours in the woods. Unless you are willing to buy multiple detectors and switch to use lighter or more balanced, weight & ergonomics should be high on your list of factors to consider. Another factor to consider is the overall design of the detector. If you have to hipmount the control housing to be able to use it for extended periods of time or it requires that the battery pack be attached to your belt, is this really going to work when you're slogging through thick underbrush a mile or two from the nearest road?

Interchangeable coils are a must when selecting a relic detector and you want to see what the largest coil is that can be used on the detector you are looking at. The brand-specific sections of the Buyers Guide cover what coils are available for each model both from the factory as well as third party vendors. Larger coils allow you to cover more ground with each sweep and are invaluable when trying to find a possible site among acres of fields or woods plus they detect targets deeper than stock coils. On the other hand, once you find a site, a smaller coil may enable you to find relics in between trash or amongst rocks or fallen trees.

Some serious relic hunters have opted to use detectors typically used on beaches or in shallow water which are fully waterproof or water resistant. Despite their higher price tag and increased weight, they can be invaluable if you are miles from your vehicle and get caught in inclement weather that might suddenly pop up. Most of the high-end beach / water detectors are in fact simply waterproofed versions of the land detectors produced by the same manufacturer and can in fact make excellent relic detectors.

RELIC HUNTING BASICS

Taking the information you have uncovered through your research and other techniques provided throughout this book, you should have identified several potential sites to search. Before you head out into the field, you will probably have to spend a little more time actually pinpointing the site's location so as to narrow down your search area. The State-of-the-Art Treasure Hunting Techniques chapter will cover the use of old maps, computer programs and GPS units to help in this task; however, there are a few tips that you may find helpful in defining your search area.

- Military camps would typically be located near a source of water for the troops. This is especially true if the cavalry was present because the horses needed to be cared for in order to take part in the day-to-day activities. Settlers would have looked for the same area as they needed water for their family and livestock. When you are looking over a topographical map, pay particular attention to areas near streams, lakes or rivers that would have provided a source of water. If they had a choice, they would prefer to set up home or camp close to the same level as the water so they did not have to carry it back up hill.
- High ground was highly sought after as vantage points by military commanders. If you are searching for a camp or battle site, see if there is high ground in the area. Even if most of the activity occurred in the lower areas, there would have been troops stationed on the higher ground as lookouts or to direct the course of the battle and in many cases these sites have not been hunted.
- Most relic hunters focus on specific sites like battlefields, well-defined camps or ghost towns. Keep in mind that the people or troops had to move from point 'A' to point 'B', and unless there were railroads available, they marched from point to point. If you can pinpoint two locations on a map, try to determine the most likely path that they would have taken between them. Does the route pass along a stream or river? If so, they may have stopped for a rest and to collect water. A number of outstanding finds have been made by relic hunters searching sites that by all accounts should not have had anything since there were no camps or battles in the area; however, those passing through lost artifacts that astute detectorists found.
- Maps – both old and new – are an invaluable research tools for relic hunters. A few years ago my brother Chris came down to Georgia for a visit. We went out relic hunting a few times and he found a number of artifacts. As we talked about the research I had done on the area, he looked at the topographical maps I had marked up to indicate battle sites and skirmishes. Having a surveying background, he was extremely familiar with reading maps and pointed at three or four spots that appeared to be perfect observation areas or spots where troops may have rested near water. We tried two of them the following day and at both sites we found Civil War artifacts that

would probably still be there. What research had my brother done? None other than reading the maps and identifying likely sites based on what I told him had produced well in the past.
- The least amount of discrimination should be used when hunting for relics . . . note that this does not say NO discrimination should be used at all times. As the discrimination level is increased, the potential for a rejected target; i.e. one below the setpoint of the selected discrimination, to override the signal from a good target also increases. If the signal from the rejected target is stronger either because it is shallower or larger than the good target, you may not receive a signal. This is why many heavily hunted sites are still producing valuable relics for hunters who are willing to dig a little more trash in order to be sure they do not inadvertently miss a "keeper". The actual discrimination level you use in the field should be selected based on the amount of trash present and how much "patience" you have at the time which can and will change from day-to-day or site-to-site.
- Try using different search coils to hunt the sites you know have produced in the past. Remember the Equipment chapter? Each coil has its advantage and simply changing coils may reveal dozens of artifacts that you may have been unable to detect with the standard coil that came with your metal detector. A year or so ago Bobby Ellis visited a well-hunted mining camp in central Idaho and decided to try using a smaller coil in a particularly trashy section near the remains of the saloon. A few hours of searching turned up a handful of coins and tokens including this beautiful $1 gold piece. Over the next few weeks he recovered even more relics from this site using the smaller coil. The Brand-Specific chapters cover optional search coils available for each model.
- If you search sites that contain fallen trees and branches, take the time to move them out of the way and search the ground beneath them. Very few relic hunters take the time to do this and the natural debris often hides many relics. One of my hunting partners, Denny Koutouzis, and I hunted a site near Kennesaw, Georgia that had been heavily hunted for years. While the open areas were quite clean in terms of signals, we found a number of bullets and other artifacts after moving some of the larger fallen trees that were strewn throughout the area.
- Before you move the trees and larger limbs away to check underneath them as described in the tip above, sweep your coil over them to see if there might be a bullet or shell fragment embedded in the tree. During the battles, bullets and shells flew everywhere and many wound up in trees on or around the battlefield. As the trees died and fell to the ground, relic hunters have found them by carefully checking old trees that are now just decaying away. Be sure to check all sides, especially as you move them aside to check for any relics hidden beneath them.
- If you gain access to a field that is still being farmed on a regular basis, plan to revisit the site after it has been tilled. Artifacts that may have been beyond the detection depth of your detector or situated at an angle that prevented it from being detected may now be easily located. Productive fields can be hunted year after year with a continual harvest of relics being recovered. If you hear about a field that had produced a number of relics years ago and is now thought of as "hunted out", get out there at the first opportunity after the ground has been turned over and see what might still be there.
- Keep an audible threshold on your detector. If your detector has a search mode with an audible threshold, try using it when relic hunting. Unless you are hunting in all-metal, when you pass over objects that fall within the area(s) you have marked to be rejected, you will start hearing the threshold disappear or null out. Often if you are looking for a camp site or skirmish area, the first indication will be ferrous items such as nails, tacks or small pieces of rusted iron. When you come across signals that null out, slow down, tighten up your search pattern and see what turns up. This may help you focus in on a virgin site.
- A tip that will be repeated throughout this book and covered in detail in the Identifying Your Finds chapter is to not discard <u>ANYTHING</u> you find until you are sure it has no intrinsic or historic value.

A few years back, fellow relic hunters Ed & Brenda Williamson came over and looked through my "junk" box containing miscellaneous finds. They picked out several buttons and asked why I had them in with the rest of the items. When I asked what was special about the buttons they had picked out, they stated that they were from the Civil War and fairly rare. A Confederate Navy button and a Musician button were rescued from being tossed in with "junk" and have assumed a prominent place in one of my display cases. I thought they had come from modern coats and were worthless!

So what is the best way to setup your detector for optimal results when relic hunting? Again, as mentioned in previous chapters, there are no "hard-and-fast" rules when it comes to how to set your detector but there are some tips and techniques that have been shown to consistently produce relics at sites worldwide. Read through the information presented and try those settings that seem like they might work for you. Combine those that you find to be effective and experiment in the field to see what results you can get.

As discussed earlier, when it comes to any form of relic hunting the saying "Less means More" holds true when it comes to discrimination settings used. Bart, an active member of one of the popular Internet forums, made the following post about relic hunting. This statement does a great job of summarizing why increasing the amount of discrimination you use will result in the number of relics you find going down.

> *"The problem with relic hunting (if you want to call it a problem), is that any metal object, of any size, at any depth, and of any type of metal, can be historically interesting - even those pesky square nails. Heck, relics are even made of aluminum. I recently found an aluminum condom can produced by the Three Merry Widows company made from the late 1800's to the 1930's which is an interesting find in itself. Silver, gold, platinum, iron, steel, bronze, lead, copper, aluminum, tin, nickel, all of these metals and alloys have at one time or another been formed into objects of historical interest. To discriminate any metal objects out might cost you a unique or very interesting find. Of course, the downside is that you will dig your fair share of junk. That's the price you pay for relic hunting. To minimize the junk items, try to find sites that have seen very little human activity for about the last 50 or 60 years. Maybe it's just me, but I see nothing interesting in aluminum foil, drink cans, and pull tabs. Good luck in your search for history!"*

As anyone who has spent even one day relic hunting knows, there are probably no sites which hold relics that also are not infested with ferrous trash such as nails, bolts, broken iron tools, rusted metal roofing and the like. The trick is coming up with a method of picking the good targets out from the unwanted items. While recovering every single target might sound like the best answer to ensure nothing is missed, unless you're retired and have plenty of time on your hands, it is not the most practical solution. Are there still countless relics left to find even in sites that have been hunted for decades? Yes, and working slowly from multiple directions and trying different coils is often the trick in finding them.

As experienced relic hunters know, finding the right spot to search is just as important as knowing how to set and adjust your detector – any make or model – when it comes to your overall success. There are dozens of books dealing with how to locate sites in the United States and overseas. The rest of this chapter will cover a few additional techniques to locate sites to search and then touch on some of the techniques successful relic hunters are using to help you get the most out of your in-field time.

CIVIL WAR RELIC HUNTING

The Civil War . . . The War of The Rebellion . . . The War of Northern Aggression . . . The War Between the States . . . many names for the same tumultuous period in United States history that left it's mark in the form of battlefields, campsites, field hospitals and ruined towns across nearly 20 states. This period in the early 1860's was one of the darkest in U.S. history during which brother fought against brother for more than four long years. But the silver lining in this black cloud is the myriad of relics lost for nearly 150 years still waiting for today's detectorists to recover. The number of recent television programs and movies devoted to the Civil War combined with a renewed interest in the country's history has significantly increased the interest in collecting relics from this period. The purpose of this section is to provide you with some proven tips and techniques that will help ensure you bring more home at the end of the day on a consistent basis than you have in the past.

More has been written about the Civil War than any other period of United States history and this wealth of information provides the Civil War relic hunter with the information needed to located untouched sites. The most useful set of books for today's relic hunter is called *"The War of the Rebellion: A Compilation of the Official Records of the Union and Confederate Armies"* or the OR's as they are commonly called. This set was originally published in the late 1800's and contains 128 separate books or parts, each containing 700 to 1,000+ pages. The United States government collected all of the documents they could find from the Union and Confederate Armies pertaining to the war including official reports, dispatches, telegrams, personal ledgers and even letters from soldiers. These documents were then sorted and arranged in chronological order and geographic locations. While some parts cover a several month period or a number of skirmishes, the larger battles such as Gettysburg, Richmond, The Wilderness and Atlanta are often covered in several volumes by themselves. The General Index volume contains a detailed index indicating which parts and pages contain references to a particular battle or campsite and a brief summary of what time period and area is covered in each part. By reviewing the General Index, you can determine which part(s) apply to your area of interest. As you read through the appropriate sections, descriptions of small skirmish sites, camps or supply depots can often be uncovered for additional follow-up.
Relic hunters frequently find a site referenced in the OR's which can be located that has never been searched. You can buy the OR's on CD or DVD that allow you to access them on your computer. Available for less than $100 and fully searchable by keywords such as camp, battle, skirmish and specific locations, they make a Civil War relic hunter's research activities almost enjoyable. There are even several websites that provide free access on-line to the OR's complete with full search capability that are listed in the Reference Section at the end of this chapter.

Another extremely useful reference tool is the *Official Military Atlas of the Civil War* that was designed to compliment the OR's. It is an oversized book with nearly 1,200 entries including more than 800 maps drawn by both Union and Confederate forces during the war, 100 engravings of forts and 200 drawings of weapons, equipment and uniforms. Many of the maps show troop positions and fortifications in great detail that can be easily transposed onto modern topographical maps in order to quickly locate the site. Beneath each map is the section of the OR that provides additional information on the particular battle of activity depicted so follow-up research is simplified. This book has been reprinted several times and copies are available for under $100. While it is somewhat pricey, it is a good investment if you plan on doing much Civil War relic hunting. It is also available on CD for your computer and compliments the electronic version of the OR's; however, the hard copy is easier to use in terms of looking up sites and comparing the old maps to the more current ones.

Regimental histories are another source of information that can be extremely helpful in locating new and productive sites. Virtually every regiment that fought in the Civil War published one of these books detailing the campaigns they were involved in, casualties, camp stories and personal remembrances from the soldiers. While many of the stories of their victories were exaggerated, the mention of a small skirmish or a camp that was occupied for one or two nights might be just enough to lead you to a true hot-spot. The OR's or a book entitled *"Authentic Civil War Battle Sites – Land and Naval Engagements"* by E.S. LeGaye will identify the regiments that fought in specific battles and this will in turn help you select the regimental histories that will be useful in locating sites in your area. Many book dealers, including those listed in the bibliography at the end of this chapter, carry or can obtain copies of these regimental histories. Some have begun to show up on Internet web sites and can be viewed for free. Try hitting a few of the Internet search engines and see what you can turn up.

If you live near the site of battle activity during the Civil War, you should check with your local historical society for information they may have on the area. Many of these organizations have an extensive research section which often contains personal diaries of local soldiers who fought in the war that may have been donated by surviving family members. You may also find newspaper accounts of battles or troop movements, local family histories that describe the war in the community and publications put out by the historical society that cover this period. Local history books may also contain information that will help locate potentially productive sites to search. A brief mention of troops camped on the edge of town may be sufficient to lead you to a site never before hunted. Most Southern states have state run historical societies that publish quarterly newsletters often containing previously unpublished information related to the Civil War. If your local society cannot get copies of these newsletters, you can often join the state organization for a nominal fee and receive copies directly through the mail.

With the increased competition among relic hunters' research, is the key if you want to be successful. With a little effort you will be able to locate sites that have not been heavily hunted and you may in fact be the first relic hunter to search the site.

EUROPEAN RELIC HUNTING

Metal detecting in the majority of sites throughout the United Kingdom, Europe, or Asia is unlike detecting done at sites in the United States or even at sites in these regions such as swimming beaches, schools or public parks. In these types of sites, the targets being searched for are well known and with a little practice, detectorists can easily recognize the signals produced by keepers. Even at older military skirmish or camp sites in the US, the targets being searched for fall into a few categories such as bullets, buttons, artillery shells or cannon balls. Seasoned hunters have learned what these targets sound like. That's why discrimination settings and patterns work as well as they do when conditions allow. Now when it comes to sites outside the U.S., the good targets start to fall all over the board in terms of the signals they produce. After all, you have had people on the sites being searched for 1,000's of years losing a myriad of objects. Many of these items were made from metals that vary greatly in composition. Plus being buried under ground for all that time, they have been further altered due to corrosion from the soil and fertilizers used over the centuries. This beautiful enameled plate brooch with a sunburst decoration dating from the 2nd Century AD located by Adam Staples in a field on the eastern side of England is just one example of what can be found on sites that date back 1,000's of years.

Over the countless years that have passed, entire civilizations have been born, lived and died on the same piece of ground. Metal detectors have truly become time machines as they locate and bring to light remnants from groups such as the Celtics, Saxons, Romans and Barbarians as well as periods such as the Bronze Age, the Iron Age, the Middle Ages and Victorian England. It is often hard for U.S. hunters to imagine the history that lies beneath the soil in other countries when we have only a few hundred years of modern history to search through and finds dating back a mere 100+ years are considered old. As a result of the wide range of artifacts that await discovery, the need to use less discrimination than say a person hunting for coins in the local schoolyard or recently lost pieces of jewelry on the beach might use is clearly evident. On the other hand, with the centuries of activity on virtually every square inch of land in the U.K. and Europe, there is an immense amount of trash present, primarily ferrous in nature. This trash that would drive most detectorists crazy if they had to listen to (not to mention recover) each and every target, so unless you have a great deal of patience, hunting in All-Metal is not an option that should be used at all times. This stunning 20KT gold padlock-shaped pendant with a small compartment inside was found by Wayne Burton while taking part in a club outing on an English field. The find dates to the 1830's and came out looking like it did the day it was lost.

The primary factor to consider when relic hunting non-U.S. sites is to use minimal levels of discrimination . . . typically just enough to eliminate the myriad of signals that come for small pieces of iron. Slow and methodical search patterns are also a must to ensure you do not miss something that might be next to an items being rejected or is at the edge of the detection depth afforded by your detector. Checking with some of the local metal detector dealers or clubs to see what models work best in the various price ranges is highly recommended since preferred models tend to vary in areas even a scant 100 miles apart.

Remember however, if you want to be really proficient with your detector searching for relics under these conditions, there is no replacement for time spent learning what each control does and then getting out there listening to actual signals. See if you can hunt with someone who has mastered the techniques to find those targets that often produce nothing more than a subtle change in the threshold or the faintest of beeps and check the signals they see as worth recovering. Try different settings to see what works best at **your** sites and best suits **your** personal preferences.

GHOST TOWNING

The first image that comes to mind when the term "Ghost Town" comes up is a run-down old town in the mountains of the American West with a saloon door swinging on its hinges as tumbleweed rolls down the main street. Well, there are plenty of old sites that fit that description; however, ghost towns are far more than just that. According to Dictionary.com, a ghost town is defined as "*a town permanently abandoned by its inhabitants because of a business decline or because a nearby mine has been worked out.*" There are ghost towns in virtually every corner of the globe including towns set up to recover coal, precious metals, lead and even salt; lumber camps, fishing settlements, trading posts, military outposts, construction camps for train tracks, roads, and dams. There are also ghost towns of a sort that are actually part of an existing community that may have been many times its current size at the height of whatever activity founded the town in the first place. In 2004 I had the opportunity to go out with a group of Minelab employees including the company's president, Gerry Brannigan, to try some new detectors in the desert surrounding their Las Vegas facility. One location called a "ghost town" was actually little more than a run-down group of buildings, some of which were still in use. The town had sprung up in the late 1800's to support mining in the nearby mountains and had hosted over 1,000 citizens at one time. Home to less than 50 people now, there was far more ground that nature had reclaimed than was in use. We made a few inquires and were given permission to search several sections of the old town. We were rewarded with dozens of coins and artifacts dating back to when the town had been founded. Gerry found a beautiful Shield nickel in one of the lots shortly after getting started. There are many areas of the country (and worldwide) that have been adversely impacted by economic changes which have caused businesses to close or new roads being built that cause traffic to bypass an entire area. Each of these often results in the formation of a ghost town or at the very least a significant reduction in the size of what was once a busting town. Unless you live in one of the few areas where economic prosperity still reigns and building is taking place at an explosive pace, there will be sites that fall under the true definition of a ghost town not far from your home. Look back to see what businesses might have helped develop your area, and if they are no longer prominent employers, you will likely have a ghost town or section of an existing town that can be considered to be a ghost town worth searching. For U.S. hunters, a book that is invaluable in identifying 100's of sites in your immediate area no matter where you might live is called *The United States Treasure Atlas* by Thomas Terry. It is a 10 volume set with each volume covering a handful of States broken down by counties. The author spent countless hours identifying sites that range from treasure leads to ghost towns and individual spots such as parks, ferry landings, etc. He is currently working on an updated set but the original series is still a treasure trove that should be in every treasure hunter's library.

SEARCHING THE SITES & RECOVERING THE RELICS

Once you've identified some sites to search, there are a number of tips and techniques that can help you find more in less time, which should be your overall goal. It's surprising how often relic hunters who have taken the time to conduct research and locate sites do not have a formal plan or method to actually search the site once they arrive. As they say *"Even a blind squirrel finds a nut once in a while"* but hoping for the best is rarely the optimal way to be successful on a regular basis.

Let's look at campsites which are areas where troops or settlers may have stopped for a single night on the way to a distant battle or stayed for a month or more waiting for orders or camped waiting for the rest of their party to catch up. What you will be looking for are relics that were lost or discarded rather than items that were involved in a battle. It's amazing to see the variety of finds that are made at campsites ranging from personal items such as coins, jewelry and carved bullets to buttons, bullets, cooking utensils, cavalry equipment and even caches of coins and other valuables - if they had it with them, there's a good chance that you as a relic hunter may find it!

Most campsites contain a great deal of ferrous targets such as nails from boots and horseshoes, tool parts, iron pins, etc. Even if you are not interested in digging up all of these targets, the fact that they are present can help you find the right location to tighten up your search pattern and start recovering the relics you are searching for.

Let's assume that your research has identified the existence of a small campsite. You have determined the approximate area where it was located; however, it would take a considerable amount of time to thoroughly cover the entire 10 to 20 acre area. In this case the best way to try to pinpoint the campsite is to set your discrimination as close to '0' as possible and simply walk back and forth across the area. If you find certain areas contain a fair number of targets, slow down and start working a more formal pattern to ensure you are not missing anything. Unless you have no desire to recover any of the ferrous targets present such as square nails, shell fragments, horseshoes, etc., leave your discrimination low as you search. If there are numerous ferrous targets, they may 'mask' or hide good targets that may be adjacent to them. This problem is why many sites still contain valuable targets despite having been hunted for years. If your discrimination is set too high, there is a good chance that a rejected target will keep you from detecting a good target in the immediate vicinity.

Fire pits are another area worth focusing in on when you search campsites. Not only were they used for cooking, but also trash was often tossed in at the end of the day. Much of what is recovered from fire pits shows signs of being in the fire; however, a number of first-rate finds have come out of them.

This is another reason why you want to search camps with very little discrimination. A fire pit will usually contain ferrous trash and non-ferrous trash and even the slightest amount of discrimination will cause you to miss a potentially productive area.

After you have located a campsite and searched the area where it was located, don't give up and head on to the next site. If the site was occupied for more than a night or two, they would have found an area a short distance away that could be used to get rid of the camp trash. It is human nature is to carry the trash to a spot downhill from the campsite itself. After all, if you had the choice of carrying trash uphill or downhill what direction would you choose? You can either walk the area yourself or spend a few minutes looking over a topographical map to identify potential dumpsites. Remember that yesterday's trash is today's treasure. Items such as belt buckles with broken pins, threadbare clothes and other items that could not be salvaged were typically discarded with the daily trash - any of which would make a welcome addition to your collection.

Moving up let's take a look at the sites of larger battles or historic sites. Many of these have been preserved and most are designated as National Parks in the U.S. or their equivalent in other countries, which makes relic hunting off-limits within the park itself. Now before you write these sites off completely, keep in mind that these battles involved large numbers of troops on both sides and parks usually only cover a small portion of where activity associated with the battle took place. This is where research will pay off for you. For battle sites, you need to determine exactly where both sides came from before and went to after the battle since this will let you know where additional artifacts can be found. Obtain a detailed topographical map and plot the battle lines or historic site as well as the park boundaries to determine what area are likely to contain relics yet are not within the park. Contact the property owners of areas you have determined to be potential "hot-spots" and try to obtain permission to search them.

Older sites that are no longer identifiable and are not found on any maps, especially sites outside the United States or sites in the U.S. from its earliest days, tend to be somewhat harder to locate. The key fact to remember is that human needs have remained fairly constant across the millennia so areas near water, with high ground nearby for a vantage point and access to food have always been desirable. Using the wealth of mapping resources available today, it's fairly easy to pour over the material in the comfort of your house and identify potential sites to search by applying these selection criteria.

RECOMMENDED RECOVERY TOOLS & TECHNIQUES

Unless you are searching for shallow relics in a grassy area, you will need a tool that can reach down to where the relics will be found and do so without bending after a few holes have been dug. Many times the soil will be almost rock-hard which will put any digging tool to the acid test. Saving a few dollars buying a lesser-quality tool will quickly turn into an expensive mistake when you find yourself a long way from your car or truck and the digger you just bought bends or snaps in half . . . . and I've seen it happen more times than I care to remember. You know it will usually take place when you are in a great site and have been given permission to hunt it one time only. Most relic hunters use a shovel or spade designed to provide years of service in all types of soil conditions. Typically constructed entirely of metal, the only real maintenance they might require is to occasionally sharpen the edge so you can cut through roots or vines often found in wooded sites. Other options you might want to investigate include folding military shovels (just make sure you get a true surplus shovel and not an imported look-alike which rarely holds up), a hand-help pick (again, get one that is solidly built) or an all-metal gardening tool that looks like it might work in your ground conditions.

101

REFERENCE RESOURCE BIBLIOGRAPHY

Books

General Relic Hunting
- **Battles of the Revolutionary War, 1775 – 1781** by W.J. Wood
- **Battlefield Atlas of the American Revolution** by Craig L. Symonds
- **Relic Hunter, The Book** by Ed Fedory
- **The World of the Relic Hunter** by Ed Fedory

Civil War Relic Hunting:
- **An Introduction to Civil War Small Arms** by Earl Coates and Dean Thomas
- **Authentic Civil War Battle Sites** by E.S. LeGaye
- **Civil War Battles And Skirmishes** Edited by Katherine Slocum Moody (Complied from the archives of the US and the various states soon after the secession of hostilities at the instruction of the government, this is the most complete and accurate list available)
- **Civil War Relic Hunting A to Z** by Robert Buttafusco
- **Finding Civil War Campsites in Rural Areas** by Rural Relic Hunters
- **In Search of the Civil War** by Bob Trevillan
- **Insiders' Guide To Civil War Sites In The Eastern Theater** by Gleason
- **Insiders Guide To Civil War Sites In The Southern Theater** by McKay
- **The Civil War In The Western Territories** by Colton

European Relic Hunting:
- **Deserted Villages** by Trevor Rowly & John Wood
- **Discovering Battlefields of England and Scotland** by J. Kinross
- **Discovering Local History** by David Iredale & John Barrett
- **Fair Sites in England & Scotland** by Brian Cross
- **Finding Hammered silver coinage in England, Scotland & Wales** by Brian Cross
- **Hill forts in England and Wales** by James Dyer
- **Roman Buckles & Military Fittings** by Andrew Appels & Stuart Laycock
- **Simple Site Research for Serious Detector Users** by Brian Cross
- **Site Research for Detectorists, Field Walkers & Archeologists** by David Villanueva

Ghost Towning:
- **Dust in the Wind – A Guide to American Ghost Towns** by Gary B. Speck
- **Ghost Town Treasures – Ruins, Relics & Riches** by Charles Garrett
- **Hunting the Ghost Towns** by H. Glenn Carson
- **Researching Ghost Towns** by Daryl Townley
- **United States Treasure Atlas** by Thomas Terry (10 volume series covering the U.S.)

Magazines

- **American Digger Magazine**; Excellent magazine covering facets not found in other treasure hunting magazines as well as some great find photos to get you motivated; http://www.americandigger.com/
- **Blue & Gray Magazine;** http://www.bluegraymagazine.com/
- **Civil War News;** http://www.civilwarnews.com/
- **Civil War Times;** http://www.historynet.com/cwti/
- **Detection Passion**; The leading French treasure hunting magazine; http://pagesperso-orange.fr/detection.passion/cadrsomm.htm
- **North & South Magazine;** http://www.northandsouthmagazine.com/
- **North South Trader's Civil War Magazine**; Dedicated to the Civil War; http://www.nstcivilwar.com/
- **The Coin Hunter**; A Netherlands-based magazine; http://www.thecoinhunter.com/
- **The Searcher**; A monthly treasure hunting magazine from the UK; http://www.thesearcher.co.uk/

- **The Treasure Depot Magazine**: Full-color publication covering all forms of treasure hunting; http://www.thetreasuredepot.com/tdmag/treasure_depot_magazine.htm
- **Treasure Hunting**; A monthly UK treasure hunting magazine; http://www.treasurehunting.co.uk/

Computer Programs

- **The Civil War CD-Rom: The War of the Rebellion, A Compilation of the Official Records of the Union and Confederate Armies** (Contains all 127 volumes on one CD); http://www.hbar.com/
- **The Civil War CD-ROM II; Official Records of the Union and Confederate Navies in the War of the Rebellion** (Contains 30 volumes of Naval records); http://www.hbar.com/
- **Confederate Military History CD-ROM** (Contains 12 volumes with each focusing on a Southern state)
- **The American Indian CD-ROM (C**omprehensive CD on American Indian history)

Internet Resources

Forums
- **Civil War Quest**: Comprehensive forum covering all aspects of this period ranging from finds to research; http://www.civilwarquest.com/community/
- **Find's Treasure Forums – Relic & Bottle Hunting Forum**: http://www.findmall.com/list.php?30
- **TreasureNet – Civil War Forum**: http://forum.treasurenet.com/index.php/board,15.0.html
- **TreasureNet – Relic Hunting Forum**: http://forum.treasurenet.com/index.php/board,7.0.html
- **TreasureNet – Revolutionary War Forum**: http://forum.treasurenet.com/index.php/board,88.0.html
- **Treasure Spot – Relic & Bottle Forum**: http://www.mytreasurespot.com/main/list.php?3
- **The Treasure Depot – Relic Hunting Forum**: http://www.thetreasuredepot.com/cgi-bin/relic/relic_config.pl?

Reference & Research Sites
- **Abandoned & Little Known Airfields**: More then 1,500 sites across the U.S. – just make sure you get permission before hunting any of them; http://www.airfields-freeman.com/index.htm
- **Britannia; The Roman Army & Navy in Britain 55BC – 410AD**: http://www.castra.org.uk/
- **eHistory – The War of the Rebellion**; Another site that allows you to search the OR's; http://ehistory.osu.edu/osu/sources/records/default.cfm
- **Ghost Towns**; Covers sites in the U.S. and Canada; http://www.ghosttowns.com
- **Making of America – The War of the Rebellion**; Search the entire set of OR's online at no charge; http://digital.library.cornell.edu/m/moawar/waro.html
- **National Park Service Civil War Battle Summaries**: Overview of major campaigns that allows you to look for sites surrounding the battle sites and then work to obtain permission to search them: http://www.nps.gov/history/hps/abpp/battles/bystate.htm
- **Portable Antiquities Scheme**; A voluntary scheme to record archaeological objects found by members of the public in England and Wales – this site contains a wealth of information on virtually anything you might uncover while detecting in the United Kingdom or Europe; http://www.finds.org.uk/index.php
- **Wikipedia's List of U.S. Ghost Towns**: While not a complete list by any means, it does provides dozens of sites to investigate; http://en.wikipedia.org/wiki/List_of_ghost_towns_in_the_United_States

Recovery Tools:

- **Black Ada Ltd.**: Complete line of rugged digging tools (United Kingdom); http://www.blackada.com/
- **Kellyco Metal Detector Superstore**: Assortment of digging tools including the Gator Digger line including one model that comes with a lifetime warranty, http://www.kellycodetectors.com/accessories/trowels.htm
- **Predator Tools**: A complete line of target recovery tools; http://predatortools.com/
- **Wilcox All Pro Tools & Supply**; Complete line of recovery tools; http://www.wilcoxallpro.com/
- **WW Manufacturing Company**: Rugged line of all-metal spades, shovels & hand-held diggers; http://www.wwmfg.com/

BEACH & SHALLOW WATER HUNTING

Beach hunting is probably the only form of treasure hunting where anyone can go out and find items worth $1,000's just a short drive from their house. Most importantly, one is able to do it on an on-going basis as valuable targets are continually being lost at beaches and informal swimming sites. With very few exceptions, there will be a beach or at least a spot where people have gone swimming near any location around the globe and unless pollution has rendered the nearby water unfit, you will find these sites remain popular year after year.

> One word of caution to those that have an interest of getting into this addicting and lucrative form of treasure hunting relates to your equipment. While the virtually all detectors today have waterproof coils and can be submerged up to the control housing, the electronics are not waterproof. Allowing water to reach the electronics will most likely result in a dead detector. If you plan to get serious about shallow water hunting, you should to look into getting a detector designed for that application produced by one of the manufacturers. I am not going to admit anything but suffice it to say I've learned this lesson the hard way!

SELECTING A DETECTOR FOR BEACH & SHALLOW WATER HUNTING

With few exceptions, most detectors on the market today can be used for wading in shallow water. The only vulnerable part will be the electronics in the control housing and the headphones if waterproof models are not used. Realistically though, if you plan to go much past the wet sand area of the beach or the edge of the water when looking for relics at other sites that border lakes, rivers or the ocean, investing in a water resistant or water proof detector is the only sensible way to go. So what are the important factors to consider when shopping for a detector suited for this form of treasure hunting?

- **Circuit Type**: Depending on the type of water you plan on searching in or near, certain circuits are better suited than others. For fresh water, a VLF-based detector will work just fine and many successful fresh water hunters use them exclusively. Hunting in salt or brackish water tends to give VLF detectors heartburn unless you are in areas with pure white sugar sand (no mineralization). Beaches which are stained with black sand or volcanic sand need the additional capabilities of pulse detectors or those operating on dual or multi-frequencies. Check with local water hunters to see what they are using.
- **Discrimination**: When you are water hunting, discrimination should be kept at or near zero to avoid inadvertently missing what could have been the find of the year. Thin gold rings (the ones that often hold diamonds) can be easily rejected at discrimination levels much higher than foil and items such as charms or chains can be rejected even lower. So while discrimination has its place in other applications, to find gold, minimize the level of discrimination you use.
- **Battery Type, Life & Location**: This may seem like an odd feature to place on the desired feature list but you want to minimize the opportunities water has to get inside the detector. If the unit you are thinking about gets 10 hours of life from a set of batteries and you need to open the case to replace them, you have multiple chances to not seal it properly and have a leak that can damage the electronics, especially in salt water. Having a rechargeable system that allows the batteries to be charged in the case or a unit that gets 20+ hours on a set of batteries is a real plus when selecting a particular model.

- **Coils**: Some water detectors allow you to change coils in the same way land detectors do and that is a positive feature in terms of expanded versatility. If the model you want does not offer this option but is available in different coil sizes, consider the pros and cons of each based on your preferences and the types of sites you will be searching. Smaller coils offer less drag going through the water and are better suited for trashy areas while larger coils cover more area with each sweep and detect deeper.

> **Coil Selection:** *"To me, coil choice is vital for successful beach hunting. Make it a Double-D, and go for the largest diameter that you can swing. You may think that I am talking about depth here, but I'm not. I'm talking about coverage area. Using an 8" coil on a large beach is akin to trying to remove a wall mural with a pencil eraser; you either miss too much or it takes forever. With a large diameter coil you cover more area and that maximizes your chances of finding stuff. My coil of preference is the 15" WOT from Coiltek for my Minelab detector but most of my friends have also opted for the largest coil they can get for whatever brand & model they use. Larger Double-D coils get great depth, pinpoint easily and cover a heck of a lot of ground."* **Bill Paxton, Los Angles, CA**

Talk to dealers and local beach & shallow water hunters to find out what has been proven to work best in your area . . . this is where investing in the right equipment can pay off in a big way – a single ring that an inferior detector or one not suited for the conditions in your area failed to pickup could leave a $5,000+ find for the next detectorist walking behind you to recover.

THE BASICS

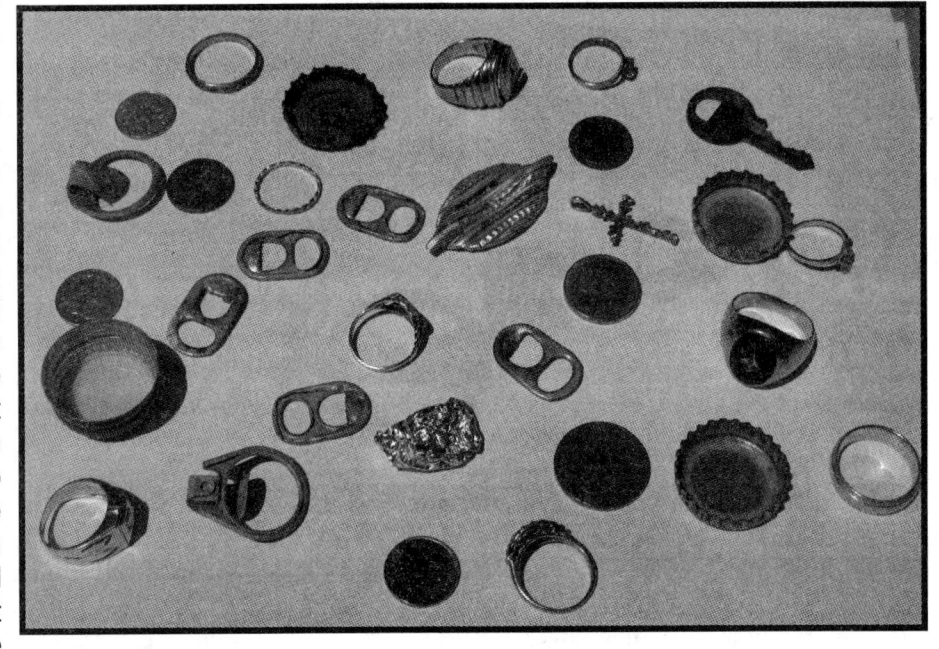

The adjacent photo shows what beach hunters can expect to come across in their searches – gold jewelry, coins, pull tabs, screw caps, foil and more – both the good and the bad. Unfortunately, until metal detectors can actually show you what's under the coil, you can't differentiate the good from the bad with 100% accuracy and you will need to dig some trash to find all the treasure. Having a clear picture of the type of targets most often encountered will dictate what settings will work best for this type of hunting. As one might expect, coins will be quite common. Performing an air test and setting up a test garden will help you determine where specific coins are accepted. Jewelry is also common as many successful beach & shallow water hunters will attest to. But, unlike coins where one could develop a comprehensive list detailing a specific denomination and the expected target ID value for each along with the discrimination setting that rejects it, jewelry covers an extremely wide range due to a number of factors. Pure gold is extremely soft, so in order for it to be fashioned into jewelry that does not wear excessively, it must be alloyed with other metals for strength as well as to vary its natural yellow color. Pure gold is recognized as being 24KT, and most jewelry ranges from 10KT (less than 50% pure) to 22KT (just over 92% pure). The remaining percentage is made up of other metals such as copper, zinc, silver, nickel, cadmium, aluminum and even iron to name but a few. Now when you vary the size of items from say a tiny pinky ring to a man's college ring or large gold pendant, it is easy to see that gold can register across a wide range of the spectrum. Unfortunately, unless you are searching a private beach which limits the type of beverage containers patrons can bring, you will also find an amazing amount of trash targets such as pull tabs, screw caps, cigarette packs and bottle caps to name just a few. As with gold jewelry, there are countless varieties of each and most will overlap the area where gold falls making it virtually impossible to ignore one while recovering the other. When you factor in the trash you are bound to encounter, expecting discrimination or target identification to allow you to only dig good targets and reject the unwanted ones is clearly unrealistic. Referring back to the analog meter on page 53, one can see that pull tabs and gold cover almost the same area.

> **Trash Often Equals Treasure:** If you come across a beach area where all you seem to be finding are pull tabs or screw caps, you might just have stumbled across a potential gold mine that others have created. Often, detectorists with little patience or understanding of what they are hoping to find get frustrated when they dig piece after piece of trash and either leave or turn up their discrimination to eliminate the unwanted targets. While they may feel satisfied that they found $10 in recently-lost clad coins and dug no trash, they will have also left most of the gold jewelry behind which registers in the same range. Work the area carefully focusing on those types of targets and you could be rewarded in a big way - several gold rings sure beats a few dollars of new coins any day of the week!

Searching swimming sites – both those still in current use as well as those long-since abandoned – is the most popular form of beach and shallow water hunting. After all, finding a handful of gold rings at today's gold prices while enjoying an afternoon at the local beach is about as close to nirvana as you can get. Toss in a generous sprinkling of collectible coins and artifacts from older sites or a pocketful of modern coins to offset the cost of filling your tank and it's little wonder beach hunting is the fastest growing segment of treasure hunting today. The following photo shows just what can be found.

You Can Find Gold on a Beach!

1 x 10K Earring
5 x 14K Rings
24 x 10K Rings
1 x 1k Bracelet

29 Gold Rings 2009

So what can one hope to find with the right equipment and search techniques? John from Edmonton, Canada is an avid detectorist who uses a Garrett Gold Scorpion and Infinium and did quite well in 2009 as evidenced by this photo he provided . . . the value of just the gold alone is over $2,000!

Formal swimming beaches are relatively easy to identify. If they are still in use, county, state or national travel directories and websites will usually list them along with details of the facilities available at each. Those that have been closed down for any one of a number of reasons may take a bit more detective work to find but the Research chapter should get you focused on the right material that will help you find several sites to search.

Informal swimming sites are much harder to find, especially if you are not from the area, but they are often unsearched by other shallow water hunters and can hold a surprising amount of treasure. To show the power of the Internet in finding sites that 95% of the competition is unaware of, there is a website that provides information on more than 1,000 swimmin' holes across the United States. The site is geared towards people looking for out-of-the-way swimming sites but it can easily be used by beach and shallow water hunters to find an informal site or two in their local area. If you are not from the area you currently live in, this is where seeking out the oldest residents and asking them where they went to swim when they were younger can be a veritable goldmine in terms of potential sites to search. Over the years I have found out about a number of such sites that even research would not have turned up. One site on a small creek in central Pennsylvania required a half-mile hike to reach. Never extremely popular or crowded, the finds were limited but 4 gold class rings and more than $8 in silver coins were recovered in the few trips it took to search the area. This site had come from an older gentleman who had asked me what I had been doing when detecting a nearby high school. A 15-minute conversation identified the swimming hole along with two one-room school houses that had been torn down decades earlier and the man was able to get me permission to search them . . . but that is a story for another day.

> **Tides & Storms:** If you search sites on the ocean, pay particular attention to changes in tidal action or passing storms as they can often unlock the "vault" containing valuables that have lain hidden for decades or longer. Coins and jewelry being heavier than the surrounding sand tend to sink ever deeper reaching depths far beyond the detection range of a metal detector. Storms have been known to strip feet of sand away in mere hours causing what is known as a "cut". Beach hunters have recovered hundreds of coins and dozens of pieces of jewelry in a short period of time from these areas. Tidal action changes in the winter months and can also bring treasure close enough to be detected. Learn to know what the normal level of sand is on your beaches and when that drops, be out there with a vengeance and see what Mother Nature has exposed for you.

The "Find-of-a-Lifetime" Found on a Florida Beach

Gary Drayton, an avid beach and shallow water hunter on the east coast for Florida made the "find-of-a-lifetime" early one morning in 2005 while searching a stretch of beach known to contain the remains of the Spanish galleons that sank in the hurricane of 1715. Significant erosion had taken place from storm surge which made for ideal search conditions. A few modern coins turned up but Gary still had high hopes for the day. The next signal produced this amazing find . . . . a 22KT Inca gold ring from the 1715 Plate Fleet containing 9 near-flawless Columbian emeralds!

Relic hunting is another form of shallow water hunting that some detectorists have gotten involved in with great success. Veteran relic hunter Charles Harris wrote about his experiences several years ago in which he and his partners waded the rivers and creeks near battle sites and found an impressive assortment of Civil War relics including bullets, belt plates, gun parts, canteens and more. Since the bottom can be irregular and drop off suddenly, it is highly recommended that you only hunt these sites with a partner. Searching the shallow water off industrial sites, amusement parks, shipping piers and cities can often turn up some very interesting items. Bob Afina, a detectorist from the Boston area with more than 25 years of experience hunts the river banks near his home when levels drop in the summer. While he comes up with a pile of trash, he also finds items dating back 100's of years including coins, buttons, old fishing lures, boat brass and more. I've talked with several "river hunters" in England who search the banks of the rivers when the tide goes out and they also make recoveries that have me thinking about planning a trip over there every time I get a few digital pictures E-mailed to me.

RECOMMENDED RECOVERY TOOLS & TECHNIQUES

For beach hunting, scoops are the "tool-of-choice". In the dry sand, a hand scoop is the best piece of equipment for the job unless bending over poses an issue for you. Scoops today range in construction from lightweight plastic (which are handy as you can pass the scoop across the coil and see if the target is in it) to rugged metal scoops made from steel or aluminum. Some dry sand beach hunters opt for a lightweight scoop with an adjustable handle which is easier on the back.

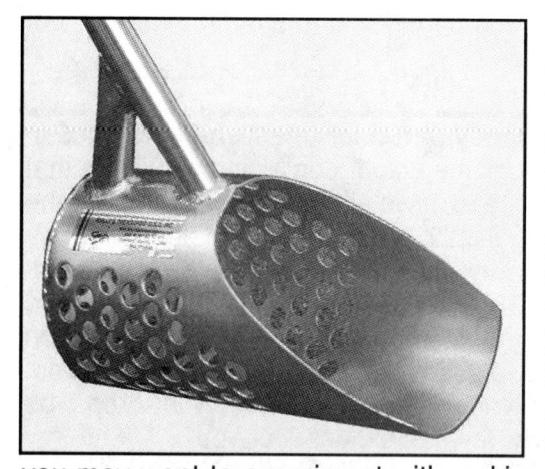

If you venture into the water, a long handled scoop is a necessity and if you plan to be serious about it, one that will hold up to the rigors resulting from digging deep holes in compacted soil, sand or rocks is worth the investment. My primary scoop cost almost $100 when I bought it back in 1985 but other than it looking a bit battle-scarred, it works just as well today as it did 25 years and 1,000's of holes ago. This is one tool where spending a little more upfront will pay off in spades with the increased efficiency you will have in recovering targets and the durability of the scoop itself. Some people have opted to make their own, and if you have one to copy along with access to the right metal working equipment such as bending machines and welders, you may want to experiment with making one. There are several companies that build scoops using designs proven under decades of serious use in a wide range of sites so see what's available and use what is comfortable and does the job you are asking from it.

Magnets: On virtually any beach or shallow water stretch you might search, you will come across a myriad of small iron items including fish hooks, nails, hair pins, bits of steel cans and more. These tiny items can drive you nuts trying to locate them as they tend to slip through the holes in your scoop and drop back into the water. Attach a magnet to the back of your scoop with a plastic wire tie or cable wrap to catch them and reduce the time it takes to find a target and move on to the next one. Farm supply stores sell what are called "cow magnets" that are well-suited for this application.

A floating sifter is another item that can increase your productivity by reducing the time spent trying to find a target in a scoop filled with material from the bottom. There are some commercially available models or you can make your own using a gold pan screen & inner tube or a 2 foot square made from 4" thin-wall PVC pipe and hardware cloth. Towed behind you in the water, one simply dumps a scoop of bottom material into it and the movement through the water will leave the target visible while allowing you to move on to the next target.

Talk to some of your fellow beach & shallow water hunters to see if they have any additional "specialized" equipment for local conditions that might help you find more in less time. Just be ready to get hooked on this form of treasure hunting once you see that first glint of gold in your scoop!

REFERENCE RESOURCE BIBLIOGRAPHY

Books & Magazines

- **Beach and Water Treasure Hunting with Metal Detectors** by Dan Berg (eBook)
- **Beach Detecting in Surf and Sand** by Jay Schofield
- **How to Search: Sand and Surf** by Charles Garrett
- **Pulsepower: Finding Gold at the Shore with a Pulse Induction Metal Detector** by Clive James Clynick
- **Site Reading for Gold and Silver; Understanding Beach, Shore and Inland Metal Detecting Sites** by Clive James Clynick
- **The Beach Bank - Your Treasure Teller** by Kevin Reilly
- **Treasure Recovery Sand and Surf** by Charles Garrett
- **Water Hunting: Secrets of the Pros** by Clive James Clynick

DVD's & Videos

- **Shallow Water Hunting Explained** (Filmed in Europe but applicable to sites worldwide)
- **Treasure Recovery Sand & Sea Video** by Charles Garrett

Internet Resources

- **Find's Treasure Forums – Beach & Water / Scuba Detecting Forum**: http://www.findmall.com/list.php?26
- **The Treasure Hunter Forum – Beach & Surf Hunting**: http://www.treasurehunterforum.com/forum35/
- **TreasureNet – Beach & Shallow Water Forum**: http://forum.treasurenet.com/index.php/board,10.0.html
- **Treasure Spot – Beach & Water Forum**: http://www.mytreasurespot.com/main/list.php?4
- **The Treasure Depot – Sand & Sea Forum**: http://www.thetreasuredepot.com/cgi-bin/surfandsand/ss_config.pl
- **Treasure Quest Beach & Underwater Forum**: http://www.treasurequestxlt.com/community/beach-water-underwater-metal-detecting/

Beach & Shallow Water Recovery Tools & Supplies:

- **Garrett Metal Detectors**: Assorted hand held scoops; http://garrett.com/hobby/hbby_recovery_tools.htm
- **Gauss Boys Super Magnets**: Variety of strong magnets for your scoop; http://www.gaussboys.com
- **Jimmy Sierra's Metal Detecting Accessories**: Sand scoops; (415) 488-8131; http://www.jimmysierra.com
- **Kellyco Metal Detector Superstore**: Assortment of short & long handled scoops, (888) 535-5926, http://www.kellycodetectors.com/accessories/shorthandscoops.htm
- **Radio Shack**: Assorted magnets for use in scoops; http://www.radioshack.com/
- **Reilly's Treasured Gold**: High-quality line of short & long handled scoops; (954) 971-6102, http://rtgstore.com/
- **Sun Spot Products**: Highly-rated rugged long-handled scoops; http://www.gold-scoop.com/
- **Super Magnet Man**: Magnets for scoops; http://www.supermagnetman.net/

<u>Dive gear (wetsuits, boots, gloves, etc.)</u>
- **Divers Supply** (Dive equipment): (800) 999-3483 ; http://www.divers-supply.com
- **LeisurePro** (Dive equipment): (888) 805-3600; http://www.leisurepro.com
- **Simply Scuba** (Dive equipment – United Kingdom):; http://www.simplyscuba.com

UNDERWATER TREASURE HUNTING

Searching for treasure with an underwater metal while diving is certainly not something for the faint of heart. Visibility in even the clearest of water can quickly go to zero when silt is stirred up on the bottom and running into some obstruction can give even a seasoned diver cause to panic. Many people I know who have been diving for years are not comfortable when they find themselves in these conditions. However, if you are not bothered by low or no visibility dive conditions or can get acclimated to them, diving will open up additional areas which 95% of your competition will be unable to search.

EQUIPMENT OPTIONS

Before you think this is a great form of treasure hunting and rush out to buy a truckload of gear, there are a few factors you need to consider and decisions to make. There are two options you have as far as the actual dive gear is concerned which are conventional scuba tanks and a surface air supply system or what is more commonly called a hookah system.

Scuba tanks are entirely self-contained and allow complete freedom underwater; however, the downside in their use for treasure hunting is the ongoing cost associated with refilling them. A standard 80-ft^3 will provide between 1 and 2.5 hours of bottom time depending on your depth and air consumption rate. The typical cost to refill a tank is between $4 and $5. There is also the cost of annual and 5-year inspections that are required in order to be able to have the tanks refilled. Many underwater treasure hunters who use scuba tend to have multiple tanks so that they can spend a weekend underwater rather than driving to find a dive shop that may be many miles away. An 80-ft^3 tank will cost about $150 from your local dive shop. In addition to the tank(s), you will need additional equipment such as a regulator / gauge / octopus system, buoyancy compensator, weights, etc. This is one area where buying strictly on price is a bad idea as your life literally rests on the equipment you use and the care you give it. Some dive gear can be purchased used; however, unless you know the person that you are buying from and have the equipment serviced prior to use, avoid buying items such as regulators and BC's on the secondary market.

An alternative to scuba that has gained in popularity over the past decade among treasure hunters is the hookah system. Consisting of a small gasoline engine and a low-pressure air compressor mounted on a flotation system that supplies clean, filtered air through conventional regulators, a hookah allows up to four divers to stay under water for little more than the cost of the gas it uses. With a hookah system, hunting time is no longer limited by the number of tanks you have along since a few gallons of gas will provide a weekend full of diving for multiple divers. Another advantage a hookah has over scuba tanks is the actual operating cost which is substantially less than tanks since the only cost will be the gas used for the engine. Hookahs have been around for years; however, the newer models are much more dependable than their predecessors and have been designed to ensure you have an extremely safe piece of equipment to use in your searches. They are well suited for treasure hunting since most of the sites you will work are in less than 30 feet of water.

The cost of both options should be weighed and compared to your planned use. You can buy two sets of dive gear for less than the cost of a hookah system so if you are not planning on taking the same partner with you each time and can share the cost of a hookah, tanks may be the lower-cost option. If you intend to be under the water a good deal of the time, figure what the cost for air fills plus the cost of the equipment versus the cost of a hookah and several gallons of gas is and see which option is more advantageous. Regardless of your decision, make sure to read the following caution!

> **GET TRAINED:** No matter which option you choose – scuba or hookah – make sure you get the proper training to ensure you are aware of the dangers of diving and how to respond to them if you are faced with issues underwater. Any dive shop offers a full range of certification classes and training programs have now been developed for hookah systems. Dive professionals recommend that even if you plan on using a hookah that you take as a minimum the basic diver certification class to avoid a potentially life-threatening situation once you slip under the surface.

SELECTING A DETECTOR FOR UNDER WATER TREASURE HUNTING

Not to sound flippant but obviously the most important factor of any detector that you plan on using when diving with is its pressure rating. There are some models that are advertised as being "water resistant" or "splash-proof" and while these may be fine for searching the beach or even wading in the surfline, the pressure exerted on them once you get below 15 feet will quickly show you why a rugged, pressure-tested case is essential. The Underwater Detector section of the Buyer's Guide Comparison Tables chapter covers all the current detectors capable of being used for diving. Factors that are key in selecting an underwater metal detector include the same ones covered in the Beach and Shallow Water Hunting chapter. Take a look at that section of the previous chapter to aid in selecting the right detector for your needs.

UNDERWATER COIN & JEWELRY HUNTING

While it's true that the number of water hunters has increased dramatically over the past decade or so as more and more hobbyists learned what could be recovered from the beaches near their homes, the amount of coins and jewelry being lost on a continuing basis provides for a never-ending supply of targets to search for and retrieve. I am an avid water hunter myself and have been a certified diver since the early 1970's. Back then there was literally no competition when diving with a metal detector and the finds we made were truly amazing. Well, times have changed and one has to work a little harder to make high quality finds on a consistent basis; however, as we discussed in the previous chapter on beach and shallow water hunting, the rewards more than make up for the effort.

Underwater treasure hunting involves the use of dive gear to venture out past the range of where the waders can search. But there are many times when you can find yourself in water 3' to 4' deep due to the hard, rocky bottom which negates the ability to use a scoop to recover targets. Diving extends your range to be able to reach areas under docks, platforms, diving boards and rope swings to name just a few of the productive areas that are typically deeper than one can get to by wading alone.

Rather than repeating the types of sites covered in the previous chapter and described in some of the books listed in the Reference Resource Bibliography, use your imagination to think of where you might be able to find lost coins, jewelry and other valuables. Formal swimming beaches are obvious producers but informal sites such as a rope swing on a county creek or a wide section of the river where the current drops off can be just as productive with far less competition. A few years ago I dove just such a pool on a large creek near our old home in central Pennsylvania. There was a rock face on one side and a rope hanging from on a tree on the other. The water was about 15 feet deep and the second signal I received turned out to be a 1944 Walking Liberty half dollar. The very next signal was a 1950 high school class ring! Most of the local formal beaches were hunted on a regular basis but none of the informal sites I came across appeared to have ever been searched. Think outside the box, master your equipment and you will find there is an amazing amount of treasure waiting to be recovered!

UNDERWATER RELIC HUNTING

For the more adventuresome relic hunters, searching waterways such as rivers, streams and lakes for artifacts is an area that has proven to be quite productive. Relics can range from military artifacts lost when troops fought around bodies of water, common items lost by people crossing the water to what was once common trash dumped into the water yet is now considered collectible.

As far as military relics go, armies had to get across rivers when they moved and often lost a significant amount of supplies off the side of temporary bridges or ferries. This was especially true if they were in a forced retreat and more interested in saving their own lives rather than a few supplies. Then there were many battles fought next to bodies of water and items ranging from artillery shells and bullets to swords, bayonets, buttons and more all found their way beneath the surface. The land surrounding the site may have been heavily hunted for years; however, the ground under the water will rarely have received much if any pressure from relic hunters. A pair of relic hunters from Monteagle, Tennessee purchased a pair of underwater metal detectors several years ago and started diving a section of the river near their homes. In a four-month period they recovered more artifacts than they had in the previous six years of hunting land sites surrounding the same area. Some of their better finds included a Confederate sword, a brass bugle, six - yes six – Confederate belt buckles and dozens of uniform buttons.

Even campsites which held entire armies can now be found underwater thanks to dam building projects that flooded large areas throughout the south. As a matter of fact, the bottom of the Tennessee River that runs through Chattanooga, Tennessee contains the remnants of camps of both the Union and Confederate armies. When the Tennessee Valley Authority dammed the river for flood control and power production more than 50 years ago, the river expanded from its original narrow course to a wide, slow-moving expanse. During the Civil War, both armies were camped in Chattanooga along the banks of the river. They stayed there for months – losing and discarding a wealth of artifacts related to daily life in the camps. Today relic hunters dive what was once farmland along the riverbanks searching the old campsites. I have talked with some of the relic divers who report that they have come across intact trenches and even picket posts or Civil War-era foxholes as they swam across the bottom. Visibility is at best 5 feet on a good day and there are submerged obstructions such as fallen trees that must be avoided but divers are finding many items that would otherwise have remained lost in the soft mud on the bottom of the river. Not quite like diving in the Caribbean; however, it does offer the opportunity to search for relics in an area most would ignore.

Bottle collectors have discovered that rare and valuable examples of glassware can often be found just a short distance offshore of towns, villages and private homes located on or near the water. In northern areas, piles of household trash were often placed on the ice during the winter months and as the ice thawed, the trash fell to the bottom. Over the years most of what was lost has disappeared but the bottles, glassware and metallic relics remain. Swimming along the shore near old hotels can often produce large numbers of bottles as well as other items lost or tossed in by patrons. If you live near rivers, consider searching around the old pilings marking the locations of piers where ships once docked. Not only can you uncover relics but if people used the piers, you will likely come across coins and other valuables as well.

One of the most productive pier-type sites for divers was the site of the old Euclid Beach Amusement Park located on the shore of Lake Erie that opened in the 1890's. The pier served ships filled with patrons from Cleveland and surrounding cites, and remained a popular part of the park even after the ships stopped using it. Over the years, thousand upon thousands of coins, rings, tokens and the like dropped into the water beneath the pier. When most of it finally fell down and was removed, a few adventuresome divers started searching the site and could not believe what turned up. I know some of the early divers that searched Euclid Beach and their finds were amazing - silver coins, gold rings, keys, cuff links - often finding multiple targets in one hole. While this site was one for the record books, there are many sites where piers or docks once welcomed people by the 1,000's that hold similar treasures waiting for divers to recover them. If you are a diver, do a little research and see if you can find an untouched site like Euclid Beach in your area and see what turns up.

RECOMMENDED RECOVERY TOOLS & TECHNIQUES

Tools used to recover targets located with an underwater metal detector are nothing as substantial as those used in other forms of treasure hunting. For one thing, trying to drag a large tool underwater with you and use it while holding the metal detector in the other just is not practical. Secondly, digging by hand in most areas will be the easiest way to actually recover a target you've located with your metal detector. If you are using a VLF or dual / multi-frequency detector for your searches, an inherent characteristic will be extremely useful when you start to recover a target. On these detectors, the search coil needs to be in motion, albeit slight, in order to pick up an object. Once you have zeroed in on the target by using one of the techniques described in the Pinpointing chapter, stop the coil above the bottom where the target is located and tilt it up just enough to get your hand under it. Fan your open hand back and forth to remove the sand, mud, silt or gravel beneath the coil. Listen for the signal to reappear – this means that the target is now moving since the coil has remained stationary; i.e., the target is now free and in the bottom of the hole. Grab a handful of the bottom material and pass your hand past the coil. If you get a signal, you have it in your fist. Simply place whatever you have in your mesh dive bag and after checking to make sure there is nothing else in the hole, move on to the next target. If you are searching a rocky bottom, move the rocks away one at a time until the target is exposed. If you come across a bottom that consists of a hard, dense sand or clay mixture, a small hand tool such as a 3-pronged claw used for gardening works well. Experiment to see what works for your type of bottom . . . you may find that a tool designed for some entirely different use works best.

Again, this is not a form of metal detecting that is for everyone. Many areas are muddy, have dangerous currents, contain submerged obstructions and are far from medical attention if required. However, if you are a proficient diver willing to work under these conditions, you might just find yourself in an area that has not been hunted before and contains a virtual treasure-trove of artifacts.

REFERENCE RESOURCE BIBLIOGRAPHY

Equipment Suppliers:

- **Airline by J. Sink** (Hookah systems & supplies): (877) 207-3235; http://www.airlinebyjsink.com
- **Brownie's Third Lung** (Hookah systems & supplies): (800) 327-0412; http://www.browniedive.com
- **Powerdive International** (Hookah systems & supplies): +618 9385 6500; http://www.powerdive.com
- **Divers Supply** (Dive equipment): (800) 999-3483 ; http://www.divers-supply.com
- **LeisurePro** (Dive equipment): (888) 805-3600; http://www.leisurepro.com
- **Simply Scuba** (Dive equipment – United Kingdom):; http://www.simplyscuba.com

Books & Magazines:

- **Beach and Water Treasure Hunting with Metal Detectors** by Dan Berg (eBook)
- **Shipwreck Diving** by Dan Berg (eBook - visit http://www.shipwreckexpo.com for download details)
- **Sunken Treasure - How To Find It** by Robert Marx
- **The Sports Diver's Guide To Sunken Treasure** by David Finnern
- **Treasure Diving with Captain Dom** by Yvonne Addario

Internet Resources:

- **Find's Treasure Forums – Beach & Water / Scuba Detecting Forum**: http://www.findmall.com/list.php?26
- **Treasure Quest's Underwater Metal Detecting Forum**: http://www.treasurequestxlt.com/community/underwater-metal-detecting/
- **TreasureNet's Shipwreck Forum**: http://forum.treasurenet.com/index.php?board=5.0

<u>Hookah Training Courses</u>:. If you plan on using a hookah, take one of these <u>first</u> along with a basic Scuba training course at your local dive center!
- **Surface Air Supply Systems Home Study Course**: This is a free on-line hookah usage training program; http://www.airlinebyjsink.com/userfiles/files/SASS home study.pdf
- **Brownies Third Lung Training Course**: They also offers a free on-line training course with the purchase of one of their systems or you can purchase an access key for $75 if you already have a system; http://www.browniedive.com./training/index.shtml

PROSPECTING

There are many people who when they hear the term "PROSPECTOR", immediately think of a grizzled old man with a scraggly beard wearing tattered clothes leading a mule up an isolated canyon. That might have been the picture 100 years ago but today, thanks to the allure of searching for precious metal in the great outdoors and the high-tech equipment that is readily available, prospectors come from all walks of life and all age groups. I've come across people prospecting chest deep in a mountain stream or miles from the nearest road in the desert who were successful doctors, stock brokers, homemakers or just the "average Joe" from down the street. Prospecting has become an activity enjoyed by all types of people and for most part, the finds are secondary to the camaraderie and excitement the activity provides.

There are probably more books written on the subject of prospecting than any other form of treasure hunting and with good reason. With centuries of experience from which to draw, there is a wealth of information available to today's prospectors.

Most precious metal will be found in one of two different forms and each has their own techniques to find, recover and process the metal. The most common form is placer or alluvial deposits. The raw metals are often intertwined with indigenous rock and as erosion from water or wind grinds the rock away, the metal is freed. It can then be found in streams or river beds (both active and ancient), dry washes in the desert or gravel beds at the base of hills or mountains. Placer mining is the easiest form of mining simply because Mother Nature has already done much of the hard work by separating the precious metal from the rock and concentrating it due to its higher specific gravity. Records dating back 1,000's of years show early miners using some of the same techniques and basic equipment that modern placer miners use. Since placer deposits tend to hold nuggets, they are what most electronic prospectors tend to spend their time searching for. To recover precious metals from placer deposits located in streams or rivers, equipment such gold pans, sluice boxes and motorized suction dredges are commonly used. Placer deposits located on dry land are usually easier to work with equipment such as metal detectors, gold pans, high bankers and dry washers.

The other form in which precious metals can be found is within lode deposits, still locked within the rock it was originally formed in. Many of the original mines dating back 100 years or more started with the discovery of a placer deposit and then turned into hard rock mines as miners followed the source of the ore deep into the earth. While there are still hard rock miners working today, very few are recreational miners due to the investment of time and equipment required to make it pay off. If you have an interest in trying your hand at hard rock mining, hooking up with an experienced miner is highly recommended for many reasons with the primary one being personnel safety if you start venturing into mine shafts, particularly those long-since abandoned.

SELECTING A DETECTOR FOR PROSPECTING

In almost every case, the areas that contain gold, silver, copper or other targets such as meteorites will also contain some of the most challenging conditions in terms of mineralization one can imagine. Until the introduction of some of the specialized metal detectors that handle these conditions far better than the detectors used for coin, beach or relic hunting, obtaining depths of more than 6 inches or so was little more than a pipe dream. More than 20 years ago, Garrett Electronics introduced what was called the Groundhog circuit that outperformed anything on the market in the Australian gold fields and the resulting finds – literally pounds per person per week – spurred one of the greatest gold rushes in the past 100 years. Even today, as new detectors are released that offer even a slight enhancement to their detection capabilities (either in overall depth or sensitivity to smaller specimens), prospectors will revisit areas considered to be worked out and continue to make impressive finds. The point is that unless you are fortunate enough to have found an area that has not been searched with a metal detector before – which is hard to find nowadays – sticking with a newer model incorporating cutting edge technology will provide an edge that far outweighs any savings you might realize buying a decade-old model.

Discrimination is a feature that will have little use to the electronic prospector since even a slight amount of discrimination can reduce overall detection depth and cause small nuggets to be rejected. It may be frustrating to dig 100 nails or boot tacks from the area surrounding an old mine littered with trash but it is from those areas that the prospector with perseverance makes those memorable finds you see or read about. In the mid-90's, my family and I had been metal detecting a creek which had been heavily mined in the 1800's near our home in Georgia at the time. Small nuggets could still be found but even they were few and far between. I had picked up several beer cans in the creek bed and after digging the 10th one, I just knew the loud signal I had just picked up was yet another one and left it there. Well, not more than two weeks later a good friend of mine, Bill Boye, came over with a large Tupperware container and a smile that went ear-to-ear. Removing the top, the yellow metal visible across the face of the foot-long piece of quartz was unmistakable. Bill told me about how he had found it near the base of a large rock on the edge of a nearby creek - yes, the same rock on the same creek where I had passed up what I had thought was just another beer can. The nugget I had first detected and Bill subsequently recovered was found to be the largest specimen found in Georgia since the 1800's . . . . I internalized an important lesson that I had drilled into others yet neglected myself but it shows that despite a small army of prospectors scouring an area, super finds still await discovery. As veteran miner Dave McCracken said a few years ago, "*Did you know there is still a lot of gold to be found today? It's true, experts say that only 5% of all gold has been found.*"

To be able to handle the highly mineralized ground you will be searching in, a detector with a precise ground balance circuit is essential. Some of the top-of-the-line models have circuits that can analyze the ground and automatically make the adjustments needed to provide optimum performance as conditions change. Do not discount the lower-priced models because while they may require a little more in the way of manual adjustments as they can offer detection depth and sensitivity that approaches that of their bigger brothers. Several manufacturers have recently introduced models in the $500-to-$800 range that provide performance that will more than meet the needs of many potential electronic prospectors under virtually all conditions they might come across. The one type of detector that will really not serve you well for prospecting is one with a fixed or preset ground balance since the mineralization will severely limit its performance. A detector with a true all-metal, non-motion search mode is the ideal prospecting detector as this will offer the greatest sensitivity to tiny targets and allow you to slowly scan in and amongst larger rocks where nuggets are often found. There are some models that serve dual purposes by providing a prospecting mode that meets the requirements called for above and then with the flip of a switch or click of a knob, activates a search mode that offers a full range of discrimination and acts like a detector one might use in the park, on the beach or relic hunting. While detectors that are designed to fulfill a single purpose will provide a higher level of performance for the application, if you are someone who may only get to do some prospecting a few times a year or during the cooler months, a dual purpose detector can let you hunt year round without the expense of having to purchase multiple detectors.

No matter what claims you may read or hear, there are physical limitations as to how deep gold, silver or any metallic ore can be located when size is taken into consideration. A flake-sized piece does not have sufficient mass to affect the field being transmitted by the detector's coil to any great degree and expecting to detect something that small much more than 6" to 8" is not being realistic. Larger pieces can be detected deeper with ounce+ sized pieces being detectable at depths that will often challenge you to recover them in hard-packed soil. Besides size, another factor that greatly affects the detection depth of any metal detector is the ground mineralization and moisture content. Often re-hunting a site after a soaking rain can turn up targets that would otherwise have gone undetected.

> **TIP**
>
> **Learn the Sound:** For the most part, the typical nugget you will come across is in the gram-size rather than ounce+ size. The response you will receive from a small nugget, especially if it is at any appreciable depth will be little more than a whisper or subtle change in the threshold audio level. When looking at buying a metal detector for electronic prospecting, it is strongly recommended that you bring samples of what you will be looking for to test the various detectors as the response may be vastly different among them. If the gold in your area is flake-sized, then this should be what you use to test the detectors. On the other hand, if small-to-medium nuggets are fairly common, investing in a sample or seeing if the dealer has one would make more sense. Use these samples to practice with at home so when you get out in the field, you can get the most out of your detector.

Search coil size is another factor that is extremely important to prospectors when it comes to their overall success. Since gold in many areas can be quite small, opting for an oversized coil may cover more ground with each sweep but it may also cause you to miss far more than you detect depending on the size of the gold in the area. Other forms of precious metal can fall into the same trap.

> **TIP**
>
> **Different Coils Can Make The Difference:** Getting your coil as close to the metal you are searching for as possible may seem like an obvious point to make; however, many prospectors fail to do just that. If the area you are searching is rocky, either look at moving the rocks out of the way or switch to a different coil – either smaller in size or elliptical in design. You'd be surprised at the amount of gold and other precious metal that has been found just under the surface that had been hidden by a large rock everyone simply worked around or in a narrow crevice that a conventional round coil could not fit into. Sometimes a small change can reap big rewards.

ELECTRONIC PROSPECTING TIPS & TECHNIQUES

As mentioned earlier in this chapter, there is a wealth of information – in both printed and electronic form – available on all types of prospecting and how to get the most out of the equipment currently on the market. The Reference Resource Bibliography at the end of this chapter provides some highly recommended material that can quickly improve your skill and increase what you find at the end of the day no matter what type of prospecting you are interested in.

This section will provide some tips and techniques provided by several very experienced and successful electronic prospectors that can be easily put into practice in your area.

The importance of properly ground balancing your detector can not overstated. If the adjustment is off even slightly, mineralization can adversely affect your detector's performance and good targets will be missed. If your detector has an automatic ground balancing circuit that tracks changes in the ground, be careful when sweeping back and forth over a particular spot trying to determine if you've found a target or are just hearing changes in ground conditions. An auto-tracking detector can actually see what it thinks is a change from ground mineralization and tune it out if the coil continues to be swept over the target causing the signal to disappear and you to leave the target for someone else. Very subtle changes in the threshold need to be investigated and it is often worth disabling the auto-track feature while you check the signal or move a few feet away from the target and then come back to keep the detector from tuning a valid signal out. When you start to dig a hole to recover what your detector has located, try to make the hole wide enough that the coil can be put down into it.

Sweeping the coil over the ground and then having the detector "see" empty air can cause false signals; however, keeping the coil at the same height above the ground will eliminate most of these false signals. A trick many successful detectorists use is to ground balance their detector slightly positive which means there will be a faint increase in the threshold sound as the coil is lowered to the ground. While it will require more patience and care to keep the coil at a constant height to avoid false signals, positive ground balancing will help you pick out tiny nuggets or weaker signals more clearly.

Remember the suggestion to listen to different detectors when you pass the type of target you will be searching for across the coil when buying a detector? The reason was to find one that had an audio response that you could listen to for extended periods and hear the subtle changes indicating the type of targets you were searching for. You want to run with an audible threshold and really focus on the sound listening for that slight change. Due to the subtle change in the audio that often indicates a small or deeply buried nugget, headphones are an absolute necessity when prospecting. A gust of wind, the rustle of leaves or the crunch of gravel under your boots can easily mask what could be the best find of your trip. This is where trying a pair on before you buy them is almost a must since you will be wearing them for hours at a time and an uncomfortable pair will quickly take any enjoyment you might be having away. If you spend time searching areas where snakes are prevalent, DetectorPro makes a set of headphones which only covers one ear leaving the other able to hear the warning rattle of a snake you might be coming upon. If you hunt year round, it is advisable to pick up a pair for the summer months and another for the cooler months. Refer back to the Equipment chapter for a list of headphone suppliers.

In many areas that contain placer gold, there will be pockets containing concentrations of black sand which is all that remains of mineralized rocks that at one time contained the gold itself. While not a sure fire indication that there will be gold in the area, if you are in a known gold producing region, pockets of black sand are often indicators of where heavier material has been deposited – including gold, silver or copper. Even the best detector available will not hit a flake sized nugget at 18" but black sand is readily detectable by locking the ground balance setting and running the threshold a bit higher than you would normally have it. Passing over a pocket of black sand will cause the threshold to decrease or disappear altogether which alerts you to investigate the area further. Remove layers of the dirt and rescan the area every few inches. As you approach bedrock, you are more likely to start to detect actual nuggets that were initially beyond the detection range of your detector. The gold found throughout the southeast is typically flake sized and very hard to pick up with a metal detector unless the coil gets quite close to it. Many of the prospectors I know who search in the Carolinas, Georgia and Alabama seek out areas containing black sand along the creeks and do quite well working those discrete spots with a combination of gold pans, sluice boxes, dredges and metal detectors.

If you are searching an area where there are tiny pieces of gold along with small pieces of trash such as lead shotgun pellets, tacks, nails and minute scraps of non-ferrous metal, don't waste valuable hunting time looking for every little piece of metal you come across. As you remove dirt from the hole, either pass a handful of dirt over the coil (remember, it detects from both sides) or use a plastic hand shovel in the same manner. Once you have it out of the hole, put the small amount of dirt in a bucket or similar container and go through it later when you are back at home or the campsite. Remember, it all comes back to simple math and your overall success will be driven by how many targets you recover per hour. Taking 15 minutes to find a miniscule piece of metal – gold or not – will take away from the time you have to find the next target which may just be that $1,000,000 find. This photo shows just how small some of the gold people are finding with their detectors can be so think of how best to maximize searching time while minimizing recovery time.

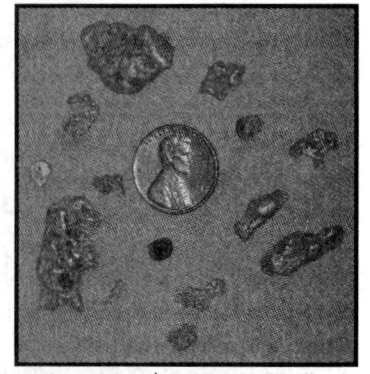

Most prospectors always carry a small, powerful magnet with them to quickly remove a tiny piece of rusted metal that is often virtually impossible to see. The Reference section in the Beach & Shallow Water Hunting chapter provides some excellent suppliers of magnets to fit anyone's needs.

PROSPECTING CLUBS, ASSOCIATIONS & GROUPS

Prospecting is not all that difficult but it is truly a form of treasure hunting that is much easier to master when you have someone who knows what they are doing showing you rather than trying to read a book and interpret what the author means. There are a number of videos available that can help you learn the tricks of the trade but getting involved with one of the prospecting clubs, associations or groups that exist is invaluable and will make your time in the field far more enjoyable (and profitable). Many of the larger groups offer the added benefit of having property available for you to prospect on at no additional charge. Without owning land yourself, it is often quite difficult to find productive ground to search without finding yourself at the business end of a rifle or spending time chatting with the local police department. Having immediate access to hundreds of acres that have been proven to contain gold and other precious metals removes one of the challenges to being successful which is finding the right place to search. These groups also offer workshops and group outings where you can learn the correct way to use a wide range of equipment in a short period of time. The Reference Resource Bibliography that follows contains several well-established and well-respected groups that can help you get into prospecting no matter what type you might be interested in exploring.

REFERENCE RESOURCE BIBLIOGRAPHY

Books

- **Advanced Dredging Techniques Volume 2, Parts 1 and 2** by Dave McCracken
- **Diving and Dredging for Gold** by Dick Anderson
- **Finding Gold Nuggets II** by Jimmy "Sierra" Normandi
- **Gold Panning is Easy** by Roy Lagal
- **Gold Mining in the 21st Century** by Dave McCracken
- **Gold Prospectors Handbook** by Jack Black
- **Modern Prospecting, How to Find, Claim and Sell Mineral Deposits** by Roger McPherson
- **Modern Electronic Prospecting** by Charles Garrett and Roy Lagal
- **Recreational Gold Prospecting for Fun and Profit** by Gail Butler
- **Rocks from Space** by O. Richard Norton
- **The Modern Goldseekers Manual** by Tom Bryant
- **You Can Find Gold With A Metal Detector** by Charles Garrett & Roy Lagal

Magazines

- **Alaska Mining eMagazine**; Free on-line resource; http://www.alaskamining.com/
- **Gold Prospectors Magazine**; http://www.GoldProspectors.org
- **ICMJ's Prospecting & Mining Journal;** http://www.icmj.com
- **Miners News**; http://www.MinersNews.com

Videos

- **Chris Gholson's Nugget Hunting Essentials – Volume 1 & 2** (http://www.arizonaoutback.com/)
- **Gold Panning is Easy** by Garrett Video Productions
- **Gold Nugget Prospecting – Metal Detecting with the Pros** by Larry Sallee, Bob Gutowski, Floyd Allen and Glen Anderson
- **Jack Lange's Nugget Finding Secrets #1, #2, #3 & #4** by Jack Lange
- **Modern Gold Mining Techniques** by Dave McCraken
- **Prospecting for Gold** by Roy Roush
- **Successful Gold Dredging Made Easy** by Dave McCraken
- **Sure-Fire Gold Panning Methods** by GPAA

Maps

- **AZ-Gold Maps**: (maps showing gold & meteorite locations in Arizona & California) http://www.az-gold.com
- **Big Ten, Inc.**, Maps showing where gold has been found in most gold-bearing states + sites that could hold relics & coins dating back 100 years or more. (321) 783-4595   http://goldmaps.com

Equipment

- **Camel Mining Products**: (Automatic gold panning machines) (800) 331-5311; http://www.Desfox.com
- **Century Mining Equipment**, (Spiral gold recovery system) (800) 458-8889; http://www.GoldMagic.com
- **Dahlke Dredge Mfg.**: (Dredges ranging from 2.5" to 6") (509) 839-4444; http://dahlkedredge.com/
- **Dalyn Enterprises**: (Gold VAC dredges); (402) 736-4455; http://www.dalynenterprises.com/goldvac.html
- **Gold Screw, Inc.**: (Gold panning machines) (800) 835-4653; http://www.GoldScrew.com
- **Keene Engineering**: (Complete line of mining equipment) (800) 392-4653; http://www.Keeneeng.com
- **Proline Mining Company**: (Dredges & high bankers); (209) 878-3770; http://www.prolinemining.com/

Internet Resources

- **Nugget Hunting Forum:** Excellent source of information; http://www.nuggethunting.com/forums/
- **The Gold Miners Headquarters**, Dedicated to the small scale & recreational miner; http://www.goldminershq.com
- **The Treasure Hunter Forum, Prospecting & Nuggetshooting**: http://www.treasurehunterforum.com/forum20/
- **TreasureNet – Gold Prospecting Forum:** http://forum.treasurenet.com/index.php/board,33.0.html
- **TreasureNet – Meteorite Forum**: http://forum.treasurenet.com/index.php/board,27.0.html
- **The Prospector's Cache**: Forums, classifieds, how-to info and more; http://www.tomashworth.com/
- **The Treasure Depot – Prospecting Forum**: http://www.thetreasuredepot.com/cgi-bin/gold/prospecting_config.pl
- **Gold Mining Links**: A wealth of links to useful and informative prospecting-related websites; http://goldmining.tripod.com/goldlinks.html

Mining Clubs & Groups

- **Arizona Association of Gold Miners**: Providing access to prime sites in Arizona's "golden triangle" along with planned outings, lessons and more; http://www.arizonagoldprospectors.org/
- **Gold Prospectors Association of America**; Premier nationwide gold prospector organization offering access to 1,000's of acres for prospecting. The Lost Dutchman's Mining Association is a sub-organization that offers additional properties and benefits; http://www.goldprospectors.org/
- **The New 49'ers**: Founded by legendary prospector Dave McCracken, this organization offers access to high-grade gold mining sites as well as equipment and training; http://www.goldgold.com/
- **Washington Prospectors Mining Association**: Providing access to sites in California, Washington & Oregon along with workshops and group outings; http://www.washingtonprospectors.org/
- **Weekend Gold Miners**; One of the few prospecting clubs on the east coast with acres of properties available for members to use, located in the heart of the Georgia gold belt; http://www.weekendgoldminers.com/

CACHE HUNTING

Cache hunting is a form of treasure hunting that many of us have dreamt about yet very few actually take the next step and engage in. A big factor contributing to that "lack of action" is that most treasure hunters have a misconception of what a cache is and as a result, do not know how to get started in finding one. Hopefully you will see that there are literally 1,000's of caches - many of them quite near your home - still waiting for an astute treasure hunter to recover.

Let's start out with the definition of a cache. If you ask 100 treasure hunters what constitutes a cache you'll probably get 150 different answers; however, most will say a cache consists of hidden valuables amounting to $10,000's or more . . . a bank robber's loot, Spanish gold or prospectors hoard for example. I say this based on having given presentations on cache hunting at a number of clubs across the United States and these are the answers I typically get when I ask that question. The most basic definition of a cache – which applies to what we as treasure hunters will be looking for - is simply *"something that someone has hidden from others and has value to the person who hid it"* . . . and nothing more! So while a cache can consist of the high-value items listed above, it can also be as small as a child's baseball card collection secreted away decades ago, a wife's "milk money" stashed behind a cabinet or a jar of coins placed in the rafters above a basement workshop. When I was growing up in New York, my brother and I played pirates one summer and buried "treasure" in the form of a canning jar borrowed from my mother filled with what we felt was valuable at the time. A few coins (silver), colored rocks, a lucky key chain, Tootsie Toy cars, metal Cracker Jack prizes and a few other items went into the jar which was buried in the woods near the house. We even made a treasure map to find it again. Well, we grew up and moved away, forgetting the hidden treasure. A few years ago I was in the area and even without the map, was able to go back to the site and with the help of my detector, recovered the treasure chest buried decades earlier. No real value but to me it was priceless. The example to be made is that there are countless of other caches that have been hidden by all sorts of people over the years that have never been recovered.

The late Bill Mahan, founder of the now-defunct D-Tex Electronics and an extremely successful treasure hunter in his own right, was an avid cache hunter. A primer that he penned nearly 40 years ago was entitled "*I Find The Little Treasures*" and is a booklet I have found myself referring to many times over the years since receiving it from him at a show in 1971. He said that it was far more profitable and far less frustrating to spend one's time searching for and finding smaller caches than spending a small fortune and years looking for the legendary hoards that may have already been found or possibly never hidden in the first place. Another statement which has been proven true time and time again since he made it is that nearly 1 in 5 homes has a cache of some form hidden in or around it.

So focus on the small caches that can be found anywhere people have been. Who hides caches? Some of the groups include:

- **Housewives**: This group is probably the largest contributor to hidden caches awaiting treasure hunters. Whether the wife of a farmer in the country or a businessman in the city, women are notorious for squirreling away spare change or loose bills for a "rainy day" that in many cases never came.
- **Farmers**: Most farmers would keep some of their savings secreted around the farm for next year's seeds or other expenses. Before banks were federally insured, a failure or robbery of the bank would wipe out all of their depositors and farmers were a big part of that group in rural banks.
- **Business Owners**: Much like farmers in the country, business owners would keep money around in urban settings again, since bank deposits were not insured.

- **Gamblers**: Gamblers are notorious cachers. Often, if they would win a sizable amount, they would hide some or all of their winnings on the way home (or in the garage when they got home) to keep their spouses from finding about their windfall.
- **Criminals**: While not a group you want to interact with, criminals have been hiding cash and other valuables almost as long as their "trade" has been in existence. With banks not being an option in most cases, hiding it was the only option other than carrying it on them which was not a desired practice.

Whenever I give talks on cache hunting at clubs or shows, the first question I get asked once I go over the aforementioned group of "cachers" is *"Why would these caches still be there decades after they were hidden?"* Well, illnesses, sudden death or simply forgetting about the cache are all factors that combined with the secrecy of hiding it in the first place contribute to so many caches remaining. If a gangster was killed in a gunfight, the location of all of his hidden caches would go to the grave with him. Similarly, if a farmer died due to a farming accident or a business owner was killed in a car accident on the way to a meeting, their heirs or partners would never even know about the hidden wealth they left behind. When looking for leads to possible caches, searching the obituaries in newspapers dating back 100 years or so can produce surprising results. A number of years ago I was looking through some papers in the archives of newspapers from the late 1800's. This story in the obituary section dated October 25, 1898 caught my eye for good reason. My immediate thought was if people had found $1,750 in coins around Mr. Umholtz's house in 1898, what had they missed that might have been hidden just underground. It took a little bit of research to find the actual location of the old Umholtz farm, but thanks to some census records and old county maps, it wasn't long before my partners and I arrived at the site of where the house had once stood. We spent some time talking to the farmer who owned all of the land in the surrounding area and after looking over the maps we had, told us where he thought the foundation of the old house was located. With permission granted, we hiked into the area, found the foundation and laid out a grid using string. In less than an hour a small container was recovered and from the weight, we had high hopes. Not to be disappointed, it contained just over $400 with more than half being $5 and $10 gold pieces.

> **HIDDEN GOLD**
>
> Since the funeral of William Unholtz, an aged resident of near Columbia who was killed when kicked by one of his mules in the barn, $1,750, mostly in gold coins, has been found about his home in out-of-the-way places. Of this amount, $1,000 in gold was found in an old crock covered with timothy weed beneath the rear steps of his home. Mr. Unholtz had been reported to be in financial need at the time of his death.

Forgetting where one hid a cache seems highly unlikely but it happens more often than you might think. A few years ago, well-known treasure hunters Mike Scott, the late Wayne Otto and Scott Warner were contacted to see if they could find several containers of silver coins that had been buried by a family member some 30 years earlier. The house was being sold and the family wanted to see if they could be located and recovered. Well, the containers turned out to be milk cans buried more than 5 feet deep containing more than 1,000 pounds of silver coins! Not that caches of this size are waiting on every corner but they do exist and are more common than you might think. If the cache has been well hidden it could remain undetected for decades or longer if undisturbed. Many caches have been found accidentally when homes have been renovated or property graded for a new project.

Now that you can see that countless caches have been hidden and subsequently forgotten over the years by a wide range of people, the next question that will probably have is *"What do these caches consist of?"* Remember the beginning of this chapter? These caches are **NOT** truckloads of cash, coins or gold bars. They usually consist of coins or paper money with a face value of $100 or less. Yes, many will be several times that but remember that a cache hidden 50+ years ago will contain coins worth many, many times their face value to collectors. Two years ago a friend of mine found a small jar hidden behind a false panel in the cupboard of an old house in eastern Oregon that contained nothing but pennies, nickels and a few dimes. The face value of the cache was just under $20 but more than half the pennies were Indian Heads and all of the nickels were either V's or

Buffalos. One of the Indian Head's was dated 1908-S and based on its excellent condition, was worth $150 adding to the cache's actual value being more than $300! My wife had a similar experience in the late 90's when we were living near Atlanta. Hunting around a long-abandoned sharecroppers shack, she hit a signal near the porch post (which was facing away from the road but more about selecting where to search later). From about 8" down, she retrieved a jar filled with coins – again, all small denomination but their age made the cache quite valuable.

The type of caches you should be focusing on can range from a few coins or bills up to several hundred dollars. While there are larger caches waiting to be found, you will find far more smaller ones than larger ones and by having a larger population of targets, your odds will improve in terms of recovering one (or more).

So far we have discussed who hides caches and what an average cache you should be focusing on might contain. Now we need to look at where you might find these caches; i.e., inside or outside or structure, the type of structure, buried or not, the type of container, etc.

When it comes to location, there's a saying among successful cache hunters that "*There's not a single cache location that has not been used by many other hoarders before.*" People stashing valuables will spend hours pondering over a location that no one has ever thought of and what they come up with is probably simply #14 on the list of the top 100 cache hiding spots. The late Jim Warnke published an excellent book on the subject of cache hunting entitled simply "*Search!*" The book contains dozens of documented hiding locations that Jim identified over the years he spent caching hunting and what he found was that the consistency of their use was universal wherever he found himself. Based on feedback received from other cache hunters across the country, they were used elsewhere as well. If you have an interest in trying your hand at cache hunting, I highly recommend picking up a copy of Jim's book along with those listed in the reference section as they will put you ahead of the competition that might be trying it haphazardly.

Caches can be found both inside and outside of a structure. There are many possible hiding locations so trying to provide a comprehensive list here would be an effort in futility. However, there are a few simple guidelines that have proven themselves over the decades by cache hunters around the world which can help you zero in on the most likely locations caches might be found.

- Outdoor caches would never be hidden in plain view of a road passing by the property or a neighbor. Someone planning to hide valuables would not want to be observed either placing the cache or retrieving it. If you are scoping out a potential site, start out by crossing off those areas that are directly visible by passer-bys or inquisitive neighbors.
- With few exceptions, most caches will not be buried very deep. A person hiding a cache would want to be done with the task as quickly as possible. Digging a large hole and then covering it up and hiding signs of the excavation under the cover of darkness precluded digging more than a foot or so.
- The person would have wanted to be able to find the cache quickly and would not have had the advantage of a metal detector to help them do so. Start searching areas near large trees, rocks or wells, beneath tree limbs that appear to have odd scars cut into them or nails driven into the bottom, or mid-way between landmarks such as the house & barn, the house & chicken coop or the house & well.

Try and put yourself in the mind of the person that initially hid the valuables you are hoping to find . . . people tend to think alike and you may be surprised at how easy it actually is to find one of these smaller caches.

> ⚠ **GET PERMISSION!** An important point to remember is that no matter how dilapidated a structure may appear, permission from the property owner should be obtained before entering and it should be left in the same condition you found it in. Do not interpret permission to search it as permission to destroy it!

CACHE HUNTING EQUIPMENT

A specialized piece of equipment that is well suited for searching for caches buried outside of a structure is the two-box detector. These are well suited for cache hunting due to the depth at which they can locate targets, the amount of ground they can cover in a short period of time and by their nature, tend to ignore smaller targets such as individual coins, pull tabs, nails and other unwanted items. Two-box detectors operate on the same principle as conventional metal detectors; however, as the name implies, the transmit-and-receive coils are contained in separate boxes which are connected by a long center rod. You simply walk in a straight line keeping the two boxes parallel to the ground. By walking a grid pattern, you can quickly cover an area and ensure you have not missed any target of interest. There are several models of two-box detectors currently on the market including an innovative attachment for the Garrett GTI 2500 which allows you to connect an assembly consisting of a pair of coils and convert the standard detector to a two-box unit.

Another piece of equipment that has proven to be invaluable to cache hunters who search the interiors of structures is a hand held detector or even a pinpoint probe. These can easily locate valuables hidden behind walls or under flooring and are very simple to operate. Look at the offerings from many of the manufacturers and if the company has a separate security division, they may have a hand held unit under that banner that will meet your needs.

Conventional metal detectors work for both inside and outside searches; however, you need to be aware of what types of targets you will be picking up in addition to caches. Opting for a smaller coil when searching inside or a larger coil held off the ground 6" or so to avoid picking up smaller, unwanted targets are options to consider.

> ⚠ **THINK ABOUT SIGNALS YOU RECEIVE** If you search inside a building and use a metal detector, think about the signals you receive before tearing into the structure expecting to find instant wealth. Check the opposite side of the wall, floor or ceiling to make sure there is no electrical box, switch, pipe or outlet. If the structure is not completely abandoned, make sure that you don't cut into a live power cable as you try to uncover what you've detected.

REFERENCE RESOURCE BIBLIOGRAPHY

Books

- **Cache Hunting Volumes I & II** by Glenn Carson
- **SEARCH!** By James Warnke
- **The Successful Cache Hunter's Handbook** by Robert Katt
- **Treasure Caches Can be Found** by Charles Garrett

Internet Resources

- **TreasureNet – Cache Hunting Forum**: http://forum.treasurenet.com/index.php/board,3.0.html

COMPETITION HUNTING

Competition Hunts or Rallies as they are known in Europe have been a unique part of the treasure hunting community for more than 40 years. Despite their longevity in the hobby, there are many detectorists who have never attended one. Others may have never returned based on their initial experience. These events are not for everyone but they are a whole lot more enjoyable when you come home with a pocketful of collectible coins, accessories, gift certificates or even a new metal detector. The purpose of this chapter is to provide you with some tips & techniques that have been proven to boost your success at a hunt if you decide to check one out.

Before we jump into the "nuts-and-bolts" of how to get the most out of participating in a hunt, let's take a minute and make sure we all have a good understanding of exactly what a hunt or rally entails. Most hunts are either a one-day or two-day event with a few larger ones taking place over a period of up to a week. Attendance can range from 30 entrants for a local club hunt to several hundred at the larger events. The hunt can be set up as either a seeded event where coins and tokens are buried by the organizers, or one at a site that contains coins and relics lost decades or even centuries ago. This chapter will focus on the seeded or planted hunts since the techniques used in the non-seeded hunts will be similar to those covered in the Relic Hunting chapter.

Depending on the number of entrants, the organizers will be burying upwards of 5,000 coins per day, and in some hunts, considerably more. For hunts in the U.S., these coins will usually include an assortment of silver coins such as Roosevelt dimes, Mercury dimes, Standing Liberty quarters, half dollars and silver dollars, copper coins such as wheat cents, Indian Head cents and even an occasional large cent, nickels, and prize tokens. This photo shows what you might bring home after a successful day at an organized seeded hunt.

The way each event unfolds throughout the hunt is quite similar. All of the contestants line up on the perimeter of the hunt field containing the planted targets. When the signal is given, the hunters begin to scour the field in an attempt to recover as many targets as possible within the allotted time which ranges from 30 to 60 minutes. There are a few tips that can help make anyone more successful in these events and while some might appear to be common knowledge, you'll be surprised at how often a small handful of hunters wind up with the vast majority of the goodies buried on the field.

My son Paul internalized these techniques at an early age opting to compete in the adult hunts from when he was 10 years old. He often finished in the top 5 in terms of coins and tokens recovered, leaving many hunters shaking their heads as he made trip after trip to the prize table! While luck does come into play since your coil has to pass over a coin or token, Paul learned the secrets that allowed him to consistently find more in less time than the vast majority of those he competed against.

TIPS FOR SUCCESS IN AN ORGANIZED HUNT

In soliciting input from competition hunters worldwide, there are a few tips and techniques that are common to most successful hunters and they are listed here to help you

- **Don't sweat the deep stuff:** Remember that the organizers have to bury every one of the targets. Do you think that even with several people helping with special tools that the targets will be buried more than an inch or two beneath the surface? Think SHALLOW! You'll be surprised to see how many hunters have holes 6+ inches deep in search of a target. There is definitely something there but whatever it is, it was not buried as part of the hunt . . . you can always come back later to see what it is. Don't worry about those deep signals! Run with the sensitivity set no higher than mid-level to reduce the response to deeper, non-planted targets and minimize the interference from nearby detectors

- **Time is of the essence in an organized hunt . . . PRACTICE!:** Most of the targets are recovered within the first 30 minutes or so. When you get a signal, being able to recover that target and then get back up and find the next one will be the key to your overall success. Again, it's a matter of math! The less time it takes you to detect and recover a target, the more targets you will have at the end of each hunt. Your ability to quickly pinpoint the targets you've detected will be critical to how many targets you recover during the hunt. What many seasoned hunters find is that pinpointing a newly buried coin just under the surface is often a lot more challenging than finding a silver dime at 10" that's been there for 100 years, especially with a Double-D coil. Before you send in that entry fee and make your travel arrangements, hit your backyard or the local park and have a friend bury a handful of coins to practice pinpointing. Use a knife, cut a slit in the grass at an angle and drop a coin in the slit. Then spend some time practicing until you can consistently put your finger on top of (or at the very least, extremely close to) each coin and be able to do it quickly. Once you have the technique down, you will find your coin count will go up dramatically in any hunt you enter

- **Specialized gear can tip the scales in your favor:** Hunting styles in these events differ greatly from how you search a park, battlefield or ghost town. As we've said, speed is critical in recovering targets. The faster you can find and recover a target you have detected the faster you can be off finding the next one. When you are in a hunt held on a field, look at using one of the electronic probes like those covered in the *Target Recovery – Remember the Math* chapter. The one word of caution is get proficient in its use BEFORE going to your 1st hunt as even a few seconds wasted trying to figure out a new piece of equipment can cost you that grand prize token or other valuable target. Remember, none of the planted targets should be any deeper than one of these probes can detect. If the hunt is being held on a beach or sandy area such as some in the desert are, plan on using a light weight but solidly built hand scoop and what is known as a hipmounted sand sifter to maximize the number of targets you recover in the hunt window. By quickly taking a scoop of sand and dumping it into the sifter, you can be moving onto the next target while the sand passes back to the ground without you needing to shake the scoop and pick each target out. Suppliers of these sifters are provided in the Reference Resource Bibliography section at the end of this chapter.

- **Know what you are looking for:** In virtually any hunt you enter, you will know beforehand what type of targets have been buried. One hunt might be only silver dimes while another may be old coins including Buffalo nickels, wheat cents and silver. Other hunts may include prize tokens, the composition of which may or may not have been disclosed. The point here is that you need to use the capabilities of your detector to your advantage. By adjusting the discrimination levels depending on the type of target(s) hidden on the field, you can get an edge over most of your competition that will set their detector for little or no discrimination and get bogged down digging trash.

"CHERRY-PICKING" THE FIELD IN A COMPETITION HUNT

This section is one that some purists might feel gives hunt participants with programmable detectors such as the Minelab Explorer and E-Trac or, White's XLT, DFX and Spectra V3 an unfair advantage. I won't deny that there is some truth to that concern. However, if you own a detector that has those capabilities, shouldn't you be allowed to use them? Some organized hunts have started to bury items that are typically viewed as trash such as screw caps or pull tabs with numbers stenciled onto them designating them as prize tokens as a way of discouraging selective target recovery. A few questions up front can tell you if you might need to be a bit less choosey in what you recover.

Okay, it's up to you whether or not you want to set your detector to be able to "cherry pick" the field in a seeded hunt but if you are one that wants to give it a try, let's continue. In seeded hunts, the organizers will have planted a number of targets which are typically listed on the hunt flyer and include items such as silver coins, old pennies, prize tokens and the like.

A section of a typical hunt flyer is shown below that lists what types of targets will be buried for each event.

Lone Star Treasure Hunters Club
35th Annual Open Hunt
October 17th 2009

8:15-9:15 Registration	1:00-1:30 Silver Quarter/Half Hunt
9:30-10:00 DOLLAR HUNT	1:45-2:00 Fundraiser Hunt
10:30-11:00 21 HUNT	2:00-3:15 Cake Auction
11:30-12:00 ALL DETECTORS HUNT	3:30-4:15 Main Hunt
12:00-1:00 Lunch	4:30 Prizes Awarded

Review the signs or flyers that describe what type of targets will be buried in each hunt of the day. If you know your detector, it is usually quite simple to program it and create custom patterns that will accept only the type of targets that have been hidden. Take a few minutes and program it for each hunt before each event or quickly alter a base program between hunts.

The only unknown can be what the prize tokens will be so it is worth asking the hunt organizers if they can or will provide you with that information.

THE HUNT "EXPERIENCE"

If you have never experienced the feeling of being in the midst of 100+ hunters all running around like madmen to find targets in a short period of time, you owe it to yourself to attend at least one organized hunt and see things in action.

One of the first things you need to realize is that while the thrill of digging up silver and gold coins along with prize tokens is a definite reason to attend an organized competition hunt, it should not be the ONLY reason you decide to attend one. Many people have said they felt "cheated" when they finished the day with less in terms of coins and prizes than what they paid in entry fees. It's true that almost every club or group that puts on an organized hunt returns close to 100% of the entry fees collected with coins buried on the hunt field and prizes awarded throughout the day. In addition, manufacturers and dealers often provide additional prizes for free or at greatly reduced prices which further drives up the value of what attendees can take home. Still not everyone who enters can be the big winner in terms of finding dozens of silver coins or winning a new metal detector. A lot depends on luck as you can win a top prize by finding a single token while someone finding 20 tokens may only win a few accessories, books or other smaller prizes.

What you should consider are the other benefits you receive by attending an organized hunt which include:

- **Improving your treasure hunting skills**: In many cases, dealers and other experienced treasure hunters will be available at the hunt site to answer questions and possibly conduct informative seminars, These sessions are free and you can usually pick up several ideas or tips that can immediately be put to use to improve your success in the field regardless of the type of treasure hunting you might be involved in. What would it be worth if you learned how to get another few inches out of your detector or do a better job of discriminating out certain types of trash targets? Even if you did not find anything in the hunt you'd be ahead of the game in terms of future finds!

- **Meeting fellow treasure hunters**: One thing I've found is that when you get together with a bunch of other treasure hunters, everyone learns something from each other. Even if you're a seasoned veteran, a novice will often have a new or different perspective on certain subjects that may just open a whole new area for you to search. These events make great places to find a new treasure hunting partner as well. You'll find that the friendly competition between two friends spurs each one to hunt just a little harder which often means better finds for both at the end of the day.

- **Picking up some new equipment**: Most hunts have displays from local dealers and manufacturers for attendees to browse through. You can usually get a good deal on a new detector or that accessory you've been looking for, often saving you more than what you paid in entry fees.

So, while finding the winning prize token or a pocketful of coins should be in the back of your mind when you head out on the hunt field, think about the other benefits you get from attending organized hunts. There's only one thing you should be aware of - more than one treasure hunter has gotten hooked after attending their first organized hunt and can be found traveling 100's of miles from hunt to hunt throughout the year. As discussed in this chapter, developing the correct techniques is essential to ensure you are successful. Spend a little time practicing your pinpointing and recovery skills, send in your entry fee and most importantly, plan to have fun!

REFERENCE RESOURCE BIBLIOGRAPHY

Books

- **Competitive Treasure Hunting** by Jack Lowery: If you want to be successful in an organized hunt, this is the only book you need!

Competition-Hunt Equipment

- **Jay's Cache**: Frequency shifter that changes the frequency of your detector to eliminate interference from nearby detectors); P.O. Box 472531, Garland, TX 75047 or jayscache@juno.com
- **Reilly's Treasured Gold:** Hipmounted beach hunt sifter & scoops; 2003 West McNab Rd. #10, Pompano Beach, Fl. 33069, (954) 971-6102, http://rtgstore.com/
- **Kellyco Metal Detector Superstore**: Sand scoops, baskets and probes, (888) 535-5926, 1085 Belle Ave., Winter Springs, Florida 32708, http://www.kellycodetectors.com/accessories/detectoraccessories.htm

Internet Resources

The following websites contain schedules of upcoming competition hunts or rallies – check them out to see if there are any planned for your area or plan a vacation, meet new friends and pick up some tips!

- **Federation of Metal Detector and Archeological Clubs**; http://fmdac.org
- **Lost Treasure Magazine**; http://www.losttreasure.com
- **Metal Detecting Rallies in the United Kingdom**: http://www.detecting.org.uk/html/Metal_Detecting_Rallies_In_The_United_Kingdom.html
- **The National Council for Metal Detecting**; http://www.ncmd.co.uk
- **TreasureNet Event Directory:** http://forum.treasurenet.com/index.php/board,42.0.html

BOTTLE HUNTING

While bottle hunting could take up an entire book all by itself, this chapter will cover the basics and provide a few twists not found in other books. The popularity of this form of treasure hunting has cycled over the years with the real peak taking place in the late 1960's and early 1970's. Growing up, one of our neighbors was an avid bottle hunter and I remember being invited to accompany him on several digs at nearby foundation sites recovering bottles and other items from dump sites dating back 150 years or more. While the overall popularity may have waned a little, there are still many avid bottle collectors spending their time locating old dump sites and recovering beautiful and valuable bottles around the world.

Bottles and glassware in general have been in circulation for 100's of years which affords today's bottle hunters with countless specimens to search for and collect. The added bonus to bottle hunting is that areas where bottles are fond often contain other artifacts including coins, jewelry, tokens, tools, porcelain, household utensils and more. So even if you are only moderately interested in bottles, you can usually find enough other items to keep your interest high.

BOTTLE HUNTING BASICS

The thing to keep in mind is that when the bottles were originally used, they were considered trash when they were empty and discarded without a second thought. What you will be looking for will be sites where trash was dumped in years past. Larger cites had formal dumps such as they do today, but what you want to find are the smaller undocumented dumps that were used by single families, a small group of homes or a community that may have been swallowed up by urban sprawl. Another site that is a veritable goldmine despite what the name might imply is an old outhouse or privy as they are commonly called. Don't worry, any objectionable material will have long since decayed away leaving little but dirt and artifacts for you to recover.

So where do you start looking for sites that might contain old bottles, glassware and the like? Well, you need to find sites that would have been in use when the bottles you are hoping to find were in use. While collecting all types of bottles may be the way you start out, after your garage starts to overflow with boxes of bottles you've brought home, you will probably start to specialize and focus on one or two specific types or styles. Many bottle diggers who find themselves in this situation trade unwanted bottles or duplicates to continue building their collection focusing on a particular style, vintage or locale.

One of the best ways to find bottle digging sites when you are starting out is to let your friends know about your interest. Ask them if they own a house that dates back 100 years or more, have property where an old house once stood or know others who have property that fits this criteria. Revisit the chapter on Research and you will quickly find sites that will keep you busy for months or longer. One of the ways that I've found a number of pre-1900 dump sites is to mention what I'm looking for to hunters or fishermen and offer them a store credit at a local outdoor store if they provide me with a lead that I can gain access to. A common site for old dumps was along a creek or river and they are often readily visible by people passing by with a canoe or kayak. Some of the best sites I've worked over the years have been accessible only by boat and had never been searched before.

Once you have identified a site that is worth searching for a possible outhouse / privy or dump location, getting permission is often the hardest part of the hunt. The General Treasure Hunting chapter provided several techniques to gain access to private sites and they can be used for bottle hunting just as easily as searching the grounds with a metal detector. Since you will be digging – and often fairly deep – make sure you stress that you will leave the property in the same condition you found it in. You may have to come back once or twice to refill holes that have settled but it will be worth it in the long run if you want to receive permission to other sites in the area and use the first ones as references. Offering the property owner some of the bottles and other items you might recover often helps break the ice and get permission . . . although many times the owner will say thanks for the offer and decline anything you find. Remember, even if you have to give a portion of what you find, 50% of something is better than 100% of nothing.

As you scout out potential sites to dig for bottles, keep an eye out for signs of old buildings long since gone, indentations around abandoned structures, or piles of debris indicating what might be an old dump. Depressions in the ground that do not look natural may indicate a well or outhouse that was filled in when no longer used, often with trash, and has subsequently settled.

Scouting along creeks and tributaries to larger rivers downstream of villages and settlements is another way to locate bottles that may have been washed out of the bank and deposited along the shoreline. Brian Phillips, an avid bottle hunter from Painesville, OH has recovered several fairly valuable bottles dating back to the mid-1800's in just that manner.

Once you have a site that warrants additional attention, a bottle probe should be used to define the perimeter of the area you plan on excavating. Unless the dig is going to be very shallow, you should taper the sides out so that any potential for a cave-in is eliminated. Until you get additional experience in bottle digging, limit the depth of any hole you are digging for this reason. The tools you will use for actually digging to where the bottles will be will vary depending on the type of soil you are working in, how compacted the soil is and how much time you have to complete the excavation.

When you get into the layer containing bottles and other items, continue digging until you don't find any further evidence of manmade items. The soil will usually change color when you hit that spot indicating undisturbed dirt. Carefully rake the dirt off the sides of the hole looking for bottles as you go. When you find a bottle – even if you cannot tell if it is intact – work under the assumption that it is. Carefully dig around the bottle and try not to touch it with your digging tool as even a slight tap can crack something that has been buried for many years. When you remove the dirt from the hole make sure you don't pile it where you will need to move it later if you have to expand the excavation. There's nothing more frustrating than moving the dirt time and time again over the course of a dig. Keep your eye out for loose rocks, bricks or stones as you expand the hole. On more than one occasion a rock has come free breaking what would have been the best find of the day. Be careful when you toss a rock out of the hole so that it does not roll back and hit you or something you are working to dig free in the hole.

> **SAFETY!** Never dig alone! Always tell someone where you'll be hunting or digging. Carry a phone with you, if possible. A small first aid kit should be packed and can come in handy. While digging, never tunnel or leave overhanging dirt or debris. Always dig straight down and use caution. Insects can cause injury - bees, spiders and ants have been a set back in many of my digs. Digging in city areas or bad neighborhoods poses different hazards, such as mugging and robbery – be aware of your surroundings! **Rick 'Meech' Burchfield, Virginia**

UNDERWATER BOTTLE HUNTING

As the Underwater Treasure Hunting chapter discussed, bottle collectors have started combining their passion in bottles with diving to reach bottles that might otherwise have gone undisturbed for years. In the colder areas of the world, trash including bottles and other glassware was often placed on the ice in the winter and allowed to sink to the bottom when the spring thaw came through. Other productive sites include popular piers – especially those no longer standing – where patrons tossed empty bottles into the water, steamboat landings, the water off the shore of hotels, motels, parks and the like. Littering is not a new issue . . . the only thing to note is that the older trash has become valuable as collectibles and worth seeking out. Even diving out in front of older homes built along the water can turn up beer, soda and medicine bottles that can be worth a small fortune to collectors. If you happen to come across a wreck on the bottom, bottles and other artifacts are often hidden just under the sand. The photo here shows Captain Dan Berg and fellow diver, Jimmy Faz, with a collection of old bottles recovered from the sand surrounding the wreck of the Oregon in the waters of New York's Long Island Sound.

The one problem many of us have found is that once you start finding some of these colorful treasures, you tend to start a collection of your own and are not willing to part with what you bring home. On more than one occasion I've gotten the comment that I'm bringing home stuff that others threw out decades before me . . . and they did so for a reason! But the finds still hold a prominent position throughout the house and I can relate the story behind virtually every one.

A PROVEN TECHNIQUE TO FIND PRODUCTIVE DIGGING LOCATIONS

How would you like to have a map that pinpointed the location of possible bottle digging locations in virtually every town and city across the country? Well, there is a collection of maps that will do just that called Sanborn Maps. Remember the Maps section of the Research chapter? The following figure shows a sample map from the Sanborn collection and annotates the location of an outhouse associated with the structure on the lot. Since the maps were drawn to exacting standards, the precise locations of features such as outhouses, garages, barns and the like can be easily transferred to current maps using the various techniques covered throughout this book. Once you know a well, privy or other likely site exists, it's a simple matter of trying to get permission to locate the area and excavate it. Many successful bottle hunters have used these maps to find untouched locations containing literally boxes of beautiful specimens . . . often just a short distance from their homes. Keep your eyes open for entire sections of towns or cites that may be slated for renovation as you might be able to search a dozen or more lots that are being cleared without the need to ask for permission from individual property owners.

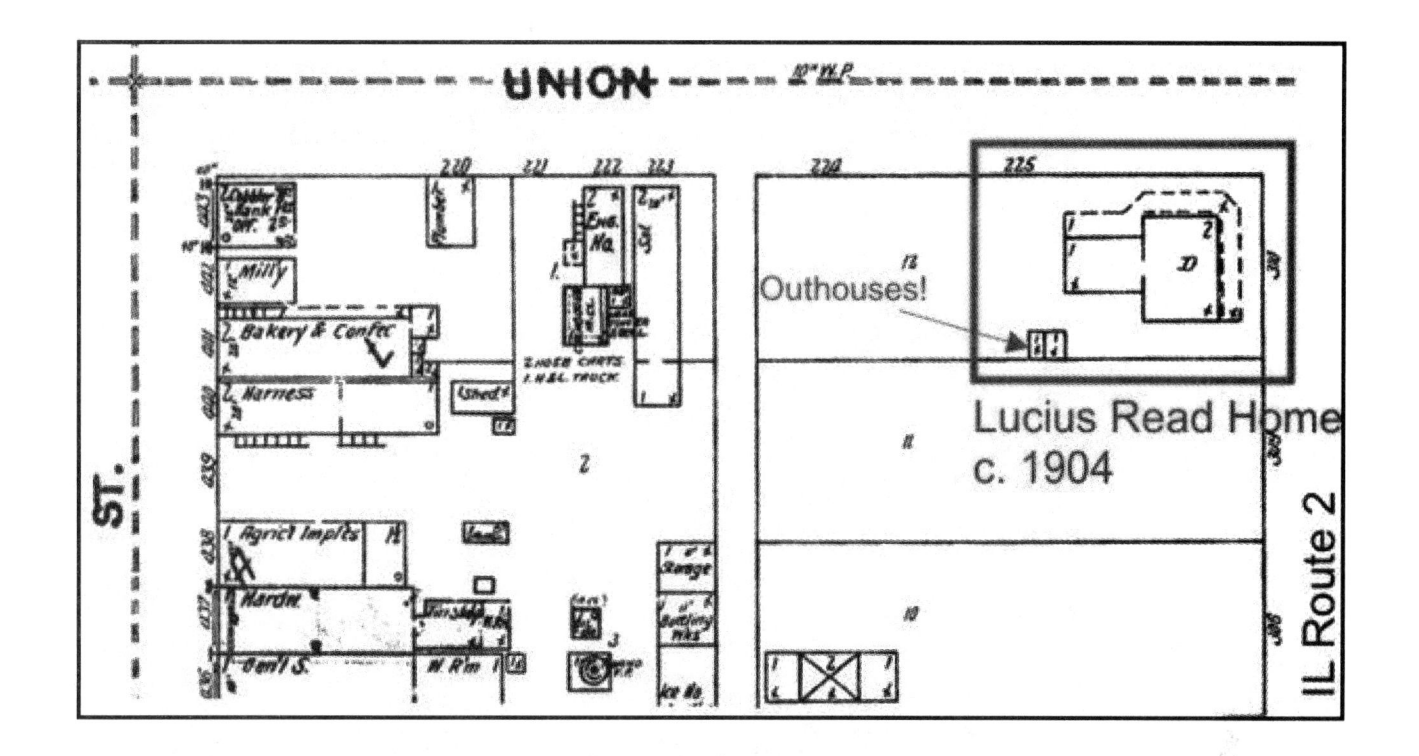

RECOMMENDED RECOVERY TOOLS & TECHNIQUES

Bottle diggers probably have the largest and most varied collection of tools to locate and recover bottles and other items from their resting places. I've known several fanatical bottle diggers who have outfitted entire trailers with all sorts of equipment that allowed them to excavate wells and privies down to depths of 20 feet or more . . . far beyond the depth any recreational digger should even consider going to without a good deal of experience and assistance. To start with, unless you happen to come across an old dump site that is visible and has not been excavated before you (which is extremely rare anymore), you will need a probe to find potential areas to investigate. After you've found a spot to dig, you'll need a sturdy shovel to remove the overburden that usually does not contain anything of interest. Once you reach the material of interest, you'll need to switch to tools that are less likely to damage anything of value, a flashlight to check out the dark corners of your excavation and a 5-gallon bucket to remove dirt from the hole.

> **BE MINDFUL OF THE DEPTH OF YOUR HOLE!** Serious bottle diggers have been known to dig down to extreme depths following urban wells or privy holes; however, they have specialized equipment that provides the necessary protection. Digging below the depth at which you can see over the edge of the hole can have dire consequences in the event of a cave-in. Be sure you don't experience a life-changing event while out in the field!

Rick 'Meech' Burchfield, an avid bottle digger and editor of the Richmond Area Bottle Collectors Association's newsletter, provided the following photo depicting his recommended assortment of tools for general bottle digging. He carries this gear with him in his truck so he's always ready to check out an interesting site he might come across. The items include 1) a hard hat since some construction sites that have exposed old foundations require a hardhat to access an active jobsite; 2) sturdy short-handled shovel; 3 & 4) bottle probe with extension probe; 5) prong rake to free up dirt around bottles. The lettered items all fit into the backpack and include B) flashlight; C) knife; D) keyhole saw to cut through roots; E, F & G) handheld probes of varying lengths; H) 3-prong digger; J) disposable coveralls (never know when you might come across a site that will be paved over in the morning); K) leather gloves and a tarp to put the dirt on making it easier to refill the hole when you are done. The specific tools you bring will depend on the soil you will be digging in which can range from soft sand to hard-packed clay and rocks.

Many bottle hunters also use a sifter to screen all of the dirt when they refill the hole to recover smaller items such as coins, buttons, marbles, stoppers, clay pipes, etc.

Make sure you bring along something to pack your finds in such as a plastic milk crate as well as something to protect them for the trip home. A pile of newspaper, old clothes that have been tossed into the rag bag or bubble paper if you have some from packages you may have received are some of the options that work well.

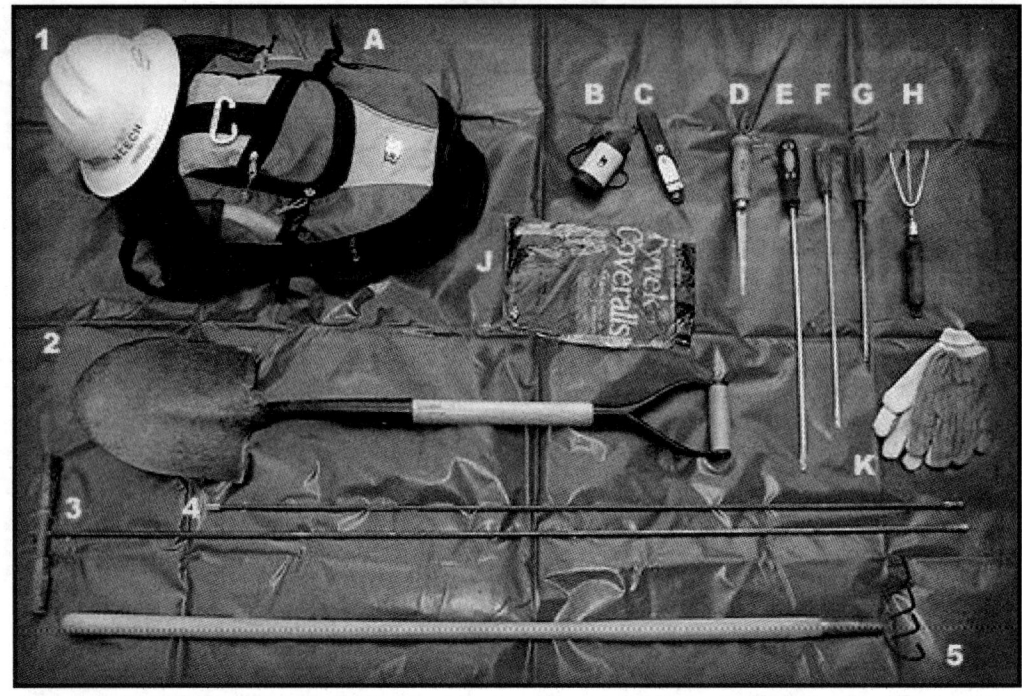

REFERENCE RESOURCE BIBLIOGRAPHY

Books

- **Digger O'Dell Publications**: Complete series of books for bottle hunters; http://www.bottlebooks.com/

Internet Resources

- **Antique Bottle Collector's Haven**: the leading Internet site for finding, buying, selling and learning about Antique Bottles; http://www.antiquebottles.com/
- **Antique Bottle & Glass Collector Magazine & Glass Works Auctions**: Compilation of on-line articles, pricing guides and photo albums; http://www.glswrk-auction.com/
- **Bottle Collecting Sites**: http://baltimorebottles.com/pages/links.html
- **Collectible Detective.com**: The largest vintage and antique guide on the web covering all aspects of bottle collecting and digging; http://www.collectibledetective.com/s/50/antique-bottles.html
- **Clubs for Antique Bottle Collectors**: http://www.antiquebottles.com/clubs.html
- **Find's Treasure Forums – Relic & Bottle Hunting Forum**: http://www.findmall.com/list.php?30
- **Flaschenjager Bottle Hunter**: Informative site for bottle hunters including how-to tips, book lists & more; http://mysite.verizon.net/flaschenjager/bottles.html
- **The Treasure Depot's Bottle Forum**: http://www.thetreasuredepot.com/cgi-bin/bottles/bottles_config.pl
- **TreasureNet – Bottle Hunting Forum**: http://forum.treasurenet.com/index.php/board,16.0.html
- **Treasure Spot – Relic & Bottle Forum**: http://www.mytreasurespot.com/main/list.php?3

Equipment

- **Bottle Digging "Privy" Probe**: http://www.cowboyblacksmith.com/probe.htm

DOWSING

Dowsing is probably the most controversial form of treasure hunting because people either believe in it and can demonstrate success in its use or dismiss it as being little more than a parlor trick. Before simply skipping on to the next chapter in the book, take a few minutes and read this chapter and see if you are at least swayed to learn a bit more about this centuries-old form of locating items.

Dowsing, on a high level definition, is simply the art of finding hidden things. There are documented examples of people using various tools such as sticks, rods and pendulums to find all sorts of items going back to before the birth of Christ. Cave drawings dating back more than 8,000 years have been found in the Tassili Caves of North Africa showing tribesmen surrounding a man with a forked stick dowsing for water. Similar drawings have been found in Asia and Egypt. Records from the Middle Ages report dowsers were used to find deposits of coal as well as sources of water throughout Europe. When the Spanish conquistadors arrived in the New World, dowsing was one of the methods they used to locate and extract vast quantities of gold and silver. Even in modern times, dowsing for water, oil and other hidden items is an accepted practice in many areas of the world. I remember meeting an older gentleman in upstate New York in the late 1970's who was well-known throughout the local area for being "the person" to call when you needed to sink a new well and wanted to know where to dig it. I watched him locate exact locations that produced flowing wells on more than one occasion and all he used was a forked stick he had cut from a tree.

There are many theories on how dowsing works but they are just that . . . theories. It is believed that there is a correlation between the dowsing reaction and changes in magnetic flux in the area around the object being sought. The jury is still out on exactly how dowsing works; however, it has been shown to work and has produced some amazing results in a wide range of applications.

There are two forms of dowsing – one is dowsing for items located in one's immediate area and the other is dowsing for items located a distance away using a map, drawing or sketch. Dowsing for an object hidden in the area around you can be done using a range of tools such as those shown below. There are a number of simple tests you can try at home using some basic equipment to see if you can get a response – many of which are detailed on the websites listed at the end of this chapter. A few years ago I had my daughter try an experiment. I took four plastic cups filled with sand and placed a gold ring in one of them. Then I had her come into the room and using a pendulum, see if she could determine which cup held the ring. She held the pendulum over each cup and mentally asked herself if the ring was in the cup. Time after time, the pendulum would swing in a circle over the cups holding nothing but sand; however, when she was over the one holding the ring, it changed and would swing back-&-forth. Being an engineer I can't offer up an explanation but I have seen dowsing work time and time again inside as well as out in the field.

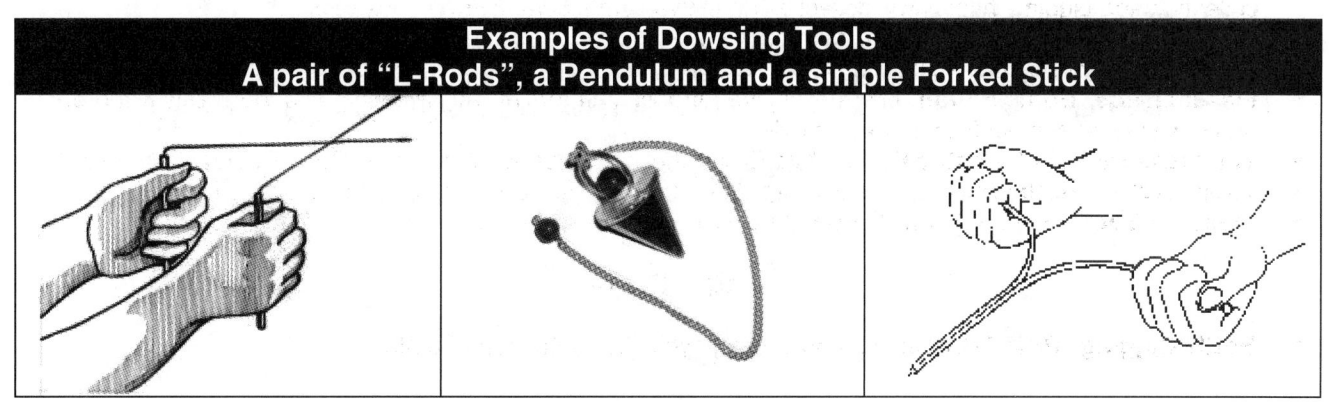

Examples of Dowsing Tools
A pair of "L-Rods", a Pendulum and a simple Forked Stick

What becomes harder for many to accept is that dowsing can also be performed over distances . . . . ranging from miles to around the globe. For those who are able to obtain consistent results, distance itself seems to have no bearing on the results. This type of dowsing is clearly not for everyone but if you have an interest in this type of treasure hunting and an open mind, there are many resources that can help you delve further into this area.

> **WORD OF ADVICE:** There are a number of devices that have been advertised & marketed over the past 20 years or so offering the user the ability to locate all forms of valuables at distances that of 10 miles or more. They claim to use electronic components which would lead one to believe that the technical basis behind dowsing or long range locating has been conclusively identified and documented. If that were true, the theory would be available for public review and the devices patented (not just a design patent but one that covered how the device worked). Despite the extensive marketing that has been done, no basis for how they work that can stand up to scientific scrutiny has ever been provided. These devices range in cost from 100's to 1,000's of dollars and the question often posed to those who are looking into buying one these "electronic" locaters is *"If you had a device that could locate gold, silver, and other valuables at a range of 10 miles, would you sell it for a few $1,000 or spend every waking minute out there using it recovering treasure?"* You should take a minute thinking about that question if you are considering buying one of these devices!

There are a number of people and companies that can supply you with quality, reasonably-priced dowsing equipment if you want to give it a try along with detailed courses and handbooks to get you started. If you think about it, how many times have you arrived at a site and for some unknown reason, walked to the exact spot that held the best find of the day? Could it have been a form of dowsing that pulled you there?

REFERENCE RESOURCE BIBLIOGRAPHY

Equipment

- **American Society of Dowsers Bookstore**; (802) 684-3417; http://www.dowsers.org/store/
- **Fisher Creek Dowsing Supplies:** (828) 507-4196; http://www.dowsingsite.com/
- **Simmons Scientific Products**: (910) 686-1656; http://simmonsscientificproducts.com/
- **Stewart Research Labs**: (423) 282-4124; http://www.losttreasure.com/stewartresearch/

Books

- **Adventures of a 21st Century Dowser** by John Baker
- **Do's and Don'ts On Dowsing** by Fred Stewart
- **Dowsing for Treasure** by Russ Simmons
- **The Dowsing Manual** by Fred Stewart
- **The Revised Professional's Complete Dowsing Course** by Russ Simmons
- **The Diviner's Handbook – A Guide to the Timeless Art of Dowsing** by Tom Graves
- **The Successful Treasure Hunter's Essential Dowsing Manual** by David Villanueva

Internet Resources

- **American Society of Dowsers**: http://www.dowsers.org/
- **The British Society of Dowsers**: http://www.britishdowsers.org/
- **TreasureNet – Dowsing Forum**: http://forum.treasurenet.com/index.php/board,200.0.html
- **Diving Mind**: Dowsing tools and information for beginners and pros; http://www.diviningmind.com/
- **International Society of Dowsers**: Forums and articles on the subject; http://www.dowsingworks.com/

Documenting Your Searches

You've just come home from a long day in the field where you searched several sites found through some focused research. Your pouch has a number of first-rate finds in it and you proudly show them to your spouse after rinsing them off. As you put your gear away in the garage and turn off the light, you start thinking about the next time you can hit some of the sites again. Well, between unexpected demands for your time at work, the family vacation, your daughter's high school graduation and several of your buddies inviting you to some other local hot spots in the area, time seems to slip by and it's months later when you think back to those sites. While the day had been productive, some sites and more specifically, certain areas had been better than others. Memories tend to fade no matter how memorable a hunt might have been and as you reflect back on the different sites you hit that day, they start to run together and the ones that were really productive become mixed with those that were mediocre. As you drive from one to the next, you start to remember where you found the better targets but you feel that you wasted a good deal of time that could have been spent hunting rather than driving. Sound at all familiar? Well much the way many treasure hunters feel about research, documenting hunts soon after getting home is often something that is way down on the list of things that actually get done.

Having documentation of where you search and what you find can pay off in multiple ways. First, by compiling information on each of your hunts that includes details on the site, what you found, special conditions you encountered, settings that worked exceptionally well (or did not work and information on the surrounding area, you will be able to determine what sites are worth returning to at specific times of the year (moisture content, underbrush, crowds, etc.) or based on what specific types of targets you have found. Many relic hunters in the Northeast who hunt farm fields for Colonial artifacts know exactly what fields and more importantly, what areas of the fields are worth searching as soon as the farmer turns the ground in preparation for planting. The window of opportunity is very small since hunting will not be allowed once the seeding is done so having a record of each productive field, contact information, and areas that have produced well in the past ensures they are at each field as soon as it is ready. There are literally miles and miles of fields that could hold artifacts but knowing exactly which areas do is the difference between a hunter who is successful on a regular basis and one who simply relies on luck to bring home a find or two. Over the years I have collected binders filled with records of hunts that have spanned the globe as well as entered data into computerized programs and spreadsheets to help me retrieve details on hunts used to develop future plans. If I am making plans to do some Civil War relic hunting, reviewing records of sites I've visited in the area that show finds were made up to a section containing thick underbrush or the property line beyond which we had not been able to secure permission, I might plan my trip in the dead of winter when the underbrush has died off or if I hear that the adjoining property has been sold for development. Another effective use of hunt logs would be to look at revisiting sites after a period of rain soaked the ground that turned up a fair number of older copper coins such as Wheat cents or Indian Head pennies. Silver is easier to detect when the ground is damp and finding copper coins is a good indication that silver coins are also present. But without having specific records that allow you to go back and dissect information, it is virtually impossible to be able to quickly identify sites worth revisiting as conditions change or you have a sudden interest to search for something different.

Another reason to document what you find and where you find it is to help preserve the history that would otherwise be lost if the artifacts were left where they lay or were simply removed haphazardly. The model of how documentation can be used to preserve history for generations to come can be found in the United Kingdom. Recognizing the value that hobbyists could provide in the recovery and documentation of artifacts that tell the history of the area, a program called The Portable Antiquities Scheme was implemented. It is a voluntary program designed to promote the recording of archaeological objects found by members of the public ranging from metal detectorists to people gardening, excavating or simply walking outdoors. The Treasure Act passed in 1996 addressed how significant finds of certain items were to be treated; however, many items that could tell a story and preserve of piece of the United Kingdom's history were not included and hence not captured in the government's database. A pilot program was started soon after the Treasure Act was made into law and the results were overwhelmingly positive. In the first year, over 13,000 individual artifacts were entered into the Portable Antiquities Scheme's database. Currently administrated by the British Museum, the Portable Antiquities Scheme has become a shining example of how archeologists and hobbyists can work together and the value amateurs can provide in preserving history through their efforts. Since 1997 the Portable Antiquities Scheme Finds Liaison Officers have examined and documented over 100,000 objects, many of which would have otherwise gone unrecorded. More and more hobbyists have started to volunteer their services to professional archeologists working side-by-side on projects around the world ranging from small local surveys to well-publicized excavations on historically significant sites. By properly documenting the results of these efforts, history is preserved and the hobby will be seen in a more positive light in the years to come. Detectorists in the U.S. can pick up some good documentation techniques by reviewing the PAS website.

The specific type of information and the level of detail you record will vary based on personal preferences, the type of hunting you are engaged in and the intended use for the information. For example, if you are a coin hunter who frequents local parks and playgrounds, simply recording the site name, the area(s) you searched, how long you hunted it, the time of day you visited the area along with the crowds present and the specifics of what you recovered; i.e., # of coins by denomination and other items, you will capture the information you need to plan future trips. On the other hand, beach hunters will need additional information such as tide levels, sand erosion and overall conditions which change each trip to get value out of reviewing search logs. If you are searching on or near a historically significant site, details of the precise location of each target (depth, orientation, etc.) along with details of the item itself will be a key part of preserving the object's pedigree for use by historians as papers are assembled about the project.

There are some commercially-available computer programs designed to allow hobbyists to document what they find in a fairly detailed fashion. Some of the programs have trial versions you can download to see if they meet your needs. If they don't do what you want, you can always opt for a paper log using forms such as those provided in this chapter designed for coin hunters or if you are handy with a computer, design a database that can capture the information you need for future retrieval. Whatever method you opt to use, getting into the habit of documenting your finds as soon as you get home will pay off in many ways including putting more in your pouch at the end of the day!

REFERENCE RESOURCE BIBLIOGRAPHY

Computer Software

- **Coin Collectors Assistant**: Comprehensive United States coin database with current values provided by Coin World; Carlisle Development Corporation; http://www.carlisledevelopment.com/coinGrading.php
- **Coin Elite**: First-rate program to track, identify and appraise coins in your collection. Covers all U.S. and worldwide coins, including ancient coins; (Trial available);Trove Software, http://www.trovesoftware.com
- **Exact Change**: Coin collecting program containing 60,000 coins from 240 countries (Trial available); Wild Man Software; http://www.exactchange.info/
- **I-Detect**: Premier program to record details on your equipment, sites and finds; CMH Software, (Trial available)http://www.ginkgoware.com/
- **K8!**: Fully customizable program to track your finds with a number of templates available for the base program (Trial available); Niche Software; http://www.collectiblessoftware.com/

SITE MAP & FIND SUMMARY

Site Information / History: _____

_____

_____ continued

Conditions / Comments: _____

_____

_____ continued

Valuable / Old Coins Found: _____

_____ continued

Jewelry Items Found: _____

_____ continued

Other Items or Artifacts Found: _____

_____

_____ continued

SITE FIND LOG

Site Name: _____ Date Hunted: _____

Time Spent: _____ Hunted With: _____

Equipment Used: _____

Site Conditions When Hunted: _____

_____

=======================================

Type of Coin	# Found	Face Value	Actual Value
_____	_____	_____	_____
_____	_____	_____	_____
_____	_____	_____	_____
_____	_____	_____	_____
_____	_____	_____	_____
_____	_____	_____	_____
_____	_____	_____	_____
_____	_____	_____	_____
_____	_____	_____	_____
_____	_____	_____	_____
_____	_____	_____	_____
_____	_____	_____	_____
TOTAL:	_____	_____	_____

Jewelry: _____

_____

_____continued

Artifacts: _____

_____

_____

_____continued

■

Identifying Your Finds

It's often surprising how many treasure hunters take the time to find productive sites, learn how to use their equipment to squeeze the most performance possible from it and then fail to take the time to identify their finds at the end of the day. I know over the years I've found things that I had thought had little or no value yet later found that they were in fact quite valuable. One example that I still think about some 40 years after it took place deals with a dozen or so pieces of sterling silver flatware that my brother and I have had found around an old house in upstate New York. We made regular trips to the local flea market to sell our finds and brought the silverware with us. Shortly after unpacking what we had brought, a dealer setup nearby walked over, looked at the silverware and asked us how much we wanted for the entire lot. We told him $2 a piece and without batting an eye, he handed us the money and picked up his purchase. Several weeks later we found another fork from the same set around the old house and took it to the next flea market. Another person looked at it and wanted to know if we had anymore like it. We told him that we had sold several pieces the month before and he asked if we knew anything about it. We said no and he said that the marks on the piece indicated it came from the silversmith shop of none other than Paul Revere! He paid us more than double what we had received for all the other pieces combined for the one fork and asked us to call him if we ever found anymore . . . which of course we never did!

Common items such as modern coins and jewelry are easily identifiable by virtually anyone so let's look at some of the other types of items recovered by hobbyists around the world and how best to identify them but first . . .

> **PROTECT YOUR FIND UNTIL YOU KNOW WHAT YOU HAVE:** A point that can't be overemphasized is to avoid inadvertently damaging an item you recover through careless digging, placing it amongst other items while in the field or by improper cleaning methods once you arrive home. As previously mentioned, protect your finds and do not clean them other then under running water until you have identified it and determined what it might be worth! Refer back to page 82 for some proven tips from detectorists on how to handle your finds.

COINS & TOKENS:

Coins of recent origin are usually easy to identify and their value can be determined using one of the on-line or printed pricing guides. There are some varieties and mint strike errors that you can read about in these sources so make sure you take the time to closely inspect any coin that might be a possible known error as some are worth many times what the common variety might be worth. In 2008, I had found the location of an old one-room schoolhouse that was no longer standing. After getting permission to search the area from the property owner, I spent several days there and did fairly well considering the students attending these schools often had very little to lose. One of the coins I found was a wheat cent in decent shape dated 1922. Not being one of the more well-known key dates in the set such as 1909S VDB, 1914D or 1931S, I simply brushed it off under running water, placed it in a 2x2 holder and slid it into one of the binders containing the year's finds. A few months later as I was preparing an article for Lost Treasure Magazine, I looked at the PCGS on-line coin pricing guide and saw that in fact the most valuable wheat cent was a 1922D without the mintmark. Officially, no pennies were made that year without the D mintmark yet due to an error at the mint, some were released that way. After sending my coin off to be authenticated, it turned to be one of those errors with an estimated value of more than $1,000! It's amazing how much difference a small letter "D" can have on the value of something . . . $20 versus $1,000+.

Tokens are another item commonly found by detectorists that can have mind-boggling values. Before 1900, it was common practice for business owners to have tokens produced that promoted their business and encouraged patrons to remain loyal customers (since the tokens were not accepted anywhere else). In the U.S., tokens were most common in states that were on the edge of the frontier but they were found at businesses throughout the country. Internationally, tokens have been found dating back 100's of years. With the wide variety of tokens available, it is only natural that people could collect them and with that collectibility, the value of tokens has continued to climb. Most tokens are fairly plain in shape and design which would make one think they are not worth much; however, if you find one from a business that is highly sought after or in fact is extremely rare, the token can be worth far more than a coin from the same time period. Tom Bennington found the token shown here while searching a vacant lot with a metal detector near his home. It is an example of a previously unknown saloon token from Tyler, Texas. The true value to a collector has yet to be determined but what initially might look like nothing more than an interesting trinket may in fact be worth $100's if not $1,000's . . . emphasizing the importance of identifying anything you might find that is not readily recognizable. (Credit to TexasTokens.com). There are a number of very active token collector groups that can help you identify tokens you may uncover. Make sure you keep good records as to where it was located as that information can add to the value of the find.

INTERNET FORUMS . . . AN INVALUABLE RESOURCE:

The Internet has given everyone with a computer access to a wealth of information that can be used to identify even the most obscure finds that are unearthed. Resources include websites that contain 100's or even 1,000's of photos of collectibles grouped by very focused types of items such as 18th century farm implements, medicine bottles, tokens from a particular state or type of business that can be used to identify what you've found and forums where collectors of specific items congregate who can quickly identify posted finds. A year ago I found a small key with a Ford logo on it on the grounds of a local college and was interested in finding out what it might be from. A quick Internet search turned up several forums setup by collectors of Ford Motor Company memorabilia and after posting a photo of the key, I received the first reply less than 30 minutes later. Several other people replied over the next few hours and what had simply been a "neat old key" was quickly identified as being from a Model T, Ford's first model and a piece of American history! The Collector Online website contains links to more than 2,000 collector sites covering virtually any type of collectible you can imagine where you can ask for help identifying your finds and often receive a great deal of information regarding the item, its history and value.

BOOKS & MAGAZINES . . . . . TIME-PROVEN REFERENCES:

A quick check at your local bookstore will reveal a number of books and magazines that focus on the collector market and provide photos of items and in many cases, current prices for each. It's amazing to see just how many different niches there are in terms of what people will collect but as they say "variety is the spice of life". If you specialize in a form of treasure hunting where you find items from a specific group such as Civil War relics, mining relics, Indian artifacts or bottles for example, picking up an identification guide is highly recommended. Several avid hunters I know keep a copy of the guide in their vehicle to check on any item they might come across in the field.

> **TIP**
> Two excellent books that can help you identify your finds are reprints of old catalogs. Sears catalogs dating as far back as the late 1800-s have been reprinted and contain 1,000's of everyday items pictured with short descriptions. Bannerman, a military surplus dealer that operated from soon after the Civil War through the 1970's produced catalogs that detailed countless military items spanning centuries. Both of these make for interesting reading and can help identify almost anything you might come across.

Since specialized identification / pricing guides can be fairly expensive due to their limited market, if you only occasionally come across something that you would need to look up, you might want to check to see if your local library system has a copy available or can request one for you. Many treasure hunting clubs have established a club library and purchasing one of these books through the club for members to use may be an option to explore. A word of advice when using one of these guides to determine the value of what you've found: remember that the prices may be somewhat dated (the actual price may have gone up or down) and the price shown may not reflect a regional demand that can often drive the price substantially higher. As the Cashing In or Selling Your Finds chapter will cover, make sure you know exactly what your item is worth <u>before</u> accepting any offer you might receive for it.

> **TIP**
> The combination of documenting the details of your find along with actually identifying what it is can often make a big difference in placing a value on the item. For example, a common Civil War bullet may be worth just a few dollars but if you can document its pedigree tying it to a major battle or well-known commander, the value can go up dramatically. The same holds true for virtually anything you might come across . . . . even if the increased value is just to local collectors. If you don't plan on selling your finds, having the additional historical background will make your collection more interesting to your and those you show it to.

REFERENCE RESOURCE BIBLIOGRAPHY

Books

Coins & Tokens
- **A Catalog of Modern World Coins, 1850 – 1964** by R.S. Yeoman
- **Bannerman Catalogue of Military Goods**: (Several years were reprinted, each containing 100's of pages)
- **Latin American Tokens; 1700 – 1920** by Russell Rulau
- **Standard Catalog of World Coins** (Several editions covering coins dating back centuries)
- **Sears & Roebuck Catalog Reprints**: (Several years were reprinted, each containing 700+ pages)
- **United States Tokens; 1700 – 1900:** by Russell Rulau (Over 1,000 pages containing 5,000+ photos of U.S. tokens along with pricing)
- **The Official Red Book, A Guide Book of the United States Coins** by R.S. Yeoman

Relics
- **American Military Belt Plates** by Michael J. O'Donnell & Duncan Campbell
- **Arrowheads & Stone Artifacts** by C G Yeager
- **Bennet's Artefacts of England and the United Kingdom**, 1st and 2nd editions
- **Civil War Artifacts, A guide for the Historian** by Howard R. Crouch
- **Civil War Bullets and Cartridges** by James and Dean Thomas

- **Civil War Collectors Guide to Albert's Button Book** by Daniel J. Binder
- **Civil War Projectiles 2 (Small Arms & Field Artillery with Supplement)** by W. McKee & M.E. Mason
- **Civil War Relics of the Western Campaign 1861-1865** by Charles S. Harris
- **Confederate Belt Buckles & Plates** by Steve E. Mullinax
- *Detector Finds 1, 2, 3, 4, 5, & 6* by Gordon Bailey (European finds)
- **Field Artillery Projectiles of the American Civil War** by George Dickey & Peter C. George
- **Guide to Civil War Artillery Projectiles** by Jack W. Melton & Lawrence E. Pawl
- **The Illustrated History of American Civil War Relics** by Sylvia & O'Donnell
- **Indian Artifacts of the East and South** by Robert Swope, Jr.
- **Interpreting History from Relics Found in Civil War Campsites** by Rural Relic Hunters
- **North American Indian Artifacts** by Lar Hothem
- **The Padlock Collector** by Franklin M. Arnall
- **Plates And Buckles Of The American Military 1795-1874** by Sidney Kerksis
- **Record of American Uniform and Historical Buttons** by Alphaeus H. Albert
- **Roundball to Rimfire – A History of Civil War Small Arms Ammunition Part 1** by Dean Thomas
- **Treasury Of Frontier Relics** by Beitz (This book contains hundreds of photos of frontier relics, along with adequate description and prices to give you an idea of what they might be worth to help you identify the finds of the last century that you make with your detector)
- **Warman's Civil War Collectibles** by John Graf

Bottles
- **Bottles: Identification and Price Guide** by Michael Polak
- **Bottle Pricing Guide** by Hugh Cleveland
- **Kovels' Bottles Price List** by Ralph and Terry Kovel

Internet Resources

- **Antique Bottle Collector's Haven**: A wealth of information related to all aspects of bottle and glassware identification; http://www.antiquebottles.com/
- **Collector Online**: Directory of over 2,100 antique & collectible clubs from around the world . . . great to pose questions on your finds to help identify them & determine a value: http://www.collectoronline.com/cgi-bin/clubs.cgi?groupKey=7
- **Don's Coin World Gallery**: Over 26,000 photos of coins from around the world; http://worldcoingallery.com/
- **Dirty Old Coins**; Interesting site dedicated to Roman-era coins; http://www.dirtyoldcoins.com/
- **Historic Glass Bottle Identification & Information Website**: Detailed website designed to help you identify and date bottles and other glassware; http://www.sha.org/bottle/
- **UK Detector Finds Database**: Photos of finds from throughout the United Kingdom fully searchable by type, detector used, location and more. http://www.ukdfd.co.uk/

Computer Software

- **Coin Collectors Grading Assistant**: Comprehensive United States coin database that helps identify and grade your finds containing all U.S coins minted since 1793; Carlisle Development Corporation; http://www.carlisledevelopment.com/coinGrading.php
- **Collectors Assistant – World Coin Database**: Add-on package containing world coin grading information
- **20th Century Coin Grading**: Add on package that also works alone providing high resolution photos of 19th & 20th century US coins; Trove Software, http://www.trovesoftware.com

Cleaning, Preserving & Displaying Your Finds

OK, so you've recovered that keeper, restrained your curiosity long enough to pack it away to prevent damaging it and you've arrived back at your house – now what? The first thing you should do is soak the finds you want to look at in warm soapy water (dish soap works well) for 30 minutes or so. After allowing them to soak, rinse what dirt comes off under running water, repeating as needed. Once you can see a date or any markings on the object, you will be able to decide how much cleaning you should do based on its approximate value. Coins can be easily valued using one of the on-line coin pricing guides and other collectibles have similar websites devoted to helping determine what their values are.

> **CAUTION:** Never clean anything you find other than rinsing any loose dirt off the surface until you know for sure what the item's value might be. Improperly cleaning an item can irreparably damage it and turn what was a valuable object into something worth little or nothing. You can find people skilled at cleaning virtually any collectible through a search on the Internet or by asking your fellow treasure hunters in your local club or on one of the many metal detecting forums available on-line. Use the following techniques only after you have determined an item's value!

The first thing you should do is to sort out your items based on their metallurgical content as the method you'll use to clean each one differs considerably.

Let's start out with silver. The condition it comes out of the ground in varies based on the mineral content, moisture content or salt content in which the item is found. I'm sure you've found silver coins in a schoolyard or around an old foundation that came out just as shiny as the day they were lost yet coins found near the ocean or in wet soil will be coated with black oxidation. The less destructive your cleaning techniques are, the more you will usually be able to get for anything you try to sell. Since professionals face the same challenge, we will take a look at some of the cleaning methods used by antique dealers and museum curators. Once of the most amazing tools I've ever seen used is called a precious metal cleaning plate. This is a sheet of specially formulated metal that is placed in your sink with hot water and some of the activator compound that comes with the system. Simply place the oxidized silver into the solution and the tarnish immediately starts to bubble off. The compound is non-toxic and the plate lasts indefinitely . . . simply rinse it off until the next use. I've used this on all types of silver and with the exception of some heavily blackened pieces that had been in salt water for more than a century, it has always done a great job removing black surface tarnish from my finds. The best part about this cleaning device is the price - about $25 for the complete system. Another non-destructive technique for cleaning lightly to moderately tarnished silver uses aluminum foil, baking soda and salt, all common ingredients found around the house. Start by placing a sheet of aluminum foil in the bottom of a pot or pan and then add a few inches of water, 1 teaspoon of baking soda and 1 teaspoon of salt. Bring this solution to a boil and then add the silver items you want to clean, making sure the items are fully submerged. After a few minutes, remove the items, rinse them off and buff them dry with a soft cloth. If there are some stubborn spots, you can repeat as necessary.

There are two non-destructive cleaning devices that work on all types of oxidized or encrusted items. The first is called electrolysis. This uses a small electrical current to remove the oxidation with little actual impact on the item itself. To start with, you will need a power source. Some people use a power supply such as one from a portable phone or tape player but their limited current output will require more time to clean items. The best source is a motorcycle battery charger that you can pick up at an auto parts store or a somewhere like Target, Wal-Mart or K-Mart. It should have a 6 volt / 12 volt selector switch so you can vary the power as needed based on the encrustation present. The object to be cleaned is connected to the negative lead from the power supply and a stainless steel item such as a spoon is connected to the positive lead. Put both leads in a solution of water, salt and lemon juice, ensuring the two leads do not touch each other. When the power is turned on or plugged in, you will see bubbling start on the item being cleaned. After 5 minutes or so turn the power off and take it out of the solution. Rinse it off and if required, repeat the process until the oxidation and surface debris is gone.

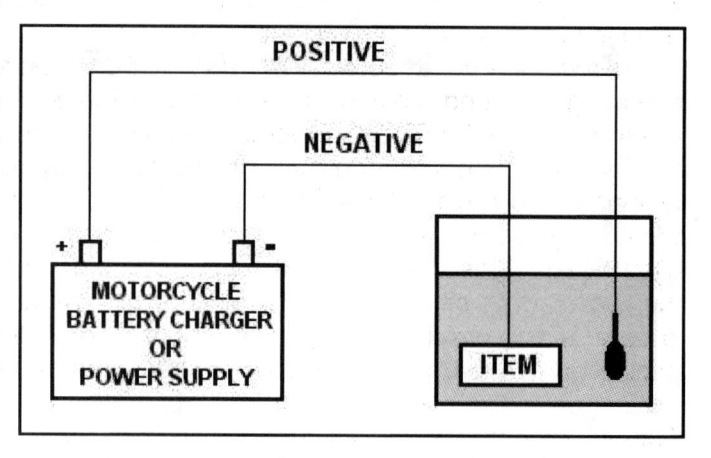

The second device is an ultrasonic cleaner that uses high frequency sound waves to create microscopic bubbles which remove dirt and grime from objects in a matter of a few minutes. An ultrasonic cleaner is best suited for doing final cleaning on items that simply have mud or dirt caked on them since it is simply cleaning the surface with tiny bubbles and not removing corrosion. Once the item has been cleaned, simply rinse it off and it should look 100% better than it did before you started. These devices can be purchased for between $30 and $100 at jewelry stores or on-line suppliers.

If you have some really stubborn spots that will not come off using one of the techniques described above, you might need to try an abrasive cleaner such as commercial polishes or cleaners designed for specific types of metals such as silver, brass, copper, etc. Another cleaner you can try is common toothpaste and a soft-bristled toothbrush. Just make sure you stop as soon as the stain is gone since over-cleaning can damage the item and greatly reduce its value.

Several years ago I had the opportunity to take the family to Spain and go metal detecting with a few archeologists who worked with the University in Madrid. We hunted sites that dated back to the time when the Romans had settlements all along the coast. Several of the coins we found were clearly from this period but we could not tell what was on them in order to date them. Two tricks they shared with me were so simple I wondered if they would actually work but they did and I've used them numerous times since. The first made be cringe initially. They laid a few of the coins on wax paper and then spread a thick layer of white glue like Elmer's over each coin. Then, after the glue dried overnight, they took the edge of the dried glue and peeled it off the coin and what came off was a layer of encrusted dirt. They said that this would never take any of the objects itself off and ensured the object was not harmed. It took several tries to get most of the 2,000 year old dirt off but after a few days, the details of the coin were plainly visible and identification was a snap! The other trick they showed me was to soak the object - we used both coins and other artifacts - in distilled water (which you can get at the supermarket). Let it sit in the water for a few hours so the water can permeate the hard surface encrustation. Then put the item in the freezer - yes the freezer - and leave it there overnight. The water will expand when it freezes and crack the surface dirt off the item - again, without damaging it object itself. You can repeat the process as needed to completely clean the item.

A great way to clean common date coins and smaller items that do not have real value is with a rock tumbler. The rubber barrels are large enough to hold 100 or so coins and can clean even unrecognizable coins in a matter of hours. Tumblers come in either a single or double barrel design and while both will do the job, having two allows you to clean more of your coins at once. It's important to separate the items you want to clean so that you do not place copper items in the same barrel as other items since the copper will leach out and give everything an orange tinge – sort of like washing a bright red towel with your whites. After you load the coins you want to clean in the barrel, you will need to add some aquarium gravel, a tablespoon or two of liquid dishwashing soap, a tablespoon of scouring powder and enough warm water to just be visible in the gravel. Another highly-recommended option is a patented kit containing special gravel and cleaning powder called Magic Tumble Clean distributed by Finch Products. Allow the tumbler to run for a few hours and check the results. If they are not as clean as you want, leave them in and continue tumbling them. Very dirty items may take up to 12 hours to clean completely. Rinse them off when you are done and save the gravel to reuse the next time. One point to remember is to keep the gravel used to clean copper separate from that used to clean other items or the copper color issue will come up again.

Another trick to remove stains from common coins is to put 100 coins or so in a container of white vinegar. Add some salt and agitate the mixture for several minutes. Check on the progress and continue until the coins are acceptable for use. They will not look like new but they will be passable if you simply plan on cashing them in at the local bank or dumping them into a coin counting machine.

So, once you've either cleaned the items you have found the right way or had them cleaned, what's next? Well, protecting your finds is essential and makes your collection more interesting and valuable. For coins, there are several options including the standard Whitman folders where you have a place for one example of each date and mintmark of a specific type of coin, 2"x2" cardboard holders where you staple the coin inside or plastic holders for the more valuable coins in your collection. If the coin is worth more than $100, you may want to have the coin appraised and encapsulated in a plastic holder with the grading on it through ANACS. The nominal fee charged for this service is well worth knowing exactly what the coin's grade is to determine its value at any point in time.

For other artifacts, many detectorists place their finds in cases called Riker mounts which preserve them and make for a nice display when friends come over, putting on an exhibit at a historical society or local library or giving a talk at a club meeting. They are available in a wide range of sizes and depths to hold almost anything you might come across and are quite reasonably priced. To add some "character" to the display, try placing a piece of colored felt on top of the white fiber lining before adding your finds. If you have some items that you are particularly proud of, there are display cases made of wood which are perfect for those special finds.

Iron artifacts need to be protected once they have been removed from the ground or from underwater as rapid deterioration will start as soon as they come in contact with the air. Electrolysis does a great job of removing loose surface rust from iron artifacts; however, if the object is severely corroded, you may find that there is in fact nothing except for rust holding it together. I've seen the results of people trying to clean what could have been an interesting artifact and winding up with nothing more than a pile of rust in the bottom of the cleaning solution. Once you have cleaned an object with electrolysis, you need to ensure the item is dry before sealing it or further damage may occur. Placing it on top of a heater vent or even in the oven set at the lowest setting for a few hours will remove water from within the cracks and crevices on the object. If you have something that you do not want to use electrolysis on, another effective technique to clean items is with a brass wire wheel mounted in a hand-held drill or a smaller tool such as a Dremel – again, using a brass wire brush. Be sure to wear eye protection as the rust will be flying once you start cleaning the object. After the rust has been removed and the item dried, a coat of clear spray-on lacquer can be applied to prevent any further rust from occurring.

As has already been stated, before cleaning and preserving ANY artifact you've recovered; make sure you know what its value and historical significance might be. What might at first seem to be nothing more than a piece of rusted iron or twisted brass could in fact be extremely valuable or significant, possibly changing history as it's currently written!

A great example of this can be seen in a photograph and story provided to me by John Benfield, a detectorist from the United Kingdom, when I was working on another book. He had been searching the grounds surrounding the Old London Road Bridge thought to be the actual location of the "Bridge of Bodies" left in the aftermath of the Battle of Towton fought on March 29, 1461. This was the largest and bloodiest single day of fighting ever fought on British soil. Nearly 550 years later, John discovered a double-bitted axe and a few months later, found the remains of a flail mace in a streambed. According to John, no examples of double bitted axes or flail maces had been found in the United Kingdom before which is why both are currently being evaluated by the Royal Armories Museum in Leeds. They show what a metal detector can unearth and why it is so important to research and preserve your finds to preserve important pieces of history.

REFERENCE RESOURCE BIBLIOGRAPHY

Books

- **Cleaning Coins & Artefacts** by David Villanueva
- **Cleaning and Preservation of Coins & Medals** by Gerhard Welter
- **Saving Stuff; How to Care for and Preserve your Collectibles, Heirlooms and Other Prized Possessions** by Don Williams and Louisa Jaggar – This is "the book to have" as it covers all types of objects and was written by the Senior conservator of the Smithsonian Institute
- **Coin & Relic Cleaning and Preservation,** by Granville
- **Cleaning and Restoring Coins and Artefacts** by Michael Cuddeford

Cleaning, Preserving and Display Supplies

- **Riker Mounts**: The #1 source of display cases for treasure hunters; http://www.rikermounts.net/
- **Collectors Display Case Company:** A wide assortment of display cases; http://www.usadisplay.net/
- **Fetpak, Inc.**: Complete assortment of jewelry boxes to showcase your finds; http://www.fetpak.com/whstore/main.pl/fl?16
- **Finch Products:** Developers of the Magic Tumble Clean system; http://finchproducts.com/
- **Jewelry Display, Inc.**: Complete assortment of jewelry boxes to showcase your finds; http://www.jewelrydisplay.com/
- **Hammacher Schlemmer Precious Metal Cleaning Plate** (Cleans gold, silver & silver plate without damaging the item); (800) 321-1484; http://www.hammacher.com/Product/65593
- **Harbor Freight**: Several different tumbler systems; http://www.harborfreight.com/
- **Kellyco Metal Detector Superstore**: Several different tumbler systems; http://www.KellycoDetectors.com

Internet Resources

- **TreasureNet – Cleaning & Preservation Forum**: http://forum.treasurenet.com/index.php/board,70.0.html
- **Cleaning Coins**: An extremely informative web resource; http://rg.ancients.info/guide/cleaning.html

Cashing In or Selling Your Finds

Many of us never sell anything we find because the memories they evoke far outweigh what they might bring on the open market. There are some finds that have little sentimental value or may duplicate others finds already in one's collection which can be sold and the proceeds used to purchase more equipment, cover travel costs to new destinations or simply pay some bills. Treasure hunting is in fact the only hobby that has a high likelihood of paying for itself and then some once the initial investment in equipment has been made.

Before you should even start to think about selling any of your finds, you need to determine exactly what they are worth so that you can decide if you are getting a good offer or are you being taken advantage of. Let's breakdown finds into a few different categories and cover how to determine what they are worth and then how to sell them if you desire for the best possible price.

PRECIOUS METAL FINDS

As gold, silver and other precious metals have soared in prices over the past year or so, you've probably seen many ads from businesses wanting you to sell them your valuables. The downside of selling scrap to local stores such as pawn shops and jewelers or the companies that advertise on a national scale is that they need to make a profit when they sell to refineries and that simply means less money in your pocket in their offers. You can sell directly to the refiners and net considerably more than you might otherwise. Another option is to come into the local stores armed with knowledge; i.e., knowing what the items are actually worth. Once you get an offer, see if they will negotiate with you or decide if you are willing to take a bit less to save the effort of sending it in to a refiner.

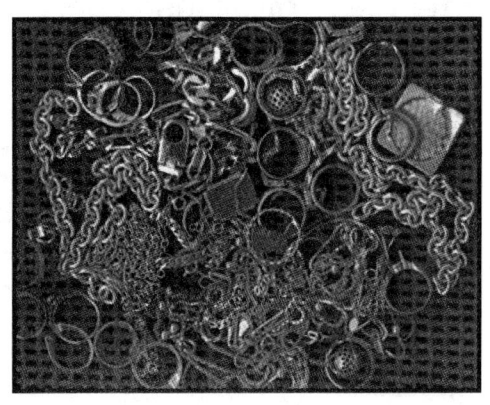

To start with, precious metal such as gold, silver and platinum are sold by the Troy Ounce. Many people don't realize that an ounce of gold (and other precious metals) is weighed using a different system and a troy ounce is more than the typical ounce found at the grocery store which is called an avoirdupois ounce.

Troy Weight Information
▪ One troy ounce = 480 grains or 31.10 grams.
▪ There are also 20 pennyweights to a troy ounce.
▪ A troy pound contains 12 troy ounces which is equivalent to 373.24 grams.
▪ 32.15 troy ounces = 1 kilogram

WEIGHING YOUR FINDS: To calculate the value of your finds, you need to figure out what they weigh. A quality digital scale is the best piece of equipment for this use. Recently, the prices of these scales have really come down and you can get one that will serve your needs for under $30. Do an Internet search for "DIGITAL SCALE" or check out some of the companies listed in the reference section of this chapter . . . you will have plenty to choose from. When using the scale, make sure to zero it out before putting the items you are weighing on it and be sure to note the scale selected; i.e., grams, ounces or dwt. **NOTE:** Unfortunately you will be paid for only the metal content without any stones so if you have a piece with a precious or semi-precious stone, you would do better selling it intact as a piece of jewelry rather than simply scrapping it out. Otherwise you need to remove the stone to weigh the piece and scrap it out.

CONVERTING WEIGHT TO ACTUAL CONTENT: When you weigh the items you find, be sure to sort them first into piles by content; i.e., 10KT, 14KT, 18KT, Sterling, Platinum, etc. Once you weigh each type, you will need to convert the weight to reflect the actual pure metal content. This conversion is done as follows:

GOLD STAMPINGS (pure gold is 24KT)
- 10KT = 10/24 = 0.4166 or 41.66% pure
- 14KT = 14/24 = 0.5833 or 58.33% pure
- 18KT = 18/24 = 0.7500 or 75.00% pure
- 22KT = 22/24 = 0.9166 of 91.66% pure

PLATINUM STAMPINGS (pure platinum is 1000 parts)
- 900P = 900/1000 = 0.9000 or 90.00% pure
- PLAT = 950/1000 = 0.9500 of 95.00% pure
- 950PLAT= 950/1000 = 0.9500 or 95.00% pure

STERLING STAMPINGS
- STERLING / STER = 925/1000 = 0.9250 or 92.50% pure

WHAT WILL YOU ACTUALLY BE PAID? As discussed earlier, selling directly to a refiner eliminates one or more intermediate step and hence a higher percentage of the actual value winding up in your bank account. But you need to be realistic and understand that even the refineries need to make some profit on the purchase of your items. The actual amount paid varies but it will range from 90% to 95% of the value based on the spot price at the time the transaction is completed. When you select a refiner to deal with, make sure you ask what their discount is so you can compare one to another and be sure you are comparing like-for-like factors.

EXAMPLE

You have a nice haul of jewelry with 71.4 grams of 10KT gold, 53.8 grams of 14KT gold and 157.5 grams of Sterling silver. What should you expect to get from one of the refineries listed in the reference section of this chapter (depending on what the spot price is the day it is processed)? Let's assume gold spot price is $1,050 per ounce and silver is $17 per ounce and you are being offered between 94% and 95% of the true value (compared to 50% at many local shops).

YOUR PAYMENT = 10KT GOLD + 14KT GOLD + STERLING

- ▶ **10KT**: (71.4 grams / 31.10 grams / ounce) x (0.4166) x $1,050 x 0.95 = $954.05
- ▶ **14KT**: (53.8 grams / 31.10 grams / ounce) x (0.5833) x $1,050 x 0.95 = $1006.53
- ▶ **Sterling**: (157.5 grams / 31.10 grams / ounce) x (0.925) x $17 x 0.94 = $74.86

YOUR PAYMENT = $954.05 + $1006.53 + $74.86 = $2,035.44

A simple spreadsheet sent in with your metals will ensure a smooth transaction!

PURITY	# of PIECES	TOTAL WGT
10 KT	11	71.4 gm
14 KT	8	53.8 gm
Sterling	19	157.5 gm

A great way to sell your gold, silver and platinum finds directly, especially if they hold stones, is to spend a little time polishing them – a Dremel tool works well – and package each one in a box like what you find at a jewelry shop. Price them somewhere between what you would get for it as scrap from one of the refiners and what the item would sell for in a store. Bring them to work before holidays such as Christmas, Valentines Day or Mother's Day or spend a day at the local flea market and watch how quickly they sell. It's a win-win for both parties, you get more than you would have by simply scrapping them out and they get a great piece of jewelry at a nice discount. You can order the boxes from one of the companies listed at the end of this chapter.

COINS

Recovered coins can be sorted into two distinct groups when it comes to cashing them in – common, everyday coins and collectible coins.

Common coins worth nothing more than face value can be cleaned with hot water and tumbled as described in the chapter on cleaning your finds. Obviously the easiest way to cash in your everyday coins is to take them to your bank or one of the coin counting machines found in most department and grocery stores today. A twist that many coin hunters have been practicing for years is to convert the money received from the clad coins into something that has value such as gold or silver bullion or even collectible coins. At the time this book was drafted, silver was in the neighborhood of $18 per ounce and silver bullion was selling for between $18.50 and $20 per ounce. If you believe that precious metal prices will continue to rise, picking up some one-ounce silver bars with clad coins found at the local park might be worth looking into. I remember talking to a successful coin hunter a few years ago at a large show who told me he was picking up silver rounds (1 ounce coin-shaped ingots) at the rate of 5 or 6 a month. With silver prices higher now that has probably dropped off but he had built up a nice "nest egg" over the years from searching sites that held primarily common date coins. For some time now, I've converted bags of clad coins at the end of the season into cash that I've used to buy collectible coins including Indian Head gold pieces, silver dollars and even high-grade Indian Head cents, Buffalo nickels and tokens.

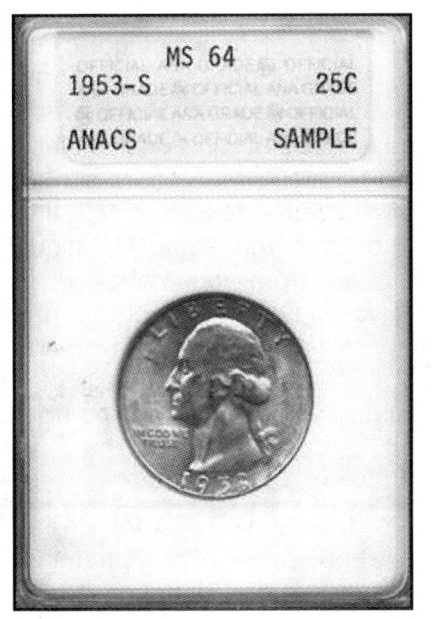

Collectible coins are another story altogether. Gold or silver coins tend to come out pretty much unaffected by the ground other than a bit of tarnish on the silver. Before you do anything other than rinse the loose dirt from them, check out the value of the coin using one of the books or on-line resources. Something that might appear totally harmless such as gently rubbing the coin can produce scratches that will drop the value by half or more. If the coin has collectible value, consider having it evaluated and protected by ANACS which is the only coin grading service that works with unearthed coins. I've used them for some of the more valuable coins I've found over the years and the nominal cost to have to them evaluated and encased has been well worth it even though I have not sold any of them. On the other hand, if you do want to sell a collectible coin, having it evaluated by a well-respected service such as ANACS is a requirement if you want to get the most for it. If the coin is worth $1,000+, some of the numismatic auction houses may help you market the coin. If you want to look for other options, there is always E-Bay or one of the coin auction sites that can be found with a quick Internet search or listed in the back a coin magazine. If there is a coin show in your area, you may find a dealer willing to make you an offer on the spot.

PROSPECTING FINDS

As discussed in the chapter on prospecting, finds can include gold, silver and copper nuggets, gold or silver ore samples and meteorites to name just a few. Most prospectors tend to hang on to every speck of precious metal they find but there may be times when a need for the money the finds are worth outweighs the desire to continue building a collection. You may also simply want to buy some new equipment and cashing in some of your finds is an easy way to do so.

If you are a prospector and have a fair amount of fine flake and flour gold, a great way to sell this type of gold is to make jewelry out of it by placing it in small glass locket available from jewelry suppliers. A&D Jewelry is one such supplier that caters to prospectors and has a wide variety of lockets and related supplies available. A small amount of flakes in a locket can easily be sold to friends, co-workers or at a flea market netting a decent profit for your time and effort. If you have larger specimens, do not base your asking price strictly on what the weight of the piece is. Specimens that are collectible quality can sell for 2-3 times the actual gold content value or more. Check with a reputable gold dealer or jeweler to find out what you should expect to receive before you wind up giving away what you worked so hard to recover.

Other prospecting finds can usually be sold on one of the prospecting or rock collecting forums found on the Internet or on one of the auction sites if you have a good idea as to what it is worth. Before listing your finds, spend a little time looking over what similar items have sold for recently.

RELICS & OTHER ARTIFACTS

A key factor in placing a value on any relic or artifact is its pedigree. An old square nail might seem like something that would typically get tossed in the trash can; however, if it is documented as having come from a structure of historic significance – even in local circles – that same nail now has value to collectors. Get in the habit of keeping your finds separated by where they came from not only to enhance their value but to preserve the story they can tell about a specific location. Most of my relics have been placed in Riker mounts which are inexpensive frames of various sizes with details on where they were found taped to the back of each. An example of how pedigree can boost an item's value can be seen in the adjacent photo. The Minnie ball is a common Civil War find and without any information on where one came from, typically sells for a few dollars. By placing one of these bullets into a Riker mount costing less than $2 along with a card printed on a home computer, it can now be sold for upwards of $15. If you find artifacts from sites that might have local interest, this same technique can help you generate a nice sideline income from your hobby while preserving the history that goes with it. If you have an artifact that has wide-spread interest such as something from one of the major wars, selling it through an on-line auction site will likely net you the most in terms of the final sales price. If your item has more of a local interest, either an advertisement in a newspaper or trade paper serving your area or setting up a booth at a flea market or collectors show will be the best way to market it.

> **TIP**: While donating your finds will not put money in your pockets directly, you can take a tax deduction on your income tax return by doing so. Think about preserving your finds, putting them in a Riker mount along with documenting its pedigree and donating it to a local historical society or museum. Adding your name to the display will help build credibility in local circles and possibly get you access to additional sites.

A final note on selling finds that you might feel are worthless. There are collectors of virtually anything today. Items such as old cereal box premiums, Cracker Jack prizes, automobile keys, saloon tokens, padlocks . . . the list is endless . . . can be worth far more than one might think. E-Bay is a great resource to check on the value of some of your finds. For example, an old Tom Mix decoder ring that came in a cereal box that was found by a detectorist recently sold for more than $100, a Cracker Jack prize from the 1920's sold for more than $50 and a Model T car key sold for $30! So before you inadvertently add a valuable collectible to one of your Riker-mount collections and give away what could have been the most valuable item you found this year, make sure you know what anything you put up for sale is really worth.

REFERENCE RESOURCE BIBLIOGRAPHY

EQUIPMENT

- **A&D Jewelry**: Supplies to make jewelry from your prospecting finds; http://andjewelry.com/
- **American Weigh Scales**: Complete line of digital scales; http://www.americanweigh.com/
- **FetPak Inc.**: Wholesale supplier of jewelry display boxes and related items – great source if you plan on selling your jewelry finds rather then scrap them out for bullion content; http://www.fetpak.com/
- **Gem World**: Diamond testers; http://www.gemworld.com/DiamondTesters.asp
- **Kellyco Detector Accessories**: Gold & Diamond testers and digital scales; http://www.kellycodetectors.com/accessories/Scales%2BGold-tester.htm
- **National Jewelers Supplies**: Gold & Diamond testers, digital scales and more; http://www.nationaljewelerssupplies.com/
- **Novel Box Company Ltd.**: Wholesale supplier of jewelry display boxes and related items; http://www.novelbox.com/
- **Save-on-Scales**: Complete line of digital scales; http://www.saveonscales.com/
- **Scales-n-Tools**: Digital scales and gold & diamond testers; http://www.scales-n-tools.com/

Internet Resources

- **ANACS Coin Grading Services:** This is the only service that will grade "dug" coins with environmental damage. If you have a coin that you believe has value, protect your find through the ANACS grading and preservation services; http://www.anacs.com/
- **Kitco**: The #1 site for real-time spot prices, historical trends and reference material for all forms of precious metals; http://www.kitco.com/
- **Precious Metal Calculator**: Simple to use tool that computes what your precious metal finds are worth based on current spot prices and the refinery discount; http://www.dendritics.com/scales/metal-calc.asp
- **Theanto.com**: Want to know what the bullion value is for you US, Canadian and Mexican silver coins? This handy application will give you the current values: http://www.thentao.com/CoinBullionValues.xls
- **Wildwinds**; Online reference and value determination for ancient Greek, Roman and Byzantine coins; http://www.wildwinds.com/

Refineries

- **123 Precious Metal Refining, LLC.**; (888) 939-0123; http://www.123preciousmetal.com/
- **Midwest Refineries, LLC**; 4471 Forest Ave., Waterford, MI 48328, (800) 356-2955; http://midwestrefineries.com/
- **Northern Refineries** 29509 Sierra Point Circle, Farmington Hills, MI 48331 (800) 882-7729 / (248) 231-2800; http://www.northernrefineries.com/
- **Specialty Metals Smelters & Refiners, LLC**; 2490 Black Rock Turnpike, Fairfield, CT 06825, (800) 208-2608 / (203) 366-2500; http://www.goldrefiner.com/

"State-of-the-Art" Treasure Hunting Techniques

Global Positioning System (GPS) Units

The use of the Global Positioning System or GPS for short has become an invaluable tool in locating and mapping areas worldwide over the past decade. Consisting of 24 satellites orbiting the earth, the system allows anyone with a handheld receiver to pinpoint their location to within a few feet anywhere in the world. While the military has been using this technology for many years, a random error signal had been added to the system which civilian receivers could not eliminate resulting in a large inaccuracy in the readings obtained in the field. Once that error signal was removed, it allowed civilians to purchase low-cost receivers that were accurate to within a few feet anywhere in the world. So what does this mean to the treasure hunter looking to improve their success rate? Well, the most obvious use is to log sites you may have worked that were off the beaten path such as foundations in the woods, battle sites, productive spots found prospecting or simply parts of large parks that you want to record for future reference. All GPS units have the ability to record a precise location with one or two keystrokes and then allow this information to be downloaded to a computer and saved. You can even share these saved locations with fellow detectorists and they will be able to walk to the exact spot you marked with ease. You can also capture a record of the exact path you followed in the field and transfer it to a map on your computer. OK, so that covers marking the location of a site that you have found and want to come back to but that really does not help you find sites that might have otherwise gone undetected. This is where adding one or two additional steps can really pay off in terms of you being able to be the first person to hunt a site that has lain undisturbed for decades or even centuries.

Map Calibration Software

Let's look at an example. Steve has spent the afternoon in the local library and was fortunate to have come across several topographical maps from the early 1900's covering the area surrounding his home showing a number of potential sites. In addition to the topographical maps, he also found a few older maps from the 1800's showing sites such as mills, an old stagecoach stop, two taverns and a tollgate. He realizes that some of these sites may in fact have never been hunted but that roads on the old maps do not look at all familiar and he is having a hard time figuring out where the sites on the old map might be in relation to a new map he brought with him. After an hour, he gives up and heads for home disappointed that he was not able to find out where the sites were and make plans to head to the local park once again. Sound like you might find yourself in this situation? Unless you live in an area where roads have not changed much in the last 100 years and little or no development has taken place, trying to transfer a location from a map even 50 years old to a current one can often be an exercise in futility but there is now an easy way to accomplish just that. Computers have made tasks that might have been impossible a decade ago child's play and this is the case in transferring the location of sites from old maps to current maps.

There is some equipment needed but most of us already have it at home. A computer, scanner and ideally a handheld GPS unit will be all that is required. Once you find an old map, and it can be any map, it is scanned into the computer. It is then analyzed by one of the several low-cost programs designed to calibrate the scan and allow you to obtain coordinates from any point on the map. The way this is done is to identify two or three points on the old map that you can obtain coordinates for from a new map or a directly from a GPS unit. What you are looking for is a location that would not have changed from one map to the other such as an old graveyard, church, fork in a road or river, a mountaintop, etc. By telling the program what the precise location is for the two or three points you know the coordinates for, it will then be able to give you the coordinates for any other location on the map. You simply move the cursor over the site(s) you are interested in and read off the precise coordinates in the window provided. If you have a GPS receiver, enter the coordinates into it and head off to see what you can find (with permission of the landowner of course). If you don't have a GPS unit, you can enter the coordinates into a computer-based mapping program such as those listed in the Reference Resource Bibliography section of the Research chapter or simply enter them into an on-line mapping service like Google Maps (http://www.google.com/maps/) or Bing maps (http://www.bing.com.maps). You can then print out a map with directions to find the locations obtained from the old maps. The full versions of the two mapping packages listed at the end of this chapter have an additional valuable feature which is the ability to obtain aerial photographs, street maps and current topographical maps with the click of a mouse showing the coordinates of the sites you have scanned in making them all you need to find sites not hunted by dozens before you.

Remember the example of Steve and his frustration? Well, a year ago a friend of mine, Jim Harnick, came across several old topographical maps of his area and scanned them into his computer. Using the calibration software, he used some points that he could recognize from a modern map and quickly calibrated the old map. Picking off five old one-room school houses, some farmhouses long since forgotten and a drive-in theatre, he transferred the coordinates to his handheld GPS unit and headed out to see what he could find. According to the GPS, the first schoolhouse he visited was in the middle of a field that had recently been harvested. Obtaining permission from the landowner, Jim walked out to where the school was to have been situated and started hunting. The first few signals were rusted nails but then a 1912 Barber dime turned up. Over the next few hours, he recovered 18 coins from the late 1800's to the early 1900's along with items including an old whistle, a charm bracelet and a silver religious medal. As he left, he could tell that the site had not been hunted before and would be worth revisiting many more times in the future. Finding the site took very little effort and the rewards were there once he started searching the area. There are countless sites worldwide that have yet to be searched with a metal detector and leveraging evolving technology will help you locate them.

Aerial Photography & Street-Level Photo Mapping

Less than a decade ago, the use of aerial photography for anything other than classified government operations would have been prohibitively expensive to even consider for everyday treasure hunting. Well like many things in the high-tech arena that were initially priced so only those with deep pockets could afford them, this technology has become readily accessible and is being used by successful hunters worldwide. Imagine being able to "fly over" any area you might be interested in and look for indications of a site worth searching. The time saved is immeasurable. If you are looking for sites that might have been used decades or even centuries ago yet are now in largely undeveloped areas such as fields or woods, an aerial photograph of the area can quickly be scanned for any sign of previous use. Being able to plan a day in the field without having to leave your house by simply using the Internet shows just how helpful today's technology can be in field. I have located several old foundations dating back to the mid-1800's in remote wooded areas of South Carolina that might otherwise have gone undetected through the use of these photographs. Both Google and Bing mapping applications are extremely useful for this purpose. Many other detectorists, bottle collectors and cache hunters have done the same thing in their local areas, spend a little time exploring the on-line mapping capabilities that exist and see what you can turn up.

To provide another example, I recently pulled up aerial photos of a few towns I was interested in visiting and spent a few hours "flying over" the locations while sitting at my computer. When I saw something that looked promising, I zoomed in and in many cases was able to pull up street level photos that provided a clear picture of what the site looked like – almost as if I was standing there in person! The screen shot to the right shows a vacant lot that I found in a town that dated back to the mid-1800's that caught my eye with what appeared to be several paths or walkways on one side. While the picture below might look like a photo taken with a digital camera, it is in fact a street level image I was able to pull up through Goggle Maps of the area highlighted with the white outline. It clearly showed that a house had once stood there and a after driving to the town, a 4-hour search turned up a number of coins dating back more than 100 years including a sliver half dollar and a few trade tokens from local businesses.

The use of the aerial photographs is not limited to searching for something as insignificant as an old foundation, well or bridge. In early 2009, a man living in California was looking over aerial photographs covering a section of the Texas coastline when something caught his attention. The outline of a ship was visible and it was determined to be in the vicinity of where a Spanish barkentine believed to be carrying gold and silver ran aground and was lost in 1822. Although this find is currently tied up in court while the person that found it and the land owner attempt to come to some agreement, it shows the power of what can be located through the use of this tool.

Remember, the best part of these tools is their cost . . . . they're FREE!

REFERENCE RESOURCE BIBLIOGRAPHY

Internet Sites

- **Find's GPS Classroom**: Great place to ask your questions; http://www.findmall.com/list.php?16
- **MapTools**: Excellent site to maximize the potential of your GPS unit: http://www.maptools.com/
- **TopoFusion Users Forum**: Master this calibration program; http://www.topofusion.com/forum/
- **TopoGrafix Forums**: Covers ExpertGPS & other programs; http://forums.topografix.com/
- **TreasureNet – GPS Forum**: http://forum.treasurenet.com/index.php/board,310.0.html

GPS Resellers

- **GPS Planet**: Supplier of GPS units from all major manufacturers offering buying assistance and technical support; http://www.gps-planet.com/
- **The GPS Store**: One of the leading suppliers of GPS units and accessories from all major manufacturers, pre-buying & after-the-sale technical support is available; http://www.thegpsstore.com
- **Tiger GPS**: Supplier of GPS units from all major manufacturers offering buying assistance and technical support; http://www.tigergps.com/

Internet Mapping Tools

- **ACME Mapper**: Powerful free online mapping tool that provides multiple views of selected areas and generates the GPS coordinates of any point of interest you come across; http://mapper.acme.com/
- **Bing Maps**: Street level and aerial photo mapping for the world. Many locations have street views that allow you to scout out a new area from your keyboard. GPS coordinates can be entered to get directions to sites; http://www.bing.com/maps
- **Google Maps**: Street level and aerial photo mapping for the world. Many locations have street views that allow you to scout out a new area from your keyboard. GPS coordinates can be entered to get directions to sites; http://maps.google.com/

Computer Software

- **ExpertGPS**: Full-featured mapping application including the ability to convert locations from old maps to GPS coordinates (Trial version is available); http://www.expertgps.com
- **TopoFusion**: Full-featured mapping application including the ability to convert locations from old maps to GPS coordinates (Trial version is available); http://www.topofusion.com/

Treasure Hunting Trips & Outings

Hopefully the preceding chapters have provided you with the information you were looking for to be more successful on a consistent basis in the forms of treasure hunting you have chosen to follow. But what if you live in downtown New York City or the panhandle of Texas and are caught up in the chapters covering prospecting for gold, searching the fields of Europe for artifacts spanning 1,000's of years or diving for treasure on a long-lost galleon? Well, there are companies and organizations that have put together trips to allow you to try those forms of treasure hunting out without investing a fortune in equipment, conducting endless hours of research and hoping you get lucky on your first attempt. The following companies have eliminated all of the guesswork and developed packages that will virtually ensure you find what you are seeking. Visit their websites and see if their offerings might just fit your upcoming vacation schedule.

GOLD PROSPECTING TRIPS

- **Alabama Gold Camp**: Located in the heart of Alabama's gold belt with miles of creek to pan, sluice, dredge, high-bank, and metal detect, the Alabama Gold Camp offers a great destination to search for that yellow metal. Cabins with heat & A/C are available as are tent sites along with a general store containing offering gear and other supplies. http://www.alabamagoldcamp.com/
- **Arizona Gold Adventures**: Unique individual prospecting trips in Arizona where you can search for gold and meteorites. Guides, instruction and equipment are provided as part of the packages offered. http://www.arizonagoldadventures.com/
- **Chicken Gold Camp & Outpost**: Built on site of a camp built in the 1930's by the Fairbanks Exploration Company, you will have plenty to keep you busy - exploring this mining community, touring the nearby historic gold dredge & actual working on-site gold mine, panning your own gold or mining on their claims and even enjoying a cappuccino! http://www.chickengold.com
- **GPAA**: The world's premier gold prospecting organization offers several different trips to gold producing areas across the United States. http://www.goldprospectors.org/
  - **Alaska Expedition** Since 1982, the GPAA has been escorting prospectors north to mining camps on 2,300 acres of the beautiful Seward Peninsula near Nome, Alaska; providing them with food, shelter, mining equipment, and mining techniques in the form of classes and seminars conducted by knowledgeable experts.
  - **Mother Lode Expedition**: The Mother Lode Expedition is divided into three one-week adventures and will accommodate groups of 20 comfortably for the one-week stays at the campsite located near Columbia, California.
  - **Outings**: For over thirty years, the GPAA has been running common gold operations designed for the members to come together and find gold. There are 3 and 5 day outings where the participants work shifts and all the gold found is split between the participants on the final morning, normally Sunday. Outings are held at sites across the United States.
- **Oregon Gold Trips**: Since 1995 this firm has provided guided and outfitted gold mining trips in Oregon. Choose from the popular Wine's Camp or the remote Emily Camp deep in the south Oregon wilderness. Enjoy an Oregon gold trip and get away from the city life! At both camps, you are provided with cooked meals, cabin accommodations, & equipment plus you keep the gold you find! Trips are limited to 12 guests http://www.oregongoldtrip.com/
- **Paradise Valley**: The ultimate remote gold mining package. Located above Alaska's Artic Circle, Paradise Valley has been hosting individuals & groups for 25 years. The only access is via bush plane which means many areas have never been searched. Spend your stay in a rustic cabin in the middle of the gold fields. http://www.akpub.com/akttt/parad.html

- **Roaring Camp Mining Co.**: Roaring Camp is something special in the way of family recreation. It is an old gold mining camp on California's Mokulmne River which used to be accessible only by horseback. Roaring Camp was once a camp for Forty Niner's, and since it was so inaccessible, most of the gold still remains. Visitors can see the operating gold mine and mine their own gold by panning, sluicing, dredging, and dry washing; http://roaringcampgold.com/

METAL DETECTING TRIPS TO ENGLAND

- **Jimmy Sierra's Discovery Tours**: For nearly 20 years, Jimmy "Sierra" Normandi has been taking groups of detectorists to search the fields of England. All fields are carefully researched and selected. You will hunt on farmer's private fields that were originally the locations of, or near, ancient villages, market places, villas, forts, roads or other populated area and find coins and relics dating back over 2000 years. All of your finds are identified by experts. Every recordable find is identified by their museum accredited staff archeologist with written detailed descriptions. http://jimmysierra.com/tour_info2.htm
- **Gerry's Detectors England Detecting Adventures**: Have you ever dreamed of digging up ancient coins & artifacts on a seven, ten or fourteen-day long detecting trip to England? All the legwork to gain access to sites is already taken care of and you get to choose which fields you want to hunt. The package includes all transportation, most food, lodging, access to sites, an export license and a 30+ year professional detectorist there to help make sure you are doing the right things to make your chances of success that much greater.; http://www.gerrysdetectors.com/england_trips.asp
- **England Detecting Adventure**: Offering either seven or ten day packages that include ground transportation, lodging, meals and services of local experts. Small groups - 10 or less - ensure personal service and increase your chances for success. http://metaldetectingtours.com/
- **England Detecting Vacation & Tours**: The organizers have exclusive permission to bring small groups of detectorists to large country farm estates that normally have a no metal detecting policy and do not allow other detectorists access to their lands. There are many historic features on these huge estates; ancient settlements and monuments have been recorded either on or close to these carefully selected venues. As a tour member, you will not only have access to these estates but you will also benefit from their extensive local knowledge & expertise in researching maps and archaeological documents. 10-day tours are offered. http://www.englanddetectingtours.com/

RELIC HUNTING TRIPS

- **Diggin in Virginia**: An invitational hunt held on private lands with the permission of the land owner at sites in Virginia twice a year. Dates for signing up for upcoming hunts will be posted on the website along with details of the hunt. http://www.mytreasurespot.com/main/list.php?5
- **Grand National Relic Shootout**: The GNRS is an annual relic hunt founded by Larry Cissna in 1998. Teams consist of individuals using their preferred brand of detector participate in an organized competitive relic hunt. The number of members on each team may change year-to-year due to the specific site chosen for the event. The hunt takes place on a real, un-seeded, relic site. http://www.thetreasuredepot.com/GNRS/gnrs.html

UNDERWATER TREASURE HUNTING TRIPS

- **Gold Hound Treasure Divers**: Ever dream of discovering sunken treasure? Here's your chance with Gold Hound Treasure Divers. Search with the Gold Hound Treasure Divers crew for the 1715 Fleet mother lode or simply come along for the ride. Treasure hunts are semi-private with no more than two visiting divers in the water at any given time. Divers entering the water must be at least open water certified. http://www.goldhoundtreasuredivers.com/

Metal Detecting Clubs

Like any other hobby, sport or interest that has a number of people who share a common interest, treasure hunters have had clubs since when there were little more than a handful of people taking part in the treasure hunting. Why join a club? People probably have 100 different reasons for joining but the biggest factors include being with a group that shares your passion, seeing what others are finding to get you fired up to find more, picking up some new techniques or tips from presentations at the meetings and gaining access to new sites to search. While all treasure hunting clubs are social in nature, many also provide services to the community to help promote a positive image of the hobby to those not involved in it. Some of these activities include:

- Offering to provide assistance to law enforcement agencies in searching for evidence associated with crimes. Some agencies now have their own equipment; however, many do not and often welcome the offer to work with detectives in recovering crime scene evidence.
- Providing a free recovery service to people that might have lost something such as a ring, set of keys, billfold, etc. A few well-placed announcements offering this service will garner a great deal of positive publicity and help people recover what they had given up for lost.
- Working with local historical societies or universities conducting archeological surveys of sites in the local area. Funding is tight and equipment is often not available so the expertise provided by the club is usually welcomed with open arms.
- Putting on talks or demonstrations for groups such as the Boy Scouts, senior citizen centers, Rotary, Kiwanis, etc. Often these talks result in new productive sites being identified and permission extended to search them which benefit all club members.

If you are planning a trip to another part of the country or a destination in another part of the world, contacting a club in the local area can serve two purposes. First, you might be able to get connected with a member who is willing to take you out hunting while you are in the area. Second, you can find out if there are any restrictions you should know about before getting into hot water out of ignorance as well as ask if there are any issues such as ground conditions that might dictate a different choice in equipment you are planning on bringing. The metal detecting organizations covered in the next chapter as well as those below all contain club listings to help you find a local group to contact

Clubs are another source of information that may help you get the most out of all your equipment. If you have one in your area and don't yet belong to it, stop in for a visit. Not all clubs are created equally but most are made up of fellow treasure hunters willing to share techniques. If there is no club locally and you have the initiative, think about starting one yourself or with some of your hunting partners.

REFERENCE RESOURCE BIBLIOGRAPHY

Internet Resources

- **Bounty Hunter's Find-a-Club Service**: http://www.detecting.com/clubs/
- **Gold Miner's Headquarters Metal Detecting and Treasure Hunting Clubs & Organizations;** Extensive list of clubs and organizations across the US; http://www.goldminershq.com/clubs/metal1.htm
- **Go Metal Detecting.com**: List of clubs worldwide – not an all-inclusive list but a good place to start; http://gometaldetecting.com/links-clubs.htm
- **Metal Detecting Clubs & Organizations in the UK**: http://detecting.org.uk/forum/index.php?board=11.0
- **TreasureNet – Clubs & Friends Forum**: http://forum.treasurenet.com/index.php/board,55.0.html

Worldwide Metal Detecting Organizations

When I first started treasure hunting some 45+ years ago, there were very few people using metal detectors and even fewer restrictions on where one could use them. Unfortunately as the hobby gained in popularity, the misplaced actions of a small but quite visible number of fellow hobbyists caught the attention of legislators at all levels worldwide and laws were written to limit when and where detecting could be done. Thankfully most of us obey the laws that exist and when possible try to get those that are overly restrictive repealed or at least modified. In order to help create a consistent appearance and position for detectorists worldwide, several organizations have been created to help reduce the number of restrictions we face and develop a more amenable relationship with the legislators and archeologists that see the hobbyist as an adversary rather than a partner. If you are active in the hobby it is in your best interest to join one or more of these organizations. Even if you are not a "club-type" person, your support will help provide the resources they need to ensure we all have areas to hunt for years to come. The section below provides an overview of the larger organizations currently in operation.

The Federation of Metal Detector and Archaeological Clubs (United States)

The mission of the FMDAC is the Preservation, Promotion, and Protection of the recreational use of metal detectors

The Federation of Metal Detector and Archaeological Clubs or the FMDAC as it is commonly referred to, was organized in 1984 as a legislative and educational nonprofit organization and is currently made up of about 150 metal detecting clubs with more than 5,500 members. The FMDAC strongly supports metal detecting clubs in every state through the establishment of seven FMDAC Chapters. Each FMDAC Chapter is assigned seven to eight states within a specific region. The primary objective of each chapter is to provide club support, recognition, education, and grow FMDAC Club membership. For those that do not live near an active club, the FMDAC has established the

Independent Membership program and is not intended to by-pass any local metal detecting club but rather promote the hobby for all that want to help keep the hobby alive.

The FMDAC has established a Code of Ethics for the proper use of a metal detector which has been endorsed by most metal detector manufacturers and adopted by many clubs worldwide. A number of hobbyists have the code printed on small cards they can give to property owners when seeking permission to search it to show how they operate and will treat the property.

FMDAC and Treasure Hunter's Code of Ethics

- I will always check federal, state, county and local laws before searching. It is my responsibility to "know the law"
- I will respect private property and will not enter private property without the owner's permission. Where possible, such permission will be in writing.
- I will take care to refill all holes and try not to leave any damage.
- I will remove and dispose of any and all trash and litter that I find.
- I will appreciate and protect our inheritance of natural resources, wildlife and private property.
- I will as an ambassador for the hobby, use thoughtfulness, consideration and courtesy at all times.
- I will work to help bring unity to our hobby by working with any organization of any geographic area that may have problems that will limit their ability to peacefully pursue the hobby.
- I will leave gates as found.
- I will build fires in designated or safe places only.
- I will report to the proper authorities any individuals who enter and or remove artifacts from federal parks or state preserves.

For more information on the FMDAC, visit their website at
http://www.FMDAC.org

National Council for Metal Detecting (NCMD) (United Kingdom)

The National Council for Metal Detecting is a representative body of elected volunteers formed in 1981 to provide a venue for responsible metal detector users to be able to discuss problems affecting the hobby and to provide an authoritative voice to counter ill-informed and frequently misleading criticism of the hobby. It does not represent the trade or archaeological interests.

The NCMD has gained Government recognition as an organization which represents metal detector users countrywide. It has played a major role in representing the views of those metal detector users to Government Departments regarding legislation affecting the hobby. The National Council for Metal Detecting has a written constitution which is available to all members.

What are the benefits of joining the National Council for Metal Detecting?

- The National Council seeks the opinions of its membership on matters affecting the hobby as they arise and keeps them informed on developments. The NCMD offers advice on various matters via its national officers and individuals with long experience in the hobby.
- The National Council provides a means whereby the consensus views of its membership can be represented both at Local and National Government level, with the Local and National Press, and any other organizations which may have an interest in hobby activities.
- The National Council provides excellent Civil Liability Insurance free of charge to all of its registered members.
- The National Council holds meetings attended by regional representatives at least quarterly. It has an Annual General Meeting for the election of officers, to give reports on its activities and to present audited annual accounts far the scrutiny and questioning of all of its membership.
- Various social events, rallies, exhibitions etc. are arranged by NCMD regions
- The National Council maintains an archive of documents relating to events affecting the hobby for the use of its membership.

The National Council for Metal Detecting Code of Conduct

- Do not trespass. Obtain permission before venturing on to any land.
- Respect the Country Code. Do not leave gates open, damage crops or frighten animals.
- Wherever the site, do not leave a mess or an unsafe condition for those who may follow. It is perfectly simple to extract a coin or other small object buried a few inches below the ground without digging a great hole. Use a suitable digging implement to cut a neat flap (do not remove the plug of earth entirely from the ground), extract the object, reinstate the grass, sand or soil carefully, and even you will have difficulty in locating the find spot again.
- If you discover any live ammunition or any lethal object such as an unexploded bomb or mine, do not disturb it. Mark the site carefully and report the find to the local police and landowner.
- Help keep Britain tidy. Safely dispose of refuse you come across.
- Report all unusual historical finds to the landowner, and acquaint yourself with current NCMD policy relating to the Voluntary Reporting of Portable Antiquities.
- Remember it is illegal for anyone to use a metal detector on a protected area (e.g. scheduled archaeological site, SSSI, or Ministry of Defense property) without permission from the appropriate authority.
- Acquaint yourself with the definitions of Treasure contained in the Treasure Act 1996 and its associated Code of Practice, making sure you understand your responsibilities.
- Remember that when you are out with your metal detector you are an ambassador for our hobby. Do nothing that might give it a bad name.
- Never miss an opportunity to explain your hobby to anyone who asks about it.

For more information on the National Council for Metal Detecting, visit their website at:
http://www.NCMD.co.uk

Federation of Independent Detectorists (FID)
(United Kingdom – Worldwide Members Welcomed)

The Federation of Independent Detectorists or FID was formed as a non-profit organization dedicated to promoting the hobby in a positive light and working to ensure areas remain open to detectorists in the future. FID has been organized primarily for the individual precluded from normal club membership, through distance, age or illness, employment or home ties; however FID membership is open to all detectorists who support its aims. By becoming a member of FID you can make a valuable contribution to the future of the hobby. If you own a metal detector, or are about to get one, then now is the time send for an application form to join *The Federation of Independent Detectorists (FID)* and become a member of the worlds largest metal detecting organization.

Some of the benefits afforded by FID membership include:

- Quarterly postal bulletins keeping you up to date with all the news
- Your own personal identity card with your photo on it
- If you live in the United Kingdom you also have free public liability insurance for £5,000,000

THE FEDERATION OF INDEPENDENT DETECTORISTS "CODE OF CONDUCT"

- Get permission before detecting on private land. Never Trespass.
- Make an agreement on sharing finds with the landowner to avoid any later misunderstandings.
- Report all your finds to the landowner, even those that must be declared to the Coroner as well.
- Remember to shut all gates, never walk through standing crops, do not startle animals or nesting birds.
- Fill all holes, even on ploughed land or beaches. Never leave a mess or damage grass, a sharp trowel will cut a neat plug and once replaced and firmed in, the find spot will almost be invisible.
- Most metal rubbish can be recycled. The planet belongs to all of us, so dispose of your unwanted iron, lead, cans, silver paper etc. With care for the environment, and never leave junk on the site.
- Never detect on a scheduled archaeological site, to do so is a criminal offence unless you have permission from the Secretary of State for National Heritage.
- Report all gold or silver artifacts over 300 years old to the local Coroner, also hoards of coins or plate of any age or material.
- All bombs, mines, ammunition or chemical containers, should have the find spot marked and be reported to the Police. Never attempt to move them yourself.
- As a FID member you have a lot to be proud of, so always be friendly to people who ask about your hobby, help them find lost metal objects when requested and never break this "Code of Conduct" or give the hobby a bad image.

For more information on the Federation of Independent Detectorists, visit their website at:
http://fid.newbury.net/

Treasure Hunting Laws

As the introduction to the previous chapter alluded to, laws relating to the use of metal detection equipment and restrictions on where searching is allowed or what items are deemed protected have been passed since the hobby first took form more than 60 years ago. Unfortunately, more continue to be enacted on a regular basis worldwide. The metal detecting organizations profiled in the previous chapter were founded to promote the positive aspects of the hobby and work with government agencies at all levels to keep unfounded laws and restrictions from being passed. While some of the laws may seem arcane or over-reaching on the part of the agency that enacted tem, they are still the law and as such need to be respected or we all face the consequences. The reason some recent laws have been drawn up has been a direct result of the inappropriate actions of a very small but visible segment of hobbyists and we all suffer the consequences with more and more areas either having limitations as to when they can be searched or closed off altogether.

Due to the fact that laws are continually changing with some being repealed, some being modified and new laws enacted, coming up with a definitive list is an effort in futility. This chapter will cover some of the laws that will not be changed in the near future and provide links to sources of information that can be used to check on what the current restrictions might be. If the sources of information appear to be somewhat dated, contact the agency in charge of the area you are interested in searching and see what the current restrictions might be. Most local dealers should be able to answer any questions you have as well and this is a resource that can be extremely helpful when traveling to another state or country.

> ⚠ Never search a site without knowing what the restrictions are hoping to plead ignorance if challenged. While that may have worked decades ago, there have been too many violations of laws that are on the books to expect nothing will happen if one is caught. Fines and / or jail time will likely result from being caught searching on restricted grounds!

The United States

There are laws pertaining to metal detecting and artifact collecting at the federal, state and local levels as well as on land deeded to Native Americans. On the federal level, the first law passed to address the collection of artifacts on federal land was The Antiquities Act of 1906. Passed by President Roosevelt, it authorized permits for legitimate archeological investigations and penalties for persons taking or destroying antiquities without permission. Two laws passed in the 1970's - The Archeological and Historic Preservation Act of 1974 and The Archaeological Resources Protection Act (ARPA) of 1979 – strengthened the definition of what constituted "archeological resources", expanded the enforcement powers of National Park Service and Indian Land personnel and specified penalties for anyone found to have violated the new laws. These penalties include a fine of up to $10,000 and / or one year in prison for the first offense and up to $100,000 and / or 5 years in prison for subsequent occurrences. Needless to say, none of us want to be the next "poster-child" for having been apprehended for violating one of these laws . . . and yes, there are people who have found themselves on the wrong side of the law and discovered that the federal government is serious about protecting their archeological resources.

For the most part, laws on the state and local level do not have penalties as severe as those mandated by the federal laws; however, violations can come with stiff fines and will likely lead to more restrictions being placed on the rest of the hobby. Take the time to research what restrictions might exist BEFORE you even bring a detector onto the site. For the most part, sites like schools, parks and beaches are generally open to metal detecting but even these are not absolutes. Some states have banned metal detecting in all or most of their state parks . . . even areas such as playgrounds or beaches. Some have restrictions that limit when you can search these areas; i.e., only after the park closes for the season or when no one is using the facility.

A good reference book for laws and restrictions within the United States was written by "Doc" Grimm. It contains letters received from the head offices of State Parks and federal agencies regarding the use of metal detectors on the lands under their control. As mentioned earlier, laws can and often do change so while this book will give you a picture of what the laws were at the time it was written, it pays to contact the office that Doc wrote to directly for a more current ruling on what restrictions might now be in place if you intend to visit one of the areas or sites.

The following sources will provide a good overview of restrictions on the federal and state level – just remember that there may be additional laws that need to be followed in order to search sites you may be interested in. You will still need to contact local police, school or parks personnel or fellow hobbyists to determine what restrictions might exist on a local level.

> **National Park Service's Federal Historic Preservation Laws**: This is a website that contains an electronic version of the National Park Service's publication of the same name that includes 23 Federal laws and portions of laws that pertain to the preservation of the Nation's cultural heritage. Arranged chronologically, the laws trace the evolution of historic preservation and cultural resource management philosophy from the Antiquities Act of 1906 through the American Battlefield Protection Act of 1996; http://www.nps.gov/history/history/hisnps/fhpl.htm
>
> **FMDAC State Park Regulations Compendium**: The FMDAC has attempted to compile all restrictions on the use of metal detectors in state parks across the country. This page provides a summary of the restrictions, if any, and contains links to the state's website that has the most current regulations: http://www.fmdac.org/parks/parks.htm

Worldwide

If you thought that rules and regulations related to the use of metal detectors and collecting artifacts in the United States were confusing with restrictions at the federal, state and local levels, imagine how much more confusing the regulations are throughout the rest of the world. In Europe where one can cross multiple countries in the course of a drive lasting but a few hours, one can find themselves dealing with literally dozens of laws – each with stiff penalties if violated. This is where knowledge is essential in ensuring you do not inadvertently find yourself in front of a magistrate trying to extricate yourself from a legal situation that can in short order become extremely expensive.

Use the information provided by the following references and build on it from there. Check with local metal detector dealers and detectorists in the area you are planning to search. They should be able to tell you what laws exist and what permits or permission might be required before you get there and find out you are not able to unpack your detector. The NCMD & FID can also help you determine what restrictions might exist in your area of interest

Standing Conference for European Metal Detecting: This organization was established with the goal of controlling the enacting for laws designed to curtail the use of metal detectors throughout Europe. Working to implement controls such as those in the United Kingdom, their website contains a listing of laws in many countries throughout Europe. Again, check with local hobbyists or dealers for the most current regulations. http://www.ukdetectornet.co.uk/scemd.htm

Laws Regarding Metal Detecting Outside the United Kingdom: Another compilation of laws by country. As stated on their website, "*This report has been written to provide available information on the law in other countries. Every effort has been made to verify its correctness but anyone wishing to metal detect overseas should satisfy themselves of the legal situation at the time they intend traveling*"; http://www.ncmd.co.uk/law.htm

War Relics Forum; A European website that provides a section that covers restrictions on the use of metal detectors throughout Europe and the former Soviet Union and provides a forum for posting questions on specific restrictions; http://warrelics.eu/forum/search-technology-metal-detecting/laws-pertaining-metal-detecting-10209/

> **TIP**: If you find that an area does allow metal detecting or collecting of artifacts, printout the webpage that contains that statement or obtain a letter from the office that manages the area. There's nothing worse than driving 100 miles to search a site you know allows it and having a ranger or other employee tell you to leave. With something official, you can often get right back to hunting after clearing it up with the individual.

Unless you are looking to sign up for the vacancy shown below, ensuring you are aware of <u>all</u> applicable laws and regulations prior to unpacking your gear is essential. We should all work to stem the number of restrictions being enacted by educating those that make the laws and presenting a positive image of what our hobby provides to its members and the public.

2010 Treasure Hunting Equipment Buyers Guide

The Buyers Guide portion of this book covers all of the models available from the major manufacturers around the world. There are some "boutique" or "in-house" brands that are not included based on their limited availability or user-base which impacts the ability to gather information on their use under different conditions. The previous chapters in this book have provided proven tips and techniques used by successful treasure hunters worldwide to locate productive sites and then conduct effective searches of them. You should be able to duplicate their success by following the guidance contained in these chapters. The next portion of the book will help you narrow down your choices and select the right detector for your specific needs and preferences.

The truly successful treasure hunters are not always the ones with the latest and most expensive equipment but rather those who know how to adjust their detector and understand what it is telling them and have selected the equipment best suited for the specific needs in their search area(s).

The final information that will help guarantee you are successful in the field is contained in the following chapters. Each brand as well as models in their current product line is covered. In addition, there are certain accessories that also enhance the ability of the detector to locate specific targets. The sections are written with a standard format and contain the following information:

- **Contact Information**: The beginning of each chapter contains the address, phone number, fax number and Internet web site for the manufacturer. This can be used to contact the manufacturer, request additional information if desired or find a local dealer.

- **The Product Line**: This section covers all of the models in the manufacturer's current product line and provides a summary of features and pricing along with photos of the units themselves.

    NOTE: While the product line was accurate at the time the book was printed, new models may be added, existing models discontinued throughout the year or pricing changed. A quick check of the manufacturer's website will alert you of any changes when you are ready to make a purchase. Pricing, particularly on models produced outside of the United States which can be affected by the dollar conversion, may change throughout the year . . . . check with your local dealer or the manufacturer for the latest pricing on models you are looking at.

- **Finds Showcase**: What are the users of each brand finding in the field? Many treasure hunters provided photos of the finds made while using metal detectors from a particular brand and this section shows what can be found with the right equipment and techniques.

- **Brand / Model-Specific Accessories**: Metal detector manufacturers design their equipment to perform well under a wide range of conditions and for different applications right out of the box. However, there are a number of accessories - both from the manufacturer itself as well as third parties - that can be used to significantly enhance the detector's performance for specific applications. This section covers accessories you might want to consider adding to your "treasure hunting arsenal" for increased success in the field.

- **Brand / Model-Specific Books, Videos and Internet Resources**: Despite the best efforts by the manufacturers in assembling a manual for each model that instructs owners how to best use the detector, many fail to answer the difficult questions that typically come up in the field. After all, each area will be different in terms of ground conditions and the type of target being sought. Well, luckily there are additional books, instructional video tapes and Internet web sites that one can use to help get the most out of a specific detector. Each brand-specific section that follows compiles those that can be of value to anyone - novice or seasoned detectorist – looking to get the most out of their detector.

The comparison tables at the end of the individual manufacturer sections provide a standardized compilation of information that allows comparisons to be made including intended use, operating characteristics, specific features, weight, batteries, and more.

As you go through the Buyers Guide, take a close look at what's currently available as there may brands you are not familiar with that may meet the needs for your specific form of treasure hunting and the conditions you will be searching under.

Aquascan International, Ltd.

Aquascan International Ltd.
Aquascan House, Hill Street, Newport, Gwent, NP20 1LZ
Wales, United Kingdom
Tel: +44 1633 841117
http://aquascan.co.uk/

E.O. Industries, LLC
(Authorized U.S. Agent for Aquascan International Ltd)
134 Fifth Ave. Suite 103, Indialantic, FL 32903
Tel: (435) 881-8240
http://www.eoindustries.com/

COMPANY PROFILE:

Aquascan International Ltd was incorporated in 1982 for the purpose of designing and manufacturing specialized underwater electronic detection instruments. Since the incorporation the company has maintained a stable but small workforce. Based in a customized facility in Newport, South Wales; the company has gradually broadened the range and sophistication of the instrumentation it produces and has included the provision of customer training and the supply of specialized survey services to its clients. The market place for the company's products and services is truly world-wide with a high proportion of the business being export-based. The USA forms an important part of the export business and is served by a sales & service outlet. Sales to the rest of the world are in general carried out on a direct basis, although a level of business is carried out through trade outlets. Technical services to the marine industry have also formed an important part of the Aquascan business over recent years, with a number of survey contracts being completed in a number of overseas countries. Many professional salvage companies use Aquascan products on their projects with great success.

PRODUCT LINE:

Aquascan AquaPulse 1B 15' / 10" / 8" coils   LIST: $1,460 / $1,385 / $1,325

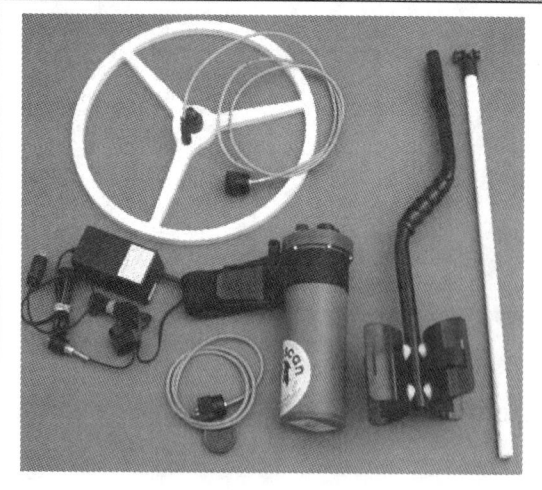

The AQUAPULSE 1B underwater metal detector has been used in every conceivable underwater application around the world in the past decade with an exceptional degree of success.

The AQUAPULSE 1B is an underwater metal detector employing a search head mounted on the end of a telescopic arm and can detect objects up to a range of 10ft.

In addition to the sensitivity control, the 1B underwater metal detector has an additional control to enable the whole range of AQUAPULSE coils (8", 10" & 15") to be used with it and the same control is used to reject surface clutter such as pull tabs, cigarette foil, etc., often found buried in the sand or mud. The internal "Ni-Cad" battery pack provides 10 hours operation.

Aquascan DX200 Underwater Magnetometer   **LIST: £1,900 / $3,155**

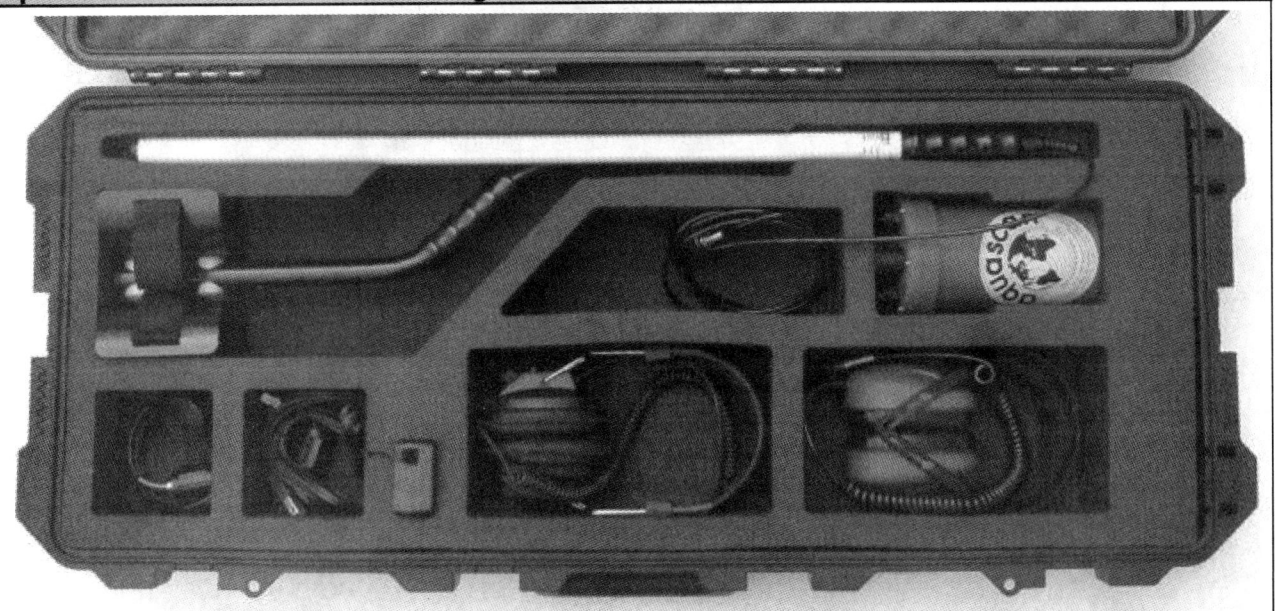

The AQUASCAN DX-200 has been developed as a powerful detection tool for the diver. It compliments a towed magnetometer where indication from the surface survey is met with an apparent debris-free seabed. A diver can use the DX-200 to quickly pinpoint the buried ferrous anomalies. Target response is via an audible tone allowing the diver to determine the distance to a target by the increase in the tone. The system consists of a robust electronic module together with a one meter long detection probe, a slim Bonephone (or optional U/W headphones) and a universal battery charger. Connections are made to the control unit with Ikelite connectors. The charger, Bonephone & headphones are identical to those supplied with the Aquapulse 1B family, allowing existing owners to interchange these items. The NiMH battery pack gives a minimum of 12 hours operation and can be charged at any time without the drawback of "memory" effects. A Low, Medium and High sensitivity mode can be selected that allows the system to be progressively de-sensitized as a target is investigated. The audible output can be preset to be silent or at a low frequency such that a minor change in pitch can be observed to allow for the presence of metallic items to be identified.

FACTORY ACCESSORIES:

The right accessory can greatly expand the versatility and performance of any detector as search conditions or the type of target being sought changes. The following accessories are available for the Aquascan line of equipment:

Search Coils:
- 8", 10" and 15" round coils with standard cable length
- 15" round coil with 20 meters (65 feet) of cable to allow surveys to be done from a boat
- 1" probe in multiple lengths

Headphones
- Land headphones with an Ikelite connector
- Underwater headphones with an Ikelite connector

Other Items:
- Optional shafts of various lengths (for diving or land use)
- Replacement battery packs & chargers

Bounty Hunter

First Texas Products, LLC.
1100 Pendale, El Paso, TX 79907
(915) 633-8354
http://www.Detecting.com

COMPANY PROFILE:

Bounty Hunter is a name that has been familiar to treasure hunters for many years although the actual company has changed hands and locations a few times since it was originally founded in the 1970's in the mountains of Oregon. Bounty Hunter or Pacific Northwest Instruments as it was originally known – moved to Phoenix, Arizona in the late 1970's to expand their manufacturing capabilities and quickly become a respected name in the treasure hunting industry. As the business landscape changed, the company was sold and became part of the original Teknetics brand which was based back in Oregon. Incorporating some innovative concepts developed by chief engineer George Payne, the Bounty Hunter Big Bud models became extremely popular among treasure hunters. Unfortunately issues tied to the management of Teknetics / Bounty Hunter in the mid-1980's forced them to shut their doors but the intellectual assets were acquired by First Texas and the Bounty hunter line resurrected. Today, First Texas continues to produce Bounty Hunter metal detectors and their goal is to provide hobbyists with affordable equipment that performs where it counts . . . in the field!

BOUNTY HUNTER FIND SHOWCASE:

Historic Finds Can be Made With a Low Cost Detector!

Stuart Rainford has been metal detecting sites throughout England since 1977 and wanted to get a detector his wife could use as well as not breaking the family budget. After researching his options, he selected a Bounty Hunter Fast Tracker and it has not disappointed Stuart or his wife. Searching one field that many had hunted before over the years, the Fast Tracker turned up a number of buttons, a fob seal, a small buckle and a hammered silver penny depicting King Edward I from the 1280's. Stuart's impression, "*A big congratulations to First Texas Products, you've got a winner in the Fast Tracker!*"

PRODUCT LINE:

Bounty Hunter Gold Digger — LIST: $99

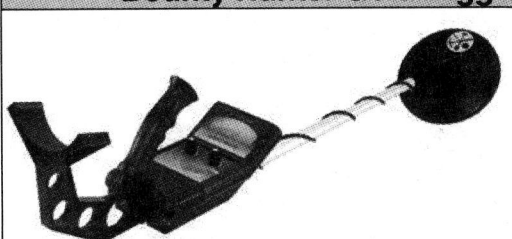

The stylish Gold Digger metal detector will detect all kinds of metal from iron relics, coins and household items to precious metals like silver and gold. For more privacy when treasure seeking, the Gold Digger comes complete with headphones and 1/8" headphone jack for immediate use. It uses a motion all-metal mode for detecting all types of metal and runs on two 9-volt alkaline batteries.

Bounty Hunter Tracker II — LIST: $129

The Tracker II is one of Bounty Hunter's classic metal detector packages, but with completely redesigned graphics and electronics for the best features and performance. The Tracker II combines the ease of automatic ground balancing with manual settings for some of the most challenging types of soil. Whether sifting through the sandy beaches for lost items or searching for silver, the Tracker II can do it all. It features a 7" waterproof search coil and uses two 9-volt Alkaline batteries.

Bounty Hunter Fast Tracker — LIST: $129

The Fast Tracker is a user-friendly instrument, offering tremendous value for the money, while delivering effective performance over a wide range of conditions and applications. The Fast Tracker works in extreme ground conditions ranging from saltwater beaches to highly mineralized inland sites with no operator adjustments to the circuitry and with no loss of sensitivity. The Fast Tracker has offers 2-tone target identification for fun, easy searching.

Bounty Hunter Tracker IV — LIST: $139

The stylish metal detector will detect all kinds of metal from iron relics, coins and household items to precious metals like silver and gold. Streamlined in appearance, with only two operating controls and a mode selection switch, the Tracker IV has eliminated the most difficult aspect of metal detector operation: Ground Balancing. With built-in Automatic Ground Trac, the Tracker IV balances for mineralization while you detect. The Tracker IV will detect in extreme ground conditions from salt wet beaches to highly mineralized inland sites with no operator adjustments to the circuitry and with no loss of sensitivity.

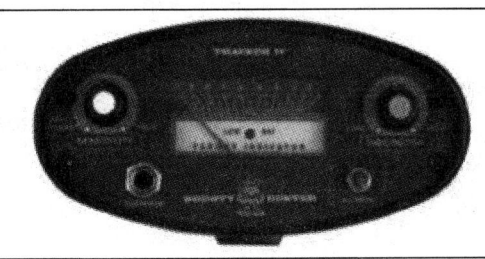

Bounty Hunter Quick Silver — LIST: $149

The Quick Silver features fully automatic ground balance with Squelch-Tech to eliminate false signals; push-button discrimination and one-touch depth control making it easier to use; 4 segment digital target ID and three tone audio feedback & an easy-to-view LCD display that is readable at varying distances.

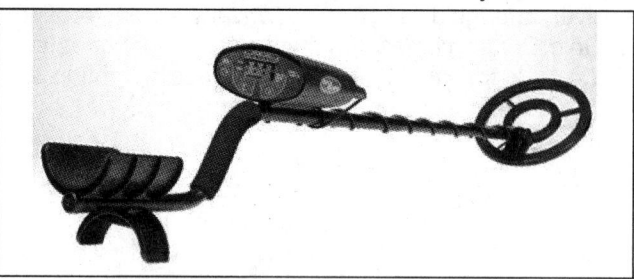

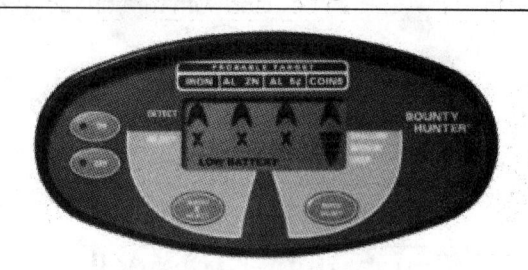

Bounty Hunter Pioneer EX — LIST: $149

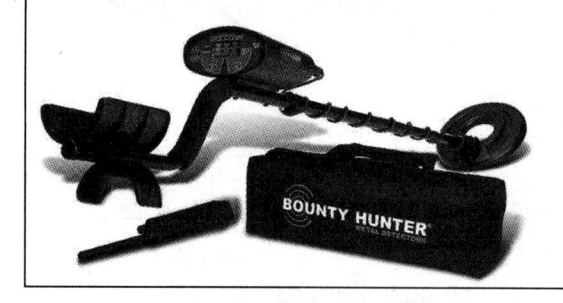

Hit pay dirt when you scour any terrain with the Bounty Hunter Pioneer EX metal detector combined with a Pin Pointer and carry bag. The push-button discrimination and one-touch depth control provide the help you need whether you're coin shooting, gold prospecting, or searching for jewelry. Features include fully automatic ground balance, push-button discrimination and one-touch depth control, 4-segment digital target identification and 3-tone audio feedback, easy-view LCD display and a carry bag for storage.

Bounty Hunter Discovery 1100 — LIST: $149

The Bounty Hunter Discovery 1100 Metal Detector has all of the convenient features you're looking for in a metal detector. The easy-to-use push-button discrimination and one-touch depth control make it great for beginner treasure hunters. The submersible search coil allows you to access coins and items under water, giving you a wide range of area to scour. Plus, an easy view LCD display is readable at varying distances.

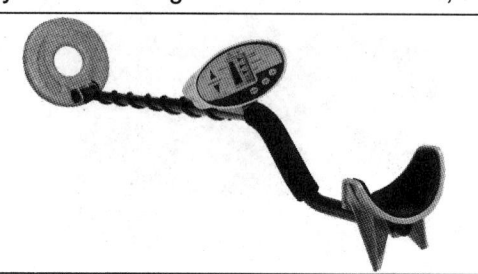

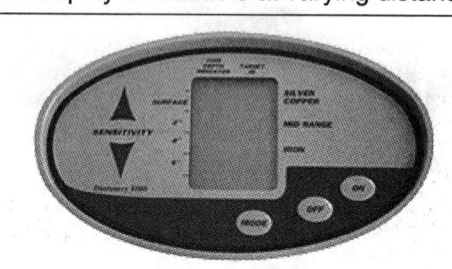

Bounty Hunter Lone Star — LIST: $199

The Lone Star is an advanced technology metal detector, designed for a variety of applications including coin shooting, relic hunting, and general purpose detecting. The unit provides target identification and mode in an easy to read LCD display. Standard features include a built-in speaker, headphone jack and adjustable aluminum stem with an ergonomic S-Rod handle and armrest and all of this is backed by Bounty Hunter's exclusive five-year limited warranty.

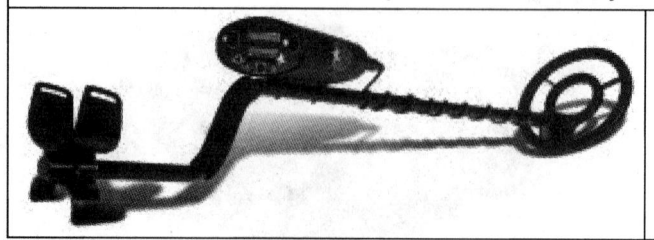

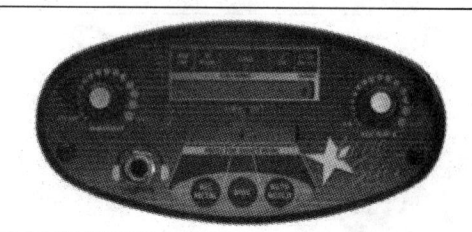

| **Bounty Hunter Commando** | **LIST: $199** |

Offering a streamlined design with only 2 controls. Built-in Automatic Ground Trac balances for mineralization while detecting. It detects in extreme ground conditions from salt wet beaches to highly mineralized inland sites with no operator adjustments required and no loss of sensitivity. The sensitivity meter helps determine signal strength. User controlled sensitivity and discrimination knobs for varying conditions. The headphone jack with 1/4" plug can be used with most headphones

| **Bounty Hunter Quick Draw II** | **LIST: $249** |

The Quick Draw II is equipped with a powerful Micro-chip computer circuit, which combines with Bounty Hunter's Patented Technology to offer more features, performance and value than any other detector in its price range. Whether sweeping the searchcoil ultra fast or ultra slow, the Quick Draw II will detect targets with tremendous accuracy.

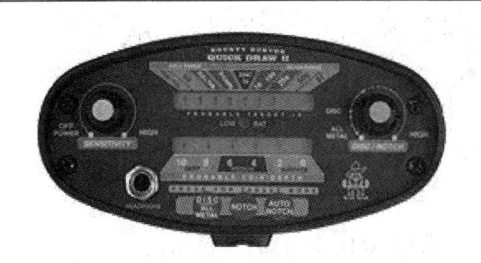

| **Bounty Hunter Pioneer 202** | **LIST: $249** |

The Bounty Hunter Pioneer 202 This is a great detector with all the accessories you will need to get treasure hunting. The Pioneer 202 metal detector incorporates patented microprocessor-controlled technology to detect coins at up to 10 inches and larger objects up to 4 feet and offers digital depth and target display, 4 modes of operation, tone target identification, fully automatic ground balance and interchangeable coils.

| **Bounty Hunter Discovery 2200** | **LIST: $249** |

The Bounty Hunter Discovery 2200 Metal Detector is feature packed and easy to use. Its standard motion all-metal mode detects all types of metal, while the progressive discrimination control eliminates iron and other unwanted items. As the coil nears a target, the Discovery 2200 three-tone audio feedback aids in distinguishing between valuables and undesirable metals. This model also comes equipped with a 1/4 " headphone jack compatible with most headphones for privacy while treasure hunting

| Bounty Hunter Discovery 3300 | LIST: $349 |

The Bounty Hunter Discovery 3300 Metal Detector is feature packed and easy-to-use. It operates on two 9-V batteries and is designed to be lightweight and ergonomic for easy handling and comfortable use. The standard motion all-metal mode detects all types of metal, while the progressive discrimination control eliminates iron and other unwanted items. As the coil nears a target, the Discovery 3300 three-tone audio feedback aids in distinguishing between valuables and undesirable metals.

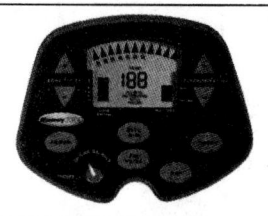

| Bounty Hunter Pioneer 505 | LIST: $349 |

Hit the treasure trail with the Professional Series Pioneer 505 metal detector and leave others eating your dust! The Pioneer 505 metal detector must be one of the best kept secrets out there. You just can't find a better, all-purpose metal detector for all kinds of deep treasures. Minutes after assembling your Pioneer 505, you can get out and start finding coins, gold and silver rings, artifacts and more. It's one of the best all-purpose metal detectors for its price!

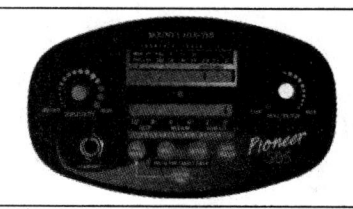

FACTORY ACCESSORIES:

The right accessory can greatly expand the versatility and performance of any detector as search conditions or the type of target being sought changes. The following accessories are available for the Bounty Hunter line of equipment:

Search Coils:
- 4", 7", 8" and 10" round concentric coils with standard cable length / coil covers for coils

Other Items:
- Pinpointer Probe
- Spare lower rod to expedite switching search coils in the field
- Bounty Hunter carrying case
- Bounty Hunter headphones

REFERENCE RESOURCE BIBLIOGRAPHY

Internet Resources

- **Find's Treasure Forums – Bounty Hunter Forum**: http://www.findmall.com/list.php?60
- **The Treasure Hunter Forum – Bounty Hunter**: http://www.treasurehunterforum.com/forum9/
- **TreasureNet – Bounty Hunter Forum**: http://forum.treasurenet.com/index.php/board,210.0.html
- **The Treasure Depot - Bounty Hunter Forum**: http://www.thetreasuredepot.com/cgi-bin/bounty/bounty_config.pl?

C.Scope Metal Detectors

C.Scope International Ltd,
Kingsnorth Technology Park, Wotton Road, Ashford, Kent
TN23 6LN   United Kingdom
Tel: +44 (0)1233 629181 • Fax +44 (0)1233 645897
http://www.cscope.co.uk/

COMPANY PROFILE:

C.Scope International Ltd. has been one of the leading European manufacturers of high-quality metal detecting equipment for more than 25 years and has earned the reputation of producing powerful and reliable metal detectors at an affordable price. Their metal detectors for the hobby market (C.Scope also produces equipment for the utility and security markets) are ideal for those who want to get into the hobby with a metal detector that doesn't cost too much yet but is powerful enough to find real artifacts and will not need to be upgraded if one's interest in the hobby grows. C.Scope detectors are designed for the unique soil conditions found in the UK; however, they have proven to be effective at sites around the world. C.Scope's excellent reputation for customer care, support after the sale and the ability to take care of any detector they have ever produced – even those dating back 25 years – are reasons to give C.Scope careful consideration when buying your next metal detector.

FACTORY ACCESSORIES:

The right accessory can greatly expand the versatility and performance of any detector as search conditions or the type of target being sought changes. The following accessories are available for the C.Scope line of equipment:

Search Coils: .... 6" round concentric coils for the CS1220XD

Other Items: ...... Search coil covers for all available coils, D/L Headphones optimized for the C.Scope models, Rechargeable battery system (battery + charger), Carrying bags for detectors and accessories

PRODUCT LINE:

C.Scope CS440XD   LIST: £99 / $165

The CS440XD is a perfect way to start metal detecting. The powerful non-motion circuitry is super sensitive to the deepest targets and is possibly the deepest metal detector in its price range! The discrimination control enables you to reject trash items such as iron nails, foil, etc. It's equipped with the new 8" polo search head for added performance. You are buying a finely tuned metal detector capable of many years service and not a gimmicky toy as is all too often seen in this price bracket.

C.Scope CS770XD — LIST: £119 / $198

The CS770XD is the perfect way to start metal detecting. The powerful non-motion circuitry is super sensitive to the faintest whispers denoting deep targets and is possibly the deepest detector in its price range. Automatic discrimination with advanced two-tone audio identification gives a high tone for good targets and a low tone for targets such as iron nails and foil but you get to make the decision as to whether you dig or not. Now equipped with the new 8" polo search coil for added performance. The CS770XD is ideal for searching inland sites or adjust the control for equal performance at the beach.

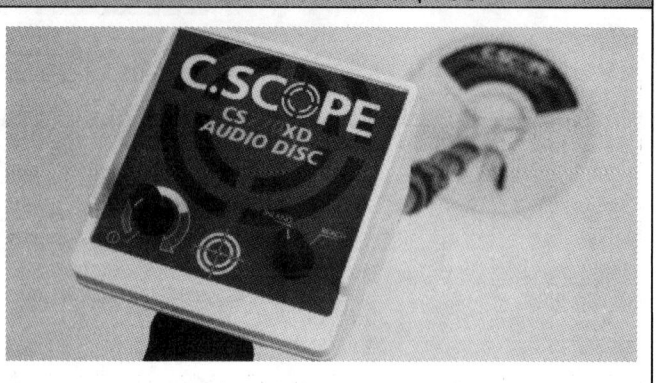

C.Scope CS1MX — LIST: £159 / $265

Light weight, excellent depth and sheer simplicity of operation make the CS1MX an ideal choice for beginners and professional detectorists on a tight budget.

Controls include: On/Off /Sensitivity, fully variable Discrimination & Auto –Retune. It also features an adjustable stem, counterbalanced stem with integral armrest and headphone socket.

C.Scope CS3MX — LIST: £249 / $415

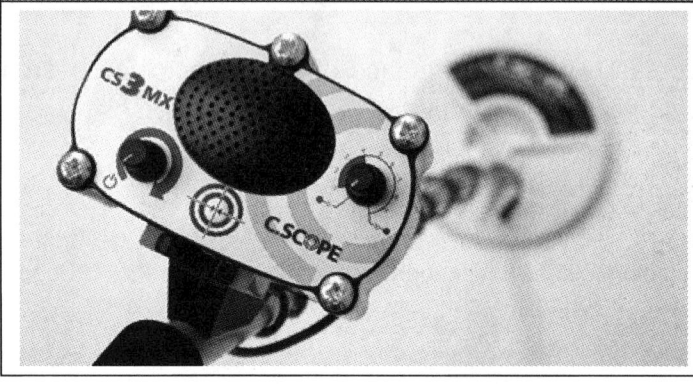

The CS3MX is the definitive professional metal detector. No frills, excellent depth, straightforward operation. It's built to withstand demanding hobby use.

Ideal for professional and amateur detectorists alike for all forms of detecting.

It has a weatherproof design which is ideally suited for hunting year round.

C.Scope CS4PI — LIST: £259 / $430

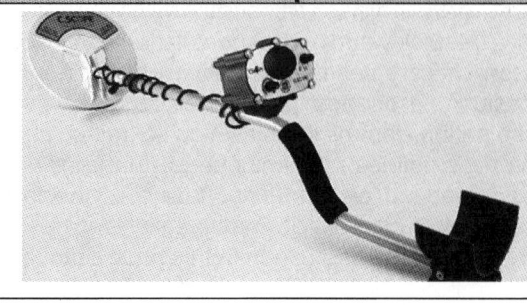

The CS4PI is a rugged, tough metal detector with a dust and shower proof control box, specifically designed for metal detecting on beaches. It operates on the pulse induction principle which is unaffected by the kind of conductive minerals found on the beach such as wet salt & black sand. By the very nature of Pulse Induction it is a very simple detector use and so can be operated efficiently by anyone. This is the perfect metal detector for anyone wishing to specialize in beach work.

C.Scope CS5MX — LIST: £359 / $595

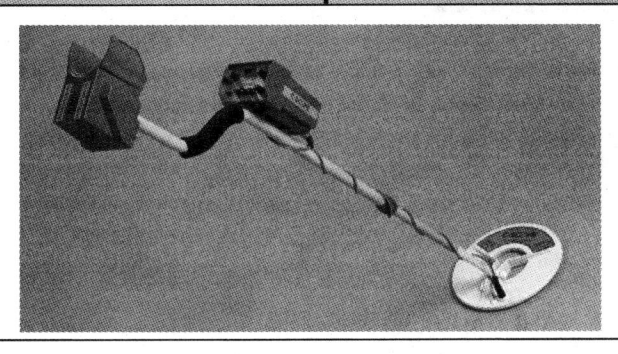

The CS5MX is power detecting at its best. With an easily understood discrimination system it's a classic maximum depth detector for serious metal detecting enthusiasts.

The CS5MX is a more effective deep search detector than some competitors at twice the price

C.Scope CS1220XD — LIST: £369 / $615

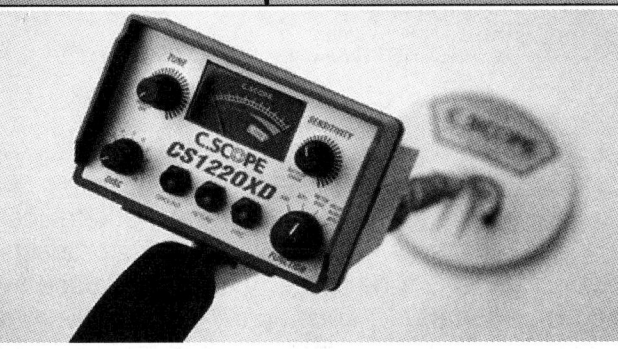

The CS1220 is a design classic in the world of metal detecting. This unique machine was originally conceived by C-Scope more than a decade ago & the design has been refined and honed to perfection. The audio discrimination feature allocates a tone to every target object, which rapidly becomes a language which you can interpret. The CS-1220-XD also features metered discrimination on a nice big, clear, meter display; and two factory preset ground settings. The CS-1220-XD is extremely good at identifying iron rubbish - the well known curse of almost all farmland sites. The CS-1220-XD won't waste your time and is highly recommended for serious metal detecting enthusiasts of all abilities.

C.Scope R1 — LIST: £499 / $830

Switch on the R1 and the opening screen tells you it is ready to go, select program mode and there's nothing to adjust except the volume. The R1 is optimized and automatic. There are two powerful computers, each carrying out one million operations every second. The first carries out all of the signal and target analysis. The second controls the user interface. This takes the data produced by the first processor and presents it to the user on the display.

C.Scope CS9000HPX — LIST: £499 / $830

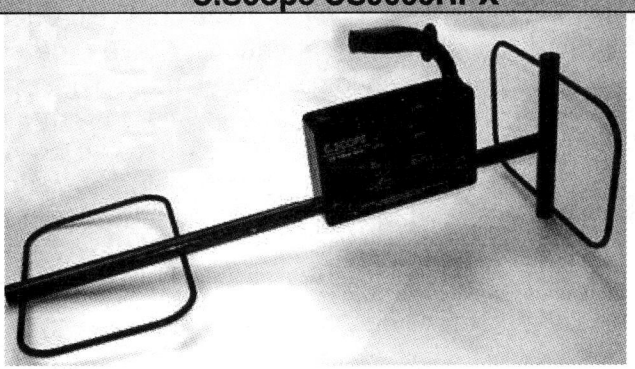

Are you looking for a treasure cache or any large deep metal objects? If so, then this is the perfect choice. The CS9000HPX is a 'two box'" detector designed to locate large deep objects. Sensitivity to objects less than 4" in size is very poor but those larger than this can be located at great depths (depth is relative to object size.) For instance a coffee jar size object can be located at 30-40cm while an object the size of a small car may be detected at 5+ meters. Applications include treasure hunting for hoards, aircraft archaeology where parts can be at great depths & industrial applications such as locating and tracing metal pipe lines.

DetectorPro Electronics

Route 44, Pleasant Valley, NY 12569
Tel: (800) 367-1995 or (845) 635-3488
http://www.detectorpro.com

COMPANY PROFILE:

DetectorPro is one the newest metal detector and accessory manufacturers to enter the marketplace; however, since they opened their doors in 1996 they have introduced a number of innovative products that have proven themselves where it counts . . . in the field under a wide range of conditions used by novice and veteran treasure hunters alike. When Gary Storm started the company his goal was to build quality equipment that addressed many of the equipment-related comments voiced by hobbyists around the world. The most common issues or comments that came up were weight, balance, durability, complexity and cost. With these issues in mind DetectorPro developed what has turned into a full line of more than a dozen headphones designed specifically for the treasure hunter, several unique detectors and two target pinpointing probe systems. The performance and features found in DetectorPro's products typically cost hundreds of dollars more on other detectors. Despite the success realized by DetectorPro, they are not resting on their laurels and have more products in the pipeline!

DETECTOR PRO FIND SHOWCASE:

Gold & Diamonds Turn-up the Second Time Out

Steve Alter had thought about getting into shallow water hunting for a few years but living in central Idaho, he felt there weren't enough swimming sites nearby to justify the cost of a high-end water detector. Well, when the Pirate Pro was introduced, Steve ordered one as a backup to his land unit and did some research to find a few beaches to search. The first one he came across dated back to the early 1900's and Steve had high hopes of what he might find. On his second trip to the beach, he recovered this unique diamond ring with a total of 1.2 carats of sparking ice along with 6 silver coins and several wheat pennies.

Super Finds Made Over a Six-Month Period

Lloyd Sadler has been metal detecting since 1975 and has tried many detectors over the years. Since using DetectorPro detectors, he has done extremely well in finding jewelry as this photo can attest to. All of the pieces in the picture were found in a 6 month period with the total value in excess of $8,600. The one in the center was appraised at $4,500, the two on the sides – found 100 miles and one month apart – at $1,500 each and the chain at $600 . . . . . as Lloyd says, *"I guess the Detector Pro's are DECENT on jewelry – Whatcha think?"*

PRODUCT LINE:

DetectorPro Headhunter Pirate — LIST: $329

The Headhunter PIRATE features two-knobs, turn-on-and-go simplicity and the electronics mounted inside the integral headphones.

Its family friendly and packs easily in the trunk of your car for vacations. This is a metal detector that is really light-weight, powerful, hunts in the rain and water on the beach, made of quality materials, simple enough for everyone in the whole family to use and easy on your budget.

DetectorPro Headhunter Pirate Pro — LIST: $439

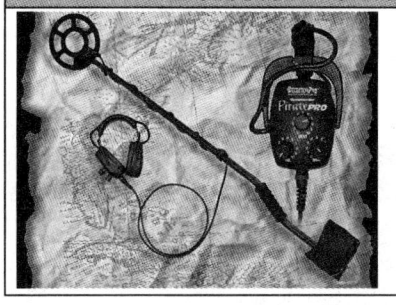

The Headhunter PiratePRO is the newest addition to the DetectorPro line. It incorporates all the great features of the popular Pirate model with an added sensitivity control and arm cup comfort strap. It has "family friendly turn-on-and-go" simplicity and goes anywhere with very little effort to pack and stow!

This is a metal detector that is really light-weight, powerful, hunts in the rain and water on the beach, made of quality materials, simple enough for everyone in the whole family to use and easy on your budget.

DetectorPro Headhunter Wader (8" / 10" coil) — LIST: $650 / $699

You are looking at the most compact amphibious metal detector in the world. Not only does this metal detector contain today's most innovative electronics, it is the first detector that has all the electronics built into the headphones. By eliminating the control housing, the weight of the detector is significantly reduced and so is your arm fatigue. When you travel, the Headhunter also takes up very little luggage space. All of this is possible because of our innovative micro circuitry and packaging. The Headhunter has been engineered to perform in both salt and fresh water, but it is also just as effective on land as well. The headhunter is a true universal application metal detector and will open up a whole new world of excitement for you.

DetectorPro Headhunter Pulse (8" or 11" coil) — LIST: $799

The Headhunter Pulse was designed to do one thing very well - punch deep in highly mineralized sand and salt conditions and find GOLD! Newly engineered pulse circuitry now fits into DetectorPro's acclaimed headphones making it the most compact underwater PI metal detector in the world today. The Headhunter Pulse has been engineered to perform in both salt and fresh water. The Headhunter pulse circuitry is controlled by a unique new Frequency control that re-tunes the sensitivity of the Headhunter Pulse to be responsive to selected metals without losing its depth toward the selected metal. Unlike other PI detectors, turning the frequency control back from the higher frequency position will not result in a loss of depth for the detector.

DetectorPro UniProbe — LIST: $350

You are looking at a value-added industry first from DetectorPro! The first compact all-in-one probe/headphone/pulse inductance metal detector in the world famous DetectorPro design. The UniProbe is a new high-powered pulse inductance probe that can be switched on or off during hunting and retrieval with your metal detector. It can be used just as a set of high-quality detector headphones... Or with an optional PI searchcoil and shafts, it can be turned into a complete PI metal detector! Not only does this probe contain today's most innovative Pulse Inductance electronics, it is the first probe that has all the electronics built into the headphones. All of this is possible because of our innovative micro circuitry and packaging. The UniProbe has been engineered to perform in all ground minerals and on both salt and fresh water beaches too with up to 5-6" depth on coins in the retrieval hole.

UniProbe is a true universal application probe/ metal detector and will open up a whole new world of accurate retrieval for you. Too many valuable coins, relics and jewelry are damaged everyday by the detectorist's inability to accurately pinpoint with large search coils.

FACTORY ACCESSORIES:

The right accessory can greatly expand the versatility and performance of any detector as search conditions or the type of target being sought changes. The following accessories are available for the DetectorPro line of equipment:

Search Coils:
- 8"' and 11" pulse coils to convert the UniProbe to a Headhunter Pulse PI detector

---

REFERENCE RESOURCE BIBLIOGRAPHY

Internet Resources

- **Find's Treasure Forums – DetectorPro Forum:** http://www.findmall.com/list.php?11
- **The Treasure Hunter Forum – DetectorPro:** http://www.treasurehunterforum.com/forum16/

Fisher Research

**FISHER LABS
SINCE 1931**

1465-H Henry Brennan Dr., El Paso, TX 79936
(915) 225-0333 ext.118
http://www.fisherlab.com/

COMPANY PROFILE:

In the late 1920's, Dr. Gerhard Fisher, a German immigrant who studied electronics at the University of Dresden, obtained the first patent ever issued on aircraft radio direction finders. He was working as a Research Engineer in Los Angeles, California at the time and his work attracted the interest of Dr. Albert Einstein. After a demonstration of Dr. Fisher's equipment, Einstein enthusiastically and correctly predicted the world-wide use of radio direction finders in the air, on land and at sea. When using such direction finders during those early years, aircraft pilots found that errors would occur in their bearings when metal objects came between the transmitter and receiver, or whenever they passed over certain areas. Different pilots flying different planes always observed the same errors over the same places. When Dr. Fisher investigated this phenomenon, he found these errors to be the result of highly conductive, mineralized areas. Dr. Fisher concluded that a portable electronic prospecting instrument could be developed that used the same principle to detect the presence of small buried objects and ore deposits.

He continued his research into this phenomenon, and in 1931 he founded Fisher Research Laboratory in a garage behind his home in Palo Alto, California. He and four employees began producing the "Metallascope," starting each unit as a new order came in. The "Metallascope" was a rugged, easy-to-use metal detector. By today's standards, it was an ungainly device consisting of two large, flat wooden boxes containing simple copper coils, five vacuum tubes, and a few assorted components. It soon captivated the imagination of the country, and within a short time, the world. By 1936, sales had increased to the point where the garage was no longer large enough. Fisher Research Laboratory moved to a small building in Palo Alto. Shortly thereafter, Dr. Fisher was granted a patent for his "Metallascope." The "Metallascope" was soon nicknamed the M-Scope, and as such, became an accepted standard for all types of electronic metal detection: geologists located ore, treasure hunters found treasure, utility companies located buried pipes, lumber mills located metal inclusions in sawn logs, and law enforcement agencies used it to locate abandoned or hidden weapons.

In 1939, just prior to World War II, Fisher moved to an even larger building in Palo Alto. During World War II and the subsequent Korean Conflict, the company was called upon to contribute its technical competence to the war effort, but the M-Scope business was never neglected. With the increasing popularity of the M-Scope, and with Fisher's patent rights expiring, numerous competitors began producing similar equipment. Due to relentless efforts to incorporate every available technical advancement - and in particular, by keeping in close contact with countless users to utilize their vast in-field experience in the design of new models - Fisher maintained its position of solid industry leadership. Over the years, Fisher has designed and produced such sophisticated products as Geiger counters, radio communication systems, voltage detectors and cable fault locators.

In 1961, Fisher moved to an even larger production facility in Belmont, California. In 1967, Dr. Fisher retired, having firmly established his name in the annals of electronic history. The company continued to grow, and in 1974, Fisher Research Laboratory moved 90 miles southeast to Los Banos, California. In 1990, Fisher built a spacious, modern manufacturing plant in the Los Banos Industrial Park, where the world's oldest metal detector business resided until it was acquired by First Texas Products in 2006.

FISHER RESEARCH FINDS SHOWCASE:

Four Gold Rings in Four Hours!

Dennis Jones from Ontario, Canada had a banner day while hunting a small local beach with a friend who also is a Fisher user. The beach had recently been scraped and Dennis took his time scanning the sand piled up with his Fisher F-75. Opting for the DE mode with a discrimination level of "6", he dug anything that registered above "20" and was rewarded with these four beautiful gold rings in a 4-hour hunt including the one in the lower left which was stamped 22KT gold and the one in the lower right containing diamonds!

Sidewalk Construction Turns Up Gold!

William Jeffers lives in a small town near Lincoln, Nebraska and noted some sidewalks being replaced in the city center section driving to work one day. Stopping to try and get permission to hunt the area later, the foreman gave him access to the entire work site once the workers knocked off for the day. William had high hopes for the site looking at the age of buildings that bordered the sidewalks. Using his trusty F-5, he picked up a few coins in the first block but shortly after he started the next one, he received a solid signal which turned out to be an 1899 $10 gold piece in amazing shape. *"Keep your eyes open"* is the lesson William wanted to impart.

A New Fisher F-75 LTD Has a Great First Day!

Josep Mandek from Gdansk, Poland, unpacked his new F-75 LTD, read over the operating manual, and headed out to see what he could find at a site he had scouted out while waiting for his detector to arrive. Less than 15 minutes after starting his hunt, a repeatable signal came through Josep's headphones and after digging down nearly 10" in the dark soil, a coin was visible. Dated 1668, it was a hammered silver 6 Grozhen coin depicting King Jan II. Not a bad start to what Josep hopes will be a hobby that continues to allow him to touch his country's history.

PRODUCT LINE:

Fisher F2 — LIST: $299

The sensitivity of the Fisher F2 has earned rave reviews from both first time users and experienced detectorists. It has found items as deep as 10" in various soil types with medium sensitivity. Meanwhile the Pinpointing feature allows you to quickly hone in on specific items. The Fisher F2 features a large control panel with seven big push buttons and an equally big display. The control panel is very simple to operate, making this an excellent detector for beginners. The light weight of the Fisher F2 combined with the adjustable arm cuff will keep you hunting for hours!

Fisher F4 — LIST: $449

The Fisher F4 metal detector features a waterproof 11" open search coil with "Double D" technology to ensure maximum depth and signal strength. The large digital face plate and easy-to-see push buttons putting even the most advanced features at your fingertips! An 11-segment digital target identification system will help you SEE your target BEFORE you start to dig. Operating at a 5.9kHz frequency, the Fisher F4 boasts four search modes designed to help you sniff out treasure in any ground conditions! Search in "Auto Tune" for all metals, the "Discrimination" mode to manually tune out the metals you don't want to detect, the "pinpoint" feature to hone in on the smallest treasures and know exactly where to dig, or the "notch discrimination" to focus on specific targets of interest!

Fisher F5 — LIST: $549

Fisher proudly named the F5 a "Professional" metal detector due to the many professional features that were incorporated into the F5. The F5 is a high tech metal detector that is very automatic making it a detector that is easy to set up and easy to use in the field. A large visual display provides both Target Identification and Target Depth while in either search mode - all metal or discrimination. The F5 operates in all types of soils with its computerized ground balancing circuit allowing you to detect in areas difficult for other metal detectors.

Truly a professional metal detector at a budget price!

Fisher Gold Bug — LIST: $549

Fisher introduces the newest gold detector in their line – the Gold Bug! Designed to find even the smallest gold nuggets in highly mineralized soil, the new Gold Bug also offers a separate mode designed to meet the needs of coin hunters and relic hunters with full discrimination. Two independent ground balance circuits to allow for full user control in the worst conditions, the Gold Bug will find what others have missed. The easy to read LCD screen, light weight and coil designed to fit into even the smallest crevices, the new Gold Bug should prove to be a winner!

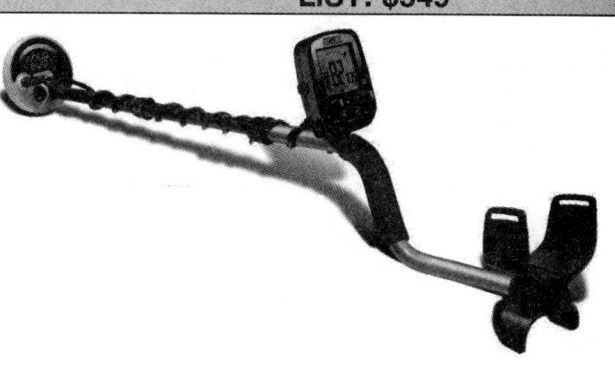

| **Fisher 1270-X** | **LIST: $700** |

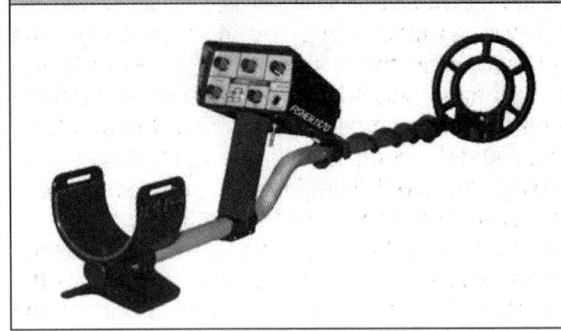

The Fisher 1270-X is made for the treasure hunter who wants an easy-to-tune, easy-to-use metal detector, with features that are easily understood and can be operated to its maximum performance level minutes after the detector is taken from its box and assembled. No meter, no bells and whistles, nothing to breakdown and slow your metal detecting experience. This metal detector is "HOT" and very powerful. Buy the 1270-X if you're looking for a super high-performance metal detector that will find valuable coins, rings, gold, etc. with minimal adjustments.

| **Fisher F70** | **LIST: $799** |

"Use your F70 right out of the box." The F70 is a very easy detector to set up and use. It is considered to be an all-around metal detector with all the features you would use for coin shooting, relic hunting, gold prospecting, cache hunting and even shallow water hunting.

Simply assemble detector, install 4AA batteries, turn the detector on, toss a coin on the ground, sweep coil back and forth over the coin a few times to get the feel for how the detector responds and you're pretty much ready to go treasure hunting.

| **Fisher Gemini III** | **LIST: $799** |

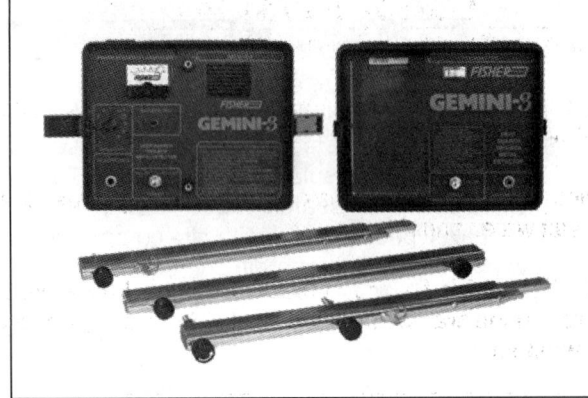

Designed to locate large, deep objects, like an iron chest, ore vein or metal pipe, the Gemini-3 is used by professional treasure hunters, prospectors, geologists and public utility company employees. Depending on ground mineralization and target size, objects may be detected as deep as twenty feet or more. Find deeper, larger targets that others overlook using equipment from other manufacturers.

| **Fisher 1280-X Aquanaut (8" / 10" coils)** | **LIST: $800 / $830** |

The 1280-X Aquanaut is an easy-to-use, high performance, land and sea metal detector that goes anywhere. It's waterproof to 250 feet, and because it's virtually impervious to sun, dust, rain and fog, it's the No. 1 choice for many land treasure hunters as well.

It features a lightweight, solid, glass-bead epoxy search coil; an adjustable, fiberglass shaft; a high-impact, injection-molded control box; a waterproof headset and a stainless steel arm rest. You have the choice of either an 8" or 10" coil. It's one tough metal detector!

Fisher Goldbug 2 — LIST: $900

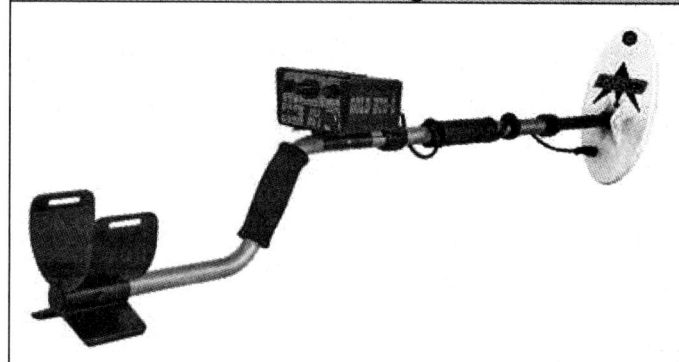

Now with an ultra-high operating frequency - the highest one on the market - combined with iron discrimination, you'll be striking it rich in no time! Using low-noise, precision-matched, temperature-compensated components and state-of-the-art circuitry, the Gold Bug 2 takes prospecting to a new level. The 71 kHz operating frequency gives increased sensitivity to smaller and deeper nuggets even in highly mineralized soil. With the Gold Bug 2's audio boost and iron discrimination mode you can now hear those faint, deep signals while avoiding hot rocks and ferrous targets.

Fisher CZ-3D — LIST: $950

The CZ-3D is engineered to provide maximum success searching for old coins and other valuables while retaining the best possible ratio of good targets vs. trash targets. In older sites, where aluminum trash is rarely found, the CZ-3D will give exceptional performance on older targets . . . simply select the "Enhanced" mode and you will see the difference.

No special or lengthy programming required, just flip the switch and see what you've been missing.

Fisher CZ-21 (8" / 10" coils) — LIST: $1,299 / $1,349

You can go anywhere with the CZ-21 even underwater!

The CZ-21 is a go-anywhere, do-anything, all-weather, target-ID machine that is leak proof to 250 feet

Its patented electronics make it deep-seeking while it ignores the destabilizing effects of salt water and black sand.

It is the perfect target ID machine for the versatile treasure hunter who wants to hunt anywhere - underwater, on the beach, in the surf, on dry land and in all kinds of weather.

Fisher F75 / F-75 LTD — LIST: $1,199 / $1,399

The F75 is an outstanding all-purpose metal detector. Its most popular uses are finding coins, rings, and jewelry. It is also well suited to find relics and for gold prospecting as well as beach hunting. Perfect for beginners to very experienced metal detector users. This top-off the line metal detector has all the important features you would expect from a Fisher detector. Light & well balanced with a large LCD screen that shows you Target Id, Target Confidence and Target Depth .You can hunt relics and artifacts with the all-metal mode, or discriminate the junk targets. The F-75 LTD takes the performance to a new level with a more powerful microprocessor and new programming with two new signal algorithms; one which substantially increases depth under most conditions, and the other designed to find large deep objects.

FACTORY ACCESSORIES:

The right accessory can greatly expand the versatility and performance of any detector as search conditions or the type of target being sought changes. The following accessories are available for the Fisher line of equipment:

Search Coils:
- **12XX Series**: 5" solid, 8" spider and 10.5" spider concentric coils
- **CZ-3D**: 5" solid, 8" spider and 10.5" spider concentric coils
- **Gold Bug 2**: 6.5" elliptical, 10" elliptical and 14" elliptical Double-D coils
- **F-Series**: 5" Double-D, 6.5" elliptical, 10" elliptical concentric and 11" elliptical Double-D coils

Other Items:
- Coil covers for all standard and optional coils
- Carrying cases; both hard sided and soft cases
- Pinpointer probe
- Spare lower shafts to simplify swapping coils in the field
- Harness system to hipmount or chest mount control housings for the 1236-x2, Gold Bug 2, CZ-3D & 1280-X
- Control housing covers (F-series,
- Instructional video (1270-X)
- Items with the Fisher logo; hats, shirts, find pouches
- Headphones

THIRD PARTY ACCESSORIES FOR FISHER DETECTORS:

- **Sun Ray In-Line Pinpointing Probes**: Pinpoint probe designed for specific detectors – probes available for CZ's, F-70/F75/F75 Ltd, ID Excel5, Coin$trike and ID Edge detectors, . Sun Ray Detector Electronics, (319) 636-2244; http://www.sunraydetector.com/
- **Sun Ray Invader CS-5 5.5" Concentric Coil**: Designed for hunting in high trash areas by providing maximum target separation (fits the Coin$trike and ID Edge detectors), http://www.sunraydetector.com/
- **SEF Search Coils**: Combining the benefits of concentric & Double-D coils, SEF coils have been proven in the field; (10"x12" & 15"x12") http://www.kellycodetectors.com/accessories/searchcoils.htm (U.S. market) or http://www.joanallen.co.uk/a_detech_metal_detectors_uk.html (U.K. distributor)
- **Straight Shaft Systems**: Designed to improve the balance & ergonomics of your detector:
  - **Anderson Detector Shafts**: Quality-built shafts for the 1280-X, Impulse, CZ-20 & CZ-21 (Two full-length sizes and a shorter Scuba shaft available); http://andersondetectorshafts.com/11.html

---

REFERENCE RESOURCE BIBLIOGRAPHY

Books

- **Deep Treasure and Cache Location with the Fisher Gemini-3** by Stephen Ryland
- **Advanced Treasure Hunting with the Fisher 'Quicksilver' Metal Detector** by Andy Sabisch

Internet Resources

- **American Relic Hunters Fisher Forum**: http://www.americanrelichunters.com/cgi-bin/fisher/webbbs_config.pl/#2
- **Find's Treasure Forums – Fisher Forum**: http://www.findmall.com/list.php?37
- **The Treasure Hunter Forum – Fisher**: http://www.treasurehunterforum.com/forum8/
- **TreasureNet – Fisher Forum**: http://forum.treasurenet.com/index.php/board,210.0.html
- **The Treasure Depot – Fisher Forum**: http://www.thetreasuredepot.com/cgi-bin/fisher/fisher_config.pl

Garrett Electronics

GARRETT METAL DETECTORS™

1881 W. State Street, Garland, TX 75042
(800) 527-4011 or (972) 494-6151 • Fax: (972) 494-1881
http://www.Garrett.com

COMPANY PROFILE:

Garrett Electronics has a history that extends back to the early 1960's. In 1963, Charles Garrett rented a number of commercial metal detectors and found them lacking in terms of performance. He started working in the garage of his Garland home to design and build better metal detectors. In 1964, Charles and his wife Eleanor established Garrett Electronics and introduced the dual search coil Hunter - their first metal detector - to the market. In 1968, Charles established the first distributor outlet, "Bowen's Hideout," a store owned by Harry and Lucille Bowen, in Spokane, Washington and recognizing the tremendous value of a distributor network, the company began placing ads to set up dealerships across the country.

Garrett became the first manufacturer to eliminate oscillator drift as well as designing and patenting the revolutionary, independently-operated search coils which greatly improved treasure hunting efficiency. Garrett was also the first to overcome search coil drift by inventing and patenting a special coaxial search coil winding technique. These discoveries launched Garrett to the forefront of the metal detector industry.

In 1971, Garrett Metal Detectors moved into a new 15,000 square foot facility and began increasing production of its products. In 1974, the Gravity Trap Gold Pan was designed and patented by Roy Lagal and Garrett began worldwide distribution of this pan which continues to be the world's most popular gold pan today. In 1978, as gold prices soared, treasure hunters clamored for Garrett's detectors worldwide. Garrett received requests to establish international dealerships and the first one opened in London followed shortly by the first Australian dealership. By the mid-1980s Garrett Metal Detectors became one of the largest metal detector manufacturers with over 1,800 dealers worldwide. In 1983, In September, Garrett was invited to develop a walk-through metal detector for the 1984 Summer Olympic Games in Los Angeles and the company has continued to supply security detectors for subsequent Olympics as well as the 1984 National Republican Convention, the Egyptian Ramses Exhibit, the 1987 PanAm Games, the 1988 Republican GOP Convention and many other events.

In 1990 Garrett introduced the first Graphic Target Analyzing (GTA) microprocessor-driven detector with multiple notch discrimination for treasure hunting. This system is still the most efficient and desirable metal detector target discriminating method. Garrett was selected to provide security training and products for the U.S. armed forces in Kuwait during the Persian Gulf conflict known as Desert Storm.

In 1991, Garrett moved their company headquarters and detector manufacturing to the current location in Garland, Texas. In 1997, The Garrett Academy of Metal Detection was formally established to offer certification in the use of metal detection equipment in checkpoint screening applications such as airports and special events. In 2003, Garrett became the only U.S.-based manufacturer to meet TSA guidelines for walk-through and held-held metal detectors. Garrett supplies walk-through metal detectors to one-third of America's airports and to many overseas airports. In 2007 Garrett's facilities were expanded to 100,000 square feet. The new Garrett home office now houses an enlarged treasure hunting museum, a formal conference/training center for The Garrett Academy of Metal Detection training, and enlarged production and warehouse facilities.

Garrett continues to be a leader in the metal detection field and their engineering staff is always looking at using emerging technology to improve the current equipment for hobbyists and security users.

GARRETT ELECTRONICS FINDS SHOWCASE:

Treasure is Literally Everywhere!

James H. from South Texas was searching a playground near his house in the area he calls the "Momma Line" . . . . where momma stands while she's "pushin' the kids on the swing." Using his Garrett GTI 2500 fitted with a 5" Excellerator search coil to work close to the equipment, James got a signal that screamed TREASURE and this beautiful 14KT gold ring set with London blue Topaz and diamonds turned up! One never knows where treasure will be found.

The Little Ace 250 Finds Big Silver

Greg Zayas had picked up an Ace 250 hoping his wife would join him but she never really found the same thrill he did digging up a piece of the past. Rather than simply reselling his new detector, he took it to some of the sites he and his hunting partner had visited before and he was quickly surprised at the performance the little detector provided. Searching an overgrown section of a park near the outskirts of New York City, Greg started picking up wheat cents along with an occasional Indian Head penny from amongst the trash that littered the area. Pushing the coil under a bush near the edge of a field, he received a solid signal that showed it was a deep one . . . . 6 inches or more and indicating between "50c" and "$1". Hoping for a silver half, Greg was speechless when this 1922 silver Peace dollar appeared at the bottom of the hole. Needless to say, Greg said he would be using the Ace on more of his trips!

Lightening Can Strike Twice in the Same Place!

Steve Sanchez from Oklahoma City has been an avid coinhunter for more than 15 years and had always wanted to find a gold coin with his GTI 1500. Well, he obtained permission to hunt a large private estate and less than an hour into the hunt, he pulled out a 1910 $2.50 gold coin. The next day he returned and a short distance away he recovered an 1883 $10 gold piece. Two gold coins in two days – WOW!

PRODUCT LINE:

Garrett Electronics Ace 150 — LIST: $180

Garrett has managed to create the most sought after and easy-to-use series of metal detectors on the market today! Ahead of the competition in every respect, the ACE 150 is the exception to every rule. It's affordable and fun, yet still made from high quality materials we've come to expect from Garrett Metal Detectors. With a rugged appearance that features a large LCD screen you will be able to easily adjust the three pre-programmed notch search modes, three depth levels and four sensitivity settings. Clear and audible target identification will let you hear treasures while graphic target identification will put them right before your eyes! The ACE series was made to perform and provide the perfect introduction to metal detecting!

ACE 150 Control Panel

Garrett Electronics Ace 250 — LIST: $250

Garrett's taken much of the leading edge technology and well thought-out features from their GTI and GTAx lines and packaged them into the most aggressive, rugged outdoor design in the industry. These attention-stealing detectors are turning heads and sending the competition back to the drawing board. But put aside their aggressive good looks and you'll see just how much amazing technology we've packed into these NEW machines. From custom notch discrimination, pinpointing, adjustable sensitivity and depth settings to the newest addition of the PROformance coils series, these detectors will never stop impressing you - or finding treasure. Of course you'd never expect a detector with this price tag to offer so much performance.

ACE 250 Control Panel

Garrett Electronics GTAx 550 — LIST: $500

The introduction of GTA technology almost a decade ago caused a sensation among treasure hunting enthusiasts everywhere. The patented, microprocessor-driven Graphic Target Analyzer (GTA) was the first mid-range hobby detector to reveal a target's probable identity and continuously display the names of the operating mode, search aid and discrimination method in use. After years of refinements and added features, the GTAx remains in a class by itself. The detectors' unique mix of high performance, easy operation and affordability makes it a mainstay among veteran and beginners alike.

The 550 features the revolutionary Graphic Target Analyzer LCD, which reveals coin depth in pinpoint mode, displays an easy-to-read, horizontal conductivity scale, shows which targets are "notched" (accepted or rejected) for discrimination and in an instant, pinpoints targets with ease.

Garrett Electronics Scorpion Gold Stinger — LIST: $550

Based on the original Groundhog (15kHz) circuit renowned over the world for its power in driving through ground minerals to pinpoint the tiniest gold nuggets, the Gold Stinger takes performance to the next level. The Gold Stinger has been proven around the world as a universal gold detector. The Stinger offers three versatile search modes unmatched by other gold hunting detectors. It's a deep-seeking gold-finder, but this instrument also offers a hunting mode with the precise discrimination demanded by veteran coin-finders. When you're not locating gold nuggets, use your Scorpion Gold Stinger to locate coins, jewelry or any other kind of treasure.

Garrett Electronics GTP 1350 — LIST: $700

Inspired by the elite GTI line, the GTP series gives you plenty of the technology and features while providing critical target size information that other detectors in its class don't offer. When treasure hunting, knowing the size of a buried target may mean the difference between digging trash and digging treasure! That's why you need Garrett's Graphic Target Profiling (GTP) 1350. The GTP 1350 is packed with many of the same amazing technologies that are featured in Garrett's elite GTI series. And it offers exclusive profiling technology that identifies the size (Small, Medium, Large) of a target on the LCD display. The GTP also comes with Garrett's all new, highly rugged 7x10" PROformance search coil, which means you search deeper and cover more ground per sweep than with traditional coils.

Garrett Electronics GTI 1500 — LIST: $800

Designed with the serious coinshooter in mind, the GTI 1500 boasts all of the key benefits of the 2500 but at a smaller cost. The GTI 1500 also gives you instant feedback on the kind of coin you've detected and how deep it is by revealing its true size and depth graphically, again via Garrett's unique GTI display. Don't dig for aluminum cans when what you're really after are coins and rings. Rely on the TreasureVision screen to tell you if the detected target is the size of a coin & what its denomination is. TreasureVision provides extra target information to help you decide whether a target is worth digging, enabling you to spend more time digging treasure instead of trash. Only Garrett packs this much superior quality into one affordable metal detector.

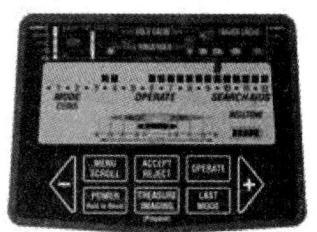

GTI 1500 Control Panel

Garrett Electronics GTI 2500 — LIST: $1,000

Garrett's top-of-the-line GTI 2500 incorporates more than a quarter century's worth of innovative metal detection technology. Backed by a powerful onboard DSP chip, the GTI 2500's unique benefits can't be beat. From the graphic identification of targets to unsurpassed depth capabilities and hunting versatility, the GTI 2500 does it all. Only Garrett enables you to "see" the real size and depth of a detected target. Garrett's exclusive GTA (Graphic Target Analyzer) and GTI (Graphic Target Imaging) technologies team up to bring you TreasureVision, a patented breakthrough system that shows you a target's identity and size via unique, user-friendly color graphics. See whether the target is a coin, pull-tab, bottle cap, drink can or large cache-sized object before you start digging. And view all of the information on one convenient easy-to-read screen!

GTI 2500 Control Panel

Garrett Electronics Sea Hunter Mark II — LIST: $750

The Sea Hunter Mark II is ideal for use in and around water . . . oceans, beaches, lakes and rivers. Having led a legendary life being involved in projects led by the late Mel Fisher, Robert Marx and many other successful treasure hunters large and small . . . the Sea Hunter has been The Master of Water Treasure Hunting for over 25 years. With its unique Discrete Trash Elimination technology, the Sea Hunter Mark II can eliminate most pull tabs and foil without significantly degrading the sensitivity of rings and coins in Discrete Elimination mode. A favorite detector for treasure hunters around the world because of its ability to ignore salt water, the Sea Hunter's electronic housing can be mounted on the hip or above, below or under the cuff in either short or long configuration.

Garrett Electronics Infinium Land & Sea   LIST: $1,250

The Infinium LS (Land & Sea) is a new direction for Garrett and treasure hunters all over the world. Considered the "go anywhere, do anything" detector, it was designed to find nuggets, coins, caches, and relics virtually anywhere in the world even at diving depths of up to 200 feet! With variable speed ground tracking, multi-channel pulse induction technology, advanced discrimination, Tone ID for enhanced target information, a fully submersible, all-environment design and interference elimination without reduced sensitivity, the Infinium LS is by far the most technologically advanced multiple frequency detector on the market. It easily surpasses the depth and discrimination capabilities of every competitor in its class. Whether prospecting in the gold fields of Australia and Arizona, hunting Civil War battlefields, volcanic rockslides of the Pacific Northwest or the black-sand beaches along Italy's coast, the Infinium LS will maintain its exceptional performance. The waterproof design of the Infinium LS makes it the first metal detector highly recommended for both land and deep water detecting. Three controls are all you need to successfully hunt for relics, jewelry and gold. The Infinium *LS* features Advanced Pulse Induction™ (API) technology which many consider the industry's greatest innovation in years. This new technology, teamed with the remarkably powerful 10 x 14" DD™ search coil, provides treasure hunters with the most stable, rigid, and performance-packed detector in the world.

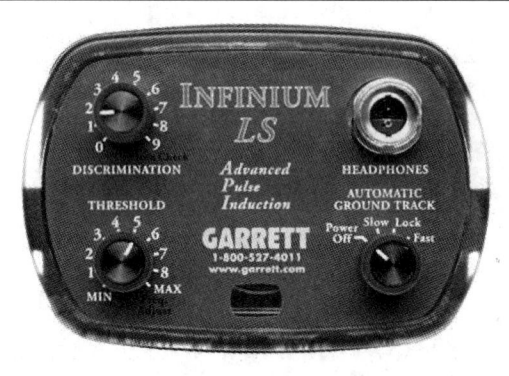

FACTORY ACCESSORIES:

The right accessory can greatly expand the versatility and performance of any detector as search conditions or the type of target being sought changes. The following accessories are available for the Garrett line of equipment:

Search Coils:
- **Ace 150 / 250**: 9"x12" elliptical concentric and 4" round search coils
- **GTI 1500 / 2500**: 10"x14" Double-D elliptical, 5"x10" Double-D, 12.5" round imaging, 4.5" round concentric search coils and TreasureHound two-box attachment
- **GTP 1350 / GTAx 550**: 9"x12" elliptical concentric, 4.5" round concentric and 10"x14" Double-D elliptical search coils

- **Master Hunter CX Plus**: 4.5" round concentric and 10"x14" Double-D elliptical search coils and TreasureHound two-box attachment
- **Sea Hunter Mark II**: 10"x14" Mono elliptical search coil
- **Infinium LS**: 10"x14" Mono elliptical, 8" mono round, 5"x10" Double-D and 3"x7" Double-D search coil
- **Scorpion Gold Stinger**: 3"x7" Double-D search coil

Other Items:
- **Control Housing Covers:** For the CX, GTAx, GTP, GTI and Ace models
- **Carrying cases**
- **Headphones:** Lightweight, padded and underwater
- **Instructional DVD's & Videos:** Training courses for the GTI 2500 / 1500; Ace 250 / 150; GTP 1350 / GTAx 550 and Infinium / Sea Hunter / Gold Stinger detectors

THIRD PARTY ACCESSORIES FOR GARRETT DETECTORS:

- **Jay's Cache**: Frequency shifter that changes the frequency of your detector to eliminate interference from nearby detectors); P.O. Box 472531, Garland, TX 75047 or jayscache@juno.com
- **Sun Ray In-Line Pinpointing Probes**: Pinpoint probe designed for specific detectors – models available for the Garrett GTI 1500, 2000 & 2500, Ace 150 & 250, GTAx 550, 750 & 1250, and GTP 1350. Sun Ray Detector Electronics, (319) 636-2244; http://www.sunraydetector.com/
- **Excellerator & SEF Search Coils**: Additional size options for several Garrett models http://www.kellycodetectors.com/accessories/searchcoils.htm (U.S. market) or http://www.joanallen.co.uk/a_detech_metal_detectors_uk.html (U.K. distributor)
- **Straight Shaft Systems**: Designed to improve the balance & ergonomics of your detector:
  o **Anderson Detector Shafts:** Quality-built shafts for the Mark II, Infinium and other water units (Two full-length sizes and a shorter Scuba shaft available); http://andersondetectorshafts.com/12.html

REFERENCE RESOURCE BIBLIOGRAPHY

Internet Resources

- **Find's Treasure Forums – Garrett Forum**: http://www.findmall.com/list.php?32
- **The Treasure Hunter Forum – Garrett**: http://www.treasurehunterforum.com/forum2/
- **TreasureNet – Garrett Forum**: http://forum.treasurenet.com/index.php/board,209.0.html
- **The Treasure Depot – Garrett Forum**: http://www.thetreasuredepot.com/cgi-bin/garrett/garrett_config.pl
- **Treasure Quest Garrett Forum**: http://www.treasurequestxlt.com/community/forumdisplay.php?s=2587a4b6f106eb2e48a965005c11227d&f=119

J.W. Fishers

JW Fishers
Underwater search equipment it pays to own!

1953 County Street, E. Taunton, MA 02718
(800) 822-4744 • (508) 882-7330 • Fax: (508) 880-8949
http://www.jwfishers.com/

COMPANY PROFILE:

For over thirty years JW Fishers has specialized in the design and manufacture of reasonably priced, high-tech underwater search equipment. The product line includes diver-held and boat-towed metal detectors, marine magnetometers, underwater camera systems, ROVs, and side scan sonar equipment.

The company was founded in the mid-1960's by current president and CEO Jack Fisher. It all started when Mr. Fisher, an avid diver, needed an underwater metal detector to use on a salvage project. Finding there was no such product available for recreational divers; he developed and built his own underwater metal detector. JW Fishers Manufacturing was formed and Mr. Fisher began offering his detectors for sale to other recreational divers. As a result of customer requests for a line of commercial quality detectors, the company designed and built more powerful models that could cover larger areas. The product line was expanded from diver-held metal detectors to boat-towed metal detectors and magnetometers. Underwater cameras were a natural follow-on to the product line as customers asked for a tool they could use to look at targets they were finding with their boat-towed detectors or simply wanted to do a visual search of an area. Next came a family of sonar devices including a line of side scan sonar (the ultimate underwater search system). JW Fishers side scan sonar is a breakthrough in a high performance, low cost side scan systems.

Today the company maintains an active R&D effort to explore and develop new technologies for underwater search in order to offer our customers the latest and most cost effective equipment available. The company offers the most complete line of underwater search products from any single manufacturer and stands behind every piece of equipment with a warranty and service that is second to none.

PRODUCT LINE:

J.W. Fishers Pulse 6X – Versions 1 & 2   LIST: $1,495 / $1,645

The Pulse 6X has the same top quality construction and 200 foot depth rating as the top-performing Pulse 8X, but with less detection range. A unique feature is that it can be upgraded to the Pulse 8X at any time. The Pulse 6X is in use by military, law enforcement, commercial, and salvage divers worldwide. The Pulse 6X is not affected by highly mineralized salt water, coral, rocks with a high iron content, or magnetic (black) sand; all of which drive conventional detectors crazy. The diver is alerted to presence of a metal target by both visual readout (shown on the meter) and an audio output (heard in the underwater earphone). The detection range for a target is unaffected by the medium between the detector's coil and the metal object. Powered by an internal 9 volt rechargeable battery pack, the detector will run all day on a full charge - recharge the battery overnight and it's ready for another full day of hunting. The Pulse 6X comes with all the accessories needed to use the detector on land and to dive including a corrosion proof PVC handle for underwater use, an anodized aluminum handle for land use, an underwater earphone, AC and DC battery chargers, a hip-mount kit for the electronics housing, and a spare parts kit. Version 2 allows for interchangeable coils to be used, while Version 1's coil is hardwired

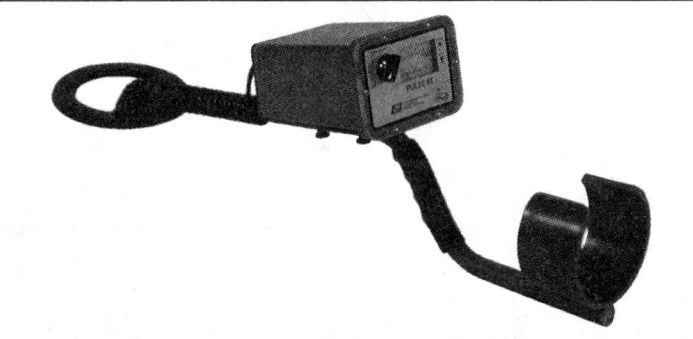

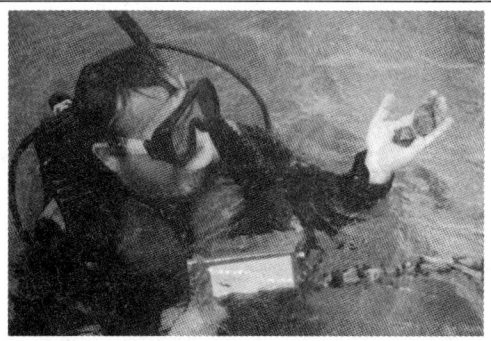

J.W. Fishers Pulse 8X – Versions 1 & 2   LIST: $1,895 / $2,045

With a 200 foot depth rated housing and a 6 foot maximum detection range, the Pulse 8X is Fishers top of the line detector. This commercial-grade metal detector is used by treasure hunters, commercial diving companies, law enforcement agencies, and military units worldwide. The Pulse 8X detects all metals from coins and jewelry, to anchors and cannons; and does it on land, or in fresh or salt water. The diver is alerted to presence of a metal target by both visual readout (shown on the meter) and an audio output (heard in the underwater earphone). The Pulse 8X comes with all the accessories needed to use the detector on land or dive including a corrosion proof PVC handle for underwater use, an anodized aluminum handle for land use, underwater and land headphones, AC and DC battery chargers, a hip-mount kit for the electronics housing, rugged Cordura carry bag and a spare parts kit. Powered by an internal 9 volt rechargeable battery pack, the detector will easily run all day on a full charge. A complete line of interchangeable coils are available which gives this detector tremendous versatility. The Pulse 8X has <u>twice</u> the power and detection range of the Pulse 6X detector. Version 2 allows for interchangeable coils to be used, while Version 1's coil is hardwired.

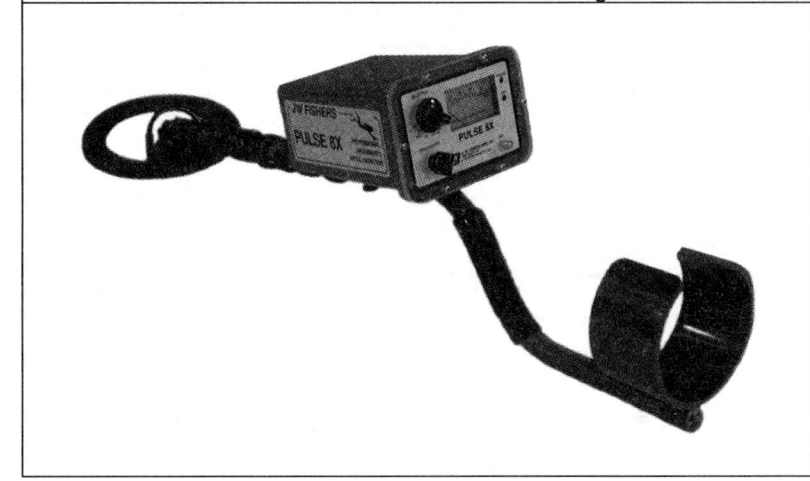

197

J.W. Fishers Diver Mag1	LIST: $7,995

The Diver Mag 1 is the highest performing diver-held ferrous metal detector on the market today. It is a top performing microprocessor driven marine magnetometer detection system with a one gamma sensitivity. This hand-held mag detects ferrous metal (iron/steel) that works equally well on land and underwater. The Mag1 will locate pipe lines, cables, cannons, dredge parts, and just about any ferrous metal object of any size. Ruggedly constructed for commercial operations, the Diver Mag1 was designed with user friendly controls for ease of operation. Out of the water, the handle grip and included shoulder strap make the Mag1 easy to carry. Operator selectable cycle times (how often a reading is taken) of 2, 5, or 10 seconds allow for a strong return signal and a fast response to detect even small targets. The readout is displayed on an easy to see 5 digit LED for murky water or night operations. In addition, an audio output allows the diver to operate the system without the need to watch the LED display. Easy to maneuver with operator adjustable buoyancy. Power is supplied by an internal 12 volt rechargeable battery that will last for two continuous hours at the 5 second cycle time. Increase the operating time by using the optional belt mounted spare battery pack. The Diver Mag1 is constructed of corrosion proof urethane and PVC to give many years of trouble free performance.

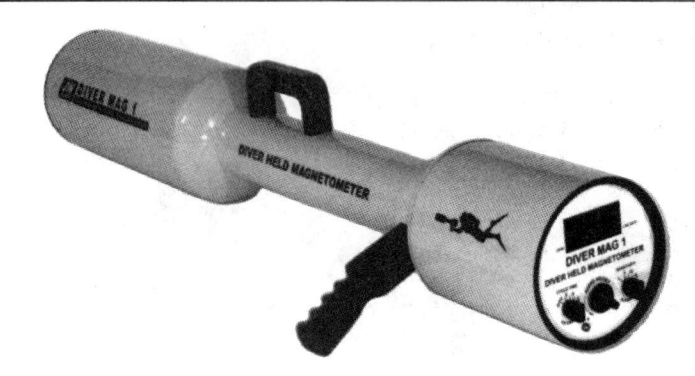

FACTORY ACCESSORIES:

The right accessory can greatly expand the versatility and performance of any detector as search conditions or the type of target being sought changes. The following accessories are available for the J.W. Fishers line of equipment:

Search Coils:
- Underwater Connector for Coil
- 5", 10" or 16" coils / 18" Coil for Boat Deployment / 8" x 48" coil, skids & 100' cable
- Extra probe coil (1" diameter x 22" long):

Other Items:
- Dual Underwater Earphones
- Carry Bag
- Extra Battery Pack
- 220vac charger (Europe)

Internet Resources

- **TreasureNet – J.W. Fisher's Forum**: http://forum.treasurenet.com/index.php/board,214.0.html

Minelab Electronics

Corporate Headquarters
PO Box 537, Torrensville Plaza SA 5031, Australia
61-8-8238 0888 • Fax: 61-8-8238 0890

Minelab USA
871 Grier Dr., Suite B1, Las Vegas, NV 89119
(702) 891-8809 • Fax: (702) 891-8810

Minelab International, Ltd.
Laragh, Bandon, Co. Cork, Ireland
353-23-8852101 • Fax: 353-23-8852106

COMPANY PROFILE:

Since its origins in 1985, Minelab has been the world leader in providing metal detecting technologies for consumer, humanitarian demining and military needs. Through devotion to research and development and innovative design, Minelab is today a major world manufacturer of hand held metal detector products. Over the past 20 years, Minelab has introduced innovative and practical technology that has taken the metal detecting industry to new levels of excellence.

Specializing in advanced electronic technologies, Minelab's competitive advantage was created early on with a highly innovative and dedicated research and development team inspired by the innovative physicist Bruce Candy. Minelab products continue to set new standards in the world of metal detecting for both performance and innovation.

In line with these high standards Minelab is an ISO 9001 Quality Endorsed Company. ISO 9001 is a worldwide quality standard certification that ensures continuous improvement is maintained in order to provide the highest level of product quality for our customers. We believe in a strong customer focus and working together to find innovative solutions that add value to our products.

It is this commitment to the development of new technologies, along with excellence in customer service that will give you a big advantage when you are out detecting, no matter what the ground or environmental conditions. With Minelab products you will have the opportunity to find more good targets more often.

In 2008 Minelab became a member of the dynamic Codan Group of Companies. The parent company, Codan Limited, is an international leader in the high frequency radio and satellite communications markets with customers in over 150 countries. In 2009, Codan celebrated its commemorative year, marking 50 years of Codan-built communication equipment.

MINELAB ELECTRONICS FINDS SHOWCASE:

You Never Know What You Might Turn Up!!!

Research had helped Randy Horton locate the site of an old picnic ground that had been used from the late 1860's to the early 1890's. To most people driving by, the site looked like any other corn field in the area but Randy knew better. He'd hunted the site for many years and each spring when the fields were turned, more coins would turn up. Arriving at the site one day, Randy & his partner hoped for the best despite the area having been "hunted to death". Using his X-Terra 705 with the 6" HF coil to avoid getting snagged on corn stalks, Randy picked up a few coins but the one that stood out was this stunning 1877 Indian Head with full Liberty on the head band. The coin – conservatively appraised at more than $2,300 – has been sent in to be preserved and sealed. As they say, never pass up a site said to be worked out!

Once You Find Your First Gold Nugget, You're Hooked!

Steve Hersbach, veteran prospector and owner of Alaska Mining and Diving, has been searching for gold since he was a teenager and in 2003, he purchased his own gold mine called Moore Creek in a remote section of Alaska well-known for larger nuggets. Using a Minelab GPX 3000 (the predecessor to the current GPX 4500), he uncovered the beautiful specimen shown here which weighed just over 2 ounces and is shot through with white quartz. It was located in tailing piles from the old mining operations and represents the type of gold lost by inefficient recovery systems being found by today's prospectors armed with state-of-the-art metal detectors.

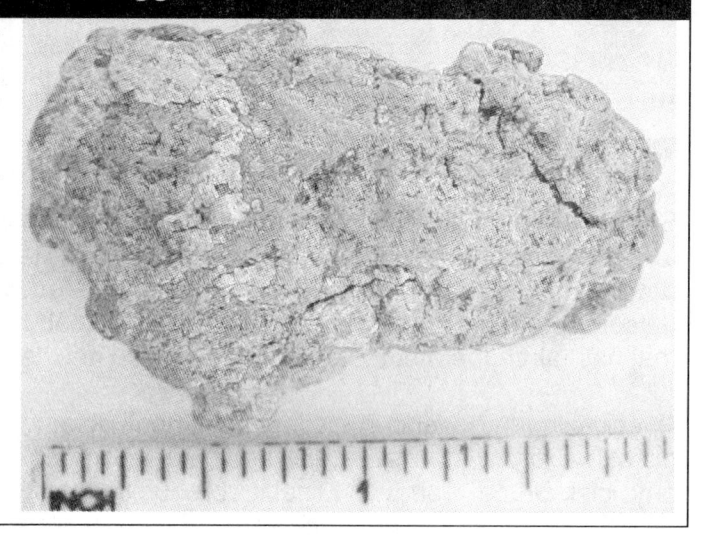

PRODUCT LINE:

Minelab X-Terra 305   LIST: $495

The X-TERRA 305 is the solid no-nonsense introduction unit in the new generation Minelab X-TERRA Series. A lightweight, easy to use, coin-and-treasure-hunting detector designed for the hobbyist who does not want or need the top of the line machine. The X-TERRA 305 is suitable for the whole family and there is even a short shaft available for youngsters. Despite being ultra lightweight and easy to use, there is no compromise on quality or performance. The X-TERRA 305 is now packed with new features, functionality and enhanced setting options. This detector delivers results, value and more…in fact some might think that we made it too good!!! A no nonsense detector perfect for those seeking a high performance entry-level detector

Minelab X-Terra 505 — LIST: $695

The X-TERRA 505 is the high performance, mid-range detector in the new generation Minelab X-TERRA Series. With advanced capability, great depth and excellent discrimination, the X-TERRA 505 is the ideal all-rounder to take your detecting experience to the next level. Equally at home on land or at the beach, the X-TERRA 505 now has full frequency capability and can adapt easily to coin & treasure and relic hunting. Compatible with low frequency (LF) 3kHz waterproof coils as well as medium 7kHz and high frequencies 18.75kHz, all seven X-TERRA coils can now be used on the X-TERRA 505. The X-505 has a number of new and enhanced features that make it an excellent choice for a wide range of applications.

Minelab Musketeer Advantage — LIST: $895

The best performing detector in its class! Ideally suited for the coin and relic hunter who needs simple solid performance. The dedicated power of this detector will amaze even the most seasoned detectorist. One of the most powerful VLF detectors on the market.

You will be amazed at the awesome depth straight out of the box! Simple. Deep, Fast. You won't find another VLF detector on the market today that will produce the incredible results of the Musketeer Advantage. Super rugged, & well balanced, this is the detector for you!

Minelab X-Terra 705 — LIST: $950

The X-TERRA 705 offers the ultimate detecting experience. Capitalizing on the versatility of the range, the X-TERRA 705 can be used for gold prospecting as well as for coin & treasure hunting, simply by switching between available pre-programmed modes. Thanks to Coin & Treasure and Gold Prospecting Modes you get a gold detector plus coin, treasure & relic detector all in one! The specialized Prospecting Mode has improved sensitivity making the detector more sensitive to small target signals. The Prospecting Mode can be used in highly mineralized, 'difficult' areas. The high frequency Double-D coils offer advantages in handling these conditions. The Prospecting Mode is ideal not only when searching for gold nuggets but also for small relics and some types of jewelry. With Minelab's proprietary "True Digital" VFLEX technology, you can change the operating frequency simply by changing coils.

Minelab Sovereign GT — LIST: $995

Minelab's BBS Technology automatically transmits 17 separate frequencies over a range from 1.5khz to 25khz which means you have more depth, greater sensitivity and more accurate discrimination. The Sovereign GT does it all! Turn it on, set the controls and start searching for coins and treasures. Only Minelab technology makes it this easy! Whatever you're looking for the Sovereign GT has the penetrating power and versatility you need. The Sovereign GT discriminates between good targets and unwanted trash with astonishing depth and can be used from the park or building site to the sandy beach. This is an all terrain detector ready for any conditions providing maximum performance every time. Perfect if you are looking for a machine offering outstanding performance in a traditional switch and knob package.

Minelab Safari
LIST: $1,195

Powered by Minelab's Full Band Spectrum (FBS) multiple frequency technology, the Safari combines deep, sensitive and accurate detecting for anyone demanding both simplicity AND performance. Safari uses advanced digital filtering to eliminate the influence of ground signals automatically so you can experience easy, seamless detecting whatever the field conditions. With its High Trash Density setting, Target IDs and audio tones are updated when sweeping over closely spaced targets FAST! This improves the recovery of deeply buried high conductivity targets in a trashy environment and allows you to more accurately identify the type of target found. Discover the adventure and excitement of detecting with a Safari today!

Minelab Eureka Gold
LIST: $1,250

The Eureka Gold is one of the world's most versatile gold nugget detectors. Operating with Minelab's exclusive triple frequency technology the Eureka Gold makes prospecting easier than ever before. The Eureka Gold gives you 6.4kHz for maximum depth, 20kHz for general detecting and the super sensitive 60kHz to find the smallest gold nuggets that others are missing. Featuring Minelab's "Accu-Trak" Digital Ground Balance with switchable two speed recovery, combined with new microprocessor controlled discrimination circuitry, it takes the guess work out of detecting so you will find more gold, more often. Hot Rocks are no problem for the Eureka Gold; it will punch through highly mineralized soil with ease. The Eureka Gold is for those of you who want solid performance in a mid-priced Minelab detector.

Minelab Excalibur II 800 or 1000
LIST: $1,395

Minelab's unique Broad Band Spectrum (BBS) technology, combined with superior ground rejection technology, makes the Excalibur II the ideal underwater machine. The unique design of the Minelab Excalibur II allows you to use it as effectively in or out of the water - this machine can move seamlessly from land, beach and wet sand conditions to 200ft underwater. Thanks to a unique method of ground canceling, you will never get false signals from detecting in salt water. Enjoy the simple yet effective discrimination and be surprised at the sensitivity and depth you uncover targets from. Whether you are a long time diver or a casual beachcomber the Excalibur II is an unbeatable choice.

Minelab Explorer SE Pro   LIST: $1,495

The Explorer SE Pro features Digital Technology providing Simple, Powerful and Fast operation.

From the world leader in metal sensing technology, the Minelab Explorer SE Pro raises the standard for metal detecting. This switch-on-and-go detector finds valuable coins, rings, jewelry and relic targets that others walk right over. Packed with exclusive features including SMARTFIND™ 2 dimensional discrimination, 28 frequencies operating together in Minelab's exclusive Full Band Spectrum (1.5 to 100 kHz) technology and now with fast operating 2nd generation software. Minelab Explorer SE Pro is the world's best performing metal detector.

Minelab E-TRAC   LIST: $1,895

Minelab's most technologically advanced detector sets new industry benchmark! The E-TRAC is Minelab's most technologically advanced detector incorporating unique Full Band Spectrum (FBS) technology and Smartfind™ discrimination. FBS technology simultaneously transmits frequencies ranging from 1.5kHz - 100kHz which allows the E-TRAC's advanced signal processing to analyze more target information so that target identification is more accurate. Its sleek, sturdy design, innovative control panel, intuitive menus, clear LCD screen, robust lightweight coil and comprehensive targeting options set the E-TRAC apart from any other detector available today. Minelab has taken the groundbreaking step of incorporating a USB interface – the E-TRAC Xchange. This enables you to connect your metal detector to your home computer to download or upload your E-TRAC settings, user modes and discrimination patterns. You never have to worry about losing your most successful settings again!

Minelab SD 2200 v2   LIST: $2,495

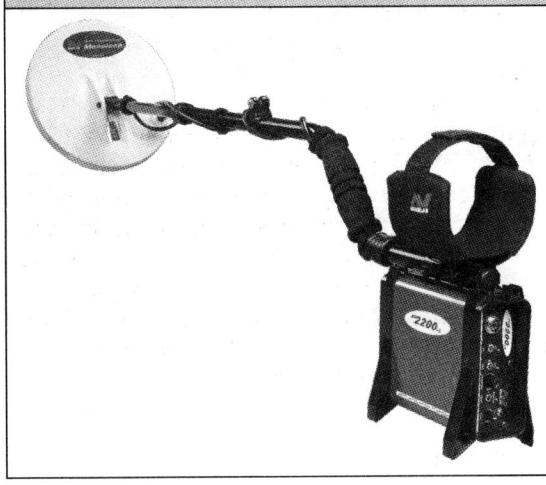

Minelab's SD2200v2 takes your detecting up a notch featuring Multi-Period Sensing (MPS) technology, the exclusive invention of Minelab, to give you depth, sensitivity and reliability. The SD2200v2 combines automatic ground balance, discrimination and automatic tuning to make it one of the world's most sophisticated and powerful gold detectors. The boost amplifier and tone control allow you to customize your detector, making hard to hear sounds clear and defined whilst the discrimination function rejects strong signals from ferrous junk, allowing more time detecting and less time digging unwanted targets. With an excellent balance of features, performance and price, the SD2200v2 offers you more bang for your buck with its surprisingly affordable price.

Minelab GPX 4500	LIST: $5,995

Stronger and more versatile than ever before, the GPX-4500 is the ultimate in cutting edge gold finding technology offering features and performance levels that other manufacturers are yet to match. Incorporating new Smart Electronic Timing Alignment (SETA) technology alongside Minelab's existing Multi Period Sensing (MPS) and Dual Voltage Technology (DVT), it is quieter and less susceptible to interference than earlier models, making it a real pleasure to use. No matter if you've never picked up a detector before or hunted for years, the GPX-4500 offers a number of pre-programmed search modes allowing you to start detecting like an expert right away! The improved discrimination, including the Iron Reject function, combined with the specially programmed Hi Trash search mode makes areas of extreme junk well worth a search. It is also great for the specialist Relic and Jewelry hunter who wants to recover smaller and deeper targets invisible to most treasure detectors.

FACTORY ACCESSORIES:

The right accessory can greatly expand the versatility and performance of any detector as search conditions or the type of target being sought changes. The following accessories are available for the Minelab line of equipment:

Search Coils:
- FBS Models: 8" and 11" Double-D coils
- X-Terra Models: 6" concentric + Double D; 9" concentric; 10" Double-D; 10"x5" Double-D
- SD, GP & GPX models: 11" Double-D, 8" mono, 10"x5" Double-D, 11" mono, 15"x12" mono, 18" mono

Other Items:
- Coil covers for all Minelab coils
- Control Housing Covers
- Carrying cases
- Headphones; Lightweight, padded and underwater
- Rechargeable battery packs & charger systems
- Upper and lower shaft sections
- Minelab logo clothing and hats

THIRD PARTY ACCESSORIES FOR MINELAB DETECTORS:

- **Sun Ray In-Line Pinpointing Probes**: Pinpoint probe designed for specific detectors – models available for the Minelab Explorer S, XS, II, SE & SE Pro, Quattro, Safari & E-Trac. Sun Ray Detector Electronics, (319) 636-2244; http://www.sunraydetector.com/
- **Sun Ray Stealth Coils**: Double-D coils for the Explorer/E-Trac/Safari/ Quattro and the Sovereign line in 5.5", 8" & 12.5" sizes. http://www.sunraydetector.com/
- **Coiltek Search Coils**: Coiltek Manufacturing Pty., Ltd.: (Contact the factory for a local dealer / distributor) 6 Drive In Court, Maryborough, Victoria, Australia 3465; (03) 5460 4700); http://www.coiltek.com.au
- **Detech / Excellerator Search Coils**: Kellyco Detector Distributors: 1085 Belle Ave., Winter Springs, FL 32708; 407-592-6159; http://www.kellycodetectors.com (U.S. distributor for Detech coils) / Joan Allen Electronics, Ltd: 190 Main Road, Biggin Hill, Kent, TN16 3BB, (0)1959 571255; http://www.joanallen.co.uk

- **Nugget Finder Search Coils**: Mono and Double-D search coils for the Minelab gold detectors – 15 sizes available;
  - **Arizona Outback**: http://www.arizonaoutback.com/nfcoils.html (US supplier)
  - **Goldsearch Australia**: http://www.goldsearchaustralia.com/search-coils.html (Australia)
- **Metal Arm Cuff Assembly**: Replacement arm cuff that offers extra comfort & durability (Fits the Explorer, E-Trac, Quattro and Safari models)
  - **Anderson Detector Shafts**: (A generic cuff is also available) http://andersondetectorshafts.com/16.html
  - **Dixie Metal Detectors**: http://www.dixie-metal-detectors.com/
  - **Krayolacuff**: Powder-coated metal replacement cuffs & shafts; http://mrkrayolacuffs.com/
  - **Jeff Herke Accessories**: http://hdwt.net/minelab.html
  - **Pro Scoops**: http://www.proscoops.com/
- **Control Housing Covers:** Protect the electronics and screen of your detector
  - **Maz Detecting Supplies**: http://members.multimania.co.uk/maz_detecting/
  - **Sun Ray Detector Electronics**: http://www.sunraydetector.com/
- **Straight Shaft Systems**: Designed to improve the balance & ergonomics of your detector:
  - **Anderson Detector Shafts:** Quality-built shafts for the Excalibur (Various sizes and styles to choose from including beach hunting, wading and diving options); http://andersondetectorshafts.com/2.html
  - **Pro Scoops:** Shafts and knob-guards for the Excaliburs; http://www.proscoops.com/
  - **Reilly's Treasured Gold:** Lightening rod for the Excalibur; http://www.RTGStore.com
- **In-Sight Target ID Display**: Unique target ID mod for Sovereigns; http://home.comcast.net/~dtekt/In-Sight/

REFERENCE RESOURCE BIBLIOGRAPHY

Books

- **The Minelab Explorer & E-Trac Handbook** by Andy Sabisch
- **Mastering the Minelab Explorer S & XS** by Andy Sabisch
- **Mastering the Minelab Quattro & Safari** by Andy Sabisch
- **Advanced Field Methods for the Minelab Excalibur: Theory & Practice** by Clive James Clynick
- **Advanced Methods for Finding Gold in the Water with the Minelab Excalibur** by Clive James Clynick
- **Finding Gold, Silver & Coins with the Minelab Sovereign & Excalibur** by Clive James Clynick

Videos

- **Practical Prospecting with Minelab's GPX Series** by Arizona Outback (http://www.arizonaoutback.com)
- **Exploring the Explorer – Advanced Edition**
- **Explorer II Training Video** by Gary Brun

Other

- **Minelab Times Factory Newsletter:** Exclusive pre-release product information, the latest news and exclusive content; http://minelab.com/usa/consumer/knowledge-base/newsletter

Internet Resources

- **Find's Treasure Forums:** Individual forums for the Explorer, E-Trac, X-Terra, Safari / Quattro and Sovereign / Excalibur models; http://www.Findmall.com
- **The Treasure Hunter Forum – Minelab:** http://www.treasurehunterforum.com/forum7/
- **TreasureNet – Minelab Forum:** http://forum.treasurenet.com/index.php/board,211.0.html
- **Treasure Quest Minelab Forums:** http://www.treasurequestxlt.com/community/forumdisplay.php?f=120
- **The Minelab Owners**; Great information on Minelab detectors and specific tips on hunting in Europe and the United Kingdom; http://www.minelabowners.com

Nautilus Metal Detectors

Nautilus Metal Detectors
29 West Lemon Street, Coats, NC 27521
(910) 897-7950

Worldwide Detectors Ltd
20 Hall Moor Road, Hingham, Norfolk, NR9 4LB
United Kingdom
Tel: +44 (0) 1953 440 041
http://www.nautilusmetaldetectors.co.uk/

COMPANY PROFILE:

Nautilus metal detectors have been manufactured for over 35 years in North Carolina, USA. They have a very dedicated following and are considered "cult machines" among U.S. Civil War relic hunters because of their superior depth, discrimination and robust construction.

What makes Nautilus detectors different? We live in a world of mass production and homogenization. Nautilus metal detectors are different and different in a positive sense as they have features found on no other detector - features that provide real benefits to the detectorist. The Nautilus DMC range is all about putting the operator back in control, giving as much or as little audio information desired in order to make that important decision - whether to dig a target or not. The analog design of the Nautilus also means the user knows exactly how their detector is set-up and operating. There is no complicated LCD menu system to navigate, just glance at the controls and you instantly know where you are. The rugged lightweight aluminum control box offers excellent protection to the electronics inside from physical shocks. The DMC system is unique to Nautilus. DMC stands for "Dual Mode Circuit" and in effect it is two detectors operating at the same time; a non-motion ground canceling All Metal detector and a motion discriminator. There are some distinct advantages to running a DMC detector because of the operating differences between All Metal and Motion discrimination modes. Most detectors today are motion discriminators and some have an All-Metal mode (which may or may not be a true zero motion All Metal mode). If a detector has a true All-Metal mode (one that operates with a threshold tone and where the volume varies according to the strength of the target signal) it goes deeper in this mode than the motion discrimination mode. However, most users will choose the motion discriminate mode over the All Metal mode and only use the All-Metal mode for pinpointing. This is because, they get fed-up with having to check each signal in the motion disc mode, whether that's changing the actual mode or referring to a target ID meter.

With Nautilus DMC detectors you get the full advantages of both systems, without any of the disadvantages.

NAUTILUS FINDS SHOWCASE:

History Preserved and Artifacts See Light After Nearly 150 Years!

Tom Perry is an avid relic hunter from Pooler, GA that uses Nautilus detectors in all his searches. The artillery shell fragments shown here came from an area that was part of the Battle of Pocotaglio fought on October 22, 1862 and were recovered by Tom while participating in the 2009 GNRS hunt on Team Nautilus. The fragments came from both Union and Confederate shells that had been fired by both sides and laid forgotten for close to 150 years until Tom and his trusty Nautilus recovered them.

PRODUCT LINE:

All Nautilus metal detectors can be ordered with your choice of shaft design and mounting configuration. The original design features a straight shaft with a "U-shaped" handle that wraps over the back of the control housing. The "S-shaped" handle allows the control housing to be mounted either under the arm rest or on top of the shaft in front of the handgrip.

Nautilus DMC IIB with 8" coil — LIST: $925

The DMCIIB has more controls than the DMCIIBa, but these do not require a lot of extra adjustment and once set can be left: It has six controls; Discrimination, Ground Balance, Discrimination Sensitivity, Ground Balance Sensitivity, Tuning and Transmit Power. The controls can also be set to the factory recommended settings, allowing the user to switch-on-and-go.

The main difference between the IIB and IIBa is that the IIB user can adjust the sensitivity levels of each DMC circuit (i.e. All Metal and Motion Disc) rather than just controlling the overall gain of the detector via Transmit Power. IIB users can also set the Search Loop Balance function manually.

Nautilus DMC IIBa — LIST: $1,050

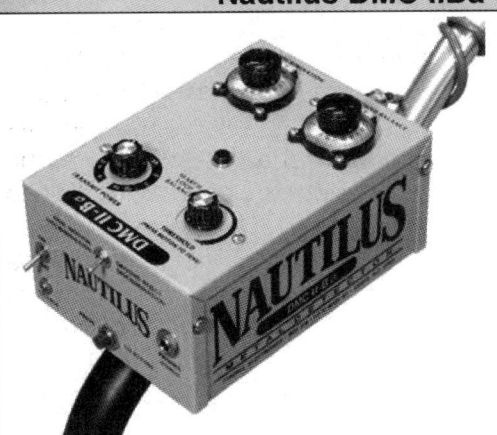

The DMC IIBa came about from customers wanting the benefits of Nautilus's unique DMC operation and pure performance, but in a simple-to-use package. The result is the DMC IIBa and it has become Nautilus's most popular detector.

The DMCIIBa features three search modes: Ground Reject Discriminate, Non-Motion Discriminate and Non-Motion Ground Balance. It has four controls, Tuning, Transmit Power, Discrimination and Ground Balance. These can be set to the factory recommended settings, making the unit virtually a switch-on-and-go detector.

FACTORY ACCESSORIES:

The right accessory can greatly expand the versatility and performance of any detector as search conditions or the type of target being sought changes. The following accessories are available for the Nautilus line of equipment:

Search Coils:
- 6" concentric coil; Excellent for getting into tight spots and places full of junk
- 8" concentric coil; A very versatile coil, lighter and gives better target separation than the 10".
- 10" concentric coil; Supplied as standard, provides excellent depth and sensitivity.
- 15" concentric coil; Surprisingly light for its size, it is ideal for use where extra depth is needed on coin size and larger objects. Not recommended for junky sites.

Other Items:
- Spare shafts; upper and lower – simplifies changing coils in the field
- NiMH rechargeable battery systems (batteries and chargers)

THIRD PARTY ACCESSORIES FOR NAUTILUS DETECTORS:

Headphones:

- Nautilus DMC detectors require headphones that are wired for true stereo due to the way Nautilus detectors operate. Most stereo headphones with an impedance of between 8-32 ohms should work; however, because of Nautilus's unique circuitry, it is recommended to have headphones with individual speaker volume controls. The DetectorPro Gray Ghost DMC headphones are recommended by the factory and endorsed by users worldwide (http://detectorpro.com/grayghostdmc.htm)

Gray Ghost DMC

REFERENCE RESOURCE BIBLIOGRAPHY

Internet Resources

- **The Treasure Hunter Forum – Nautilus**: http://www.treasurehunterforum.com/forum17/
- **Find's Treasure Forums – Nautilus Forum**: http://www.findmall.com/list.php?39
- **The Treasure Depot – Nautilus Forum**: http://www.thetreasuredepot.com/cgi-bin/nautilus/nautilus_config.pl

Nexus Metal Detectors

Avebury court, Hemel Hempstead, Hertfordshire, HP2 7TA
United Kingdom
Tel: U.K: 07909895085 / Outside U.K: +447909895085
http://www.nexusdetectors.com/

COMPANY PROFILE:

The name Nexus was announced to the metal detecting industry in October 2004 by introducing the first Nexus metal detector called Nexus Standard. The idea behind this name was created from the very principal of operation upon which the Nexus Standard is based. Nexus is a word derived from Latin, which literally means "to bind". There are several definitions for Nexus, the most popular of which is "a means of connection, link or a tie." The first Nexus Standard metal detector was based on the idea that the detector user and the metal detector in use (the Nexus) would work together for a common goal, discovering the lost treasures. The capabilities of the metal detector, the natural human senses and experience linked together would produce the ultimate results in search for lost treasures. At the end of 2006 the Nexus Standard was replaced by the Nexus Standard SE. In September 2006 the Nexus Ultima was introduced. With its dual 20" search coil, Nexus Ultima became the most powerful hand held metal detector ever made. In the beginning of 2007 the Nexus Coronado was introduced as entry level model in the Nexus metal detectors range. All Nexus metal detectors are induction-balanced and fully-tuned in electro-magnetic resonance. This fact and the original unprecedented search coil design have made the Nexus metal detectors one of a kind, the only resonant tuned metal detectors on the world market. The advantages of resonant-tuned metal detectors are well explained on the Nexus web site. The most important purpose of all Nexus designs is the aim for perfection offering unmatched discrimination, depth penetration, low weight, elegant and ergonomic design, versatility and above all long lasting performance.

NEXUS METAL DETECTORS FINDS SHOWCASE:

Deeply Buried Bronze-Age Spear Found Thanks to Nexus!

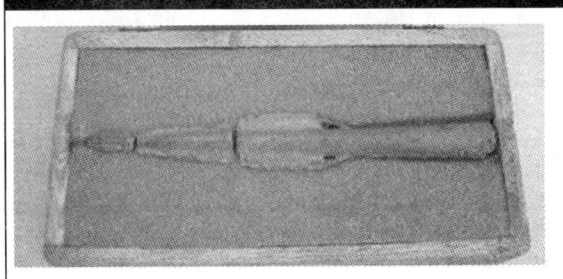

Graeme Smith from the East Devon metal detecting club in the United Kingdom have made some extraordinary finds with his Nexus detector. Graeme's said "*The spearhead is Mid Bronze Age and was around 21 inches deep in a small pasture field. The area had been searched by other detectorists in the past. My detecting friend and I had searched there the week before and found nothing; in fact we only had a couple of signals all day which made me return with the Nexus. Within an hour I had a good signal which yielded me the spearhead. I have found several other Bronze Age artifacts within a mile of this area but not so deep and using another machine. I recently got permission to search new farmland which contained a Bronze Age Settlement and which I believe is connected to my finds and am optimistic of some great finds using the Nexus.*"

PRODUCT LINE:

Nexus Coronado Ground Fix (4"/6"/9" coils)   LIST: €385 ($545) / €435 ($615) / €625

The Coronado Groundfix is a deep seeking "switch-on-and-go" type of metal detector with automatic ground balance control divided into three levels. The different levels of the automatic ground balance control are tuned for different ground mineral content. Like all Nexus metal detectors, the Coronado Groundfix is also tuned in resonance Induction Balance. The Coronado Groundfix is motion detector with fast recovery speed. Its design offers a versatile use on most inland sites and salt water beaches around the world including sites with heavy mineral deposits and black sand beaches. The Coronado Groundfix exhibits excellent depth penetration and discrimination accuracy by being able to detect a single coin (30mm) at 14" or targets as small as 1.5 mm in diameter. It is lightweight (1.3 kg with 8 AA batteries) and well balanced. It is easy to learn to use and to achieve best results, does not require previous detecting experience.

Nexus Coronado (6" / 9" coils)   LIST: €765 ($1,080) / €915 ($1,295)

The Nexus Coronado is a non-motion type of detector with fast auto tune. Its general performance is similar to motion-type metal detectors but allows users to slowly work around obstructions that might cause others to miss targets. The Nexus Coronado is an entry level unit in the Nexus Metal Detectors range. Its design allows for use on most inland sites and salt water beaches around the world including sites with heavy mineral deposits and black sand beaches. The Coronado exhibits excellent depth penetration and discrimination accuracy by being able to detect a single coin (30mm) at 14" (36 cm) depth underground or targets as small as 1.5 mm in diameter (small metal particles). The Coronado is exceptionally lightweight (1.3 kg with 8 AA batteries) and well balanced.

Nexus Standard SE (9"/ 20" coils)   LIST: €1,795 ($2,530) / €2,495 ($3,526)

The Nexus Standard SE is the flagship model from the Nexus Metal Detectors range. It came about as a result of several years of cutting edge research in the induction balance technology. Its design allows for use on most inland sites and salt water beaches around the world including sites with heavy mineral deposits and black sand beaches. The Standard SE is a non-motion type of detector with fast auto tune, with an induction-balanced resonant tuned search coil. The Standard SE exhibits excellent depth penetration and discrimination accuracy and can detect a single coin (30mm) at 18" (45 cm) or a small silver coin (18mm) at 12.5" (32cm). From all tests conducted with Nexus Standard SE around the world, the SE is has been recognized as one of the most powerful coin and relic hunting metal detectors ever made. The Nexus Standard SE is light weight (1.8 kg with 8 AA batteries) and well balanced

Nexus Ultima 5F   LIST: €3,495 ($4,950)

The Nexus Ultima is the most powerful deep seeking hand held metal detector available. With its giant dual 20 inch (88 x 52 cm) search coil, the Nexus Ultima exhibits depth penetration and discrimination accuracy unseen before and is the company's flagship model. The new Nexus Ultima 5F is designed to work on five different frequencies switchable from the search coil. The wide choice of frequency settings is undisputable advantage for reaching maximum depth in various ground conditions. With all of the accessory search coils available the Nexus, Ultima is becoming the most versatile metal detector, capable to find literally any target, small or large, shallow or deep. The Nexus Ultima is designed for use on most inland sites and salt water beaches around the world including sites with severe mineral deposits and black sand beaches. Nexus Ultima is a non-motion type of detector with fast auto-tune and an induction balanced resonant tuned search coil. The Ultima give you 55% more power than the Nexus Standard SE, which is more than twice that of other top range metal detectors. It weighs 2.7 kg with the 20" search coil

FACTORY ACCESSORIES:

The right accessory can greatly expand the versatility and performance of any detector as search conditions or the type of target being sought changes. The following accessories are available for the Nexus line of equipment:

Search Coils:
- **Ultima Coils**: Dual 4" (7.3kHz), 6" (4.2kHz, 8.5kHz & 18kHz), 9" (6.8kHz)
- **Coronado Coils:** 4" (7.3kHz), 6" (4.2kHz, 8.5kHz & 18kHz), 9" (6.8kHz)
- **Standard SE Coils:** 4" (7.3kHz), 6" (4.2kHz, 8.5kHz & 18kHz), 9" (6.8kHz), 20" (5.2kHz)

NOTE: The Nexus coils are unique in their design as the photo shows. All of the coils are manufactured using resin dipped glass fiber construction and are supplied with a coil cover for added protection. They are environmentally sealed and water tight, which makes them suitable for use on beaches and in wet conditions. Each coil is tuned in full electro-magnetic resonance for optimal performance. The size reflects the diameter of one side of the uniquely shaped coil; i.e., the overall width is nearly double the stated coil size.

Other Items:
- Replacement coil covers
- Rechargeable battery systems

Saxon Metal Detectors

Essex Metal Detectors
24 Perry Way, Aveley, South Ockendon, Essex, RM15 4RD
United Kingdom
Tel: +44 (0) 01708 866859
http://www.easytreasure.co.uk/

COMPANY PROFILE:

Essex Metal Detectors has been building Saxon metal detectors since 1979. Their first metal detectors - the Saxon and the Saxon 2 - were extremely popular in the late 1970's, being acclaimed as a "Best Buy" in a Which Magazine's test report in 1980. Since those early days of metal detecting in the United Kingdom, they have continued to develop new products over the years such as the Saxon 3, the Saxon SM30, the Saxon SM40 and the Saxon X-1 which was recognized as one of the deepest seeking metal detectors anywhere, and most recently, the Saxon SM35 and SM45. They have always given a two-year, no-quibble warranty as they are confident in the quality of construction and reliability of their detectors. Quite a few of the early Saxons are still going! As the owners of Essex Metal Detectors say *"Newcomers to this hobby very quickly get overwhelmed by the jargon, and to be blunt 'Bull' churned out by the metal detecting industry. The American metal detecting scene is completely different from in the UK. In America there is virtually nothing more than 150 years old to find and the place is vast. Fortunately for people detecting in Europe and especially England, it is a completely different ball game. We have so much to find. Just about every field will contain literally thousands of non-ferrous items, many of them interesting and valuable often going back thousands of years. Picture a piece of land just about anywhere, the size of a tennis court. And once every 100 years for the last two thousand years somebody lost something interesting. But it's not that easy of course. You need a reasonable detector, something decent to dig with and lots and lots of patience but it is a fascinating hobby."*

PRODUCT LINE:

Saxon SM35 Motion Discriminator   LIST: £230 / $380

The Saxon SM35 is an ideal beginner's detector being very simple to setup and operate. It has just one control that switches the detector on and varies the discrimination level. Apart from this simplicity of operation, the SM35 has performance that will make it attractive to more experienced users. As the 'M' in its name implies, this is a "Motion detector which means that it can discriminate and cancel out ground mineralization at the same time. The detector runs on 'silent threshold' which means the tuning is taken care of electronically, and the only sound to come from the headphones will be when the detector locates a metal object. The Saxon SM35 is a well-made machine, tough enough to take all hard knocks of field usage. The detector is well-balanced and comfortable to grip & sweep. The battery compartment of the SM35 holds 8 AA batteries & is separated from the rest of the electronics (to prevent damage in case of battery leakage).

Saxon SM45 Motion Discriminator — LIST: £350 / $580

The SM45 is similar to the SM35 but has several added features that will be helpful to the more experienced user. The addition of a gain control on the SM45 allows the sensitivity to be set a bit higher than the SM35. When searching difficult areas such as high mineralized soil or salt wet beaches the gain can be reduced a bit to avoid chattering or false signals. An all-metal pinpoint switch is also included on the SM45. The SM45 is a motion detector which means that it can discriminate and cancel out ground mineralization at the same time. The detector also runs on 'silent search' which means that tuning is taken care of electronically and the only sound normally to come from the headphones will be when the detector locates a metal object in the ground. The stem itself breaks down into three parts. This allows for easy transportation to and from sites. It also means that the SM45 will fit into a small bag or suitcase should you be thinking of traveling with it.

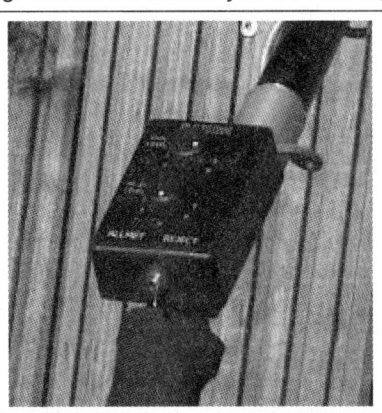

Saxon X-1 Ultra Deepseeking Analytical Detector — LIST: £1,700 / $2,825

What does Essex Metal Detectors say about the X-1? "*Until the advent of the Saxon X-1, there had been no successful attempt to produce a generally useable deep-seeking detector for many years. Regardless of claims made, all recent designs lacked adequate discrimination at depth. They could not be used effectively on the vast majority of inland sites because such sites are contaminated with iron fragments and other magnetic material. The operator of such equipment very soon lost confidence to dig anything deep. Anyone who persisted soon had scrap iron by the bucketful and virtually nothing else - apart from blistered hands and backache, that is! The Saxon X-1 was designed from start to finish as a highly accurate discriminating and ultra deep-seeking detector. In comparison to the old Arado 120b and 130 models of the late 1970's and 1980's the X-1 has very much more depth - a staggering increase in the order of 50% right across the board. Moreover, it is much more stable, easier to use, has a more rugged construction with far better balance and suffers much less from power-line interference. The X-1 does require a highly experienced operator with access to a considerable number of reasonably good sites, so that its full capabilities can be both realized and appreciated. Moreover, such operator needs to be experienced in the use of other than Motion Detectors in order to have a realistic appreciation of what is in the ground and of the various types of ground effect likely to be encountered. Without any doubt whatever, it is much easier to find large quantities of small non-ferrous metal items with the X-1, particularly on 'worked out' sites. The main problem likely to be encountered is that of fatigue, due to the effort of digging so many relatively deep holes. As this is a detector for inland use, salt-water beaches should be avoided. The Saxon X-1 provides the first real performance improvement in deep-seeking detectors for many years - and this improvement is truly massive!*"

Secon Metal Detectors

SECON Sicherheitstechnische Anlagen GmbH
Vulkanstraße 12, D- 54578 Wiesbaum/Eifel, Germany
Tel: +49 (0) 6593 / 9809990
http://www.secon-koeln.de

SECON-USA
1600 E. St. Rt. 73, Waynesville, OH 45068
Tel: (800) 895-5573
http://secon-usa.com/

COMPANY PROFILE:

Ebinger has its roots in the field of bomb disposal where the company founder introduced his first detectors some forty years ago. The refinement of a new detection principle finally led to the creation of the current company in 1969.

A large number of inventions and trend setting innovations now carry the name of EBINGER, which in the meantime has become a world-renowned brand name. Ebinger developed and produces a wide portfolio of detectors for metal detection, munitions and battle area clearance, pipe and cable locating, security, law enforcement, commercial application in industry, civil engineering, timber industry and scientific use.

Ebinger puts much emphasis on research and development of innovative techniques for an efficient and reliable detection technology intended for professional use. The Ebinger head office is based in Cologne, Germany. The company maintains a modern facility at Wiesbaum/Eifel and is represented by dealers and distributors worldwide. Their technology has to prove itself constantly under operational conditions, whether on land or under water. This challenge is their motivation. They strongly support their staff's dedication to continuous improvement and to the company's quality goals.

PRODUCT LINE:

Secon UWEX 720C — LIST: €685 / US Pricing *

Despite its small size and search head this compact, simple to use underwater metal detector offers an impressive detection performance and an outstanding separation of small metal objects buried closely to each other. The UWEX 720C detects ferrous and non-ferrous metals and alloys. The UWEX 720C operates on the Pulse Induction (PI) Principle, which is advantageous for use in fresh and saltwater. It consists of a single sided headset and a search head flanged to the detector handle with built-in electronics and battery compartment. Rotating the handle turns the detector on. Sensitivity can be adjusted through the sensitivity adjustment ring even when wearing diving gloves. The waterproof headset gives clear audio indication to allow target size and depth to be determined. It is equally at home in fresh water as it is in salt water.

| Secon UWEX 722C | LIST: €1,300 / Not Available in the U.S. |

The UWEX 722C is a highly sensitive metal detector capable of underwater and normal land use being configured in the short or long handled version. It is pressure tested up to 60m. The waterproof headset gives a clear audible signal with large frequency deviation making it easy to pinpoint the target. The UWEX 722C operates on the Pulse Induction Principle (PI) which eliminates the interference caused by to conductive saltwater or mineralized ground. Local interference or unwanted signals from small metal scrap (i.e., nails or short wires) can be strongly reduced by tuning of internal adjusters. It consists of a search head with joint, which is flanged to the detector handle containing the detector electronics. For normal land use or for working in underwater vegetation an extension rod can be screwed between search head and electronic cylinder. The detector is switched on by rotating the handle 180° in clockwise direction.

| Secon UWEX 722T | LIST: €1,500 / US Pricing * |

The UWEX 722T is designed to search for metal objects on both land or underwater. The UWEX 722T operates on the Pulse Induction (PI) Principle and can be used in fresh or saltwater. It detects ferrous and non-ferrous metals. The UWEX 722T consists of a square shaped search head with a joint, which is flanged to the detector handle containing the battery compartment and socket for the headset. The detector is switched on by half-rotation of the handle. The sensitivity can be adjusted by means of a sliding adjuster at the search head joint. For the operation on land the extension rod can be screwed between the search head and module. Size and conductivity of the objects are analyzed by the detector electronics and indicated by a modulation of the audio signal. The diver can differentiate between scrap and those objects worth excavating.

| Secon UWEX 725K | LIST: €3,927 / US Pricing * |

The UWEX 725K is a further development of the well-proven UWEX 722 metal detector. Improved detection performance and a wide auto-adaptation to interfering metal components characterize the new 725 design. It can detect shallow buried minimum amount of metal. It operates using the dynamic mode pulse induction concept. Target acquisition is indicated as a visual or audible + visual alarm. Optional search coils expand the UWEX 725K's versatility. The only external operation element is the ON/OFF & sensitivity stepping switch. The headset socket and the alarm LEDs are placed at the square section of the handle. The detector can be operated in a normal mode with audio and LED detection signals or in a 'silent mode' without headset. In this case target detection is indicated only by the two alarm LEDs on the detector handle.

| Secon UWEX 725PA | LIST: TBD / US Pricing * |

The UWEX 725PA operates on the Pulse Induction Principle with audio-coded object information. The PA designation stands for Pulse Analyzing System that analyzes and indicates the decay times and/or the object's signature of detected metal objects. Small objects and short decay times will lead to a continuous alarm signal while large metal objects or those with high electrical conductivity will lead to additional pulsing information, which is indicated by an audio and visual response. The 725PA consists of a search head with a joint that is flanged to the detector handle, extension rod and headset. The handle contains the electronics circuit board and the battery compartment. Signals are indicated by the alarm LEDs which are placed at the bottom of the handle and audio signals which are transmitted to the headset.

Secon UPEX ONE — LIST: €2,080 / US Pricing *

This is the first high performance nugget and coin detector made by Ebinger for treasure hunters. The UPEX ONE is equipped with a search coil, an S-shaped two part telescopic handle, armrest and rear-mounted control housing. The battery container fits in the rear end of S-handle, which balances the detector optimally. The UPEX ONE works by means of the Pulse Induction Principle (PI) going back to the 1970's. After further development and combined with ground compensation the detector is now using sophisticated techniques to detect targets. Ground magnetic effects are suppressed which allows for small metal parts or nuggets to be detected in even the worst ground. Thanks to the Pulse Analyzing Function the conductivity of various located metal targets is indicated by a high or low alarm signal.

Secon UPEX 728 — LIST: €2,975 / US Pricing *

The UPEX 728 is a pulse induction metal detector that can be equipped with various search heads or large loops on land or under water depending on the detection job. The detector supports two different working methods:

- **Manual detection**: standard use, audio and visual alarm signal of a detected metal object.
- **Mapping**: computerized determination and documentation (optional) of metal contaminated areas.

The UPEX 728 is equipped with ground compensation and with a pulse analyzing function (PA) which evaluates the conductivity of the detected object concerning its long or short decay time. The electronics indicate the different decay characteristics by an audio and visual signal which provides useful information on the detected object to the operator and is also fed to the detector's data port (computer assisted evaluation).

Secon TREX 204 — LIST: €1,428 / US Pricing *

The TREX 204 is used in adverse conditions such as in dense vegetation and on mineralized ground such as in the Australian Outback. The precise ground compensation, the audio coding for ferrous/non ferrous metal and the slim sensor probe are the exceptional characteristics of the 204. Small ferrous parts, nails or iron fragments are suppressed by the switchable iron filter/discriminator. Larger ferrous objects or worth excavating coins and gold nuggets produce responses. Field tests confirmed the practical value of this detector for geologists and mineralogists as it detects not only metal relics but also ore veins in old mining districts. The TREX 204 applies a TR-system (transmitter-receiver-principle) where metal objects become magnetized when subject to the alternating electromagnetic field transmitted by the detector's probe. One unique characteristic of the detector is its hockey stick shaped sensor probe. It is proven to be ideal for use in difficult terrain such as narrow trenches, earth hollows or beneath tree roots. 
The 3-part telescopic handle, which is protected against accidental twisting, consists of a handgrip and an armrest. The electronic can be fixed beneath the armrest. The handgrip and armrest can be disassembled as required and the electronics can also be hip-mounted.

* - Due to Euro-Dollar fluctuations, contact Secon-USA for the latest U.S. pricing

Teknetics

First Texas Products, LLC.
1100 Pendale, El Paso, TX 79907
(915) 633-8354 or (800) 413-4131
http://www.tekneticst2.com & http://www.Detecting.com

COMPANY PROFILE:

The name Teknetics was first introduced with the formation of a company in the early 1980's and it quickly earned the reputation of building detectors with cutting edge technology and world-class performance. Unfortunately while the products were first-rate, the management practices were not and the company faded into the history books. Years later, First Texas Products, located in El Paso, Texas, who manufactures Bounty Hunter, Fisher and related private-label metal detectors, resurrected the Teknetics moniker and attached it to the initial model in the line – the T2 – based on the high level of performance it offered detectorists. First Texas, and as a result Teknetics, has earned the reputation of producing high quality metal detectors that offer excellent value when looking at price and performance.

Lead engineer, Dave Johnson, has designed many of the industry's most popular metal detectors for several different companies, beginning with the Fisher 1260-X in 1981. If you're an avid detectorist, you probably already swing machines that are Dave Johnson's designs or adaptations of them as he has worked for companies including Whites, Fisher, Tesoro and Troy. Dave worked on incorporating aspects of the many wish lists veteran detectorists have put together into a line of high performance yet affordable detectors. The T2 was the first in the Teknetics line but the Alpha, Delta, Gamma and Omega have since followed. Dave's goal – and that of the engineering team he worked with on the projects at Teknetics – was to improve the current detectors on multiple fronts. Lighter weight, better ergonomics, better battery life, deeper detection, more accurate discrimination & target ID and an improved user interface. Based on user feedback, it looks like they accomplished what they set out to do.

TEKNETICS FINDS SHOWCASE:

The T2 & 5" Coil Unlock a Trash-Filled, Worked-Out Site

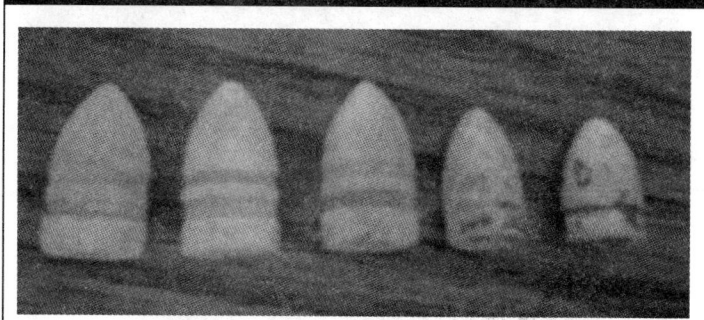

Mark Sweberg is an avid Civil War relic hunter that took his T2 equipped with a new 5" coil to a site he & others had hunted for more than 3 years. The finds had pretty much dried up but Mark thought the smaller coil would be the trick in picking up keepers from amongst the iron trash in the area. Well, the 5 dropped bullets show the results – and 3 were in the same hole with large pieces of rusted iron. Mark said *"I am very pleased with the performance of the coil and plan to make it one of my regular tools for metal detecting"*

The T2 Made Some Incredible Finds One Day

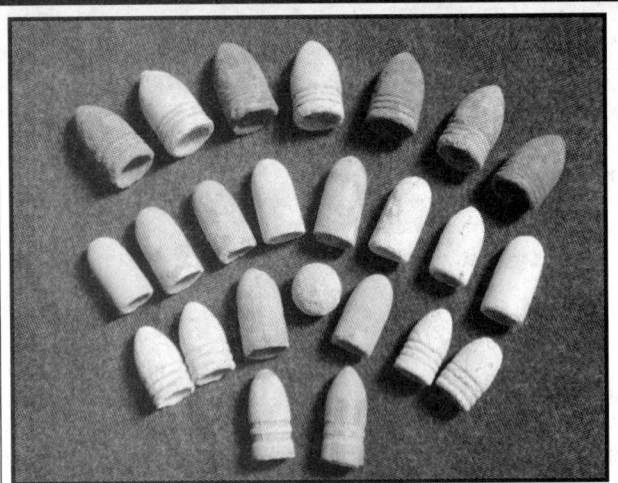

Dennis is truly sold on his T2 . . . actually both of them. In his words,

"It is without a doubt the machine for me. I've made some incredible finds with it over the last two years and it has been fun! I actually own two of them, one with the standard coil and one with that sweet little donut coil that will pick the smallest of buttons out of an iron bed. It's a great machine and First Texas has the best customer service."

The bullets shown here were found in a single outing with the T2 at a site that Dennis had found in his home state.

The New Omega 8000 Hits Silver at the Park!

Bill Sarver from central Missouri was on the way home from a site he had been hunting when he came across a small park he had never seen before. The third signal came through loud and clear which made Bill think he had detected a recently lost clad coin. Needless to say he was more than just a little surprised when you removed a shallow plug and recovered an 1891 Seated dime! A great find and a good lesson – never pass up a good signal as you never know what it might be

More Relics Come to Light Thanks to First Texas

Mike Scott, Global Director of Hobby Sales for First Texas, took part in one of the large organized relic hunts known as the Mardi Gras hunt coordinated by Larry Cissna, administrator of The Treasure Depot website. In Mike's words, here's the story behind this impressive haul of vintage relics.

"I found a spot loaded with flat buttons that the gang came over and fed on it. Tons of fun with the best group of hunters. I only wound up with the early button and a ton of flat buttons but the finds kept on coming. I found Eagles buttons, Eagle I buttons, a Rhode Island militia button, a Massachusetts button, an 1859 Flying Eagle cent and an 1852 silver 3 Kreuzer coin"

PRODUCT LINE:

Teknetics Alpha 2000 — LIST: $199

The Alpha metal detector features a large LCD display that gives you real-time read out of target depth, target ID, battery level and much more. It has preset ground balance and offers turn-on-and-go simplicity.

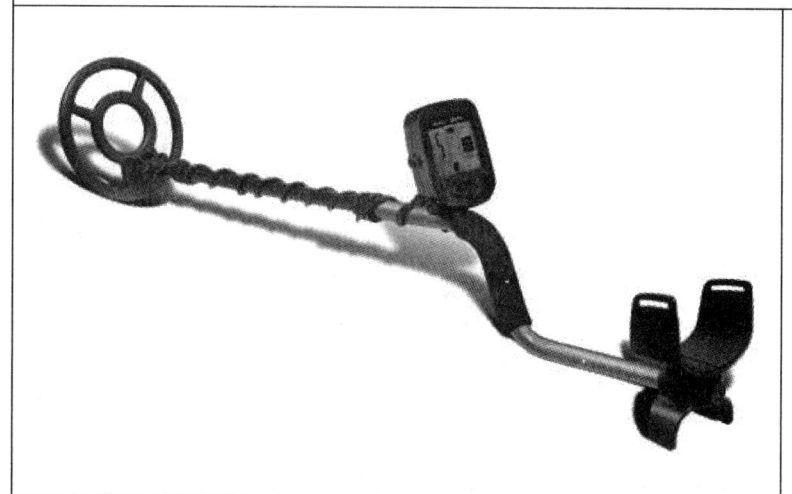

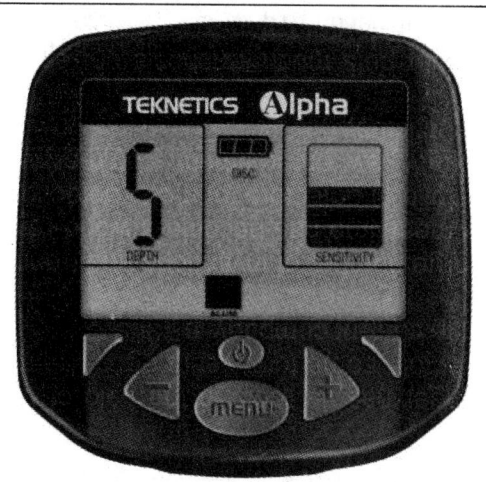

Teknetics Delta 4000 — LIST: $279

Another proud descendent in the Teknetics line. Featuring a large LCD display, numerical target identification, multiple discrimination notches, Press-n-Hold pinpoint, 5-level running depth display, three independent search modes, 3-tone audio target identification / discrimination and an overload alarm system . . . the Delta 4000 is a detector for all levels of detectorists.

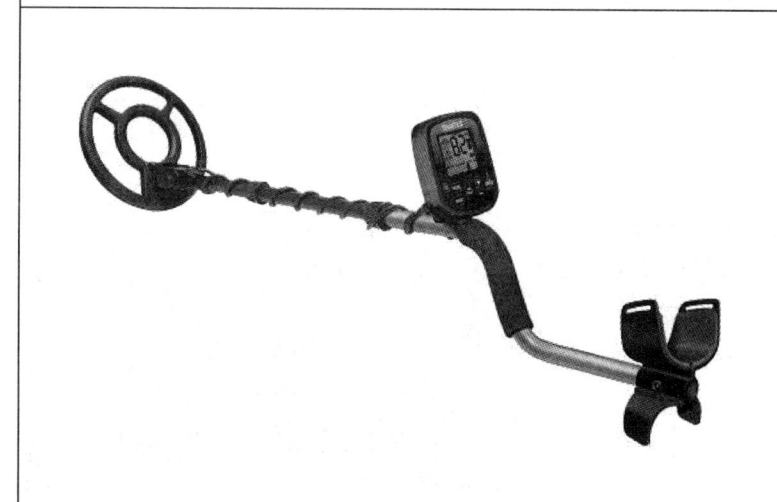

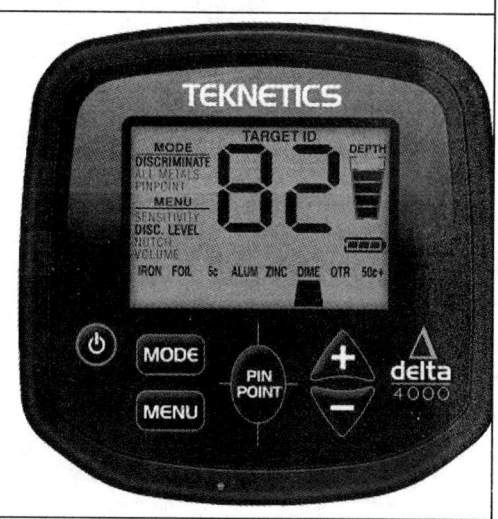

Teknetics Gamma 6000 — LIST: $499

A step above its brothers, the Alpha 2000 and Delta 4000, the Gamma 6000 has more user-adjustable features. Manual Ground Balancing will allow you to selectively tune out those pesky minerals that can give false signals. Featuring a large LCD display, numerical target identification and depth reading, 80 Levels of discrimination adjustment, Press-n-Hold pinpoint, independent search modes, 3-tone audio target identification / discrimination and an overload alarm system . . . the Gamma makes for an detector suited for all levels of detectorists. The Gamma also has "Multiple Notches," selectable by categories, so you'll be able to select pre-programmed discrimination settings and spend your time digging treasure

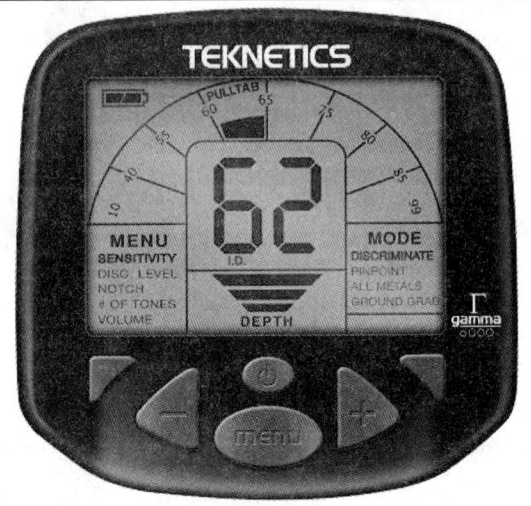

Teknetics Omega 8000 — LIST: $599

The Teknetics Omega 8000 Metal Detector features a large, crystal clear and easy to read, identification meter. This new design enables even the novice of detectorists to see the treasures they've found before they begin to dig! The large control housing of the Omega features push buttons and adjustable knobs to control the interface, numerical depth readout, an intuitive menu system, and a running depth indicator. The two-digit numerical target identification system makes identifying buried target fast and easy! Automatic and manual ground balancing makes it capable of handling even the worst conditions out there. With the Omega 8000 accuracy is improved on all targets – even those older and deeper coins

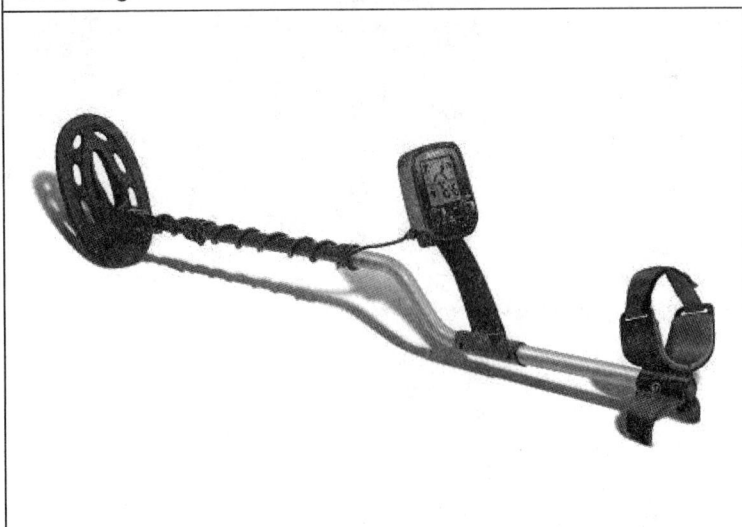

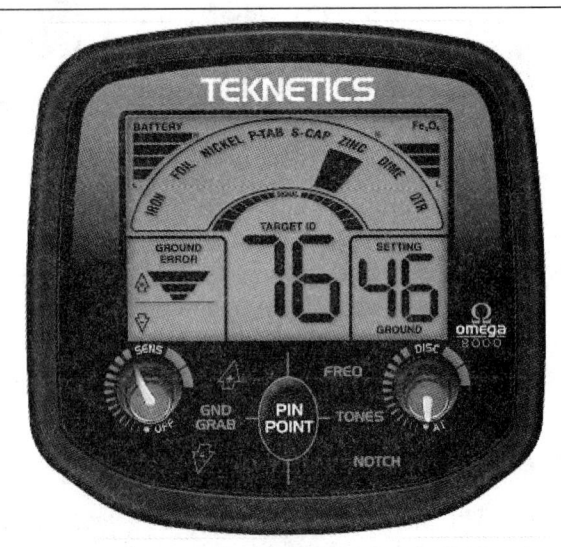

Teknetics T2 / T2 LTD	LIST: $999 / $1,199

The Teknetics T^2 is a new high-performance multi-purpose professional grade metal detector. It utilizes the latest advances in electronic technology, and its functional design represents the leading edge of the metal detector engineering art. The T^2 is easier to learn to use properly than other comparable metal detectors. Its combination of light weight and balance provides comfort unmatched by any other detector in its price range. Its most popular uses include coin shooting, relic hunting, and gold prospecting. Its large LCD Screen with Target Identification Display and intuitive User Interface makes it a snap to master. The waterproof 11-inch Double-D coil provides exceptional coverage and target separation. The LTD edition features two new search modes (Boost to detect even deeper when conditions permit and Cache Hunting to search for larger hidden valuables) and a unique camouflage paint scheme.

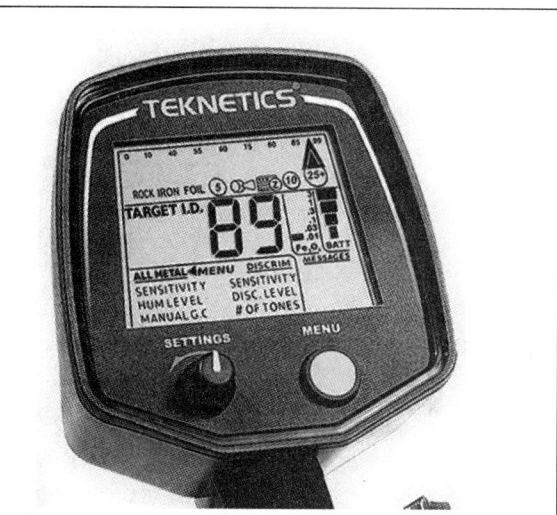

FACTORY ACCESSORIES:

The right accessory can greatly expand the versatility and performance of any detector as search conditions or the type of target being sought changes. The following accessories are available for the Teknetics line of equipment:

Search Coils:
- **T2**: 11" Double-D & 5" Double-D
- **Alpha, Delta, Gamma & Omega**: 5" Double-D, 8" Concentric, 10" Elliptical & 11" Double-D

Other Items:
- Search Coil Covers: Covers are available for all coils produced for Teknetics models
- Carry case for Teknetics detectors
- Headphones for Teknetics detectors
- Find pouch and digger combo set
- Control housing rain covers (T2)

REFERENCE RESOURCE BIBLIOGRAPHY

Internet Resources

- **The Treasure Hunter Forum – Teknetics**: http://www.treasurehunterforum.com/forum165/
- **Find's Treasure Forums – Teknetics Forum**: http://www.findmall.com/list.php?58
- **The Treasure Depot – Teknetics Forum**: http://www.thetreasuredepot.com/cgi-bin/tek/tek_config.pl?

Tesoro Electronics / Laser Detectors

Tesoro

715 White Spar Road, Prescott, AZ 86303
(928) 771-2646 • Fax: (928) 771-0326
http://www.Tesoro.com

COMPANY PROFILE:

Tesoro . . . . The Name That Means Treasure! The company was founded in 1980 by Jack and Myrna Gifford. Jack had already spent several years in the metal detector industry and had worked on some of the best known detectors on the market. In July of 1980 dealers all over the country received a letter from Jack announcing the founding of Tesoro Electronics Inc. and the first two paragraphs laid out the direction that Jack wanted the company to go and the ideas that the company still follows today:

"It has become apparent to me over the past few years that there is a place for, even a need for, a metal detector manufacturer who is dedicated to the independent dealer market. The products should utilize the best of today's technology to provide maximum sensitivity. They should be rugged, but light enough that anyone can use them. They should do their job without "bells and whistles" that only increase the cost. And finally, the company should remain loyal to their dealers and be responsive to their needs and desires. It is with these principles in mind, that TESORO was founded in May of this year.

Tesoro is the Spanish word for treasure. The Spanish certainly seemed to understand and appreciate Tesoro. Never in the history of the New World has there been a treasure hunt like the Spaniards held. It's hard to think of a better name for a company associated with treasure hunting, or a better symbol of our goals than the conquistador. As the Spaniards were yesterday's undisputed masters of treasure hunting, we at TESORO will always endeavor to meet our goal of making TESORO Metal Detectors today's undisputed masters of treasure hunting."

After many dedicated years, Jack and Myrna Gifford retired in late 2004, and the family business is now being managed by Vince and James Gifford with the same philosophy that started the company some 30 years ago. As the company enters the future, Tesoro Electronics will remain in the hands of the Gifford family, and we will continue to produce the best possible metal detectors based on the words that Jack wrote many years ago. *"As the Spaniards were yesterday's undisputed masters of treasure hunting, we at TESORO will always endeavor to meet our goal of making TESORO Metal Detectors today's undisputed masters of treasure hunting."*

TESORO FINDS SHOWCASE:

Beautiful Gold Coin Turns Up At A Construction Site

William "Billy" Ferguson was bitten by the treasure hunting bug in late 2008 when he saw a husband-and-wife team searching a construction site in the downtown area of his home town. After seeing several old coins they have found, Billy was sold and picked up a Cortes as an early Christmas present to himself. Over the next few months he gained experience and the quality and quantity of his finds steadily increased. In October of 2009 he saw another section of the old business district being excavated and after checking with the supervisor of the job, visited the area one evening after work. A few wheat cents and a Mercury dime kept Billy's interest; however, when this 1885 $10 gold piece turned up, he called it a day! Can you blame him?

PRODUCT LINE:

TESORO COMPADRE — LIST: $189

The Tesoro Compadre was designed with the idea that less is more. This machine can do a lot of the same things that its bigger brothers can do. It works great for coin hunting, competition hunting and relic hunting, but it does it without any excess knobs. Switch on the detector and you're working in a silent search, motion all metal mode. The farther you turn the knob, the more discrimination you can bring to bear on those trashy sites. The Compadre comes standard with a 5.75" round concentric coil. The depth is equivalent to the original 7" concentric, plus the new coil reduces the likelihood of target masking in extremely trashy ground. It also gives you the ability to get into and around natural obstacles like bushes, fences, and playground equipment. The Compadre has it all. One knob simplicity for the beginner and high gain circuitry and the famous Tesoro ED-180 discrimination for the advanced user.

TESORO SILVER uMAX — LIST: $299

The Silver Sabre series has had a very long history with Tesoro Electronics. First introduced in 1983 when "lunch box sized" detectors were the norm, the original Silver Sabre was perceived as a toy unit. Advertised as "strong, simple, silent", the Silver Sabre has gone through many changes over the years. The Silver Sabre Plus added a no motion all metal circuit. The Silver Sabre II added a new plastic housing and new Hybrid Circuit technology. Several years ago we introduced the Silver Sabre µMax with an incredibly small housing and Max Boost technology. Tesoro decided to bring the Silver back full circle to where it started. The original Silver Sabre was a turn on and go detector with Silent Search discrimination and all metal modes. The new Silver µMax returns to its roots and offers strong, silent and simple operation once again.

TESORO CIBOLA   LIST: $425

The Cibola combines H.O.T. circuitry with turn-on-and-go simplicity. It is designed for the treasure hunter that does not want to bother with too many controls. The Cibola is named after one of the fabled seven cities of gold that the conquistadors were searching after and will simplify the search for any treasures to be found.

The Cibola's main search mode is an ED 180 Silent Search discriminate. A threshold-based All Metal mode is accessed by the Push Button Pinpoint mode. The ease of use for the Cibola makes it the perfect detector for both the metal detecting novice as well as the treasure hunter that's been around for a while.

TESORO VAQUERO   LIST: $525

During the design phase of the Vaquero, we knew that it was going to be a very hard working detector. It is designed as an all-around detector, able to do just about everything that any detectorist could want to do. Vaquero is the Spanish word for cowboy. When we think of hard work and the ability to take on any kind of tough job, we think of the cowboys of the old west. The main part of the Vaquero's versatility is its three and three-quarters manually adjusted ground balance. This will give the detectorist the power to set up his machine to best suit the mineralization conditions that he is working in and his personal treasure hunting style. The Vaquero adds an ED180 discrimination feature to filter the trash from the treasure and a Push Button Pinpoint that makes digging up the goodies that much easier. The discriminate knob is also used to switch into a threshold-based All Metal Mode.

TESORO GOLDEN uMAX   LIST: $529

The µMax detector that you have been waiting for is here - The Golden µMax. This is a detector that only Tesoro could build - Full size detector depth, sensitivity, Four Tone Audio ID and a user adjustable Notch Filter Discriminate all placed into the lightest detector housing on the market. At less than 2.5 pounds, the Golden µMax lets you control what you want to find. The adjustable notch window lets you, not the engineers; decide how to pick through the pull tabs to find the nickels and gold rings, while the ED 120 discrimination knocks out all of the nasty iron. The tone ID will also give you a great idea of what your target is. The Golden µMax will help you define your targets and make better use of your detecting time

TESORO DeLEON   LIST: $599

The DeLeón is a Target Identification Detector. The DeLeón is designed as an easy to use, turn-on-and-go detector. The faceplate has only four controls: Sensitivity, Discriminate, Threshold & a Mode Switch. It uses the same circuitry as the Cortés, so you can expect the same depth and sensitivity from the DeLeón that the Cortés is well known for. The DeLeón's display screen is one character high by eight characters wide. It is larger and easier to read than the Cortés display but does not carry as much information. The DeLeón has a Coin Depth reading, a five segment bar graph and a two-digit Target ID Number.

TESORO SAND SHARK   LIST: $679

Our Sand Shark combines time-proven PI circuits with the latest digital technology creating the first microprocessor controlled PI detector. Pulse Induction (PI) detectors have always been the natural choice for working wet salt beaches. Their circuitry and single loop coils will not see changes in salt-water conductivity that drives a VLF-style detector crazy. Add Tesoro Electronics' exclusive interchangeable Printed Spiral coils (available in four sizes) and you create a fantastic PI detector. But we didn't stop there. The Sand Shark has two distinct operating modes: VCO and Normal. When working in the VCO mode, as targets get closer to the coil, the threshold generates a louder, higher pitched tone great for pinpointing. The Normal mode works with a single tone and is used for beachcombing and other prolonged searches. Tesoro added a microprocessor to help you customize the detector to your specific needs. The Pulse Width control allows you to tune your detector to the best balance of depth, sensitivity, and battery life. You can also change the Normal mode audio frequency. Simply use the "F" Adjust knob to set the tone and you're ready to go.

TESORO TEJON   LIST: $699

The Tejón features a high output transmit oscillator to push the signal deeper and an increased gain for sensitivity to smaller items and was designed from the ground up with the coin and relic hunter in mind. The first thing that you will notice is the lack of a mode switch on the faceplate. We have moved it beneath the control housing so that you are able to switch modes quickly. Pinpointing & checking your targets with the Alternate Discrimination is a breeze and the Tejón's two discriminate modes are fully user definable. The engineers at Tesoro have given the user the ability to set the machine for their hunting needs. Each discriminate mode uses ED180 circuitry. The regular discriminate also incorporates a full-time all metal setting. Want to hunt in all metal and check the targets for iron or discriminate out iron and perform a check for high value silver or gold targets? It's no problem for the Tejón. Simply set the Discriminate and Alternate Discriminate modes for your style of hunting and swing the coil. Then use the Trigger Switch to quickly change modes to check your targets. Push the trigger forward to activate the Alternate Discriminate or pull the trigger back to pinpoint the target. The Tejón makes it fast and easy. The Tejón has a manually adjustable ground balance that works for both the All Metal mode and both Discriminate modes. Using a three and three quarter potentiometer, the Tejón will meet and defeat all soil conditions and is suitable for any hunting style.

TESORO TIGER SHARK — LIST: $749

The Tiger Shark uses microprocessor technology to create a true dual function machine. In Normal Mode, the Tiger Shark works like any other Tesoro detector. It uses the same great ground balance and discrimination features that made past Tesoro detectors so successful. On land, the Tiger Shark can be used for coin and relic hunting and even gold prospecting. By using the four controls on the outside, you can fine tune your detector to handle whatever conditions you are working in. Working in the wet salt areas is where the Tiger Shark outshines the land detectors. In land conditions, the most crucial adjustment is using the ground balance to tune out mineralization. In wet salt conditions, changes in the conductivity in the sand cause most of the problems. The Tiger Shark uses a completely different set of internal settings in the SALT Mode than in the NORM Mode. There are no special controls or techniques to remember. The Tiger Shark continues in the tradition of other great Tesoro underwater machines by having interchangeable coils available.

TESORO LOBO SUPER TRAQ — LIST: $799

The Lobo SuperTRAQ is the pinnacle of electronic gold prospecting technology. No other detector gives you the fast, accurate and reliable ground tracking in normal and severe soils like the Lobo SuperTRAQ. Tesoro's famous discrimination circuitry lets you relic and coin hunt too. The Lobo SuperTRAQ is one of the finest gold nugget metal detectors you can buy. Tesoro's SuperTRAQ Computerized Ground Tracking System solves the detectorist's greatest problem- ground balancing. No matter where you hunt, the Lobo SuperTRAQ will quickly self-adjust to eliminate minerals letting you find more gold with ease. Discrimination circuitry with instant pinpointing at your fingertips takes the awesome power of the Lobo SuperTRAQ into every type of metal detecting you do.

TESORO CORTES — LIST: $849

The Cortés represents the best combination of current and new technologies that Tesoro has to offer. When Jack Gifford and Vince Gifford set out to create a new target ID machine they each brought with them different experience. Jack has over twenty-five years experience designing some of the best analog detectors that have been on the market. Vince brought with him a decade of computer systems experience. Together, they have been creating new technology that gives our detectors superior performance and keeps them easy to use. The new Cortés represents all phases of our new microprocessor technology combined with our tried and true analog circuits to create a detector that has all of the high end features our customers have asked for with user friendly Tesoro controls.

LASER METAL DETECTORS:

Tesoro has been producing a line of metal detectors designed to tackle specific challenges and meet the demands of the United Kingdom market for Frank Mellish, owner of Treasure World in London, under the "Laser Detectors" name since 1991. The current line includes five models (Scout, Rapier+, Trident 1, Trident 2 and Hawkeye) which derive much of their technology from other models in the Tesoro family. The Scout draws from the Compadre; the Rapier+, Trident 1 & Trident 2 from the Cibola & Vaquero platform and the Hawkeye from the DeLeon. All Tesoro search coils are interchangeable with Laser models. Treasure World can be reached at 192 Albany Street, London, NW1 4AP, England or by phone at (44) 207-387-3142. While Treasure World does not have a website, many of his authorized dealers do and additional information on the specific Laser models can be obtained from them. An internet search will identify Laser dealers in your local area.

FACTORY ACCESSORIES:

The right accessory can greatly expand the versatility and performance of any detector as search conditions or the type of target being sought changes. The following accessories are available for the Tesoro line of equipment:

Search Coils:
- **uMax Series of Detectors**: 3"x18" widescan / 4" round concentric / 5.75" round concentric / 7" round concentric or widescan / 8" round concentric / 8.5" round widescan / 9"x8" concentric / 10" elliptical widescan / 12"x10" widescan
- **Cibola, Lobo SuperTRAQ, Tejòn & Vaquero Models**: 3"x18" widescan / 5.75" round concentric or widescan / 8" round concentric / 8.5" round widescan / 9"x8" concentric / 10" elliptical widescan / 12"x10" widescan
- **Tiger Shark**: 7" round concentric / 8" round concentric / 10.5" round concentric
- **Sand Shark**: 3"x18" pulse / 7" round pulse / 8" round pulse / 10" elliptical pulse / 10.5" round pulse

Other Items:
- Padded carrying case with the Tesoro logo & detector accessory carrying bag with Tesoro logo
- Weather covers for detector control housings
- Spare lower shafts to expedite replacing coils
- Clothing items with the Tesoro logo including various hats, shirts

THIRD-PARTY ACCESSORIES:

- **Straight Shaft Systems**: Designed to improve the balance & ergonomics of your detector:
  - **Anderson Detector Shafts**: Quality-built shafts for the Stingray, Stingray II, Piranha, Tiger Shark and Sand Shark (Two full-length sizes and a shorter Scuba shaft available); http://andersondetectorshafts.com/10.html
- **Maz Detecting Supplies**: Control Housing Covers to protect the electronics and screen of your Tesoro & Laser; http://members.multimania.co.uk/maz_detecting/

REFERENCE RESOURCE BIBLIOGRAPHY

Internet Resources

- **The Treasure Hunter Forum – Tesoro**: http://www.treasurehunterforum.com/forum10/
- **TreasureNet – Tesoro Forum**: http://forum.treasurenet.com/index.php/board,213.0.html
- **Find's Treasure Forums – Tesoro Forum**: http://www.findmall.com/list.php?17
- **The Treasure Depot – Tesoro Forum**: http://www.thetreasuredepot.com/cgi-bin/tesoro/tesoro_config.pl

Viking Metal Detectors

1 Angela Street, Mill Hill, Blackburn, Lancashire, UK, BB2 4DJ
United Kingdom
Tel: +44 (0)1254 55887
http://www.metaldetectors.co.uk/

COMPANY PROFILE:

Viking is one of the best known and longest established names in the metal detecting industry. Viking Metal Detectors has been manufacturing and supplying metal detectors to hobbyists and the water industry in the UK and Europe since the 1970's. They pride themselves on being totally devoted to metal detectors and as such manufacture nothing else. Export trade is a growing side of their business and they are pleased to report that they now sell metal detectors to dealers in over 10 European countries. Their metal detectors can be used either inland or on the beach, so wherever you want to detect you can feel assured that your Viking Metal Detector will perform reliably - and make finds. It is often noted that their prices appear to be cheaper than the competition. They assure you that this is not reflected by the quality of their product and have always tried to bring value for money to their customers and aim to continue to do so. All their metal detectors come with a 2 year guarantee on parts and labor (excluding batteries) and their Customer Service is second to none.

PRODUCT LINE:

Viking 1 — LIST: £77.31 / $129

Developed from the classic Viking Metal Detector first introduced in 1976, the Viking 1 Metal Detector remains a popular model. With a shorter shaft and smaller search head than our other detectors, it is light and easy to handle and therefore a particularly suitable choice for children. It is operated by two simple controls, Fine Tuning and Coarse Tuning, in the same manner as our larger Viking 5 Metal Detector and industrial WASP models. The Viking 1 Metal Detector has earned a reputation over the years for being effective on heavily contaminated sites that can render more advanced metal detectors unusable.

| Viking 5 | LIST: £87.10 / $145 |

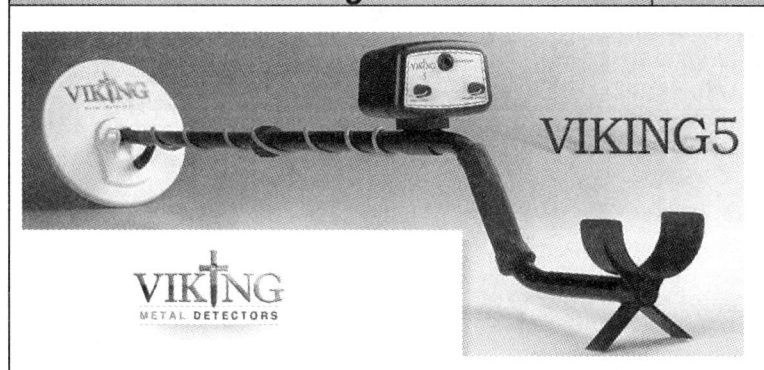

Developed from a circuit first introduced in 1976, the Viking 5 Metal Detector is one which has stood the test of time, and remains a popular choice for both beginners and more experienced detectorists. It is arguably one of the best selling and most successful metal detectors of all time. The Viking 5 Metal Detector is remarkably easy to use, having just two simple tuning controls. It has excellent sensitivity to gold, silver and copper objects, yet discriminates against small iron junk. It is often acclaimed for its ability to detect desirable objects in an area with either heavily mineralized ground or one littered with rusty iron, a feat that is often impossible for a detector costing many times the price. Along with an excellent record for reliability, these are reasons that this metal detector has established itself so successfully within the hobby. Working well on both inland sites and the beach, this metal detector represents excellent value for money.

| Viking 6 | LIST: £99 / $165 |

The excellent value Viking 6 Non-Motion Metal Detector is operated by a single tuning control, in conjunction with a memory retune button. Once initially tuned, this allows the metal detector to be brought back into tune by simply pressing the button, should it drift out of tune for any reason. The reject control can be used to make the metal detector ignore lower quality metal targets, reducing the number of unwanted objects detected. The Viking 6 Non-Motion Metal Detector has also been used very successfully on the beach where careful setting of the reject control can be used to counteract the common reaction metal detectors often have to wet sand and salt water.

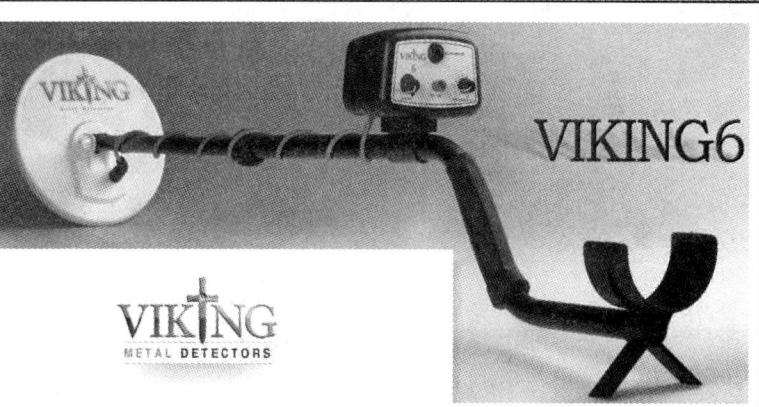

| VK 10 | LIST: £126.26 / $210 |

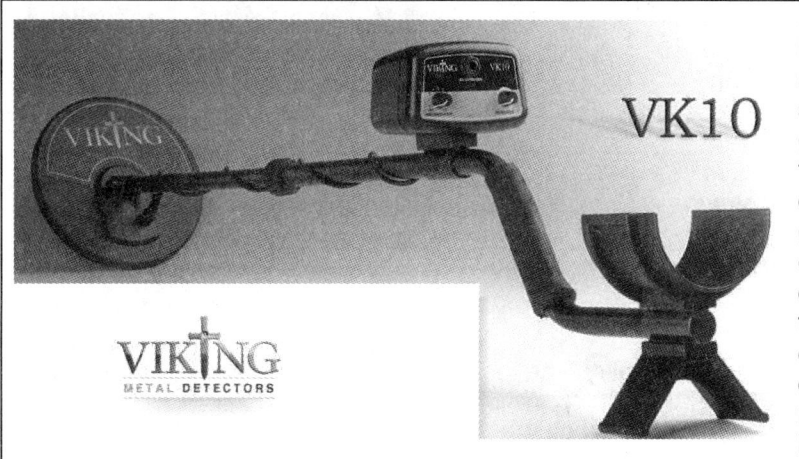

Extremely easy to operate the VK10 Metal Detector is the simplest of our motion metal detectors. It requires no tuning or setting up and is literally a 'switch on and go' metal detector. As a motion detector, the VK10 continually adjusts itself to compensate for ground conditions and gives a sharp signal whenever a target object is found. The discrimination control can be used to reject lower quality metal targets, while the sensitivity control enables the best performance to be obtained from the metal detector regardless of where it is used. The VK10 Metal Detector is suitable for beginners who require a more sophisticated metal detector than our basic non-motion machines.

VK 20	LIST: £155.62 / $260

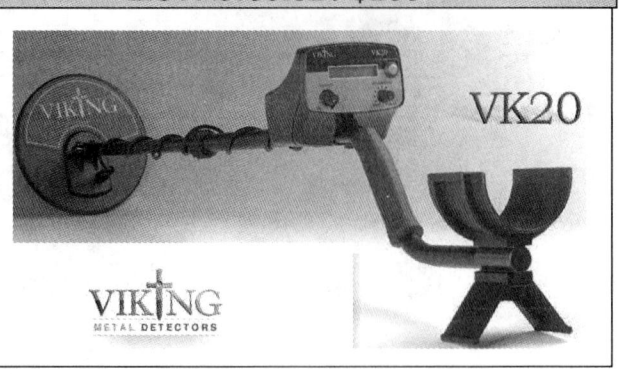

A purely motion metal detector, the VK20 Metal Detector is the first model in our range to feature the useful Target ID facility. Used in conjunction with the Discrimination control, this can help determine whether a target is worth digging or not. The display used to provide the Target ID information also shows Discrimination and Sensitivity control settings, as well as providing an indication of remaining battery power. The VK20 Metal Detector also provides a beach mode which eliminates false signals when detecting on wet sand.

VK 30	LIST: £194.76 / $325

Two detectors in one, the VK30 Metal Detector features both Motion and Non-Motion detection modes.

Use the VK30's Motion mode with Discrimination to detect and determine whether a target is worth digging, and then use the Pinpoint pushbutton to accurately locate the object. Alternatively scan the ground with the extra-sensitive non-motion mode to find a target and identify it with the Target ID. The VK30 Metal Detector also features a beach mode to reduce the negative effects of detecting on wet sand.

VK 40	LIST: £224.12 / $372

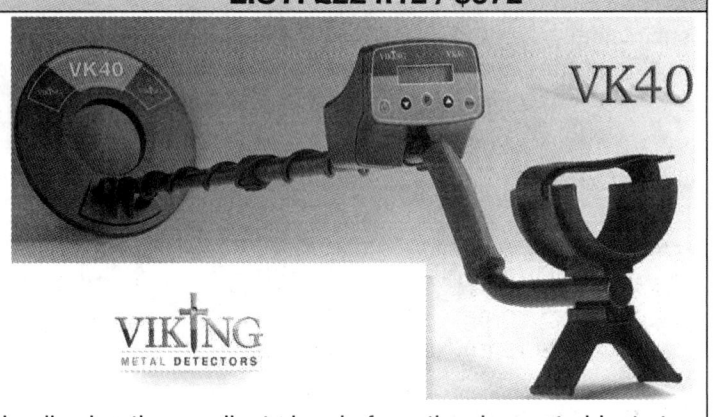

Top of our range, the features that set the VK40 Metal Detector apart from the rest of the Viking range are its concentric search head and membrane keypad control system. The large search head allows objects to be detected deeper, while the keypad allows quick switching between detection modes. Processor memory allows the metal detector to be set up as desired and retain those settings whilst not in use. The VK40 Metal Detector offers 3 modes of detection: Motion Detection for discriminating against lower quality targets, Non-Motion Detection for accurate pinpointing of objects and All-Metal Detection which is an automatically retuning Non-Motion mode allowing the smallest signals from the deepest objects to be heard.

FACTORY ACCESSORIES:

The right accessory can greatly expand the versatility and performance of any detector as search conditions or the type of target being sought changes. The following accessories are available for the Viking line of equipment:

- Search coil covers
- Carrying cases

Whites Electronics

White's Metal Detectors
"See what's in the ground before you dig!"

White's Electronics, Inc.
1011 Pleasant Valley Road, Sweet Home, OR 97386
Tel: (541) 367 6121 • Fax (541) 367 6629
http://www.WhitesElectronics.com/

White's Electronics (UK), Ltd
35 Harbour Road, Inverness, Scotland IV1 1UA
Tel: (01463) 223456 • Fax: (01463) 224048
http://www.Whites.co.uk

COMPANY PROFILE:

White's beginnings date back to the year 1950 and the uranium craze. When all the country was looking for uranium, so were Olive and Ken White, Sr. The only Geiger Counters available used headphones and Mr. White quickly learned that headphones created a problem in rattlesnake country. He invented a better product but was told his design was impossible by the leading Geiger Counter manufacturers. Deciding to manufacture the design himself, he and an employee built one Geiger Counter a day. The counters were well received and within seven years, White's had 65 employees. In 1958, the U.S. government announced it would no longer purchase uranium. All was not lost for this growing business, however. At the request of a former dealer in Tombstone, Arizona, Mr. White was persuaded to build a metal detector. On his first outing, the dealer found a Spanish spur, a large piece of silver, several artifacts and a few coins. This successful first outing was written up in a book with Mr. White's name and address. The year was 1959 and orders and requests for information poured in marking the beginning of the White's we know.

White's Electronics is a world leader in the design and manufacture of metal detectors. The company is currently led by Ken and Mary White, using the same philosophy that was so successful for Ken's father 50 years ago - give the customers quality and value, treat your employees like you would like to be treated and the future will be bright. Numerous patents are material proof of White's commitment to maintaining this leadership role. As the technology of the electronics industry has changed, so has White's technology - from vacuum tubes to sophisticated computer driven metal detectors for hobby, security and industry. White's Electronics is extremely proud of their national network of authorized dealers.

Research and development are an ongoing commitment at White's Electronics in the areas of engineering, design and manufacturing. State-of-the-art electronics performing in harsh environments demands real world engineering talent . . . talent that is finding treasure at greater depths, in all ground conditions, in high trash areas and in harsh climates. Combine this with high quality, hand-built craftsmanship that provides many years of trouble free treasure hunting. It's all here under one roof at White's Electronics. In the years to come, White's Electronics will continue to use cutting edge electronic technology to offer our customers reliable, easy to use, high performance metal detectors.

WHITE'S-ELECTRONICS FINDS SHOWCASE:

All That Glitters Just Might Be Gold

Bill Grey has been swinging a metal detector for 25 years starting with brands that are no longer in business. Switching to the White's, Bill currently uses the Beach Hunter ID 300. His finds off the beaches around his Florida home have been quite impressive and the photo below shows one season's worth of gold rings he recovered . . . one was worth $2,000 and another $2,500! Not a bad return while spending time in the sun on Florida's beaches.

A White's Prism IV Helps Return Rings Thought Lost Forever

Jerry Troiano found a pair of class rings at a site near his home using a Prism IV within months of each other. The first, a 1954 Clemson University ring had only been lost for 5 years and the owner was ecstatic when he got the call from Jerry saying he had found it. The second was a 1958 Rock Hill High School ring and it took a little longer to track the owner down. Unfortunately the owner had passed away just months before it had been recovered but Jerry returned it to his widow who was speechless at the ring being found after being lost for more than 50 years. Jerry had this to say about his actions . . . *"I attempt to return all class rings; that's just me."*

Lost Gold Coin Sees Daylight After More Than 100 Years

Martin Sykes, an avid detectorist in the United Kingdom, has found that research often reveals productive sites that might otherwise not warrant a second glance. This beautiful 1890 gold Sovereign was found in an isolated farm field miles from the nearest town using a Whites XLT operating in the stock Relic program. Martin is already planning a return visit once the crops have been harvested.

PRODUCT LINE:

Whites Electronics Coinmaster — LIST: $180

The new COINMASTER is White's most affordable detector, featuring target I.D. and target depth. Depth Reading as you hunt - once you've detected a good target, the screen shows you how deep to dig. No extra steps, it's automatically on the screen! Real-time Target I.D where the display shows the I.D. of targets as you hunt. The Coinmaster's 5-Range Discrimination control allows you to pick what you want to see and hear . . . hear and see it all, or just the good stuff. With the 9 inch spider coil and batteries, the Coinmaster only weighs 2.5 pounds!

Whites Electronics Prizm II — LIST: $250

The Prizm II is packed with turn-on-and-go features. It provides depth reading as you hunt - Once you've detected a good target, the screen shows you how deep to dig. No extra steps, it's automatically on the screen! Target I.D. Display shows I.D. of target as you hunt. Hear and see targets! Target ID circuitry shows the I.D. of targets as you hunt. Full discrimination adjusts so you pick what you want to see and hear. Hear and see it all, or just the good stuff. Hear and see targets! With the 8 inch spider coil and batteries, the Prism II only weighs 2.5 pounds!

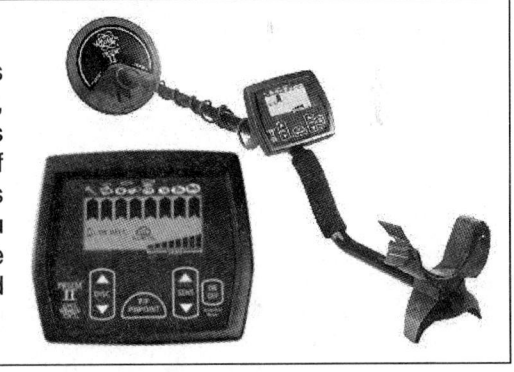

Whites Electronics Prizm III — LIST: $300

The Prizm™ III is White's affordable metal detector. Features include depth indicator and target ID. Once you've detected a good target, the screen shows you how deep to dig. No extra steps, it's automatically on the screen! Target I.D. Display shows I.D. of target as you hunt. Hear and see targets! Target ID circuitry shows the I.D. of targets as you hunt. Hear and see targets! Adjustable discrimination allows you pick what you want to see and hear. Hear and see it all, or just the good stuff. With the 9 inch spider coil and batteries, the Prism III only weighs 2.5 pounds!

Whites Electronics Prizm IV LIST: $400

The Prizm™ IV is a light weight, affordable metal detector packed with White's state of the art know-how. Smart Notch allows you to choose what targets you detect or ignore. Just push a pad and nails, foil, and tabs are in or out. The "Smart" system notches each zone based on your discrimination setting. Once you've detected a good target, the screen shows you how deep to dig. No extra steps, it's automatically on the screen! Target I.D. Display shows I.D. of target as you hunt. Hear and see targets! Better than 20 hours on a set of batteries & 2.5 pounds makes it a breeze to use for hours in the field. An instructional DVD is included with the detector to get you started on the right foot.

Whites Electronics Prizm V LIST: $500

The Prizm V is a light weight, affordable metal detector with a high performance 9.5" search coil, VCO and Multi Tone target ID - hear instantly whether it's a nail, ring, or quarter! 8 distinct audio tones - one for each discriminate zone - range from VERY LOW for nails up to HIGH for silver dollars. Just press MultiTone and listen as the Prizm V metal detector tells you what kind of treasure you've found, OR, if you prefer the Prizm 4-style 3-tone I.D., it's here, too! Once you've detected a good target, the screen shows you how deep to dig. No extra steps, it's automatically on the screen! Smart Notch allows you to choose what targets you detect or ignore. Just push a pad and nails, foil, and tabs are in or out. The "Smart" system notches each zone based on your discrimination setting. Lightweight – just 2.5 pounds – makes for a tireless time in the field.

Whites Electronics GMZ LIST: $500

The GMZ is a new lightweight instrument that operates at a frequency of 50khz which is the optimum frequency to detect small, medium, and large gold. It can be used with any Goldmaster Series search coil for maximum versatility. The GMZ is extremely lightweight & well balanced – weighing just 3.3 lbs with batteries! It features an easy-to-use manual ground rejection system and only three controls - Sensitivity, Ground Reject, and Ground toggle. The GMZ features Silent Search. It can also be used for prospecting as well as industrial "All Metal" applications where small targets and high sensitivity to all metal types are desired.

Whites Electronics ULA-3 / Sierra Madre LIST: $600

A great White's metal detector for searching large metal objects at greater depths. Use the optional 15" search coil to reach an impressive 5 foot depth. Industrial and Serious Deep Treasure Hunting. Specialized for large metal objects. Analog circuitry and fine tuning controls to reach way down. 9 1/2" search coil standard for depth. And the optional 15" search coil detects metal objects up to 5 feet.

Comes with both English and Spanish instruction manuals.

Whites Electronics M6 — LIST: $700

The White's Matrix M6 is a high performing, medium priced, easy-to-use coin and jewelry detector perfect for parks, beaches and general use in ALL ground conditions it even features a "beach mode" to hunt on wet, salty sand! It is one of the most affordable and easy-to-operate metal detectors from White's. The seven tone target identification will keep you from even having to glance at the M6's display – just listen for the sounds you want to dig! The tones and the visual display have a corresponding VDI number to help you know what you've found BEFORE you dig! Go anywhere and find everything with the Matrix M6!

Whites Electronics Prizm 6T — LIST: $700

Like all Prizm's, the 6T is rugged and lightweight for all-day hunting. See what's in the ground and how deep to dig on the easy-read display. Adjust the DISC control up and down depending on where you're hunting. Use low settings in yards and on private property. High settings filter out junk in high traffic areas.

The 6T is loaded with all of the proven Prizm features, plus the latest in metal detection circuitry and software. The result? A detector that's fun to use and finds more treasure!

Whites Electronics GMT — LIST: $800

Ground Minerals are no longer a problem as the GMT simplifies the tough task of ignoring the ground minerals found in gold-bearing areas. Whether you're brand new to searching for gold, or own another metal detector, the GMT raises the standard for electronic prospecting. Automatic Ground Balance with fast AutoTrac cancels the ground minerals in seconds and then tracks to changing conditions as you hunt. The Full-time Iron ID Bar Graph displays the percentage probability of iron. to help decide whether or not to dig a target!

Whites Electronics TM-808 — LIST: $800

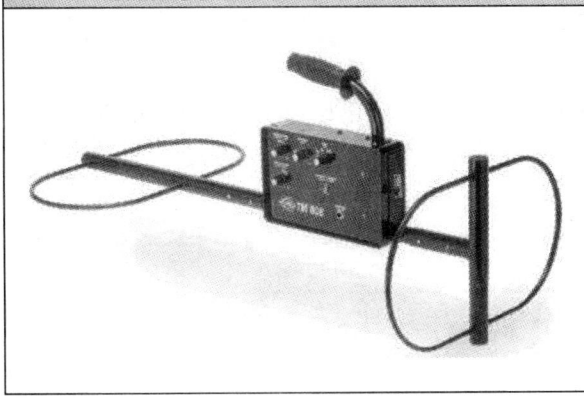

Got a map to a Treasure Chest? A serious industrial strength detector for finding lots of metal deep down. If you're after large, deeply buried treasure, chests, coin caches, hoards of gold, underground tanks or pipes, then the TM-808 is the metal detector for you. Recover buried treasure 4-20 feet (1-6 meters) deep! If you're after large, deeply buried treasure, underground tanks or pipes, then the TM 808 is the metal detector for you. Whether you're hunting for a cache of coins or you need the precise location of an underground pipe, the TM 808 does it all. It's operable virtually anywhere, regardless of interference or ground minerals.

Whites Electronics XLT — LIST: $900

The XLT Metal Detector is high-performance simplicity and versatility at its best. With 5 expertly-designed programs to choose from, you've got virtually every kind of metal detector hunting covered.

It's easy to enhance a program to suit your particular metal detecting needs starting with one of 10 Basic Adjustments or one of the 29 Professional Options. The exclusive SignaGraph from White's provides a wealth of information to help you decide to dig or not.

Completely automatic or totally adjustable.

Whites Electronics MXT / MXT 300 — LIST: $800 / $900

One metal detector with three completely separate operating modes! Just toggle between the gold prospecting, coin/jewelry or relic modes depending on what you are searching for and the MXT becomes a specialized metal detector optimized for that type of treasure. The MXT provides the flexibility to hunt for your type of treasure and do so with no fancy adjustments which means you will be finding treasure in no time! Each operating mode contains optional search and discriminate methods, i.e., Disc Notch, Mixed Mode Audio, VCO and much more. The MXT 300 features the new 12" search coil for added performance.

Whites Electronics Surf PI Dual Field — LIST: $900

The Surf PI Pro Dual Field combines turn-on-and-go ease and unbeatable depth and sensitivity. The Surf metal detector's all-new power circuit reaches new depths, especially on the most prized jewelry - smaller gold, platinum and white gold even in the worst beach conditions like black sand. Depth, sensitivity, ease-of-use, and speed combine to make the Surf PI Dual Field unbeatable on the beach. The all new, large 12" search coil can be swept quickly or slowly across wet, salty sand and water as well as highly mineralized ground with exceptional results and very little resistance.

Whites Electronics Beach Hunter 300 LIST: $1,000

The BeachHunter ID 300 is the top of the line submersible detector from one of the leading names in metal detecting. The new and improved 300 coil has near neutral buoyancy to provide excellent results, allowing you to focus your energy on treasure! Because the new 300 search coil is larger, you can cover more ground per sweep and go deeper than ever before! White's easy-to-use discrimination system features three special, color-coded lights, each of which is paired with a specific audio tone.

Whites Electronics DFX / DFX 300 LIST: $1,100 / $1,200

The Finest all-around metal detector. The DFX is simply unsurpassed in its ability to find treasure; older, deeper, smaller items that other detectors pass over. The DFX brings together sophisticated microprocessor technology, and turn-on-and go simplicity. White's patented multi frequency method partners with the target I. D. you get only from DFX to "see through" minerals in the ground and detect coins, jewelry and relics other detectors miss. Hunt in 3 kHz or 15 kHz (the two best frequencies for finding treasure) or use both together for unequalled hunting. and turn-on-and go simplicity. You're out hunting right away, but there are plenty of adjustments too. The DFX 300 features the new 12" search coil for added performance.

Whites Electronics Spectra V3 LIST: $1,500

The Spectra V3 is White's finest turn-on-and-go metal detector using 3 frequency detection to find the oldest, deepest treasures. The White's Spectra V3 features a Full-Color High Definition Display. All the target information you need now in bold, high contrast color! Bigger VDI numbers, icons and Signagraph. Use the ZOOM key to enlarge or reduce display info. Hunt using the preset color pallets or create your own custom color schemes for each program. 10 All-New Turn-on-and-Go Hunting Programs: Set up by the experts at White's. Choose from Coin, Coin and Jewelry, Salt Beach, Relic, Prospecting, Deep Silver, High Trash, Hi-Pro, Mixed Mode Pro, and Meteorite. It's as easy as turning on your TV and choosing the program you want to see (and use). The wireless headphones are another innovation from the team at Whites that really makes hunting more enjoyable.

Whites Electronics TDI — LIST: $1,600

Professional-level ground-balancing, pulse induction detection. Unlike any other metal detector on the market today, the TDI is capable of remarkable depth and extreme sensitivity in the worst grounds. TDI was originally designed for prospecting; now optimized for exceptional performance for relic, beach, even coin hunting. Full-control Ground Balance allows you to quickly balance out the iron mineralization of hot rocks, black sand, and other tough grounds. The Adjustable Pulse Delay - Settings from 10 ms (best for finding gold nuggets) to 25 ms (for relic, coin and beach hunting).

FACTORY ACCESSORIES:

The right accessory can greatly expand the versatility and performance of any detector as search conditions or the type of target being sought changes. The following accessories are available for the White's line of equipment:

Search Coils:
- **For the Spectra V3, DFX, MXT, M6**: 10" Double-D, 12" Concentric, 5.3" Concentric, 6"x10" Double-D, 9.5" Concentric
- **For the Spectra V3, DFX, MXT**: 4"x6" Double-D, 8"x14" Double-D
- **For the XLT**: 4"x6" Double-D, 5.3" Concentric, 9.5" Concentric, 15" Concentric
- **For the Prism's**: 9" Spider Concentric, 9.5" Concentric, 8" Concentric, 4"x6" Double-D
- **For the Goldmasters**: 4"x6" Double-D, 6"x10" Double-D, 8"x14" Double-D

Other Items:
- Instructional videos produced by Whites covering tips & techniques not found in the user's manuals for the Spectra V3, DFX, XLT, MXT, M6, Prism III / IV / V, Classic ID / IDX, Quantum XT / II, Beach Hunter ID, Surfmaster PI Pro, GMT, Classic I / II / III and TM 808. (Available directly from Whites or local dealer)
- Search coil covers for all factory coils
- Tall-man S-rod section for taller individuals
- Center rod sections to extend the overall length of the detector
- Tall Man or Pee Wee lower rods for children or shorter / taller adults
- Spare lower shafts to make changing coils easier by leaving the extra coil attached to a lower shaft
- Carrying cases – hard-sided and soft cases
- Rechargeable battery systems and chargers
- Complete line of clothing and hats with the White's logo

THIRD PARTY ACCESSORIES FOR WHITES DETECTORS:

- **Jimmy Sierra's Coils**: Legendary coils from the White's master; http://www.jimmysierra.com/loopsZ.htm
- **Jay's Cache**: Frequency shifter that changes the frequency of your detector to eliminate interference from nearby detectors); P.O. Box 472531, Garland, TX 75047 or jayscache@juno.com
- **Sun Ray In-Line Pinpointing Probes**: Pinpoint probe designed for specific detectors – models available for the Whites Spectra V3, DFX, MXT, M-6, XLT, Pro XL, and other older 6.592 kHz models. Sun Ray Detector Electronics, 106 N Main St, Hazleton, Iowa 50641 (319) 636-2244; http://www.sunraydetector.com/
- **Nugget Finder Search Coils**: The Mono search coils work on the Whites TDI and provide additional versatility for all applications – 10 sizes available; http://www.arizonaoutback.com/nfcoils.html (US supplier) / http://www.goldsearchaustralia.com/search-coils.html (Australia supplier)
- **Coiltek Search Coils**: Coiltek Manufacturing Pty., Ltd.: Marketed for Minelab detectors, several are interchangeable and fit on the Whites TDI. (Contact the factory for a local dealer / distributor) 6 Drive In Court, Maryborough, Victoria, Australia 3465; (03) 5460 4700); http://www.coiltek.com.au

- **Excellerator & SEF Search Coils**: Additional size options for several Whites models http://www.kellycodetectors.com/accessories/searchcoils.htm (U.S. market) or http://www.joanallen.co.uk/a_detech_metal_detectors_uk.html (U.K. distributor)
- **Straight Shaft Systems**: Designed to improve the balance & ergonomics of your detector:
  - **Anderson Detector Shafts:** Quality-built shafts for the Beach Hunter ID, Beach Hunter ID 300, Surf PI and other machines with 2.5" hole spacing (A full-length size, a shorter Scuba shaft and travel models are available); http://andersondetectorshafts.com/14.html

Books

- **XLT Field Methods and Custom Programs** by Clive James Clynick
- **XLT Ring Enhancement Programs** by Clive James Clynick
- **Understanding White's DFX** by Jimmy "Sierra" Normandi
- **Dancing with the DFX** by Howard Garr
- **DFX Gold Methods** by Clive James Clynick
- **DFX: From Beginner to Advanced** by Clive James Clynick
- **Digging Deeper with the DFX** by Jeff Foster
- **MXT Methods** by Jeff Foster

Internet Resources

- **The Treasure Hunter Forum – Whites**: http://www.treasurehunterforum.com/forum267/
- **Find's Treasure Forums – Whites Forum**: http://www.findmall.com/list.php?31
- **TreasureNet – Whites Forum**: http://forum.treasurenet.com/index.php/board,212.0.html
- **The Treasure Hunter Forum – Spectra V3**: http://www.treasurehunterforum.com/forum280/
- **Find's Treasure Forums – Spectra V3 Forum**: http://www.findmall.com/list.php?66
- **The Treasure Hunter Forum – MXT**: http://www.treasurehunterforum.com/forum15/
- **Find's Treasure Forums – MXT Forum**: http://www.findmall.com/list.php?25
- **The Treasure Hunter Forum – DFX**: http://www.treasurehunterforum.com/forum24/
- **The Whites Metal Detecting Forum**: Forum provided by White's Electronics as a service to their customers and those thinking of buying a Whites; http://forum.treasurenet.com/whites/index.php
- **Whites TDI Forum**: http://tdi.invisionplus.net/?mforum=tdi&showforum=3

XP Detectors

XPLORER
40, Chemin du Moulin; 31320 Mervilla France
+33 (0)5 61 73 63 29 • Fax: +33 (0) 5 61 73 48 39
http://www.xpmetaldetectors.com/

COMPANY PROFILE:

Since its creation in 1998, XP metal detectors has strived to continuously improve its manufacturing process and build innovative, high-performance metal detectors that have quickly become a reference among enthusiasts.

The company, based on Toulouse, France, has produced several innovative products over the past decade. Designed by our engineers in collaboration with our team of experienced detectorists, XP's range of metal detectors has been designed to respond to users' real expectations. XP's products combine power, selectivity and ergonomics to strike the perfect balance between performance characteristics!

Now with the DEUS, XP has invented a new generation of metal detectors that offers a user-friendly design and optimal performance. It introduces you to a new exploring dimension, a powerful, fully wireless metal detector!

Some of the features and technology from XP not found on other detectors include:

- Wireless headphones where the transmitter is integrated on the circuit boards of several of the newest detectors. It has been designed with two switchable channels to prevent interference from nearby detectors.
- A FREQ SHIFT switch on the front of the detectors that enables the two output channels to be toggled quickly and easily to eliminate outside electrical interference.
- New analogical filters improving the detection of targets in iron infested areas. The masking generated by the iron is greatly reduced. Targets of interest in iron infested areas can therefore be detected more easily, thus enabling targets other detectors overlook to be located and recovered

XP Detectors . . . . .
Bringing state-of-the-art technology & innovation
to the metal detecting industry!

XP DETECTORS FINDS SHOWCASE:

XP Gold Maxx Detectors Love "Worked Out" Sites & Deep Targets!

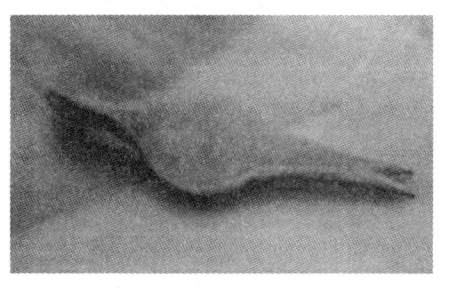

Metal detectorists in Europe, the United Kingdom and elsewhere around the world have found the XP line of detectors to excel in a wide range of applications. The finds depicted here were found at sites throughout the United Kingdom by Gary, administrator of the website "Gary's Detecting." Clockwise starting from upper left they include the remains of a purse filled with hammered silver coins, an extremely tiny hammered silver coin found with one of XP's elliptical search coils (showing how sensitive the XP detectors are), and a Roman nail cleaner found while demonstrating an XP Gold Maxx to a newcomer at a site all other local detectorists had long since given up as "worked out" and a Roman fibula dating from the 1st century AD found in a field 10" deep. Gary has many other XP finds showcased on his website showing what he and others turn up on a regular basis.

PRODUCT LINE:

XP ADX 150   LIST: €400 / $599

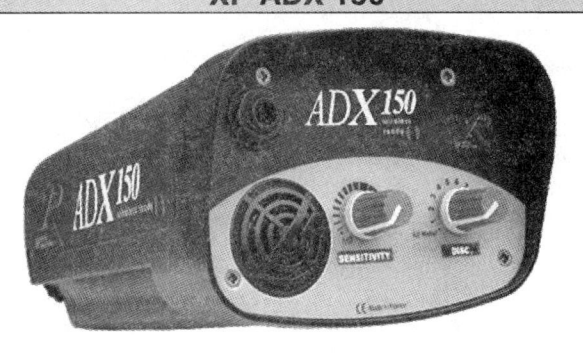

Unequalled performances and characteristics in its category! It is the detector of those which want the power without worrying about the adjustments. From the first moment you pick up an XP detector, you will find it easy to handle and use. Whether experienced or a complete novice, this detector will give you great satisfaction especially due to the basic settings for easy and quick usage. Compatible with the XP wireless headphones, it is lightweight and features a robust ABS electronic box which can be fixed under the armrest or for a maximum comfort, can also be hip mounted with the included hipmount bag included).

XP ADX 250 — LIST: €550 / $825

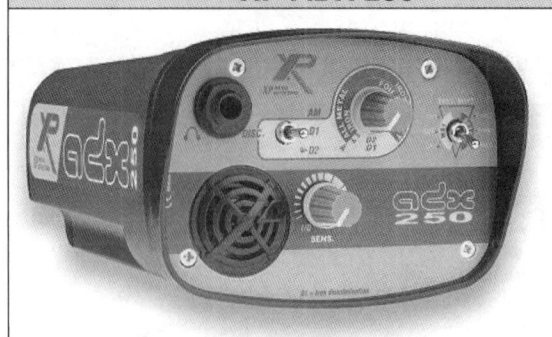

More powerful than the earlier ADX100, the 250 benefits from the technology of the ADVENTIS 2. Thanks to the presetting of the GROUND EFFECT and SILENCER circuits, it is the metal detector of those which want simplicity with optimal performances. This evolution of the ADX 250 incorporates a completely new electronic circuit and has features such as: wireless headphones, a FREQ SHIFT switch on the front of the detector that enables the two output channels to be toggled quickly and easily; new filters improving the detection of targets in iron infested areas and improvement of the gradation of the sensitivity settings to allow for more precise adjustment. The shaft assembly is identical to that used on the Gold Maxx Power.

XP Adventis 2 — LIST: €650 / $975

The Adventis 2 is a clever combination of analog/digital technology and benefits from the latest advances in the field. It is a detector which will surprise you by its reliability, robustness and detection depth. XP's knowledge of analog/digital technology has led them to integrate a microprocessor analyzing discrimination signals. This microprocessor gives the ADVENTIS 2 increased power & stability, as well as better rejection of unwanted targets. The Double D search coil provides very good ground penetration. Preset markings on the controls will allow the beginner to get started quickly. You will appreciate the sturdiness and the manufacturing quality of XP detectors. The shaft assembly is identical to that used on the Gold Maxx Power.

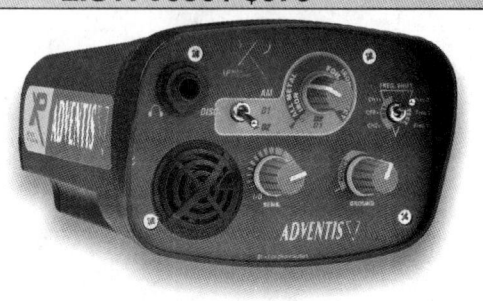

XP G-Maxx II — LIST: €800 / $1,195

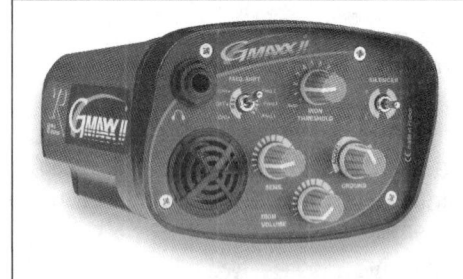

Thanks to its 4.6 kHz search frequency, the G-Maxx II is a The all new XP Gmaxx II comes with the entirely new and re-worked circuit board. This has been designed for better performance and gives higher sensitivity. The Gmaxx II will find deeper targets near iron thanks to the super fast recovery time. As with the other new detectors in the XP range, the Gmaxx II will accept the new cordless headphones with the transmitter built into the circuit board. Flexibility is provided thanks to the Multi-Tones mode, the IRON LEVEL and the new IRON THRESHOLD adjustments. The shaft assembly is identical to that used on the Gold Maxx Power.

XP Gold Maxx Power — LIST: €850 / $1,275

The Gold Maxx Power is an exceptional detector to find little targets in difficult type of soil (mineralized). Its search frequency (18 kHz) makes it a very sensitive to targets that are usually very difficult to detect, like thin coins, gold nuggets, jewels and all other small objects. An important flexibility in the set up allows you to fit in with the ground you wish prospect, thanks to the Multi-Tones mode, the IRON LEVEL and the new IRON THRESHOLD adjustments. We chose instantaneous sound signaling, rather than a LCD display because of the extraordinary faculties of analysis of the human ear compared to an LCD display. LCD displays cannot respond in real time and do not capture weak signals that are too brief or too close to other signals. Gold Maxx Power sound signaling provides real-time output of the most imperceptible signal. Our detectors use Double-D coils because this allows for better ground penetration.

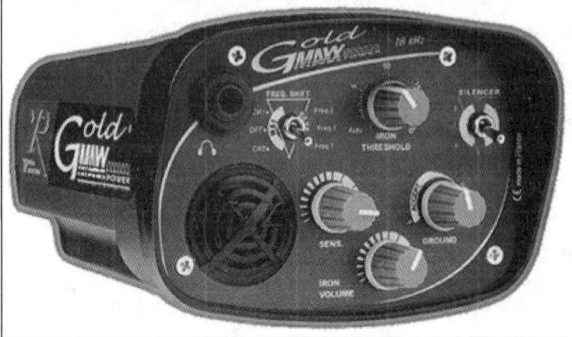

XP Deus	LIST: €1,400 / $2,095

XP invents the first wireless detector...and the first fully telescopic S-shaped stem

DEUS marks a technological breakthrough and is a real innovation in metal detector design.

The Deus's patented architecture is based on three elements: a Coil, a Remote Control and a set of Audio Headphones, which are unique in that they communicate with each other via a digital radio link. The search coil contains the essential components for processing the signals, which no longer need to be conveyed via a wire link but are digitized and analyzed directly in the coil by an ultra-miniature digital circuit, which greatly improves the quality of signal acquisition. This circuit, which is integrated in the coil, processes the information and sends it to the headphones and remote control in real time via a radio link. The headphones can control the detector alone, enabling you to go detecting with an even more portable configuration (just 875g). In the absence of the remote control, the headphones enable you to adjust all the main settings of the detector: Sensitivity, Discrimination, Ground Balance, Frequency (4 kHz, 8 kHz, 12 kHz, 18 kHz), Multi-Tones etc, - all of the settings previously created with the remote control! Deploy or fold away your stem in just 5 seconds! Change the coil in an instant! This new patented stem can be stored away instantly and is much easier to handle than a straight stem with an integral handle. It is particularly comfortable to use because of its shaped rubber handle & improved operating angle. Another first is the ability to update the software by downloading the new program and installing it via the USB port.

FACTORY ACCESSORIES:

The right accessory can greatly expand the versatility and performance of any detector as search conditions or the type of target being sought changes. The following accessories are available for the XP line of metal detectors:

Search Coils:
- 9"x8" Concentric; 15"x18" elliptical Double-D; 9" Double-D, 11" Double-D; 4.3"x9.5" Double-D

Other Items:
- Wireless headphones designed specifically for the XP line of detectors; spare lower rods to simplify swapping out coils, hipmount bag, rechargeable battery systems, carrying bags and backpacks, weather covers for control housings and caps and shirts with the XP Detectors logo.

Internet Resources

- **The Treasure Hunter Forum – XP Detectors**: http://www.treasurehunterforum.com/forum17/
- **The XP Owners Forum UK**: http://www.xp-ownersforum.com/
- **XP Metal Detector's Forum**: Run by the XP factory; www.xpmetaldetectors.com/xpforum/viewforum.php?f=5
- **Gary's XP Gold Maxx Finds Page**: http://www.garysdetecting.co.uk/gold.htm

Videos

- **XP Explained** by Norfolk Wolf; Covers the entire line of XP detectors, crammed full of great advice!

Comparison Charts

The first section of this book provided proven tips and techniques used by successful treasure hunters worldwide to select the right equipment, locate productive sites and then conduct effectively search them to find more in less time. The second section provided a "one stop shop" to see all of the metal detectors currently being marketed on a main-stream basis. The tables that follow provide a tool that allows you to compare specific features on a model-vs.-model basis to help you zero in on the perfect detector for your needs be it features, weight or budget.

The following abbreviations will be used throughout the tables denoting specific features about individual models. For more information on what the features mean, refer back to chapters such as the one, "*Your Equipment – Time to Upgrade or Simply Master What You Have*" which contains explanations that can help you interpret the tables coding or consult one of the books listed in the reference section at the end of the chapter.

Good luck in finding whatever you plan on searching for in the field!

LEGEND:

Application(s): **C** (Coin Hunting), **B** (Beach Hunting), **R** (Relic Hunting), **P** (Electronic Prospecting, **S** (Shallow Water Hunting), **D** (Diving), **G** (General Treasure Hunting), **SA** (Specialized Applications)

Circuit Types: **VLF** (Very Low Frequency, ground canceling), **VLF-D** (VLF circuit operating on two frequencies), **VLF-M** (VLF circuit operating on multiple frequencies simultaneously), **PI** (Pulse induction), **TR** (Transmit-Receive); **MPS** (Multi-Period Sensing, a form of PI circuitry found on some Minelab models)

Meter Type: **N** (No meter), **Y** (signal intensity or battery check only), **Y-ID** (Target ID meter), **Y-ID+** (Target ID along with depth indication or additional target information); **BLM**: Back-lit meter

Controls: **T/P**: Touchpads; **P/B**: Push Buttons; **K**: Knobs; **T**: Toggle switches

Features: **P**: Factory preset ground balance; **M**: Manual ground balance circuitry; **A**: Automatic ground balance circuitry
STD: Rechargeable battery system included; **OPT**: Rechargeable battery system available / optional

Depth Rating: **S/P**: Splash-proof or water-resistant, not to be used for extended periods underwater

Other: **NS**: Not Supplied .... Unfortunately not all information for all models was received by the time the guide went to print but if the unit is one you are interested in, contact the manufacturer for any missing information you might need to make an informed buying decision.

LAND METAL DETECTOR COMPARISON CHART

		B-H Gold Digger	B-H Fast Tracker	B-H Tracker II	Viking 1	B-H Tracker IV	Viking 5	B-H Discovery 1100	B-H Quick Silver/Pioneer EX	C.Scope CS440XD	Viking 6
SPECS	Retail Price	$99	$129	$129	$129	$139	$145	$149	$149	$165	$165
	Warranty	1 YR	5 YR	5 YR	2 YR	5 YR	2 YR	5 YR	5 YR	2 YR	2 YR
	Weight w/batteries (lbs)	2.4	3.0	2.6	1.9	2.6	2.4	2.5	2.8	2.5	2.4
	Overall Length - Min	35"	44"	45"	35"	45"	45"	45"	44"	36"	29"
	Overall Length - Max	45"	51.5"	52"	42"	53"	51"	53"	51.5"	53.9"	53.5"
	Application(s)	G	G	G	G	G	G	G,C	G,C	G	G
	Headphone Jack & Size	1/8"	1/4"	1/4"	1/4"	1/4"	1.4"	1/4"	1/4"	1/4"	1/4"
	Internal Speaker	Y	Y	Y	Y	Y	Y	Y	Y	Y	Y
	Hipmountable	N	N	N	N	N	N	N	N	N	N
CIRCUIT	Circuit Type	VLF	VLF	VLF	VLF	VLF	VLF	VLF	VLF	VLF	VLF
	# of Frequencies	1	1	1	1	1	1	1	1	1	1
	Frequency(s)	6.6kHz	6.6kHz	6.6kHz	8kHz	6.6kHz	8kHz	6.6kHz	7.0kHz	17kHz	14kHz
	Ground Balance Type	P	P	M	P	P	P	P	P	P	P
CONTROLS	Touchpad / Knobs	K	K	K	K	K + T	K	T/P	T/P	K	K
	Ground Balance	N	N	Y	N	N	N	N	N	N	N
	Discriminate	Y	Y	Y	N	Y	N	Y	Y	Y	Y
	Notch Discriminate	N	N	N	N	N	N	Y	N	N	N
	Sensitivity	Y	Y	Y	N	Y	N	Y	Y	Y	Y
	Volume	N	N	N	N	N	N	N	N	N	N
	Threshold	N	N	N	N	N	N	N	N	N	N
	Other	---	---	---	---	---	---	---	---	---	---
POWER	Batteries #	2	2	2	1	2	1	2	2	1	1
	Batteries Type	9V	9V	9V	9V	9V	9V	9V	9V	9V	9V
	Rechargeables	OPT	OPT	OPT	OPT	OPT	OPT	OPT	OPT	OPT	OPT
	Battery Check	N	N	N	N	N	N	N	N	N	N
	Battery Life (hrs)	20-30	20-30	20-30	20	20-30	20	20-25	15-20	40	15-20
	Low Battery Alert	N	Y	Y	N	Y	N	Y	Y	N	N
COIL	Stock Coil Size	7"	7"	7"	6"	8"	8"	7"	8"	7"	8"
	Coil Type	C	C	C	DD	C	DD	C	C	C	DD
	Interchangeable	N	Y	N	N	Y	N	Y	Y	N	N
DISPLAY INFO	Display	N	N	N	N	N	N	Y	Y	N	N
	Display Type	NA	NA	NA	NA	NA	NA	LCD	LCD	N/A	N/A
	Meter	Y	N	Y	N	Y	N	N	N	N	N
	Target ID - Audio	N	Y	Y	N	Y	N	Y	Y	N	N
	Target ID - Visual	N	N	N	N	N	N	Y	Y	N	N
	Depth Indication	N	N	N	N	N	N	Y	N	N	N
MODES	# of Search Modes	1	2	3	1	3	1	2	2	2	1
	All-Metal Search	N	Y	Y	Y	Y	Y	Y	N	Y	N
	Motion Discriminate	Y	Y	Y	N	Y	N	Y	Y	Y	N
	Non-Motion Discriminate	N	N	N	N	N	N	N	N	N	Y
	Non-Motion Pinpoint	N	N	N	N	N	N	Y	N	N	N

LAND METAL DETECTOR COMPARISION CHART

		Garrett Ace 150	White's Coinmaster	Tesoro Compadre	C.Scope CS770XD	B-H Lone Star	B-H Commando	Teknetics Alpha 2000	Viking VK10	B-H Discovery 2200	B-H Quickdraw II/Pioneer 202
SPECS	Retail Price	$180	$180	$189	$198	$199	$199	$199	$210	$249	$249
	Warranty	2 YR	2 YR	LIFE	2 YR	5 YR	5 YR	5 YR	2 YR	5 YR	5 YR
	Weight w/batteries (lbs)	2.7	2.5	2.2	2.5	3.5	3.5	2.3	2.4	2.4	3.5
	Overall Length - Min	42"	45.3"	38.5"	36"	44"	44"	40.5"	29"	45"	44"
	Overall Length - Max	51"	50.3"	52.5"	53.9"	51.5"	51.5"	50.5"	53.5"	53"	51.5"
	Application(s)	G,C	G,C	G	G	G,C	G,C	G,C	G	G,C	G,C
	Headphone Jack & Size	1/4"	1/4"	1/4"	1/4"	1/4"	1/4"	1/8"+1/4"	1/4"	1/4"	1/4"
	Internal Speaker	Y	Y	Y	Y	Y	Y	Y	Y	Y	Y
	Hipmountable	N	N	N	N	N	N	N	N	N	N
CIRCUIT	Circuit Type	VLF	VLF	VLF	VLF	VLF	VLF	VLF	VLF	VLF	VLF
	# of Frequencies	1	1	1	1	1	1	1	1	1	1
	Frequency(s)	6.5kHz	8 kHz	12kHz	17kHz	6.6kHz	6.6kHz	7.8kHz	7kHz	6.6kHz	6.kHz
	Ground Balance Type	P	P	P	P	P	P	P	P	P	P
CONTROLS	Touchpad / Knobs	P/B	T/P	K	K	T/P+K	K + T	P/B	K	T/P	T/P+K
	Ground Balance	N	N	N	Y	N	N	N	N	N	N
	Discriminate	Y	Y	Y	N	Y	Y	Y	Y	Y	Y
	Notch Discriminate	Y	Y	N	N	Y	N	Y	Y	Y	Y
	Sensitivity	Y	Y	N	N	Y	Y	Y	Y	Y	Y
	Volume	N	N	N	N	N	N	N	N	N	N
	Threshold	N	N	N	N	N	N	N	N	N	N
	Other	---	---	---	---	---	1	---	---	2	---
POWER	Batteries #	4	2	1	1	2	2	1	1	2	2
	Batteries Type	AA	9V	9V	9V	9V	9V	9V	9V	9V	9V
	Rechargeables	OPT	OPT	OPT	OPT	OPT	OPT	OPT	OPT	OPT	OPT
	Battery Check	Y	Y	Y	N	Y	N	Y	Y	Y	Y
	Battery Life (hrs)	20	20	10-20	40	15-20	20-30	20-25	15-20	15-20	15-20
	Low Battery Alert	N	Y	N	N	N	Y	Y	N	Y	N
COIL	Stock Coil Size	6.5"X9"	9"	5.75"	7"	8"	7"	8"	8"	8"	8"
	Coil Type	C	C	C	C	C	C	C	DD	C	C
	Interchangeable	Y	Y	N	N	Y	Y	Y	N	Y	Y
DISPLAY INFO	Display	Y	Y	N	N	Y	N	Y	N	Y	Y
	Display Type	LCD	LCD	N/A	N/A	LCD	N/A	LCD	N/A	LCD	LCD
	Meter	N	N	N	N	N	Y	N	N	N	N
	Target ID - Audio	Y	N	N	N	Y	Y	Y	N	Y	Y
	Target ID - Visual	Y	Y	N	N	Y	Y	Y	N	Y	Y
	Depth Indication	Y	Y	N	N	N	Y	Y	N	Y	Y
MODES	# of Search Modes	3	1	1	2	3	3	1	1	2	4
	All-Metal Search	N	N	N	N	N	Y	N	N	1	N
	Motion Discriminate	Y	Y	Y	Y	Y	Y	Y	Y	Y	Y
	Non-Motion Discriminate	N	N	N	N	N	N	N	N	N	N
	Non-Motion Pinpoint	N	N	N	N	Y	Y	N	N	N	Y

KEY: Controls - Other: (1) 3-Mode Toggle Switch; (2) "ZAP" Target accept / reject touchpad; (3)

LAND METAL DETECTOR COMPARISION CHART

		Fisher F-2	Garrett Ace 250	White's Prizm II	Viking VK20	C.Scope CS1MX	Teknetics Delta 4000	Tesoro Silver uMax	White's Prizm III	Viking VK30	B-H Discovery 3300
SPECS	Retail Price	$249	$250	$250	$260	$265	$279	$299	$300	$325	$349
	Warranty	5 YR	2 YR	2 YR	2 YR	2 YR	5 YR	LIFE	2 YR	2 YR	5 YR
	Weight w/batteries (lbs)	2.6	2.7	2.5	3.1	2.5	2.3	2.2	2.5	3.1	2.4
	Overall Length - Min	41.5"	42"	45.3"	22"	36"	40.5"	38.5"	45.3"	22"	45"
	Overall Length - Max	51.5"	51"	50.3"	49"	53.9"	50.5"	52.5"	50.3"	49"	53"
	Application(s)	G,C	G,C	G,C	G	G	G,C	G	G,C	G	G,C
	Headphone Jack & Size	1/4"	1/4"	1/4"	1/4"	1/4"	1/8"+1/4"	1/4"	1/4"	1/4"	1/4"
	Internal Speaker	Y	Y	Y	Y	Y	Y	Y	Y	Y	Y
	Hipmountable	N	N	N	N	N	N	N	N	N	N
CIRCUIT	Circuit Type	VLF	VLF	VLF	VLF	VLF	VLF	VLF	VLF	VLF	VLF
	# of Frequencies	1	1	1	1	1	1	1	1	1	1
	Frequency(s)	5.9kHz	6.5kHz	8 kHz	7kHz	17kHz	7.8kHz	10.6kHz	8 kHz	7kHz	6.7kHz
	Ground Balance Type	P	P	P	P	P	P	P	P	P	P
CONTROLS	Touchpad / Knobs	T/P	P/B	T/P	K + P/B	K	T/P	K + T	T/P	K + P/B	T/P + K
	Ground Balance	N	N	N	N	N	N	N	N	N	Y
	Discriminate	Y	Y	Y	Y	Y	Y	Y	N	Y	Y
	Notch Discriminate	Y	Y	N	N	N	Y	N	Y	N	Y
	Sensitivity	Y	Y	N	Y	Y	Y	Y	N	Y	Y
	Volume	N	N	N	N	N	Y	N	N	N	N
	Threshold	N	N	N	N	N	N	N	N	N	N
	Other	---	---	---	1	---	---	2	---	1	3
POWER	Batteries #	2	4	2	1	1	1	1	2	1	2
	Batteries Type	9V	AA	9V	9V	9V	9V	9V	9V	9V	9V
	Rechargeables	OPT	OPT	OPT	OPT	OPT	OPT	OPT	OPT	OPT	OPT
	Battery Check	Y	Y	Y	Y	N	Y	Y	Y	Y	Y
	Battery Life (hrs)	15-20	20	20	15-20	40	20-25	10-20	20	15-20	12-18
	Low Battery Alert	N	N	N	Y	N	N	N	N	Y	Y
COIL	Stock Coil Size	8"	6.5"x9"	8"	8"	7"	8"	8"	9"	8"	8"
	Coil Type	C	C	C	DD	C	C	C	C	DD	C
	Interchangeable	Y	Y	Y	N	N	Y	Y	Y	N	Y
DISPLAY INFO	Display	Y	Y	Y	Y	N	Y	N	Y	Y	Y
	Display Type	LCD	LCD	LCD	LCD	N/A	LCD	N/A	LCD	LCD	LCD
	Meter	N	N	N	N	N	N	N	N	N	N
	Target ID - Audio	Y	N	N	N	N	Y	N	N	N	Y
	Target ID - Visual	Y	Y	Y	Y	N	Y	N	Y	Y	Y
	Depth Indication	Y	Y	N	N	N	Y	N	Y	N	Y
MODES	# of Search Modes	1	5	2	1	2	3	2	2	2	2
	All-Metal Search	N	N	Y	N	Y	Y	Y	Y	Y	Y
	Motion Discriminate	Y	Y	Y	Y	Y	Y	Y	Y	Y	Y
	Non-Motion Discriminate	N	N	N	N	N	N	N	N	Y	N
	Non-Motion Pinpoint	Y	Y	Y	N	N	Y	N	Y	Y	Y

KEY: Controls - Other: (1) Inland / Beach switch; (2) Mode Select toggle; (3) Zap automatic target reject function

LAND METAL DETECTOR COMPARISION CHART

		B-H Pioneer 505	Viking VK40	Saxon SM35	White's Prizm IV	C.Scope CS3MX	Tesoro Cibola	Fisher F-4	Minelab X-Terra 305	Teknetics Gamma 6000	Garrett GTAx 550
SPECS	Retail Price	$349	$372	$380	$400	$415	$425	$449	$495	$499	$500
	Warranty	5 YR	2 YR	2 YR	2 YR	2 YR	LIFE	5 YR	3 YR	5 YR	2 YR
	Weight w/batteries (lbs)	2.8	3.1	4.0	2.5	3.3	2.2	2.9	2.9	2.4	3.3
	Overall Length - Min	41"	20"	30"	45.3"	42"	38.5"	41.5"	48"	40.5"	40"
	Overall Length - Max	51"	51"	40"	50.3"	54"	52.5"	51.5"	56"	50.5"	51"
	Application(s)	G,C	G,C	G	G,C	G	G	G,C	G,C	G,C	G,C
	Headphone Jack & Size	1/4"	1/4"	1/4"	1/4"	1/4"	1/4"	1/4"	1/4"	1/8"+1/4"	1/4"
	Internal Speaker	Y	Y	Y	Y	Y	Y	Y	Y	Y	Y
	Hipmountable	N	N	N	N	Y	N	N	N	N	Y
CIRCUIT	Circuit Type	VLF	VLF	VLF	VLF	VLF	VLF	VLF	VLF	VLF	VLF
	# of Frequencies	1	1	1	1	1	1	1	2 (1)	1	1
	Frequency(s)	6.6kHz	7kHz	14kHz	8 kHz	17kHz	14.5kHz	5.9kHz	7.5/18.75	7.8kHz	7.0kHz
	Ground Balance Type	M+A	P	P	P	P	P	M	M	M	P
CONTROLS	Touchpad / Knobs	T/P + K	T/P	K	T/P	K	K + T	T/P + K	T/P	T/P	T/P
	Ground Balance	Y	N	N	N	N	N	Y	Y	Y	N
	Discriminate	Y	Y	Y	Y	Y	Y	Y	Y	Y	Y
	Notch Discriminate	Y	N	N	Y	N	N	Y	Y	Y	Y
	Sensitivity	Y	Y	N	Y	Y	Y	Y	Y	Y	Y
	Volume	N	N	N	N	N	N	N	Y	Y	N
	Threshold	N	N	N	N	N	Y	Y	N	N	N
	Other	2	1	---	---	---	5	---	3	4	---
POWER	Batteries #	2	1	8	2	8	1	2	4	1	8
	Batteries Type	9V	9V	AA	9V	AA	9V	9V	AA	9V	AA
	Rechargeables	OPT	OPT	OPT	OPT	OPT	OPT	OPT	OPT	OPT	OPT
	Battery Check	N	Y	N	Y	Y	Y	Y	Y	Y	Y
	Battery Life (hrs)	15-20	15-20	40	20	NS	10-20	15-20	15-20	20-25	30
	Low Battery Alert	Y	Y	N	N	N	N	N	Y	Y	N
COIL	Stock Coil Size	8"	9.5"	8"	9"	8"	9"X8"	7.5"X11"	9"	8"	7"X10"
	Coil Type	C	C	DD	C	C	C	DD	C	C	C
	Interchangeable	Y	N	Y	Y	N	Y	Y	Y	Y	Y
DISPLAY INFO	Display	Y	Y	N	Y	N	N	Y	Y	Y	Y
	Display Type	LCD	LCD	N/A	LCD	N/A	N/A	LCD	LCD	LCD	LCD
	Meter	N	N	N	N	N	N	N	N	N	N
	Target ID - Audio	Y	N	N	Y	N	N	Y	Y	Y	Y
	Target ID - Visual	Y	Y	N	Y	N	N	Y	Y	Y	Y
	Depth Indication	Y	N	N	Y	N	N	Y	Y	Y	Y
MODES	# of Search Modes	3	3	1	2	2	2	4	2	2	2
	All-Metal Search	Y	Y	N	Y	Y	Y	Y	Y	Y	Y
	Motion Discriminate	Y	Y	Y	Y	Y	Y	Y	Y	Y	Y
	Non-Motion Discriminate	N	Y	N	N	N	N	N	N	N	N
	Non-Motion Pinpoint	Y	N	N	N	Y	Y	Y	Y	Y	Y

KEY: Controls - Other: (1) Ground / Beach selector; (2) Auto Notch Control; (3) Frequency selected by coil; (4) # of Tones; (5) Frequency Shift toggle

Circuit: (1) Frequency is dependent on coil used, 3 kHz / 7.5kHz

LAND METAL DETECTOR COMPARISION CHART

		White's GMZ	White's Prizm V	Tesoro Vaquero	Tesoro Golden uMax	Fisher F-5	Fisher Gold Bug	Garrett Gold Stinger	Saxon SM45	C.Scope CS5MX	Teknetics Omega 8000
SPECS	Retail Price	$500	$500	$525	$529	$549	$549	$550	$580	$595	$599
	Warranty	2 YR	2 YR	LIFE	LIFE	5 YR	5 YR	2 YR	2 YR	2 YR	5 YR
	Weight w/batteries (lbs)	3.3	2.5	2.2	2.2	2.9	2.3	3.3	4.0	3.5	2.9
	Overall Length - Min	44.3"	45.3"	38.5"	38.5"	41.5"	40.5"	42"	30"	42"	40.5"
	Overall Length - Max	49"	50.3"	52.5"	52.5"	51.5"	50.5"	51"	40"	54"	50.5"
	Application(s)	P	G,C	G,R	G,R,C	G,C	G,P	G,P	G	G	G,C,R
	Headphone Jack & Size	1/4"	1/4"	1/4"	1/4"	1/4"	1/4"	1/4"	1/4"	1/4"	1/8"+1/4"
	Internal Speaker	Y	Y	Y	Y	Y	Y	Y	Y	Y	Y
	Hipmountable	N	N	N	N	N	N	N	N	N	N
CIRCUIT	Circuit Type	VLF	VLF	VLF	VLF	VLF	VLF	VLF	VLF	VLF	VLF
	# of Frequencies	1	1	1	1	1	1	1	1	1	1
	Frequency(s)	50kHz	8 kHz	14.5kHz	10KhZ	7.8kHz	19kHz	15kHz	14kHz	12kHz	7.8kHz
	Ground Balance Type	M	P	M	M	M	M + A	M + A	P	P	M + A
CONTROLS	Touchpad / Knobs	K + T	T/P	K + T	K + T	T/P + K	T/P + K	K+T+P/B	K + T	K + P/B	T/P + K
	Ground Balance	Y	N	Y	N	Y	Y	Y	N	N	Y
	Discriminate	N	Y	Y	Y	Y	Y	Y	Y	Y	Y
	Notch Discriminate	N	Y	N	Y	Y	N	N	N	Y	Y
	Sensitivity	Y	Y	Y	Y	Y	Y	Y	Y	Y	Y
	Volume	N	N	N	N	N	N	N	N	N	N
	Threshold	N	N	Y	Y	Y	Y	Y	N	N	N
	Other	10	---	8	9	1	2	3, 4	---	6, 7	1, 2, 5
POWER	Batteries #	8	2	1	1	2	1	3	8	8	1
	Batteries Type	AA	9V	9V	9V	9V	9V	9V	AA	AA	9V
	Rechargeables	OPT	OPT	OPT	OPT	OPT	OPT	OPT	OPT	OPT	OPT
	Battery Check	Y	Y	Y	Y	Y	Y	Y	N	Y	Y
	Battery Life (hrs)	50	20	10-20	10-20	20-25	20-25	20	40	NS	20-25
	Low Battery Alert	Y	N	N	N	N	N	N	N	N	N
COIL	Stock Coil Size	6"X10"	9.5"	9"X8"	9"X8"	9.75"	5"	5"X10"	8"	10"	10"
	Coil Type	DD	C	C	C	C	DD	DD	DD	C	C
	Interchangeable	Y	Y	Y	Y	Y	Y	Y	Y	Y	Y
DISPLAY INFO	Display	N	Y	N	N	Y	Y	N	N	N	Y
	Display Type	N/A	LCD	N/A	N/A	LCD	LCD	N/A	N/A	N/A	LCD
	Meter	N	N	N	N	N	N	N	N	Y	N
	Target ID - Audio	N	Y	N	Y	Y	N	N	N	N	Y
	Target ID - Visual	N	Y	N	N	Y	N	N	N	N	Y
	Depth Indication	N	Y	N	N	Y	N	N	N	N	Y
MODES	# of Search Modes	1	2	2	2	3	2	3	1	1	3
	All-Metal Search	Y	Y	Y	Y	Y	Y	Y	N	N	Y
	Motion Discriminate	N	Y	Y	Y	Y	Y	Y	Y	Y	Y
	Non-Motion Discriminate	N	N	N	N	N	Y	Y	N	N	N
	Non-Motion Pinpoint	N	Y	Y	Y	Y	Y	Y	Y	Y	Y

KEY: Controls - Other: (1) Frequency Shift; (2) Ground Grab Auto ground cancel; (3) Mode select toggle; (4) Auto/Manual toggle (5) Tones; (6) Dual Discrimination controls; (7) Boost Hi/Normal toggle; (8) Frequency Shift toggle (9) Notch Width control; (10) Ground toggle

LAND METAL DETECTOR COMPARISON CHART

		Tesoro DeLeon	XP ADX 150	White's Sierra Madre	C.Scope CS1220XD	Nexus Coronado Ground Fix	Minelab X-Terra 505	Tesoro Tejon	Fisher 1270-X	Garrett GTP 1350	White's M6
SPECS	Retail Price	$599	$599	$600	$615	$615	$695	$699	$700	$700	$700
	Warranty	LIFE	2 YR	2 YR	2 YR	2 YR	3 YR	LIFE	5 YR	2 YR	2 YR
	Weight w/batteries (lbs)	2.9	3.1	4.3	3.5	3.5	2.9	2.9	3.6	4.0	4.0
	Overall Length - Min	38.5"	44"	44.5"	36"	(1)	48"	38.5"	42"	40"	4.5"
	Overall Length - Max	52.5"	53"	51.5"	53.9"	49.2" (1)	56"	52.5"	52"	51"	51.5"
	Application(s)	G,C	G,R	SA	G,C	G,R	G,C,P	G,R	G,R	G,C	G,C,B
	Headphone Jack & Size	1/4"	1/4"	1/4"	1/4"	1/4"	1/4"	1/4"	1/4"	1/4"	1/4"
	Internal Speaker	Y	Y	Y	Y	N	Y	Y	Y	Y	Y
	Hipmountable	N	Y	N	N	N	N	N	N	Y	N
CIRCUIT	Circuit Type	VLF	VLF	VLF	VLF	VLF	VLF	VLF	VLF	VLF	VLF
	# of Frequencies	1	1	1	1	1	1	1	1	1	1
	Frequency(s)	10kHz	4.6kHz	6.5kHz	17kHz	1	3 (2)	17.4kHz	8.2kHz	7.2 kHz	15kHz
	Ground Balance Type	P	P	M	P	P	M	M	M	P	P
CONTROLS	Touchpad / Knobs	K + T	K	K + T	K + P/B	K	T	K + T	K + T	T/P	K + T
	Ground Balance	N	N	Y	Y	N	Y	Y	Y	N	N
	Discriminate	Y	Y	N	Y	Y	Y	Y	Y	Y	Y
	Notch Discriminate	N	N	N	N	N	Y	N	N	Y	N
	Sensitivity	Y	Y	N	Y	N	Y	Y	Y	Y	Y
	Volume	N	N	N	N	Y	Y	N	Y	N	N
	Threshold	Y	N	N	N	N	N	Y	N	N	N
	Other	9	---	10, 11,12	4, 5	13	---	6, 7, 8	1, 2	14	3
POWER	Batteries #	8	8	4	8	8	4	8	2	8	8
	Batteries Type	AA	AA	C	AA	AA	AA	AA	9v	AA	AA
	Rechargeables	OPT	OPT	OPT	OPT	OPT	OPT	OPT	OPT	OPT	OPT
	Battery Check	Y	Y	Y	Y	Y	Y	Y	Y	Y	Y
	Battery Life (hrs)	10-20	50	16	NS	35	20	20-30	30-40	25	40
	Low Battery Alert	N	Y	N	N	Y	Y	N	Y	N	N
COIL	Stock Coil Size	9"x8"	9"	9.5"	8"	6" Dual	9"	9"x8"	8"	7"X10"	9.5"
	Coil Type	C	DD	C	C	C	C	C	C	C	C
	Interchangeable	Y	Y	Y	Y	Y	Y	Y	Y	Y	Y
DISPLAY INFO	Display	Y	N	N	Y	N	Y	N	N	Y	Y
	Display Type	LCD	N/A	N/A	ANALOG	N/A	LCD	N/A	N/A	LCD	LCD
	Meter	N	N	Y	Y	N	N	N	N	N	N
	Target ID - Audio	N	N	N	N	Y	N	N	N	Y	Y
	Target ID - Visual	Y	N	N	N	N	Y	N	N	Y	Y
	Depth Indication	Y	N	N	N	N	Y	N	N	Y	Y
MODES	# of Search Modes	2	2	3	2	2	3	3	3	5	3
	All-Metal Search	Y	Y	Y	Y	Y	Y	Y	Y	Y	Y
	Motion Discriminate	Y	Y	N	N	Y	Y	Y	Y	N	Y
	Non-Motion Discriminate	N	N	N	Y	N	N	N	N	N	N
	Non-Motion Pinpoint	Y	N	Y	Y	Y	Y	Y	Y	Y	Y

KEY: Specs: (1) The Nexus shaft is collapsible and extends to 49.2". Different lengths can be specified when ordering
Controls - Other: (1) Normal & Iron Discriminate controls; (2) Iron & Silencer toggles; (3) Land / Beach toggle
(4) Function / Mode Select; (5) Retune pushbutton; (6) Dual Discrimination circuits; (7) Tone adjust
(8) Frequency shift (choice of 17.2kHz, 17.4kHz or 17.6kHz); (9) Mode toggle switch
(10) High Mineral / Low Mineral selection; (11) Ground Balance adjustment; (12) Trigger switch
(13) Ground Fix selection (Low / Mid / High); (14) Target size indication on LCD
Circuit: (1) Frequency is dependent on coil used, ranges from 4.2kHz to 18kHz; (2) 3 kHz / 7.5kHz / 18.75kHz - coil driven;

LAND METAL DETECTOR COMPARISION CHART

		White's Prizm 6T	Fisher F-70	Tesoro Lobo ST	Garrett GTI 1500	White's GMT	White's MXT	XP ADX 250	C.Scope R1	Tesoro Cortes	Minelab Musketeer Advantage
SPECS	Retail Price	$700	$799	$799	$800	$800	$800	$825	$830	$849	$895
	Warranty	2 YR	5 YR	LIFE	2 YR	2 YR	2 YR	2 YR	2 YR	LIFE	3 YR
	Weight w/batteries (lbs)	3.0	2.9	3.5	4.1	3.9	4.3	3.1	4.2	2.9	4.8
	Overall Length - Min	41.4"	43.5"	38.5"	40"	44.5"	45"	44"	42"	38.5"	48.5"
	Overall Length - Max	53.8"	52.5"	52.5"	51"	51.5"	52.5"	53"	54"	52.5"	52.5"
	Application(s)	G,C,R	G,C,R	P,G	G,C,R	P	G,R,P	G,R	G,R	G,C,R	G,R
	Headphone Jack & Size	1/4"	1/4"	1/4"	1/4"	1/4"	1/4"	1/4"	1/4"	1/4"	1/4"
	Internal Speaker	Y	Y	Y	Y	Y	Y	Y	Y	Y	Y
	Hipmountable	N	N	Y	Y	N	N	Y	N	N	N
CIRCUIT	Circuit Type	VLF	VLF	VLF	VLF	VLF	VLF	VLF	VLF	VLF	VLF
	# of Frequencies	1	1	1	1	1	1	1	1	1	1
	Frequency(s)	8 kHz	13kHz	17.8kHz	7.2kHz	48kHz	14kHz	4.6kHz	NS	10kHz	5kHz
	Ground Balance Type	P	M + A	A	P	A + M	A + M	A	NS	M	M
CONTROLS	Touchpad / Knobs	T/P	T/P	K + T	T/P	K+T+T/P	K + T	K + T	K+T/P	K + T	K + T
	Ground Balance	N	Y	N	N	Y	N	N	N	Y	Y
	Discriminate	Y	Y	Y	Y	N	Y	Y	Y	Y	Y
	Notch Discriminate	Y	Y	N	N	N	N	N	Y	Y	N
	Sensitivity	Y	Y	Y	Y	Y	Y	Y	Y	Y	Y
	Volume	N	N	N	N	N	N	N	Y	N	N
	Threshold	N	Y	Y	N	Y	Y	N	N	N	N
	Other	5, 6	1, 2, 13	3, 4	---	7, 8, 9	4	13	4	11, 12	2
POWER	Batteries #	8	4	8	8	8	8	8	8	8	8
	Batteries Type	AA	AA	AA	AA	AA	AA	AA	AA	AA	AA
	Rechargeables	OPT	OPT	OPT	OPT	OPT	OPT	OPT	OPT	OPT	OPT
	Battery Check	Y	Y	Y	Y	Y	Y	Y	Y	Y	N
	Battery Life (hrs)	25	35-50	20-30	25	40	40	45	NS	10-20	10-15
	Low Battery Alert	N	N	N	N	N	N	Y	Y	Y	Y
COIL	Stock Coil Size	9"	5.5"X10"	10"	9.5"	6"X10"	9.5"	9"	10"&5"	9"X8"	10"
	Coil Type	C	C	DD	C	DD	C	DD	C	C	DD
	Interchangeable	Y	Y	Y	Y	Y	Y	Y	Y	Y	Y
DISPLAY INFO	Display	Y	Y	N	Y	Y	Y	N	Y	Y	N
	Display Type	LCD	LCD	N/A	LCD	LCD	LCD	N/A	LCD	LCD	N/A
	Meter	N	N	N	N	N	N	N	N	N	N
	Target ID - Audio	Y	Y	N	Y	Y	Y	N	Y	Y	N
	Target ID - Visual	Y	Y	N	Y	Y	Y	N	Y	Y	N
	Depth Indication	Y	Y	N	Y	N	Y	N	N	Y	N
MODES	# of Search Modes	2	5	2	6	3	3	2	2	2	2
	All-Metal Search	Y	Y	Y	Y	Y	Y	Y	Y	Y	Y
	Motion Discriminate	Y	Y	Y	N	N	Y	Y	Y	Y	Y
	Non-Motion Discriminate	N	N	N	N	N	N	N	N	N	N
	Non-Motion Pinpoint	Y	Y	Y	Y	Y	Y	N	Y	Y	Y

KEY: Controls - Other: (1) Speed; (2) # of Tones; (3) Soil Type toggle; (4) Mode select toggle; (5) Beach ground balance mode (6) Tone ID on/off; (7) S.A.T. SPEED; (8) Audio Boost toggle; (9) Ground Balance toggle; (10) Tuning (11) Notch width; (12) Meter backlight; (13) Frequency Shift

LAND METAL DETECTOR COMPARISION CHART

		Fisher Gold Bug 2	White's XLT	Nautilus DMC IIB	Fisher CZ-3D	Minelab X-Terra 705	XP Adventis 2	Minelab Sovereign GT	Teknetics T2	Garrett GTI 2500	Nautilus DMC IIBa
SPECS	Retail Price	$899	$900	$925	$950	$950	$975	$995	$999	$1,000	$1,050
	Warranty	5 YR	2 YR	2 YR	5 YR	3 YR	2 YR	3 YR	5 YR	2 YR	2 YR
	Weight w/batteries (lbs)	2.9	4.0	4.3	3.7	2.9	3.2	4.8	3.6	4.6	4.3
	Overall Length - Min	40"	44.5"	43"	41"	48"	44"	38"	45.6"	40"	43"
	Overall Length - Max	53"	51.5"	49"	51"	56"	53"	55"	54"	51"	49"
	Application(s)	P	G,C,R,B	R,G	G,C,R	G,C,R,P	G,R	G,C,R	G,C,R	G,C,R,P	R,G
	Headphone Jack & Size	1/4"	1/4"	1/4"	1/4"	1/4"	1/4"	1/4"	1/4"	1/4"	1/4"
	Internal Speaker	Y	Y	N	Y	Y	Y	Y	Y	Y	Y
	Hipmountable	Y	N	N	N	N	Y	Y	N	Y	N
CIRCUIT	Circuit Type	VLF	VLF	VLF	VLF-D	VLF	VLF	VLF-M	VLF	VLF	VLF
	# of Frequencies	1	1	1	2	3	1	17	1	1	1
	Frequency(s)	71kHz	6.5kHz	14kHz	5 + 15kHz	(6)	4.6kHz	1.5-25.5	13kHz	7.2kHz	14kHz
	Ground Balance Type	M	A	M	M	M	M	A	M + A	M + A	M
CONTROLS	Touchpad / Knobs	K + T	T/P	K+T+P/B	K+T+P/B	T/P	K + T	K + T	K + P/B	P/B	K+T+P/B
	Ground Balance	Y	Y	Y	Y	Y	Y	N	Y	Y	Y
	Discriminate	N	Y	Y	Y	Y	Y	Y	Y	Y	Y
	Notch Discriminate	N	Y	N	N	Y	N	Y	N	Y	N
	Sensitivity	Y	Y	Y	Y	Y	Y	Y	Y	Y	Y
	Volume	Y	Y	N	Y	Y	N	Y	N	Y	N
	Threshold	N	Y	Y	N	Y	N	Y	Y	Y	N
	Other	3, 4	5	---	1	6	9	7		8	---
POWER	Batteries #	2	8	4	2	4	8	8	4	8	4
	Batteries Type	9V	AA	9V	9v	AA	AA	AA	AA	AA	9V
	Rechargeables	OPT	STD	OPT	OPT	OPT	OPT	STD	OPT	OPT	OPT
	Battery Check	Y	Y	N	Y	Y	Y	Y	Y	Y	Y
	Battery Life (hrs)	25-35	15	15	20-25	20	45	10-15	35-50	25	15
	Low Battery Alert	N	N	N	N	Y	Y	Y	Y	Y	N
COIL	Stock Coil Size	6.5"	9.5"	8"	8"	9"	9"	10"	11"	9.5"	8"
	Coil Type	DD	C	C	C	C	DD	DD	DD	C	C
	Interchangeable	Y	Y	Y	Y	Y	Y	Y	Y	Y	Y
DISPLAY INFO	Display	N	Y	N	Y	Y	N	N	Y	Y	N
	Display Type	N/A	LCD	N/A	ANALOG	LCD	N/A	N/A	LCD	LCD	N/A
	Meter	N	N	N	Y-ID+	N	N	N	N	N	N
	Target ID - Audio	Y	Y	Y	Y	Y	Y	Y	Y	Y	Y
	Target ID - Visual	N	Y	N	Y	Y	N	1	Y	Y	N
	Depth Indication	N	Y	N	Y	Y	N	N	Y	Y	N
MODES	# of Search Modes	1	9	3	5	8	2	2	2	7	3
	All-Metal Search	1	Y	Y	Y	Y	Y	Y	Y	Y	Y
	Motion Discriminate	N	Y	Y	Y	Y	Y	Y	Y	Y	Y
	Non-Motion Discriminate	N	N	Y	N	N	N	N	N	N	Y
	Non-Motion Pinpoint	Y	Y	N	Y	Y	N	Y	Y	Y	N

KEY: Controls - Other: (1) Salt / Normal toggle; (2) Mode toggle + Pinpoint / Ground Adjust toggle; (3) Mineralization toggle (4) Audio Boost / Iron Disc toggle; (5) Multiple adjustments via menu system (6) Frequency selected by coil installed (3kHz, 7.5kHz, 18.75kHz); (7) Ground Trac toggle; (8) Treasure Talk (9) Frequency shift

Display (1) Optional Target ID meter provides target ID

LAND METAL DETECTOR COMPARISION CHART

		Nexus Coronado	Whites DFX	Minelab Safari	XP Gmaxx II	Fisher F-75	Minelab Eureka Gold	XP Gold Maxx Power	Minelab Explorer SE Pro	White's Spectra V3	White's TDI
SPECS	Retail Price	$1,080	$1,100	$1,195	$1,195	$1,199	$1,250	$1,275	$1,495	$1,500	$1,600
	Warranty	2 YR	2 YR	3 YR	2 YR	5 YR	3 YR	2YR	3 YR	2 YR	2 YR
	Weight w/batteries (lbs)	2.9	4.0	3.6	3.3	3.5	4.3	3.3	4.0	4.5	5.4
	Overall Length - Min	(1)	45.5"	41.5"	44"	45.6"	47"	44"	41.5"	44.5"	45"
	Overall Length - Max	49.2" (1)	51"	52.5"	53"	55"	52"	53"	52.5"	52.5"	52.8"
	Application(s)	G,C,R,B	G,C,R,P,B	G,C,R,B	G,R	G,C,R,P,B	P	G,R,B	G,C,R,B	G,C,R,P,B	P,R
	Headphone Jack & Size	1/4"	1/4"	1/4"	1/4"	1/4"	1/4"	1/4"	1/4"	1/4"	1/4"
	Internal Speaker	N	Y	Y	Y	Y	Y	Y	Y	Y	Y
	Hipmountable	N	N	N	Y	N	Y	Y	N	N	Y
CIRCUIT	Circuit Type	VLF	VLF	VLF-M	VLF	VLF	VLF	VLF	VLF-M	VLF	PI
	# of Frequencies	1	2	28	1	1	3	1	28	3	N/A
	Frequency(s)	3	3+15	1.5-100	4.6kHz	13kHz	2	18kHz	1.5-100	1	N/A
	Ground Balance Type	M	M + A	A	M	M + A	A	M	A	M + A	M
CONTROLS	Touchpad / Knobs	K	T/P	T/P	K + T	K + P/B	K + T	K + T	T/P	T/P	K + T
	Ground Balance	Y	Y	Y	Y	Y	N	Y	Y	Y	Y
	Discriminate	Y	Y	Y	Y	Y	Y	Y	Y	Y	N
	Notch Discriminate	N	Y	Y	N	Y	N	N	Y	Y	N
	Sensitivity	Y	Y	Y	Y	Y	Y	Y	Y	Y	Y
	Volume	Y	Y	Y	N	N	Y	N	Y	Y	N
	Threshold	Y	Y	Y	Y	Y	Y	N	Y	Y	Y
	Other	---	4	4	7,8	1, 2, 3	5, 6	7,8	4	4	3, 4
POWER	Batteries #	8	8	8	8	4	8	8	8	8	1 Pack
	Batteries Type	AA	AA	AA	AA	AA	AA	AA	AA	AA	Li-Ion
	Rechargeables	OPT	STD	OPT	OPT	OPT	STD	OPT	STD	STD	STD
	Battery Check	Y	Y	Y	Y	Y	Y	Y	Y	Y	Y
	Battery Life (hrs)	35	15	16	45	35-50	10-15	50	16	10-12	8
	Low Battery Alert	Y	Y	Y	Y	N	Y	Y	Y	Y	Y
COIL	Stock Coil Size	6" Dual	9.5"	11"	9"	11"	5.5"x10"	9"	11"	10"	12"
	Coil Type	C	C	DD	DD	DD	DD	DD	DD	DD	C
	Interchangeable	Y	Y	Y	Y	Y	Y	Y	Y	Y	Y
DISPLAY INFO	Display	N	Y	Y	N	Y	N	N	Y	Y	N
	Display Type	N/A	LCD	LCD	N/A	LCD	N/A	N/A	LCD	LCD	N/A
	Meter	N	N	N	N	N	N	N	N	N	N
	Target ID - Audio	Y	Y	Y	Y	Y	Y	Y	Y	Y	Y
	Target ID - Visual	N	Y	Y	N	Y	N	N	Y	Y	N
	Depth Indication	N	Y	Y	N	Y	N	N	Y	Y	N
MODES	# of Search Modes	2	7	8	2	4	2	2	4	2	2
	All-Metal Search	Y	Y	Y	Y	Y	Y	Y	Y	Y	Y
	Motion Discriminate	Y	Y	Y	Y	Y	Y	Y	Y	Y	N
	Non-Motion Discriminate	N	N	N	N	N	N	N	N	N	N
	Non-Motion Pinpoint	Y	Y	Y	N	Y	N	N	Y	Y	N

KEY: Specs: (1) The Nexus shaft is collapsible and extends to 49.2". Different lengths can be specified when ordering
Controls - Other: (1) # of Tones; (2) Program; (3) Audio Pitch; (4) Multiple adjustments via menu system
(5) Ground Track Speed toggle; (6) Signal Processing toggle; (7) Iron audio control
(8) Frequency shift
Circuit - Frequencies (1) 2.5kHz, 7.5kHz, 22.5kHz; (2) Selectable; 6.4kHz, 20kHz, 60kHz
(3) Frequency is dependent on coil used, ranges from 4.2kHz to 18kHz

LAND METAL DETECTOR COMPARISION CHART

		Minelab E-Trac	XP Deus	Minelab SD 2200 v2	Nexus Standard SE	Saxon X-1	Nexus Ultima 5F	Minelab GPX 4500			
SPECS	Retail Price	$1,895	$1,975	$2,495	$2,530	$2,825	$4,950	$5,995			
	Warranty	3 YR	2 YR	3 YR	2 YR	1 YR	2 YR	3 YR			
	Weight w/batteries (lbs)	4.8	2.2	5.3	3.9	6.5	5.9	5.3			
	Overall Length - Min	41.7"	22.8"	43.3"	(1)	30"	(1)	43"			
	Overall Length - Max	54.3"	51.2"	53.9"	49.2" (1)	40"	49.2" (1)	51"			
	Application(s)	G,C,R,B	G,C,R,B	P,R	G,C,R,B	G,R	G,R,SA	P,R			
	Headphone Jack & Size	1/4"	1/4"+1/8"	1/4"	1/4"	1/4"	1/4"	1/4"			
	Internal Speaker	Y	Y	Y	N	N	N	Y			
	Hipmountable	N	Y	N	N	N	N	N			
CIRCUIT	Circuit Type	VLF-M	VLF	MPS	VLF	VLF	VLF	MPS			
	# of Frequencies	28	1	---	5	1	5	---			
	Frequency(s)	1.5-100	2, 3	---	1	6.59kHz	1	---			
	Ground Balance Type	A	M+A	A	A + M	M	A + M	A			
CONTROLS	Touchpad / Knobs	T/P	T/P	K + T	K + T	K + P/B	K + T	K + T			
	Ground Balance	N	Y	N	Y	Y	Y	Y			
	Discriminate	Y	Y	N	Y	Y	Y	Y			
	Notch Discriminate	Y	Y	N	N	N	N	N			
	Sensitivity	Y	Y	N	Y	Y	Y	Y			
	Volume	Y	Y	N	Y	Y	Y	Y			
	Threshold	Y	Y	Y	Y	Y	Y	Y			
	Other	1		6	5	2	5	1			
POWER	Batteries #	8	1	GEL CELL	8	PACK	8	LI-ION			
	Batteries Type	AA	LI-ON	6V	AA	---	AA	12V			
	Rechargeables	STD	STD	STD	OPT	STD	STD	STD			
	Battery Check	Y	Y	Y	Y	Y	Y	Y			
	Battery Life (hrs)	16	20	15	30	8	35	12			
	Low Battery Alert	Y	Y	Y	Y	N	Y	Y			
COIL	Stock Coil Size	11"	9"	11"	Dual 9"	12"	Dual 9"	11"			
	Coil Type	DD	DD	DD	C	DD	C	DD			
	Interchangeable	Y	Y	Y	Y	N	Y	Y			
DISPLAY INFO	Display	Y	Y	N	N	N	N	Y			
	Display Type	LCD	LCD	N/A	ANALOG	ANALOG	ANALOG	LCD			
	Meter	N	N	N	Y+ID	Y	Y+ID	N			
	Target ID - Audio	Y	Y	Y	N	N	N	Y			
	Target ID - Visual	Y	Y	N	Y	N	Y	N			
	Depth Indication	Y	Y	N	N	N	N	N			
MODES	# of Search Modes	9	9	3	2	2	2	6			
	All-Metal Search	Y	Y	Y	Y	Y	Y	Y			
	Motion Discriminate	Y	Y	Y	N	N	N	Y			
	Non-Motion Discriminate	N	N (1)	N	Y	Y	Y	N			
	Non-Motion Pinpoint	Y	Y	N	Y	Y	Y	N			

KEY: Specs: (1) The Nexus shaft is collapsible and extends to 49.2". Different lengths can be specified when ordering
Controls - Other: (1) Multiple adjustments via menu system; (2) Gain control; (3) Pulse Delay
(4) Target Conductivity toggle switch; (5) VCO adjustment; (6) Shallow/Normal/Deep settings
Circuit: (1) Frequency is dependent on the coil used, ranges from 4.2kHz to 18kHz; (2) 4kHz, 8kHz, 12kHz or 18kHz
Modes (1) Per XP, this feature will be added on the next S/W upgrade which can be downloaded thru the USB port

BEACH / UNDERWATER METAL DETECTOR COMPARISION CHART

		DetectorPro Pirate	C.Scope CS4PI	DetectorPro Pirate Pro	DetectorPro H/H Wader	Tesoro Sand Shark	Tesoro Tiger Shark	Garrett Sea Hunter Mark II	DetectorPro H/H Pulse	Fisher 1280-X	White's Surf PI Dual Field
SPECS	Retail Price	$329	$430	$439	$650	$679	$749	$750	$799	$800	$900
	Warranty	2 YR	2 YR	2 YR	2 YR	LIFE	LIFE	1 YR	2 YR	2 YR	2 YR
	Weight w/batteries (lbs)	3.5	3.3	3.5	3.5	4.5	4.5	5.7	3.5	5.1	4.6
	Overall Length - Min	43"	42"	43"	43"	38.5"	38.5"	28"	43"	33"	45"
	Overall Length - Max	53"	54"	53"	53"	52.5"	52.5"	52"	53"	49"	52"
	Application(s)	G,B,S	B,S	G,B,S	G,B,S	B,S,D	L,B,S,D	B,S,D	B,S,D	G,B,S,D	B,S,D
	Headphone Type	DUAL	OPT	DUAL	DUAL	DUAL	DUAL	DUAL	DUAL	DUAL	DUAL
	Depth Rating (feet)	S/P	S/P	S/P	6'	200'	200'	200'	6'	250'	100'
	Hipmountable	N	Y	N	N	Y	Y	Y	N	Y	Y
CIRCUIT	Circuit Type	VLF	PI	VLF	VLF	PI	VLF	PI	PI	VLF	PI
	# of Frequencies	1	N/A	1	1	N/A	1	N/A	N/A	1	N/A
	Frequency(s)	2.4kHz	N/A	2.4kHz	2.4kHz	N/A	12.5kHz	N/A	N/A	2.4kHz	N/A
	Ground Balance Type	P	AA	P	P	A		A	A	P	A
CONTROLS	Touchpad / Knobs	K	K + T/P	K	K	K	K	K	K	K	K
	Ground Balance	N	N	N	N	N	Y	N	N	N	N
	Discriminate	Y	N	Y	Y	N	Y	Y	N	Y	N
	Mode	N	N	N	N	N	Y	Y	N	N	N
	Sensitivity / Gain	N	Y	Y	Y	Y	Y (*)	N	Y	Y	Y
	Volume	Y	N	Y	Y	Y	Y (*)	N	Y	Y	N
	Threshold	N	N	N	N	Y	Y (*)	Y	Y	N	Y
	Other	---	6, 7	---	---	4	5	N	1	2	3
POWER	Batteries #	2	8	2	2	8	8	8	2	8	8
	Batteries Type	9V	AA	9V	9V	AA	AA	AA	9V	AA	AA
	Rechargeables	OPT	OPT	OPT	OPT	OPT	OPT	STD	OPT	OPT	OPT
	Battery Check	N	Y	N	N	Y	Y	N	N	Y	Y
	Battery Life (hrs)	50	NS	50	50	10-20	10-20	18-22	8-12	75	25
	Low Battery Alert	N	N	N	N	N	N	N	N	Y	N
COIL	Stock Coil Size	8"	10"	8"	8"	8"	8"	8"	8"	8"	12"
	Coil Type	C	PI	C	C	PI	C	MONO	OPEN	C	DUAL
	Interchangeable	N	N	N	Y	Y	Y	Y	Y	N	N
DISPLAY INFO	Display	N	N	N	N	N	N	N	N	N	N
	Display Type	N/A	N/A	N/A	N/A	N/A	N/A	N/A	N/A	N/A	N/A
	Meter	N	N	N	N	N	N	N	N	N	N
	Target ID - Audio	N	N	N	N	N	N	N	N	N	N
	Target ID - Visual	N	N	N	N	N	N	N	N	N	N
	Depth Indication	N	N	N	N	N	N	N	N	N	N
MODES	# of Search Modes	1	1	1	1	1	3	2	1	2	1
	All-Metal Search	N	Y	N	N	1	Y	Y	Y	Y	Y
	Motion Discriminate	Y	N	Y	Y	Y	Y	N	N	Y	N
	Non-Motion Discriminate	N	N	N	N	N	N	N	N	N	N
	Non-Motion Pinpoint	N	N	N	N	N	N	N	N	N	N

KEY: Specs: (S/P) Splashproof, not rated for extended submergence
Controls - Other: (1) Frequency Adjust (sensitivity); (2) Target indication light; (3) Pulse Timing; (4) Pulse Width
(5) Tune Speed control (motion disc / all metal / all metal slow retune); (6) Pulse Frequency
(7) Signal Strength LED
(*) - These adjustments are internal to the case

BEACH / UNDERWATER METAL DETECTOR COMPARISION CHART

		White's Beach Hunter 300	Garrett Infinium L/S	Fisher CZ-21	Minelab Excalibur II	Aquascan Aquapulse 1B	JW Fishers Pulse 6X	JW Fishers Pulse 8X
SPECS	Retail Price	$1,000	$1,250	$1,299	$1,395	$1,460	$1,645	$2,045
	Warranty	2 YR	2 YR	2 YR	1 YR	2 YR	2 YR	2 YR
	Weight w/batteries (lbs)	5.7	5.5	5.7	4.6	NS	6.5	6.5
	Overall Length - Min	45"	28"	33"	32"	NS	41"	41"
	Overall Length - Max	51.5"	52"	49"	48"	NS	54.5"	54.5"
	Application(s)	B,S,D	R,B,S,D	R,B,S,D	B,S,D	B,S,D	B,S,D	B,S,D
	Headphone Type	DUAL	DUAL	DUAL	DUAL	BONE	SINGLE	SINGLE
	Depth Rating (feet)	25'	200'	250'	200'	328'	200'	200'
	Hipmountable	Y	Y	Y	N	Y	Y	Y
CIRCUIT	Circuit Type	VLF	PI	VLF-D	VLF-M	PI	PI	PI
	# of Frequencies	2	N/A	2	17	N/A	N/A	N/A
	Frequency(s)	3+15kHZ	N/A	5+15kHz	1.5-25.5	N/A	N/A	N/A
	Ground Balance Type	M	A	M	A	A	A	A
CONTROLS	Touchpad / Knobs	K	K	K	K + T/P	K	K	K
	Ground Balance	Y	N	Y	N	N	N	N
	Discriminate	N	Y	Y	Y	N	N	N
	Notch Discriminate	N	N	N	N	N	N	N
	Sensitivity / Gain	Y	N	Y	Y	N	N	N
	Volume	N	N	Y	Y	N	N	Y
	Threshold	Y	N	N	Y	Y	N	N
	Other	---	1, 2	3	---	5	---	4
POWER	Batteries #	8	8	4	8	---	N/A	N/A
	Batteries Type	AA	AA	9V	AA	PACK	PACK	PACK
	Rechargeables	OPT	STD	OPT	STD	STD	STD	STD
	Battery Check	Y	Y	Y	N	Y	Y	Y
	Battery Life (hrs)	20	10-15	40-50	14-19	10	10	10
	Low Battery Alert	Y	Y	N	Y	Y	Y	Y
COIL	Stock Coil Size	12"	10"X14"	8"	8"/10"	15"	7"	7"
	Coil Type	C	DD	C	DD	PI	MONO	MONO
	Interchangeable	N	Y	N	N	Y	Y	Y
DISPLAY INFO	Display	N	N	N	N	N	N	N
	Display Type	N/A	N/A	N/A	N/A	N/A	N/A	N/A
	Meter	N	N	N	N	N	Y	Y
	Target ID - Audio	Y	Y	Y	Y	N	N	N
	Target ID - Visual	Y	N	N	N	N	N	N
	Depth Indication	N	N	N	N	N	N	N
MODES	# of Search Modes	2	1	2	2	1	1	1
	All-Metal Search	Y	Y	Y	Y	Y	Y	Y
	Motion Discriminate	N	N	Y	Y	N	N	N
	Non-Motion Discriminate	N	Y	N	N	N	N	N
	Non-Motion Pinpoint	N	N	Y	Y	N	N	N

KEY: Controls - Other: (1) Frequency Adjust (sensitivity); (2) Ground Track Speed control; (3) Pinpoint Touch Button (4) Search Mode (power) selector knob; (5) Reject control (limited discrimination capabilities)